365 DAYS THROUGH

THE NEW TESTAMENT AND PSALMS

QUIET TIME
BIBLE GUIDE

EDITED BY

CINDY BUNCH

IVP Connect

An imprint of InterVarsity Press
Downers Grove, Illinois

InterVarsity Press
P.O. Box 1400, Downers Grove, IL 60515-1426
World Wide Web: www.ivpress.com
E-mail: email@ivpress.com

InterVarsity Press® is the book-publishing division of InterVarsity Christian Fellowship/USA®, a student movement active on campus at hundreds of universities, colleges and schools of nursing in the United States of America, and a member movement of the International Fellowship of Evangelical Students. For information about local and regional activities, write Public Relations Dept., InterVarsity Christian Fellowship/USA, 6400 Schroeder Rd., P.O. Box 7895, Madison, WI 53707-7895, or visit the IVCF website at <www.intervarsity.org>.

LifeGuide® is a registered trademark of InterVarsity Christian Fellowship.

Original source material for this book, used by permission, is acknowledged at the end of the book.

Cover design: Cindy Kiple

Cover image: chair: Tieter Estersohn/Getty Images
book with glasses: Rick Franklin/IVP

ISBN 978-0-8308-1121-2

Printed in the United States of America ∞

 InterVarsity Press is committed to protecting the environment and to the responsible use of natural resources. As a member of the Green Press Initiative we use recycled paper whenever possible. To learn more about the Green Press Initiative, visit <www.greenpressinitiative.org>.

Library of Congress Cataloging-in-Publication Data

Quiet time Bible guide: 365 days through the New Testament and Psalms
/edited by Cindy Bunch.
    p. cm.
    Includes bibliographical references and index.
    ISBN 0-8308-1121-4 (alk. paper)
    1. Bible. N.T.—Meditations. 2. Bible. O.T. Psalms—Meditations. 3.
Devotional calendars. I. Bunch, Cindy.
    BS2341.55.Q54 2005
    225'.071—dc22
                                                                                  2005004495

P   21   20   19   18   17   16   15   14   13   12   11   10   9   8   7

Y   24   23   22   21   20   19   18   17   16   15   14   13

Contents

✑

GETTING THE MOST OUT OF THE
QUIET TIME BIBLE GUIDE

Cindy Bunch and Andrew T. Le Peau

Quiet time can seem like an impossible dream to many of us. We face so many demands each day—work, family, friends, home, school, church—that we have little time left for peaceful reflection. Yet this can be one of the most renewing and vitalizing experiences of our Christian lives.

Whether you call it quiet time, devotions or Bible study and prayer, what we are talking about is a portion of your day set aside for you to connect with God and hear what he has to say to you, to study Scripture, to apply the Word to your life, to offer praise and worship to God, and pray. This may also be a time when you record in a spiritual journal what you are learning.

God is calling us to be with him. We cannot neglect this honor.

WHY A QUIET TIME BIBLE GUIDE?

The *Quiet Time Bible Guide* puts us in touch with God's Word. It leads us to discover what the Bible says rather than simply telling us what it says. In the same way, this guide does not tell us how to apply the Word to our life; rather it guides us with God's help to apply the Scripture ourselves. It uncovers questions we have, issues we face and challenges that lie ahead. In this way, God's Word becomes as current as this morning's breakfast conversations.

How does the *Quiet Time Bible Guide* accomplish all this? Not by giving you study notes, extensive background material or cross-references. Instead it helps you discover for yourself the meaning of Scripture by asking thought-provoking questions. This question format is known as *inductive Bible study*.

We tend to remember very little of what others tell us. But we remember a large percentage of what we discover ourselves. As it has been said, "Tell me, and I will forget. Show me, and I may remember. Involve me, and I will understand." This is why inductive study works so well. Even if other sources of spiritual nourishment are hard to find, if we learn how to feed ourselves from the Word of God, we will never go hungry.

The quiet times in this study are personal. The questions expose us to the promises, assurances, exhortations and challenges of God's Word. They are designed to allow the Scriptures to renew our minds so that the Spirit of God can transform us. Our goal as Christians is not just to know *about* God, but actually to know him as one person knows another. He is our Friend, our Father, our Comforter, our Helper, our Guide and our Lord. Knowing him in this way, talking with him in this way, calls for responses of joy, of worship, of repentance and sorrow, of hope and expectation. Loving God more—that's what this guide is all about.

HOW TO USE THE *QUIET TIME BIBLE GUIDE*

Because you will be making discoveries about yourself and about God as you work through this Bible guide, you may want to record what you are learning each day. You may want to note commitments that you make and keep a list of prayer concerns so you can look back and discover how God has been working in your life.

At the beginning of each book of the Bible, you will find important information on who wrote the book, who it was written to and why it was written. This introduction will also include historical background. All of this is important to understanding each book.

Each quiet time has several components:

Warming Up to God. Sometimes a question that draws you into the theme for the day, sometimes a topic to reflect on or pray about, this portion is designed to help you prepare your heart and mind for what you will be learning from Scripture.

Daily Scripture Reading. Read and reread the assigned Bible passage to familiarize yourself with what the author is saying. When you begin a new section, you may want to read the entire book along with the introduction to that book. This will give you a helpful overview of its contents. It might be good to have a Bible dictionary handy. You could use it to look up any unfamiliar words, names or places.

Discovering the Word. The studies ask three different kinds of questions: *Observation* questions help us to understand the content of the passage by asking about the basic facts: who, what, when, where and how. *Interpretation* questions delve into the meaning of the passage. *Application* questions help us to discover its implications for growing in Christ. These three keys unlock the treasures of the biblical writings and help us live them out.

Applying the Word. This is your opportunity to make the study personal. How has God's Word spoken to you? What actions do you need to take as a result of what you have learned?

Responding in Prayer. The suggestion here is to help you begin to seek God's wisdom in the area you've studied. You will also want to pray about your daily concerns, for family and friends, and about national and world events.

The studies are designed to take fifteen or twenty minutes. You'll want to set aside additional time for prayer. Feel free to work at your own pace. Sometimes you may want to spend two days on one quiet time; other times you may want to do two in one day (one psalm and one New Testament study, for example). There are a total of 365 quiet times, which will allow you to read all of the New Testament and eighty-three psalms in one year. However, this schedule should not be something you feel bound to. Go at your own pace and as the Spirit leads you. Use the checklist found on pages 11-14 to keep track of what you've read.

A reading plan follows to give you an idea of how to spread out the Gospel reading, mixing in psalms and Letters. A topical list of reading is provided on page 16. If something is weighing on your mind as you approach your quiet time, turn there to find a reading that meets your need. A more complete index of topics can be found at the end of the book.

Generally you'll find that you gain the best grasp of each New Testament book if you work through the book from beginning to end, rather than skipping around. Therefore, quiet times are organized into books of the Bible, with an introduction to the book followed by daily readings through the book. Reading through Matthew, for example, will take twenty-two days; Mark begins again with "day one."

If you are in a Bible study group, you may be interested in knowing that the InterVarsity Press LifeGuide® Bible Study Series includes companion guides on each New Testament book and Psalms. You may want to double up on your learning by using those guides, which provide studies forty-five to sixty minutes long and include leader's notes for use in a group context.

It is our hope that these quiet times will be an encouragement and a source of growth for your life with Christ. May the Holy Spirit be with you as you meet God each day.

BIBLE READING CHECKLIST

✿

Below is a checklist of Scripture passages featured in the *Quiet Time Bible Guide*. You can read in any order and check off each passage when completed to track your progress. A sample reading schedule to vary your reading and spread out the Gospels follows the checklist.

☒ Mt 1—2	☒ Mk 2:18—3:35	☒ Lk 8:1-21
☒ Mt 3	☒ Mk 4:1-34	☒ Lk 8:22-56
☒ Mt 4	☒ Mk 4:35—6:6	☒ Lk 9:1-50
☒ Mt 5:1—6:18	☒ Mk 6:6-56	☒ Lk 9:51—10:24
☒ Mt 6:19—7:29	☒ Mk 7	☒ Lk 10:25—11:13
☒ Mt 8:1—9:34	☒ Mk 8:1—9:1	☒ Lk 11:14—12:12
☒ Mt 9:35—11:30	☒ Mk 9:2-32	☒ Lk 12:13—13:21
☒ Mt 12	☒ Mk 9:33-50	☒ Lk 13:22—14:35
☒ Mt 13	☒ Mk 10:1-31	☒ Lk 15
☒ Mt 14	☒ Mk 10:32-52	☒ Lk 16
☒ Mt 15:1—16:20	☒ Mk 11:1-25	☒ Lk 17:1—18:14
☒ Mt 16:21—17:27	☒ Mk 11:27—12:27	☒ Lk 18:15—19:10
☒ Mt 18	☒ Mk 12:28-44	☒ Lk 19:11-48
☒ Mt 19—20	☒ Mk 13	☒ Lk 20:1—21:4
☒ Mt 21:1-27	☒ Mk 14:1-42	☒ Lk 21:5-38
☒ Mt 21:28—22:46	☒ Mk 14:43-72	☒ Lk 22:1-46
☒ Mt 23	☒ Mk 15:1—16:8	☐ Lk 22:47—23:56
☒ Mt 24	☒ Lk 1	☐ Lk 24
☒ Mt 25	☒ Lk 2	☐ Jn 1
☒ Mt 26	☒ Lk 3:1-20	☐ Jn 2
☒ Mt 27	☒ Lk 3:21—4:13	☐ Jn 3
☒ Mt 28	☒ Lk 4:14—5:16	☐ Jn 4
☒ Mk 1:1-15	☒ Lk 5:17—6:11	☐ Jn 5
☒ Mk 1:16-39	☒ Lk 6:12-49	☐ Jn 6
☒ Mk 1:40—2:17	☒ Lk 7	☐ Jn 7:1-52

☐ Jn 7:53—8:11
☐ Jn 8:12-59
☐ Jn 9
☐ Jn 10
☐ Jn 11
☐ Jn 12
☐ Jn 13:1-17
☐ Jn 13:18-38
☐ Jn 14
☐ Jn 15:1-17
☐ Jn 15:18—16:4
☐ Jn 16:5-33
☐ Jn 17
☐ Jn 18:1-27
☐ Jn 18:28—19:16
☐ Jn 19:17-42
☐ Jn 20
☐ Jn 21
☐ Acts 1
☐ Acts 2
☐ Acts 3
☐ Acts 4:1-31
☐ Acts 4:32—5:16
☐ Acts 5:17—6:7
☐ Acts 6:8—7:60
☐ Acts 8
☐ Acts 9:1-31
☐ Acts 9:32—10:48
☐ Acts 11
☐ Acts 12
☐ Acts 13—14
☐ Acts 15
☐ Acts 16
☐ Acts 17
☐ Acts 18
☐ Acts 19:1—20:12
☐ Acts 20:13-38
☐ Acts 21:1—22:21
☐ Acts 22:22—23:35
☐ Acts 24:1—25:12

☐ Acts 25:13—26:32
☐ Acts 27—28
☐ Rom 1:1-17
☐ Rom 1:18-32
☐ Rom 2
☐ Rom 3:1-20
☐ Rom 3:21-31
☐ Rom 4
☐ Rom 5
☐ Rom 6:1—7:6
☐ Rom 7:7-25
☐ Rom 8:1-17
☐ Rom 8:18-39
☐ Rom 9:1-29
☐ Rom 9:30—10:21
☐ Rom 11
☐ Rom 12
☐ Rom 13
☐ Rom 14
☐ Rom 15:1-13
☐ Rom 15:14—16:27
☐ 1 Cor 1
☐ 1 Cor 2
☐ 1 Cor 3
☐ 1 Cor 4
☐ 1 Cor 5—6
☐ 1 Cor 7
☐ 1 Cor 8—9
☐ 1 Cor 10:1—11:1
☐ 1 Cor 11:2-34
☐ 1 Cor 12
☐ 1 Cor 13
☐ 1 Cor 14
☐ 1 Cor 15—16
☐ 2 Cor 1:1-11
☐ 2 Cor 1:12—2:11
☐ 2 Cor 2:12—3:6
☐ 2 Cor 3:7-18
☐ 2 Cor 4:1—5:10
☐ 2 Cor 5:11—6:13

☐ 2 Cor 6:14—7:16
☐ 2 Cor 8:1—9:15
☐ 2 Cor 10
☐ 2 Cor 11
☐ 2 Cor 12
☐ 2 Cor 13
☐ Gal 1:1-10
☐ Gal 1:11—2:10
☐ Gal 2:11-21
☐ Gal 3:1-14
☐ Gal 3:15-29
☐ Gal 4:1-20
☐ Gal 4:21—5:1
☐ Gal 5:2-15
☐ Gal 5:16-26
☐ Gal 6:1-10
☐ Gal 6:11-18
☐ Eph 1:1-14
☐ Eph 1:15-23
☐ Eph 2:1-10
☐ Eph 2:11-22
☐ Eph 3
☐ Eph 4:1-16
☐ Eph 4:17-32
☐ Eph 5:1-21
☐ Eph 5:21-33
☐ Eph 6:1-9
☐ Eph 6:10-24
☐ Phil 1:1-11
☐ Phil 1:12-30
☐ Phil 2:1-18
☐ Phil 2:19-30
☐ Phil 3
☐ Phil 4:1-9
☐ Phil 4:10-23
☐ Col 1:1-14
☐ Col 1:15-23
☐ Col 1:24—2:5
☐ Col 2:6-23
☐ Col 3:1-11

☐ Col 3:12-17
☐ Col 3:18—4:1
☐ Col 4:2-18
☐ 1 Thess 1
☐ 1 Thess 2:1-16
☐ 1 Thess 2:17—3:13
☐ 1 Thess 4:1-12
☐ 1 Thess 4:13—5:11
☐ 1 Thess 5:12-28
☐ 2 Thess 1
☐ 2 Thess 2
☐ 2 Thess 3
☐ 1 Tim 1
☐ 1 Tim 2
☐ 1 Tim 3
☐ 1 Tim 4
☐ 1 Tim 5:1—6:2
☐ 1 Tim 6:3-20
☐ 2 Tim 1
☐ 2 Tim 2
☐ 2 Tim 3
☐ 2 Tim 4
☐ Tit 1—3
☐ Philem 1-25
☐ Heb 1
☐ Heb 2
☐ Heb 3
☐ Heb 4:1-13
☐ Heb 4:14—5:10
☐ Heb 5:11—6:20
☐ Heb 7
☐ Heb 8
☐ Heb 9
☐ Heb 10
☐ Heb 11
☐ Heb 12
☐ Heb 13
☐ Jas 1:1-18
☐ Jas 1:19-27
☐ Jas 2:1-13

☐ Jas 2:14-26
☐ Jas 3:1-12
☐ Jas 3:13—4:10
☐ Jas 4:11-17
☐ Jas 5:1-11
☐ Jas 5:12-20
☐ 1 Pet 1:1-12
☐ 1 Pet 1:13-25
☐ 1 Pet 2:1-12
☐ 1 Pet 2:13—3:7
☐ 1 Pet 3:8-22
☐ 1 Pet 4
☐ 1 Pet 5
☐ 2 Pet 1:1-11
☐ 2 Pet 1:12-21
☐ 2 Pet 2
☐ 2 Pet 3
☐ 1 Jn 1
☐ 1 Jn 2:1-11
☐ 1 Jn 2:12-17
☐ 1 Jn 2:18-27
☐ 1 Jn 2:28—3:10
☐ 1 Jn 3:11-24
☐ 1 Jn 4:1-12
☐ 1 Jn 4:13-21
☐ 1 Jn 5:1-12
☐ 1 Jn 5:13-21
☐ 2 Jn 1-13
☐ 3 Jn 1-14
☐ Jude 1-24
☐ Rev 1:1-8
☐ Rev 1:9-20
☐ Rev 2
☐ Rev 3
☐ Rev 4—5
☐ Rev 6
☐ Rev 7
☐ Rev 8—9
☐ Rev 10—11
☐ Rev 12

☐ Rev 13
☐ Rev 14—15
☐ Rev 16
☐ Rev 17—18
☐ Rev 19
☐ Rev 20
☐ Rev 21—22
☐ Ps 1
☐ Ps 2
☐ Ps 3
☐ Ps 4
☐ Ps 5
☐ Ps 6
☐ Ps 8
☐ Ps 10
☐ Ps 13
☐ Ps 15
☐ Ps 16
☐ Ps 18:1-24
☐ Ps 18:25-50
☐ Ps 19
☐ Ps 22
☐ Ps 23
☐ Ps 24
☐ Ps 25
☐ Ps 27
☐ Ps 29
☐ Ps 30
☐ Ps 31
☐ Ps 32
☐ Ps 33
☐ Ps 34
☐ Ps 35
☐ Ps 36
☐ Ps 37:1-17
☐ Ps 37:18-40
☐ Ps 38
☐ Ps 39
☐ Ps 40
☐ Ps 42—43

☐ Ps 44
☐ Ps 45
☐ Ps 46
☐ Ps 47
☐ Ps 50
☐ Ps 51
☐ Ps 55
☐ Ps 57
☐ Ps 62
☐ Ps 63
☐ Ps 65
☐ Ps 66
☐ Ps 67
☐ Ps 73
☐ Ps 77
☐ Ps 84
☐ Ps 86

☐ Ps 88
☐ Ps 90
☐ Ps 91
☐ Ps 94
☐ Ps 95
☐ Ps 96
☐ Ps 99
☐ Ps 100
☐ Ps 102
☐ Ps 103
☐ Ps 104
☐ Ps 107
☐ Ps 109
☐ Ps 110
☐ Ps 115
☐ Ps 116
☐ Ps 118

☐ Ps 119:1-24
☐ Ps 119:25-40
☐ Ps 121
☐ Ps 122
☐ Ps 126
☐ Ps 127
☐ Ps 130
☐ Ps 133
☐ Ps 137
☐ Ps 139
☐ Ps 142
☐ Ps 143
☐ Ps 145
☐ Ps 146
☐ Ps 148
☐ Ps 150

SAMPLE READING PLAN

Luke 1—9
Psalms 1—5
Luke 10—19
Psalms 6—13
Luke 20—24
Acts 1—12
Psalms 14—20
Acts 13—28
Psalms 21—29
1 Thessalonians
2 Thessalonians
Mark 1—9
Psalms 30—35
Mark 10—16
Psalms 36—41
Galatians
Romans

Psalms 42—50
1 Corinthians
2 Corinthians
1 Timothy
Titus
2 Timothy
Psalms 51—61
Hebrews
Psalms 62—72
1 Peter
Ephesians
Psalms 73—84
John 1—12
Psalms 85—91
John 13—25
1 John
2 John

3 John
Psalms 92—106
Philippians
Psalms 107—115
Colossians
Philemon
Matthew 1:1—16:20
Psalms 116-24
Matthew 16:21—28:20
Psalms 125—38
James
2 Peter
Jude
Psalms 139—50
Revelation

TOPICAL BIBLE READINGS

Here are some quiet times you can turn to when you are looking for answers to particular questions you're facing, when you need encouragement from God during difficult times, when you want to rejoice and praise God for the good things in your life. (More topics are listed in the index at the back of the book.)

Angels Around Us
Hebrews 1
Revelation 8—9
Psalm 91

Assurance of Salvation
Luke 13:22—14:35
2 Corinthians 1:1-11
Psalms 25, 73

Battling Temptation
Mark 1:1-15
John 18:1-27

Comfort from God
John 14
1 Peter 5
Psalms 19, 86, 145

Decision Making
1 Corinthians 3
Revelation 14—15
Psalm 119:1-24

Experiencing Burnout
Mark 6:6-56

Expressing Anger
Mark 11:1-25
Psalms 4; 18:1-24; 94; 109

Facing Pressure
Mark 2:18—3:35

Galatians 6:11-18
Revelation 2
Psalm 31

Feeling Lonely
Luke 6:12-49
John 12
2 Timothy 1
Psalms 3, 22

Finding Joy in God
Romans 5
Philippians 3:1-21
Psalms 66, 126

Grieving
2 Corinthians 6:14—7:16
Psalm 102

Handling Guilt
1 Timothy 1
Psalm 130

Loving Others
1 John 4:1-12
2 John 1-13

The Power of God
Acts 9:32—10:48

Repentance
Luke 3:1-20
Psalm 32

Sources of Hope
Luke 1
Romans 4
1 Peter 1:1-12
Revelation 1:1-8
Psalms 33, 42—43, 146

Spiritual Battles
John 7:1-52
Ephesians 6:10-24
1 John 5:1-12
Revelation 12, 13
Psalm 110

Suffering
John 18:28—19:16
Acts 8
2 Corinthians 12
Philippians 1:12-30
Hebrews 4:14—5:10
1 Peter 3:8-22; 4
Psalm 6

Thanking God
Philippians 4:10-23
Colossians 1:1-14
Psalms 47, 50, 65

Times of Waiting
Mark 13:1-37
Hebrews 9
Psalms 27, 40, 44

Introducing
the Gospel of Matthew

W hat does it mean to be a disciple of Jesus Christ? How can we effectively disciple others?

Discipleship is the application of Christian truth to the present: "What does God want me to do about this relationship?" "How can I deal with anxiety?" We need to know what God expects of us on a daily basis. Discipleship is a very practical matter.

The book of Matthew was written to teach us how to be disciples of Jesus Christ and how to disciple others. Your most important need as a disciple is to know what the Lord is like. Matthew will help you.

Practical questions are a concern of Matthew's as he writes his book. You will discover how to handle anger and envy. You will learn how to strengthen your faith, how to pray and how to grow in humility. You will gain insights into a biblical approach to evangelism. You will find out what attitudes the Lord thinks are important. And you will learn how to handle suffering and grief. In short, a study of Matthew will help you become a better disciple and disciplemaker.

The contents of Matthew divide into two equal sections: 1:1—16:20, which focuses on the identity and authority of Jesus, and 16:21—28:20, which focuses on Jesus' opposition and persecution culminating in the cross and resurrection.

From beginning to end, Matthew is an exciting and challenging Gospel. Get ready for an adventure!

Stephen and Jacalyn Eyre

MATTHEW 1—2 *In Search of the King*

HAVE YOU EVER waited with anticipation for something, only to find that when it came it was not what you wanted at all?

The long-awaited birth of the Messiah is recorded in Matthew 1—2. The nation of Israel waited for centuries for God's anointed King to be born. What a wonderful day that was to be. Jesus' birth, however, was greeted not with royal gladness by the nation and its leaders but with intrigue and conflict. The political and religious establishments felt threatened by the coming of the Messiah. It was left to foreign leaders to welcome the newborn King.

☙ WARMING UP TO GOD

Think of something you once strongly desired (a car, a special relationship or whatever). How did it match up to your expectations?

☙ DISCOVERING THE WORD

1. *Read Matthew 1—2.* Considering Matthew's purpose to portray Jesus as a heavenly king, why would Matthew include a lineage at the very beginning of his book (1:1-17)?

2. What does 1:18-25 tell us about Jesus' origin and destiny?

3. In chapter 2, how does Jesus the heavenly king contrast with King Herod?

4. How are the Magi different from the religious leaders in this passage?

5. God is the unseen actor throughout chapter 2. In what ways can we see his behind-the-scenes actions (vv. 6, 15, 18, 23)?

☙ APPLYING THE WORD

• How has knowing Jesus involved you in a search or journey?

• The responses of the Magi and Herod are typical of how people respond to Jesus today. What might cause people to respond to Jesus so differently?

• The Magi not only found Jesus, they worshiped him and witnessed to the city of Jerusalem concerning his birth (2:2-3). How has your search for the Lord resulted in worship and telling others about him?

☙ RESPONDING IN PRAYER

Spend time worshiping Jesus. Ask God to help you tell others about him.

MATTHEW 3 *Preparing for the King*

IN ANCIENT TIMES the coming of a king required special preparation. A herald was sent ahead to prepare the road on which the king would be traveling. Holes were filled, rough places made smooth and crooked sections straightened. The same thing happened when Queen Elizabeth II visited the Bahamas. In preparation for her coming, the roads she would be traveling on were completely resurfaced. In Matthew 3 John the Baptist is sent to prepare the way for the coming of the Lord. But his arrival required a very different kind of preparation.

✎ WARMING UP TO GOD

Spend some time in preparation for meeting the Lord by confessing your sins and listening for God's assurance of forgiveness.

✎ DISCOVERING THE WORD

1. *Read Matthew 3.* For Israel the desert was a place of both punishment and renewal (recall the wilderness wanderings). How does John's ministry convey both concepts (vv. 1-12)?

2. The religious leaders considered themselves children of Abraham (v. 9). According to verses 7-10, how were they abusing this privilege?

3. John calls us to produce "fruit in keeping with repentance" (v. 8). Give examples of the kind of fruit you think he has in mind.

4. Both John and Jesus have ministries of baptism (vv. 11-12). How are their baptisms similar and different?

5. What does Jesus' willingness to be baptized suggest about him (v. 15)?

✎ APPLYING THE WORD

- The coming of Christ either demands repentance or brings judgment. In what ways do you need to better prepare for his return?

- Think of people around you who have rough places or valleys in their lives. How can you help them smooth out the rough places or fill in the valleys in preparation for Jesus' coming?

✎ RESPONDING IN PRAYER

Ask God to help you show others how to prepare for Jesus.

MATTHEW 4 *The Beginning of the Kingdom*

"IS IT TIME YET?" "How much longer?" Those are the questions children ask repeatedly as Christmas approaches. It's hard on them (and their parents) to wait. But when Christmas Day comes, it's full of fun and surprises. After weeks of waiting, we all get to open our new gifts. The beginning of Jesus' ministry was like the coming of Christmas. After a long wait, the wrappings came off and the world got to see God's greatest gift.

⚬ࣿ WARMING UP TO GOD

Reflect on the last time you experienced something new—starting a new job, going to a new school, moving to a new community.

⚬ࣿ DISCOVERING THE WORD

1. *Read Matthew 4.* Look over the entire chapter to discover the locations mentioned. What do they tell us about Jesus' ministry?

2. The prerequisite for Jesus' ministry was his ability to resist temptation. What can we discover about Jesus from his encounter with Satan (vv. 1-11)?

3. Look specifically at each temptation (vv. 3-4, 5-7, 8-10). What was Satan trying to accomplish with each of them?

4. How does Jesus demonstrate his message "The kingdom of heaven is near" in verses 18-25?

5. One of Jesus' first functions as heavenly king is calling disciples. From verses 18-22, develop a brief definition of discipleship.

⚬ࣿ APPLYING THE WORD

- From Jesus' example, what can we learn about temptation and how to resist it?

- Discipleship for the first disciples meant leaving job and family and following Jesus wherever he went. How has discipleship affected your life?

- Imagine the excitement of the first disciples as they watched Jesus healing and teaching. Describe how you would feel in their shoes.

⚬ࣿ RESPONDING IN PRAYER

Recall the qualities of discipleship you saw. Pray that you will be made a faithful disciple.

MATTHEW 5:1—6:18   *The Law of the King (Part 1)*

C. S. LEWIS was once criticized for not "caring for" the Sermon on the Mount. He replied, "If 'caring for' here means 'liking' or enjoying, I suppose no one 'cares for' it. . . . I can hardly imagine a more deadly spiritual condition than that of a man who can read that passage with tranquil pleasure" [*God in the Dock* (Grand Rapids: Eerdmans, 1970), pp. 181-82].

Studying the Sermon on the Mount can be a devastating experience. It exposes the depth of our sin and the shallowness of our commitment. But the pain it inflicts is meant to heal, not destroy, us. It is the most complete summary we have of Jesus' ethical expectations for his followers. Throughout church history it has been a helpful guide and a convincing challenge.

◆ WARMING UP TO GOD

When is it hard for you to follow God's law? Talk to God about your struggles with sin.

◆ DISCOVERING THE WORD

1. *Read Matthew 5:1—6:18.* The Beatitudes describe the qualities Jesus desires in his disciples (5:3-12). Give a brief definition of each quality.

2. What do the metaphors of salt and light (5:13-16) suggest about our role in society?

3. In the rest of chapter 5, Jesus discusses various misconceptions we might have about the Law (Old Testament Scriptures). Why do you think Jesus stresses that he did not come to abolish the Law (5:17-20)?

4. How does Jesus' teaching on murder and adultery (5:21-30) differ from the traditional understanding?

5. How does Jesus want us to respond to evil and enemies (5:38-47)?

6. What do we learn about motives from Jesus' teaching in 6:1-18?

◆ APPLYING THE WORD

• Why are our motives just as important as our religious acts?

• What does this reveal to you about your motives?

• In what way do you need to experience Christ's blessing?

◆ RESPONDING IN PRAYER

Pray for Christ's blessing in the areas in which you feel needy.

MATTHEW 6:19—7:29   *The Law of the King (Part 2)*

JIM ELLIOT, a missionary killed by the Auca Indians, once wrote, "He is no fool who gives what he cannot keep to gain what he cannot lose." His words echo this portion of the Sermon on the Mount. Jesus asks us to choose between two treasures, two masters, two roads and two destinies. But he clearly explains why following him is the only wise choice.

⚘ WARMING UP TO GOD

When are earthly treasures more tempting to you than heavenly ones? Give some thought to what earthly things have a draw on you.

⚘ DISCOVERING THE WORD

1. *Read Matthew 6:19—7:29.* In 6:19-24 Jesus talks about treasures, eyes and masters. What common themes tie these verses together?

2. Worry is a dominant theme in 6:25-34. How can we escape worrying about such things as food and clothes?

3. What is the difference between judging others and being properly discerning (7:1-6)?

4. How should our knowledge of the Father affect our prayers (7:7-11)?

5. In the final section of the Sermon (7:13-27), Jesus talks about narrow and wide gates, good and bad trees, and wise and foolish builders. How do these three metaphors work together to make a common point?

⚘ APPLYING THE WORD

• What does seeking first God's kingdom and righteousness (6:33) mean practically for your life?

• Putting Jesus' words in practice is the way to build a lasting foundation against the day of judgment (7:24-27). What will the practice of Jesus' sermon require of you?

⚘ RESPONDING IN PRAYER

Pray that you will be a person of wisdom and discernment and not of judgment.

MATTHEW 8:1—9:34 *The Powers of the King*

SOMEONE ONCE commented about a U.S. president: "I don't know where he is going, but I sure like the way he leads." Leaders must demonstrate authority. But wise leaders know they must not abuse their authority. They know people follow leaders who also demonstrate integrity and compassion. In chapters 8—9 Jesus demonstrates that he is a worthy king, one in whom we can safely put our trust.

✥ WARMING UP TO GOD

Reflect on how Jesus' authority has guided you in recent days.

✥ DISCOVERING THE WORD

1. *Read Matthew 8:1—9:34.* In chapters 8—9 Jesus' miracles occur in three groups, followed by a response, or reaction. Briefly describe how Jesus demonstrates his authority in 8:1-22.

2. In 8:18-22 Jesus begins to attract would-be followers. What do these verses teach us about the cost and urgency of following him?

3. What do we learn in 8:23—9:17 about the extent of Jesus' authority?

4. What is the relationship between Jesus' claim to have authority to forgive sins and his healing of the paralytic (9:1-8)?

5. In 9:9-17 Jesus compares himself to a doctor and a bridegroom. Then he discusses garments and wineskins. What do these illustrations teach us about his ministry?

6. How do people respond to Jesus in 9:18-34?

✥ APPLYING THE WORD

- Look back over chapters 8—9. How does Jesus want us to respond to his power and authority?

- How can a knowledge of Jesus' power and authority strengthen your faith?

✥ RESPONDING IN PRAYER

Spend time praising God for Jesus' leadership.

MATTHEW 9:35—11:30 *The Messengers of the King*

DURING THE LATE 1800s, a wealthy philanthropist decided to give away all his money. He announced he would give five hundred dollars to anyone with a legitimate need. The response was overwhelming. People lined up day after day to receive their gift.

The gospel is a priceless treasure. But as we offer it to people, their response is not always enthusiastic. In this passage Jesus warns us about those who oppose his message and his messengers. But he also encourages us as we reach out to blind and needy people.

ॐ WARMING UP TO GOD

Have you ever known someone who seemed to like you only for what you could give them? Think back on how you felt about that relationship.

ॐ DISCOVERING THE WORD

1. *Read Matthew 9:35—11:30.* How and why does Jesus demonstrate compassion for the crowds (9:35-38)?

2. As a result of his compassion, Jesus sends out the Twelve (10:1-15). Describe their mission.

3. Jesus warns the disciples that their compassionate ministry will not be warmly received (10:16-25). What will they experience?

4. In 10:26-33 Jesus prepares his present and future disciples for opposition. Why shouldn't we be afraid of those who oppose us?

5. What does Jesus promise to those who are receptive to our message (10:40-42)?

6. What does 11:7-19 tell us about John and those who heard his message?

ॐ APPLYING THE WORD

• In what ways have you found rest in your life by coming to Jesus?

• What have you learned from this study about Jesus and the nature of discipleship?

ॐ RESPONDING IN PRAYER

Pray for the gift of rest in Jesus.

MATTHEW 12 *The Leaders and the King*

POWER OVER PEOPLE is not easily shared. Wars have been fought, people assassinated and elections rigged in order to gain or maintain power.

The leaders of Israel were becoming concerned over the growing reputation and following of Jesus. Like ripples in a pool of water, the ministry of Jesus and his disciples continued to have a widening impact on the Jewish nation. If Jesus' followers became too numerous, the leaders would end up losing their positions of authority. In Matthew 12 they formulate a strategy to discredit him.

❧ WARMING UP TO GOD

Recall a time untrue rumors about you were being spread around. How did it affect your relationships?

❧ DISCOVERING THE WORD

1. *Read Matthew 12.* Consider the ways that religious leaders attacked Jesus in verses 1-14. What was their strategy?

2. As you compare the Pharisees' second accusation against Jesus (v. 10) with their own response (v. 14), what irony do you see?

3. Notice the startling contrast between the religious leaders' attitude toward Jesus and God's attitude (vv. 15-21). How do they differ?

4. In verses 43-45 Jesus tells the Pharisees and teachers of the law a story. What does it reveal about them?

5. Look back over chapter 12. What factors led to the hardness and unbelief of the Pharisees and teachers of the law?

❧ APPLYING THE WORD

- How can we avoid being like the Pharisees and teachers of the law?

- What area of change in your life does this suggest you consider?

❧ RESPONDING IN PRAYER

Ask God to teach you how to read and understand his Word so that you can use it to his glory.

MATTHEW 13 *The Parables of the King*

CROWDS ARE FICKLE. One moment they follow with enthusiasm, the next they turn hostile and angry. In Matthew 13 Jesus speaks to a mixed and fickle crowd. Some are hungry to hear his message. Others are suspicious and hostile.

In this setting Jesus begins to speak in parables. These stories test our spiritual sight and hearing. They also expose the condition of our hearts.

✎ WARMING UP TO GOD

Prepare for this study by asking God to open your mind and heart to what is here for you.

✎ DISCOVERING THE WORD

1. *Read Matthew 13.* According to the parable of the sower, what responses does Jesus expect as he preaches his message of the kingdom (vv. 1-9, 18-23)?

2. In verse 10 the disciples ask Jesus why he speaks to the people in parables. Explain his reply (vv. 11-17).

3. Wheat and weeds look similar until the harvest. How does this parable explain God's delayed judgment of the wicked (vv. 24-30, 36-43)?

4. What do the parables of the mustard seed and yeast suggest about the way the kingdom grows (vv. 31-35)?

5. What do the parables of the hidden treasure and the pearl teach us about the value of the kingdom (vv. 44-46)?

✎ APPLYING THE WORD

• Jesus wants his disciples to understand the parables. How have they enlarged your understanding of the kingdom of heaven?

• Jesus also wants us to respond to what we have heard and understood. Throughout this chapter, what types of responses does he desire?

✎ RESPONDING IN PRAYER

Ask the Lord to help you respond to him in the ways you observed.

MATTHEW 14   *The Revelation of the King (Part 1)*

CRISES ARE UNCOMFORTABLE. They force us to make painful decisions, even when we don't want to decide. In Matthew 14 Jesus places the disciples in tough situations where they must act on what they have learned about him. The focus shifts from parables about the kingdom to the identity of the king.

☙ WARMING UP TO GOD

Teachers use tests. But tests are not limited to school; God also uses tests throughout our lives. Recall a time you thought you were being tested by God.

☙ DISCOVERING THE WORD

1. *Read Matthew 14.* In verses 1-2 Herod speculates about Jesus' identity. What led him to believe that Jesus is John the Baptist (vv. 3-12)?

2. How is the feeding of the five thousand (vv. 13-21) a test for the disciples?

3. Herod and Jesus, the two kings in this passage, both serve banquets. What does each king's banquet reveal about his character and authority?

4. Imagine you are in the boat with the anxious disciples (vv. 22-26). Describe what you would see, hear and feel.

5. How is Peter's trying experience on the water a vivid picture of faith and doubt (vv. 28-31)?

☙ APPLYING THE WORD

• When are you most tempted to take your eyes off the Lord and sink in doubt?

• In verse 33 the disciples worship Jesus and declare, "Truly you are the Son of God." What do you see in this incident that leads you to worship Jesus?

• How can these things help you to trust Jesus the next time you are tempted to doubt?

☙ RESPONDING IN PRAYER

Spend a few minutes worshiping Jesus, the Son of God.

MATTHEW 15:1—16:20   *The Revelation of the King (Part 2)*

EUREKA! What a relief and pleasure it is when something we have not quite understood becomes clear to us. In this section of Matthew the disciples come to a supernatural understanding of Jesus. Speaking for the disciples, Peter declares who Jesus really is. Peter's words bring us to the climax of the first half of Matthew.

✑ WARMING UP TO GOD

Think back to how you felt the first time you recognized who Jesus is and what he offers to you.

✑ DISCOVERING THE WORD

1. *Read Matthew 15:1—16:20.* Religious leaders from Jerusalem oppose Jesus by attacking the disciples (15:1-2). What is their complaint, and what does it suggest about Jesus?

2. How does Jesus respond to their accusation (15:3-20)?

3. How would you account for the unusual interaction between Jesus, the woman and the disciples (15:21-28)?

4. After Jesus heals the sick and feeds the four thousand, the religious leaders ask him for a sign from heaven (16:1). Why do you think Jesus resists them (16:2-4)?

5. In 16:5-12 the disciples misunderstand Jesus' allusion to yeast. How is their misunderstanding related to a lack of faith?

6. In 16:5-12 the disciples couldn't even grasp a simple figure of speech. How then does Peter have enough insight to confess that Jesus is the Christ, the Son of God (16:13-17)?

✑ APPLYING THE WORD

- Are there religious practices in your life that are in danger of becoming outward, empty forms? Explain.

- How can you avoid this tendency?

- Jesus' question to Peter is one that everyone will have to respond to at some point. Who do you say Jesus is, and why?

✑ RESPONDING IN PRAYER

Offer praise to Jesus Christ for who he is.

MATTHEW 16:21—17:27 *The Work of the King*

ONE OF THE RULES of good management is "No surprises." While surprises can be fun, they can also be upsetting. Good corporate leadership seeks to eliminate surprises so that everything runs according to plan.

Now that the disciples have been with Jesus for a while, he must prepare them for the true nature of his kingdom. They are shocked at the cost of his mission and his requirements for discipleship.

৬ৡ WARMING UP TO GOD

Recall an unpleasant surprise you received and how you handled it.

৬ৡ DISCOVERING THE WORD

1. *Read Matthew 16:21—17:27.* What were some of the surprises the disciples received?

2. Peter and Jesus seem to be at cross-purposes in 6:22-23. Why do you think Jesus addresses Peter as Satan?

3. What does Jesus reveal about the cost and rewards of following him (16:24-28)?

4. What would the disciples learn about Jesus by his transformed appearance, his conversation with Moses and Elijah, and the voice from heaven (17:1-8)?

5. How might this help resolve their confusion about Jesus' impending death?

6. As a result of their powerlessness, what do the disciples learn about faith?

৬ৡ APPLYING THE WORD

- How has following Jesus produced times of confusion for you?
- We don't always understand life from a heavenly perspective. How can this passage reorient your thinking?

৬ৡ RESPONDING IN PRAYER

Ask God to help you understand his ways so you can be a better disciple.

MATTHEW 18 *The Greatest in the Kingdom*

WHO IS GREATEST in the kingdom of God? How can a subject of the kingdom earn true wealth? When should we forgive? These questions dominate the thoughts of the disciples as they approach Jerusalem. They are also important questions for us. How we answer them will directly affect the quality of our discipleship.

᪣ WARMING UP TO GOD

When has someone sinned against you? Reflect on how it affected you.

᪣ DISCOVERING THE WORD

1. *Read Matthew 18.* The disciples want to know who is the greatest in the kingdom of heaven (v. 1). How does Jesus' appeal to little children answer their question (vv. 2-5)?

2. Spiritually speaking, the "little ones" are those who humble themselves ("become like little children") and believe in Jesus. What is Jesus' attitude toward those who cause the little ones to sin (vv. 6-7)?

3. How do verses 10-14 further emphasize the value Jesus places on his "little ones"?

4. Greatness in the kingdom is also dependent on living a life of forgiveness and mercy. What guidelines does Jesus give for dealing with those who sin against us (vv. 15-20)?

5. Forgiving someone once does not always guarantee that person will not offend us again. How can the parable of the unmerciful servant help us to keep on forgiving (vv. 21-35)?

᪣ APPLYING THE WORD

- Children have little status in the eyes of adults. How can we assume the status of children in our circle of friends and coworkers?

- How should the value Jesus places on his "little ones" affect the way we view ourselves and other believers?

- How does this chapter challenge your ideas of value and greatness?

᪣ RESPONDING IN PRAYER

Ask God to help you forgive those who have hurt you.

MATTHEW 19—20 *Life in the Kingdom*

WHAT IS REALLY important to you? What makes you feel important? Money? Success? Recognition? These are common answers. The values that Jesus teaches, however, have little to do with such things. In the previous study we learned that to be great in the kingdom, we must become "small." In this study we will see how the values of the kingdom conflict with the world's approach to wealth and leadership.

☞ WARMING UP TO GOD

What does success mean to you? Think about how your idea of success compares to what our culture says.

☞ DISCOVERING THE WORD

1. *Read Matthew 19—20.* How do Jesus' teachings on divorce and remarriage contrast with the values and practices of our culture (19:1-12)?

2. In 19:16-22 a young man struggles in choosing between wealth and eternal life. Why do you think Jesus required him to choose?

3. What wealth does Jesus offer those who follow him (vv. 27-30)?

4. What does the parable of the workers teach us about greatness and wealth in the kingdom of God (20:1-16)?

5. In what ways is Jesus a model of the values he teaches in 20:25-28?

6. How does Jesus' interaction with the two blind men illustrate the values he has just taught?

☞ APPLYING THE WORD

• How have you experienced what Jesus describes in 19:29?

• In what ways has Jesus' teaching on greatness and wealth (Mt 18—20) challenged you?

☞ RESPONDING IN PRAYER

Ask God to give you strength to stand against the world and to make his values your values.

MATTHEW 21:1-27 *The King Occupies His Capital*

IT IS FASHIONABLE to believe in Jesus. Surveys reveal that millions profess to be Christians. Celebrities claim miraculous, overnight conversions. Politicians boast they are "born again." Religion has become big business.

In Matthew 21 Jesus' popularity reaches its zenith. In the midst of public acclamation he occupies Jerusalem, the capital of the Jewish nation. His clash with the religious leaders reveals the difference between genuine faith and empty profession.

WARMING UP TO GOD

Today we will see Jesus enter Jerusalem to the praise and acclamation of the crowd. Imagine you have an opportunity to see Jesus. How do you feel? Express your feelings to the Lord.

DISCOVERING THE WORD

1. *Read Matthew 21:1-27.* Excitement is building and emotions are intense. What words or phrases communicate something of the electrifying atmosphere?

2. What different perceptions does the crowd have of Jesus (vv. 9-11)?

3. Jesus clears the temple in verses 12-17. How does the condition of the temple contrast with what God intended?

4. A fig tree with leaves usually has fruit. How does Jesus' cursing of the fig tree relate to his clearing the temple (vv. 18-22)?

5. How does Jesus' encounter with the Pharisees (vv. 23-27) illustrate the danger of not responding to the light God gives us?

APPLYING THE WORD

• In what ways do you see the modern church "buying and selling" like those in the temple?

• Identify one area in which your actions need to be more consistent with your beliefs.

RESPONDING IN PRAYER

Praise God for who Jesus is and for what you have seen about him in this passage.

MATTHEW 21:28—22:46   *The King Silences the Opposition*

CONFRONTATION IS never easy. Yet there are times when the situation demands it. The religious leaders refused to acknowledge that Jesus was God's Messiah sent to rule. Skillfully Jesus seeks to expose their hardness of heart and bring them to repentance. They respond not in repentance but by plotting a trap for him.

✑ WARMING UP TO GOD

From time to time we all have been involved in confrontations. Think about how you tend to feel in these situations.

✑ DISCOVERING THE WORD

1. *Read Matthew 21:28—22:46.* What does the parable of the two sons reveal about the chief priests and the elders (21:28-32)?

2. How does the parable of the tenants illustrate the character of the Father, the Son and the religious leaders (21:33-46)?

3. How is the kingdom of heaven like the banquet described in 22:1-14?

4. In 22:23-28 the Sadducees tell Jesus a story designed to refute the resurrection. How does the story illustrate their ignorance of Scripture and God's power (22:29-33)?

5. Love was the foundation of the Old Testament law (22:34-40). Why do you think we have so much trouble equating God's laws with love?

6. Jesus poses a dilemma to the Pharisees that silences them: "How can the Christ be both the son of David and his Lord?" (22:41-46). What does this paradox reveal about the Lord?

✑ APPLYING THE WORD

• What guidance does Jesus give for fulfilling our obligations to God and the government?

• How can these accounts of Jesus in conflict strengthen your faith in him?

• What do they teach you about handling conflict?

✑ RESPONDING IN PRAYER

Ask for the help you need for whatever conflict you face today.

MATTHEW 23 *The King Condemns the Rebels*

INFLUENCE IS A powerful force. Those who influence others are able to change minds and to direct actions. The religious leaders in Israel possessed the power of influence. After they decided to oppose Jesus, they tried to lead others to do the same. In Matthew 23 Jesus condemns them point-blank. They should have been the first to enter the kingdom of God because of their knowledge of Scripture and their standing in the Jewish community. Because they refuse, Jesus calls them to judgment. This passage exposes the guilt of those who do not practice what they preach.

ᴄ᷎ WARMING UP TO GOD

When have you been hurt by inconsistency in the life or teaching of an influential person you respected? Talk to God about any feelings of hurt you still have.

ᴄ᷎ DISCOVERING THE WORD

1. *Read Matthew 23.* What attitude does Jesus teach the people to have toward the religious leaders, and why (vv. 1-4)?

2. Compare the motives of the religious leaders (vv. 5-7) with the motives and attitudes Jesus requires of his followers (vv. 8-12).

3. Jesus pronounces seven woes (judgments) against the teachers of the law and the Pharisees (vv. 13-32). Summarize each one.

4. The entire generation to whom Jesus is speaking is held accountable for the "righteous blood" shed in all previous generations (vv. 33-36). Why do you think they received such a terrible sentence?

5. What responses do you have as you observe Jesus as a judge?

6. In the midst of this overwhelming condemnation, how is the tender compassion of Jesus also evident (vv. 33-39)?

ᴄ᷎ APPLYING THE WORD

- Jesus condemns the religious leaders for confusing inward and outward righteousness (vv. 25-28). In what ways are we inclined to do that today?

- Where does this point out a place that needs to change in your life?

ᴄ᷎ RESPONDING IN PRAYER

Ask God to make your Christian life consistent with your beliefs.

MATTHEW 24 *The Return of the King*

WE ALL WANT to be safe and secure. Yet many things can threaten our security: losing our job, our income, our health, our loved ones. Our ability to handle these threats depends on the source of our security. Matthew 24 focuses on the destruction of Jerusalem and the return of Christ. The true issue of Christ's return is not the hows or whens. Rather, how should we live in the present in light of this future? We must learn the true source of our security.

✎ WARMING UP TO GOD

Write down some things that give you a sense of security.

✎ DISCOVERING THE WORD

1. *Read Matthew 24.* After Jesus' statement about the temple's destruction, the disciples ask two questions (v. 3). Look through chapter 24, briefly noting ways that Jesus answers these questions.

2. Throughout history, people have set dates for Christ's return and have been mistaken. What events might deceive the disciples into thinking the end is at hand (vv. 4-8)?

3. Before the end comes, what dangers will believers face, and how are we to handle them (vv. 9-14)?

4. In 167 B.C. Antiochus Epiphanes attacked Jerusalem and set up a pagan altar in the temple—an event that anticipated "the abomination that causes desolation" spoken of by Jesus (v. 15). What occurs in the aftermath of this abomination (vv. 15-22)?

5. How will we be able to distinguish false Christs from the true (vv. 23-31)?

6. How do the parables of the thief and of the wise and wicked servants (vv. 42-51) emphasize the importance of living in light of Christ's return?

✎ APPLYING THE WORD

• Few of us have ever faced deadly peril for our faith. What types of pressure do you face for your faith in Christ?

• In what ways do you need greater watchfulness and perseverance?

✎ RESPONDING IN PRAYER

Praise God for giving you an unfailing source of security.

MATTHEW 25 *Preparation for the King's Return*

ACCOUNTABILITY CAN BE uncomfortable and inconvenient. Our desires and preferences are subject to the demands of another. Most of us would prefer to do things our own way. A rule of thumb in management is that people don't do what you expect; they do what you inspect. Jesus is coming back to inspect our lives. He holds us accountable for how we conduct ourselves in his absence. In Matthew 25 he urges us to prepare for his coming.

✒ WARMING UP TO GOD

Have you ever been in a situation where your work did not meet up to standards when it was reviewed or inspected? Think back on how you felt in that situation.

✒ DISCOVERING THE WORD

1. *Read Matthew 25.* How does the parable of the ten virgins illustrate the need to prepare for the groom's delayed return (vv. 1-13)?
2. A talent was a vast sum of money. In the parable of the talents, what were the master's expectations of his servants (vv. 14-30)?
3. How does the master demonstrate his approval or disapproval?
4. In the parable of the sheep and the goats, identify the King, the sheep, the goats and the "brothers" of the King (vv. 31-46).
5. What criteria does the King use to separate the sheep from the goats?
6. According to Jesus' teaching in this chapter, what should we be doing until he returns?

✒ APPLYING THE WORD

- What resources and responsibilities has Jesus given you?
- How can you handle them in a good and faithful manner?
- How should the material in this chapter affect your current priorities?

✒ RESPONDING IN PRAYER

Ask God to show you how to serve him.

MATTHEW 26 *The Betrayal of the King*

ON THE DRIZZLY DAY of October 16, 1555, Hugh Latimer and Nicholas Ridley, two influential English reformers, were tied to the stake and bundles of sticks were piled at their feet. The crowd strained to hear what the two men were saying. Would they recant or would they persist in dying as heretics? As the executioner pushed a torch into the wood, Latimer said, "Be of good comfort, Master Ridley, and play the man; we shall this day light such a candle, by God's grace, in England, as I trust shall never be put out." Suffering and temptation reveal the quality of our discipleship. Nowhere is this more evident than in Matthew 26, as we move into the climax of the book.

✎ WARMING UP TO GOD

Have you ever been tempted to stop following Christ? Explain.

✎ DISCOVERING THE WORD

1. *Read Matthew 26.* How do verses 1-16 set the stage for Jesus' betrayal and death?

2. In verses 17-30 Jesus celebrates the Passover with his disciples. How is this occasion both ominous and hopeful?

3. What insights can we gain about Jesus from Gethsemane (vv. 36-46)?

4. As you look over the role of Judas in this chapter, why do you think the religious leaders used one of Jesus' own disciples to betray him (vv. 47-50)?

5. Why do you think Jesus was silent for the first part of his trial (vv. 57-63)?

6. In answer to the high priest's question (v. 63), Jesus declares that he is the Christ (alluding to Dan 7:13-14). Describe the immediate—and ultimate—impact of Jesus' words on those present (vv. 65-68).

✎ APPLYING THE WORD

• When have you been confronted with the weakness of your commitment to the Lord?

• Jesus and the disciples were tempted in this chapter. How can Jesus' example and the disciples' failures help us withstand temptation and testing?

✎ RESPONDING IN PRAYER

Ask God to give you the courage to claim allegiance to Christ.

MATTHEW 27 *The Crucifixion of the King*

DO YOU EVER FEEL that God is absent when you need him most? You pray but receive no answer. You cry but no one seems to care. As Pilate and the religious leaders condemn, mock and crucify God's Son, God himself seems strangely absent. Those who trust in the midst of roaring silence will in the end discover that God was there all along.

☞ WARMING UP TO GOD

When have you felt as though God was absent when you needed him? Talk to God about how you felt.

☞ DISCOVERING THE WORD

1. *Read Matthew 27.* After the religious leaders hand Jesus over to Pilate, Judas feels remorse (vv. 1-5). How is remorse different from repentance?

2. Jesus stands before Pilate in verses 11-26. How and why does Pilate seek to avoid sentencing Jesus?

3. The soldiers viciously mock Jesus in verses 27-31. What does their mockery reveal about their knowledge of Jesus?

4. As Jesus hangs on the cross, he is repeatedly mocked and insulted (vv. 32-44). How do these insults reveal spiritual choices these people have made?

5. As death begins to engulf him, Jesus cries out to God (vv. 45-46). What does his cry and the overshadowing darkness reveal about his relationship to the Father during this torment?

6. Observe the role Jesus' followers play during the events of his crucifixion and burial (vv. 55-61). How do you think they felt?

☞ APPLYING THE WORD

- This chapter is filled with irony. Satan's "triumph" is actually his defeat. Christ's "defeat" is actually his triumph. How should this challenge our views about the way God works in our lives?

☞ RESPONDING IN PRAYER

Pray for protection so that you won't succumb to social pressure.

MATTHEW 28 *The Resurrection of the King*

VICTORY REQUIRES proclamation. Once a battle has been won, it's time to spread the word. Matthew 28 focuses on the messengers of Jesus' resurrection: the angel tells the women, the women tell the disciples, the disciples tell the nations. Even the guards tell the religious leaders. As Matthew concludes his Gospel, we are invited to join with those who throughout history have been witnesses and messengers of Jesus, the victorious resurrected Lord.

✐ WARMING UP TO GOD

Recall a joyful Easter celebration you have experienced. What elements made it joyful for you?

✐ DISCOVERING THE WORD

1. *Read Matthew 28.* The angel is the first messenger of the resurrection (vv. 2-7). What is the significance of the angel's appearance and words?

2. Consider the mission of the women (vv. 1-10). How does it undergo a radical change?

3. The Roman guard and the Jewish leaders are confronted with a miracle. How do they respond, and why (vv. 11-15)?

4. The disciples go to Galilee, where they meet with Jesus. Describe the commission he gives to them and us (vv. 16-20).

5. How does Jesus equip them and future disciples to carry out his commission?

✐ APPLYING THE WORD

• What keeps people today from believing that Jesus is the resurrected Lord?

• As you conclude this study of Matthew, how can you be more involved in making disciples and fulfilling the Great Commission?

✐ RESPONDING IN PRAYER

Pray that God will help you to be faithful to this task.

INTRODUCING
THE GOSPEL OF MARK

Democracy, at least on a large scale, is a recent development in human history. People in other eras were most accustomed to kings. When a new king came to power through natural succession or victory in battle, questions clamored in people's minds: What would the new king be like? Would he be kind and compassionate or selfish and ruthless? Would he use his power to serve his own ends, or would he seek the welfare of all his subjects?

The Jews of Jesus' day, long oppressed by foreign rulers, yearned for a new king—one whom God would use to establish his own rule of justice and peace over not only Israel but all the earth. Imagine the excitement as John the Baptist came announcing the coming of the Lord as king and as Jesus himself often announced, "The time has come. The kingdom of God is near." Yet as Jesus continued his ministry, he met a growing wave of opposition. Not everyone was pleased with the kind of kingdom he seemed to be announcing or with who he proclaimed himself to be. The religious rulers especially opposed him, but the common people heard him gladly.

Mark shows in the story of Jesus that the kingdom in its glory comes at the end of the path of suffering and service. While Matthew focuses on Jesus as the teacher from whom we should learn (Mt 11:29; 28:20) and John focuses on him as the Son of God in whom we should believe (Jn 20:31), Mark portrays Jesus as the servant-king whom we should follow (Mk 1:17). To enjoy the glories of the kingdom, we must follow the road of suffering and service.

May the Lord himself increase your understanding of who he is and of the life to which he has called you.

James Hoover

MARK 1:1-15   *Gospel Beginnings*

DO YOU HAVE any friends who begin mystery novels at the back? Like endings, beginnings tell us a lot. In them writers set the context for what is to come and often drop hints that later prove to be important. The beginning of Mark's Gospel is no exception. This passage introduces several important themes, which will be developed in the following chapters.

✺ WARMING UP TO GOD

What does it mean to you that Jesus is King? What images and feelings does that bring to mind? Meditate on Jesus as King for a while in preparation for reading Mark's Gospel.

✺ DISCOVERING THE WORD

1. *Read Mark 1:1-15.* Verses 2 and 3 combine quotations from Malachi and Isaiah. What do these two quotations have in common?

2. How does John's ministry prepare the way for Jesus?

3. How does John emphasize the greatness of the one who will come after him (vv. 7-8)?

4. Despite his greatness, Jesus came to John for baptism. What does this tell us about Jesus' relationship to us?

5. How do the events surrounding Jesus' baptism prepare him for his temptation in the desert?

6. How does Jesus summarize his mission at the beginning of his ministry?

✺ APPLYING THE WORD

• What temptations are you currently struggling with?

• What encouragement do you find here for facing your own temptations?

✺ RESPONDING IN PRAYER

Ask God to help you to find the encouragement and strength you need to face temptation.

MARK 1:16-39 *Four Portraits*

WE ALL LIVE with authority. Depending on how that authority is exercised, either we feel put upon, trapped and used, or we feel secure, free and useful.

In 1:1-15 Mark told us that Jesus came as king to fulfill the Old Testament longing for the Lord's rule over all the earth. But what kind of king is he? Rather than offering an abstract character analysis, Mark paints four verbal portraits of Jesus in action.

✑ WARMING UP TO GOD

Recall a time you were interrupted during time you had wanted to be alone. Ask God to help you balance your need to be with him with the needs of others.

✑ DISCOVERING THE WORD

1. *Read Mark 1:16-39.* What different factors contributed to the response of Simon, Andrew, James and John to Jesus' invitation (vv. 16-20)? (Don't forget 1:1-15.)

2. What might be some of the reasons Jesus tells the demon to be silent about who he is (vv. 21-28)?

3. What impression of Jesus do you get from the portrait of his visit to the home of Simon and Andrew (vv. 29-34)?

4. Thus far we have looked at three portraits of Jesus. What aspects of Jesus' character do we see in them?

5. How does Jesus exercise his authority differently from kings and dictators and other human authorities?

6. The quiet and solitude of verses 35-39 is quite a contrast from the previous events. What do these verses reveal about Jesus' priorities?

✑ APPLYING THE WORD

• How do you respond to Jesus' authority?

• Jesus' priorities are clear in this passage. What steps do you need to take to bring your priorities more closely in line with his?

✑ RESPONDING IN PRAYER

Ask God to help you evaluate your priorities in light of Jesus' kingship.

MARK 1:40—2:17 *The Clean and the Unclean*

"UNCLEAN! UNCLEAN!" The man shouted, and everyone scattered to avoid contact with the leper—everyone except Jesus. The religious wisdom of the day demanded that a holy man keep away from the common people, the "sinners." So Jesus was bound to encounter resistance as he openly welcomed them. This passage focuses on Christ's compassion toward those we normally avoid.

✍ WARMING UP TO GOD

What is it about yourself that you feel is "unclean"? Confess your sins to God and hear him declare you to be clean once again.

✍ DISCOVERING THE WORD

1. *Read Mark 1:40—2:17.* Leviticus 13:45-46 states that a leper "must wear torn clothes, let his hair be unkempt, cover the lower part of his face and cry out, 'Unclean! Unclean!' As long as he has the infection he remains unclean. He must live alone; he must live outside the camp." What risks did the leper take in coming to Jesus (1:40-45)?

2. What risks did Jesus take in responding to him as he did?

3. How does Jesus respond to the man's total need?

4. Imagine that you are the paralytic being lowered before Jesus (2:1-12). How do you feel, especially when Jesus announces, "Son, your sins are forgiven"?

5. Contrast the Pharisees' attitude toward tax collectors and "sinners" with that of Jesus.

✍ APPLYING THE WORD

- Who do you consider to be some of the "unlovely" or "unreachable" for God's kingdom?

- What steps can you take to bring your thoughts and actions toward them into line with those of Jesus?

✍ RESPONDING IN PRAYER

Ask Jesus to help you see people as he does and to act toward them as he would.

MARK 2:18—3:35 *Conflict in Galilee*

"A TRULY RELIGIOUS person wouldn't do such a thing!" "Religion is fine, but you're becoming a fanatic." Such accusations are commonly leveled at Christians. They are difficult to bear under any circumstances. But when they come from family and friends, the pain is even greater. This passage looks at some of the pressures and privileges of following Jesus.

◈ WARMING UP TO GOD

In what area of your life are you currently facing pressure or conflict? Ask God to provide you with the strength you need in that situation through his Word and the Holy Spirit.

◈ DISCOVERING THE WORD

1. *Read Mark 2:18—3:35.* On what grounds are Jesus and his disciples criticized in 2:18—3:6?

2. How are Jesus' and the Pharisees' attitudes toward the sabbath different?

3. While the Pharisees and the Herodians are plotting to kill Jesus, how are the common people responding to him (3:7-12)?

4. What charge do the teachers of the law bring against Jesus in 3:20-30?

5. How does Jesus refute it?

◈ APPLYING THE WORD

- What types of opposition have you encountered as a Christian?
- How have you dealt with experiences of opposition?
- When you are opposed or rejected by those who are closest to you, what comfort can you receive from Jesus' words in verses 33-35?

◈ RESPONDING IN PRAYER

Ask God to give you courage to follow him even when others stand against you.

MARK 4:1-34   *Kingdom Parables*

SOME STORIES WEAR their points on their sleeves, as it were. Others, to borrow from P. G. Wodehouse's definition of a parable, keep something up their sleeves that "suddenly pops up and knocks you flat." Among Jesus' stories we find a variety—from those that are easy to understand to those that are so difficult they invite our thought and reflection again and again. The stories in this passage contain vital information about God's kingdom and its subjects—for those who have ears to hear!

✺ WARMING UP TO GOD

What aspect in your life makes it difficult for you to hear the voice of Christ? Talk to Jesus about the barriers you face and ask him to show you how to remove them.

✺ DISCOVERING THE WORD

1. *Read Mark 4:1-34.* Watch especially for words and phrases that are repeated in verses 1-25. What ideas seem to dominate these verses?

2. Jesus explains the parable of the sower, or the parable of the soils (vv. 3-8), in verses 14-20. Put this explanation in your own words, describing from your experience examples of each kind of soil-seed combination.

3. On what grounds are people included or excluded from "the secret of the kingdom"?

4. How do verses 21-25 help explain verses 11-12?

5. What insights into kingdom growth do the parables of the growing seed and the mustard seed give us (vv. 26-34)?

✺ APPLYING THE WORD

- What kind of soil are you?

- What can you do to become the kind of soil Jesus is looking for?

- In this passage we see Jesus both spreading the message of the kingdom and teaching about how the kingdom grows. What lessons can we learn about evangelism both from his example and from his teaching?

✺ RESPONDING IN PRAYER

Ask Jesus to work in you to make you receptive soil.

MARK 4:35—6:6   *Desperate Straits*

"DON'T BE AFRAID; just believe." These words may ring hollow when we, and not someone else, face a fearful or life-threatening situation. Yet in the face of danger we discover just how much faith we have. In this study we find a number of people in desperate straits. Their experiences with Jesus can help us to trust him with the fearful areas of our own lives.

ᙣᶺ WARMING UP TO GOD

When do you feel afraid? Reflect on these words from Isaiah 12:2: "Surely God is my salvation; I will trust and not be afraid." Allow God to comfort you.

ᙣᶺ DISCOVERING THE WORD

1. *Read Mark 4:35—6:6.* In the first incident (4:35-41) the disciples are quite naturally afraid of the storm and disturbed that Jesus seems not to be concerned about their drowning. However, when Jesus calms the storm, they are still terrified. How does their fear after the storm differ from their previous fears?

2. Who in the next incident is afraid and why (5:1-20)?

3. Many people find it hard to understand why Jesus allowed the demons to destroy the pigs. It could have been to prevent a violent exit from the man or to show him visibly that he was now free. Even if we can't pin down exactly why Jesus allowed this, what does the fate of the pigs show about what the demons were trying to do to the man?

4. What fears are involved in the stories of Jairus's daughter and the woman with a hemorrhage (5:21-43)?

5. What is the relationship between fear and faith in each incident?

ᙣᶺ APPLYING THE WORD

- Fear can be a very powerful emotion. What kinds of fear keep you from doing some things you think you should?

- What keeps you from turning your fears into faith?

- How can Jesus' authority calm your fears and strengthen your faith?

ᙣᶺ RESPONDING IN PRAYER

Pray for your fears to become increased faith.

MARK 6:6-56   *Beyond Burnout*

BURNOUT IS ALL too common an experience among Christians. One of its most disastrous consequences is a hardened heart that keeps us from being refreshed by our Lord. In this study, as the disciples suffer from burnout, we catch a vision of how Jesus can help us to counteract its effects.

ᕫ WARMING UP TO GOD

What is pressing on you and taking away your energy? Ask God to refresh your spirit and renew your commitment. Then consider how you could better handle your responsibilities.

ᕫ DISCOVERING THE WORD

1. *Read Mark 6:6-56.* What do Jesus' instructions to the Twelve tell us about the kind of ministry they were to have (vv. 6-13)?

2. What kind of man was Herod (vv. 14-29)?

3. This flashback to the execution of John the Baptist interrupts the account of Jesus' sending out the Twelve to preach and heal. Why do you suppose Mark recounts it here?

4. What differences are there between Jesus' approach to the crowd and that of his disciples (vv. 30-44)?

5. Jesus and Herod, the two kings in this passage, both serve banquets. Compare the two.

ᕫ APPLYING THE WORD

- When has tiredness blunted your desire to care for others?

- Recognizing the contributing factors, what steps can you take to counteract burnout and a hardened heart?

ᕫ RESPONDING IN PRAYER

Ask God to help you to give of yourself while maintaining balance in your life so that you don't burn out.

MARK 7 *Violating Tradition*

ALL OF US are influenced by traditions—even those of us who by tradition don't put much stock in them! But at what point do traditions lose their value or even become counterproductive? When do religious practices become a substitute for really obeying God? In this study Jesus has harsh words for the Pharisees and the traditions they choose to observe.

✑ WARMING UP TO GOD

Consider your spiritual life. Are there any aspects of your devotional practices that you feel bound to? Consider before God whether you are putting unrealistic expectations on yourself.

✑ DISCOVERING THE WORD

1. *Read Mark 7.* What are the Pharisees concerned about (vv. 1-5)?
2. What specific complaints does Jesus raise against the Pharisees' approach to tradition (vv. 6-13)?
3. How does Jesus' view of becoming "unclean" differ from that of the Pharisees (vv. 14-23)?
4. Jesus responds to the Syrophoenician woman's request with a parable about children, bread and dogs (vv. 24-27). What is he actually saying?
5. What does the woman's response reveal about her?
6. The healing of the deaf man takes place in the Decapolis, where Jesus has exorcised the demons from the Gerasene man at the tombs (5:1-20). How do the events here demonstrate that man's success in telling about what Jesus had done for him (vv. 31-37)?

✑ APPLYING THE WORD

- What religious traditions influence your life? Is that influence good or bad? Explain.
- What traditions that we observe today get in the way of honoring God?
- In what ways do you sometimes emphasize appearance over reality?

✑ RESPONDING IN PRAYER

Now, as then, those who are spiritually deaf—whether through hardness of heart or through substituting traditions for true obedience—can be healed by Jesus. Pray for yourself and others who need Jesus' healing touch.

MARK 8:1—9:1 *Who Do You Say I Am?*

"WHO DO YOU say I am?" The whole Gospel of Mark so far has been supplying evidence for answering this question. It's a question Jesus asks each of us, and the answer we give ultimately determines our destiny. But our answer involves more than what we say with our lips. Our real answer is to be found in the way we live our lives.

✎ WARMING UP TO GOD

What need in your life has God met recently? Spend time praising God and thanking him for meeting your needs.

✎ DISCOVERING THE WORD

1. *Read Mark 8:1—9:1.* Why do you suppose the disciples, having witnessed the feeding of the five thousand, have such a hard time believing Jesus can supply the needs of four thousand here (8:1-13)?

2. What do the disciples fail to understand in 8:14-21 and why?

3. What unusual thing happens while Jesus is curing the blind man (8:22-26)?

4. How is Peter in 8:27-33 like the blind man in 8:22-26?

5. What does Jesus say it means to acknowledge him as the Christ and to follow him (8:34—9:1)?

✎ APPLYING THE WORD

• When have you acted like the disciples in 8:1-13, not expecting God to work just after he has met a need in your life?

• Is your life characterized more by seeking to lose your life or to save it? Explain.

• In what way do you need to lose your life?

✎ RESPONDING IN PRAYER

Ask Jesus to help you see more clearly those areas where you are not yet following him.

MARK 9:2-32 *Suffering and Glory*

IN A FAMOUS story, a man is given the choice of opening one of two doors. Behind one is a beautiful maiden; behind the other, a ferocious tiger. It is easy to identify with the hero of the story, hoping for joy rather than suffering, pleasure rather than pain. But what if we cannot have one without the other? This passage examines the relationship between suffering and glory, human weakness and divine power.

✐ WARMING UP TO GOD

In this passage God tells the disciples to "listen to" his Son. Ask God to give you ears to hear what Christ wants to say to you today.

✐ DISCOVERING THE WORD

1. *Read Mark 9:2-32.* What is significant about Elijah and Moses being with Jesus?

2. God's voice is heard for the second time in Mark's Gospel (v. 7; cf. 1:11). What purposes are accomplished by God's affirmation here?

3. Jesus returns to his other disciples to find them debating the teachers of the law over their failure to exorcise a young boy (vv. 14-18). Why is Jesus so harsh (v. 19)?

4. Jesus later tells his disciples again about his death and resurrection (vv. 30-32). Why do they fail to understand what he meant?

5. What details in the account of the boy's healing parallel those in Jesus' prediction of his coming suffering and victory?

✐ APPLYING THE WORD

- Which do you struggle with more: believing that Jesus *can* or that he *wants to* answer your prayers? Explain.

- How can the dialogue between Jesus and the boy's father encourage you when your faith is weak?

- The statement in verse 7, "Listen to him!" probably alludes to Deuteronomy 18:15-19. Explain how we can listen to Jesus today.

✐ RESPONDING IN PRAYER

Ask God to provide you with the encouragement you need in your life and to make you a channel of his grace to others.

MARK 9:33-50 *The First and the Last*

ALL OF US presumably struggle with the question of status and identity within a group. Where do we fit? How important are we to the group? Who is on our side? Who isn't? In this study we find out how Jesus turns conventional wisdom about status and group identity on its ear.

✎ WARMING UP TO GOD

When have you put yourself before others? Be vulnerable before God as you consider your selfishness. Let him show you your sin.

✎ DISCOVERING THE WORD

1. *Read Mark 9:33-50.* In verses 33-37, what is Jesus trying to get across to the disciples?

2. Why is a child so appropriate an illustration for Jesus' point (vv. 36-37)?

3. What perspective governs Jesus' response to John in verses 39-41?

4. Christian history has known some individuals to take Jesus' words in verses 43-47 quite literally. Why is cutting off a hand or foot or plucking out an eye not radical enough a way to deal with sin?

5. How are Jesus' attitudes about greatness and personal worth radically different from attitudes we often adopt from society?

✎ APPLYING THE WORD

• What individuals or groups are you tempted to silence because they are not "one of us"?

• When should you oppose someone in Jesus' name (if ever)?

• What attitudes and actions does this passage suggest should govern our relationships with rival individuals or groups who act in Jesus' name?

✎ RESPONDING IN PRAYER

Look to God for his wisdom as you consider how to deal with groups and individuals you know who don't uphold the truth as you understand it.

MARK 10:1-31 *Divorce, Children and Eternal Life*

FOR MANY OF us preaching becomes meddling when it impinges on how we live. But Jesus, and the whole of the Bible, never allows religion to be divorced from family life and social relationships. This passage exposes some ways the gospel transforms these areas of our life.

ᗡ WARMING UP TO GOD

Think about how a child trusts her parents. Compare that image to how you regard God. Talk to God about what you discover about yourself.

ᗡ DISCOVERING THE WORD

1. *Read Mark 10:1-31.* What differences in approach to the question of divorce seem evident between Jesus and the Pharisees?

2. On the basis of verses 6-9, some Christian churches have refused to recognize civil divorces. Do you think this is the intent of Jesus' statement? Why or why not?

3. In verses 13-16 we find that Jesus has used a child or children for the second time to illustrate a spiritual principle. What does it mean to receive the kingdom like a little child?

4. What kind of answer do you think the rich man expects from Jesus in response to his question (v. 17)?

5. How have the Pharisees (vv. 2-9) and the rich man (vv. 17-25) failed to receive the kingdom like a child (v. 15)?

ᗡ APPLYING THE WORD

• What obstacles have been hardest for you to overcome in entering the kingdom?

• What evidence has there been of God helping you overcome these obstacles?

• In what areas of your life do you most need to express more childlike faith in God?

• How have you experienced the truth of Jesus' words, "No one who has left home . . . will fail to receive a hundred times as much" (vv. 29-30)?

ᗡ RESPONDING IN PRAYER

Ask God to make you more like a child.

MARK 10:32-52 *Blindness and Sight*

THE BLIND sometimes have uncanny "sight," and the deaf sometimes "hear" what others miss. Spiritual insight and alertness arise from the heart rather than from status or position. In this passage Mark seems to delight in the irony of a blind man who perceives what the sighted cannot see.

✥ WARMING UP TO GOD

What does God want you to "see" or know? Sit quietly before him and listen for his voice.

✥ DISCOVERING THE WORD

1. *Read Mark 10:32-52.* Given what Jesus has just said in verses 33-34, what is ironic about James and John's request (vv. 35-37)?

2. What seems to motivate James and John's request?

3. When the other ten apostles hear about this status request, they become indignant. In response, what principle does Jesus bring out again (see 9:35; 10:31, 42-45)?

4. From the brief account in verses 46-52, what kind of man does Bartimaeus seem to be?

5. Why do you suppose Jesus asks Bartimaeus what he wants him to do for him?

✥ APPLYING THE WORD

- How can your life better conform to Jesus' view of greatness? (Consider your motivations as well as your actions.)

- Jesus is indeed on the road to glory, but that road will not bypass Jerusalem. Self-sacrifice and service mark the way. What are some present opportunities you have to follow him?

- What may be some of the costs?

✥ RESPONDING IN PRAYER

Tell God how you want to sacrifice for him.

MARK 11:1-25   *Palm Sunday*

THE TROUBLE WITH righteous anger is that it is so much easier to be angry than righteous. But it is possible to be both. This passage provides an example of how our emotions and attitudes can work toward God's purposes instead of against them.

✍ WARMING UP TO GOD

When have your emotions "gotten the better of you" lately? Evaluate that experience prayerfully.

✍ DISCOVERING THE WORD

1. *Read Mark 11:1-25.* What progression of moods do you see in this passage?

2. In what ways is the significance of Jesus' entry into Jerusalem reinforced?

3. Why is Jesus so angry about what is taking place in the temple (vv. 15-17)?

4. Why do you suppose Mark has sandwiched this account of Jesus' clearing out of the temple within that of the cursing of the fig tree?

5. What does Jesus teach us about prayer in verses 22-25?

✍ APPLYING THE WORD

• When is anger righteous?

• Are there activities or attitudes in your church or fellowship that get in the way of God's purposes?

• What can you do to help eliminate them?

✍ RESPONDING IN PRAYER

Respond to this passage in prayer, praising the King of peace and asking that his kingdom might be established.

MARK 11:27—12:27 *Tempting Questions*

SOME PEOPLE ASK questions because they want to know the answers. Others take delight in posing unanswerable questions and tripping up opponents. Jesus often asked questions to get his hearers to think deeply for themselves. Learning to look behind questions to motives and learning to pose effective questions can help us be better evangelists and servants.

✎ WARMING UP TO GOD

When is Jesus most real to you? Spend some time meditating on the privilege of having Christ present with you.

✎ DISCOVERING THE WORD

1. *Read Mark 11:27—12:27.* In 11:27-28 the chief priests, the elders and the teachers of the law ask a seemingly straightforward question about Jesus' authority. What does Jesus' reply and the subsequent discussion reveal about their motives?

2. The parable of the tenants is rich in meaning. If the tenants are Israel and its religious leaders, who are the owner, the servants and the son?

3. A common enemy can draw together people who are not otherwise on good terms. In 12:13-17 we find Herodians (supporters of the puppet monarchy) and Pharisees (opponents of Roman rule) joining forces. How does the question they pose to Jesus reflect their conflicting interests?

4. The Sadducees differ from the Jews because they reject the idea of resurrection. What motives lie behind their question to Jesus (12:18-23)?

5. How do the Sadducees display ignorance of the Scriptures and the power of God?

✎ APPLYING THE WORD

- How are you experiencing the truth of the Scriptures and the power of God?

- How can we get to know the Scriptures and the power of God better?

- What can we learn from this passage about answering and asking questions?

✎ RESPONDING IN PRAYER

Pray that you will be ready to answer questions about your beliefs.

MARK 12:28-44   *An End to Questions*

PEOPLE ARE MOTIVATED by many things—ambition, money, power, recognition, the desire to please God. In this passage Jesus encounters or comments on a variety of people whose lives are governed by different goals. In so doing he exposes our own motivations to his searching glance.

༒ WARMING UP TO GOD

What motivates your daily life and future plans? List each motivating factor. Reflect on your list before God.

༒ DISCOVERING THE WORD

1. *Read Mark 12:28-44.* Like the chief priests, elders, Pharisees and Sadducees of 11:27—12:27, another teacher of the law comes to Jesus with a pointed question (v. 28). What evidence is there that he is not out to trap Jesus?

2. Though Jesus is asked for only one commandment, in good rabbinic fashion he responds by adding a second to his reply. What relationship does this second commandment bear to the first?

3. To a Jew in Jesus' day, a descendant was always inferior to an ancestor. A son might call his father or grandfather "lord," but never vice versa. How can Christ be both David's Lord and his descendant (vv. 35-37)?

4. In contrast to the teachers of the law and the rich, what motivates the widow's religious behavior (vv. 41-44)?

༒ APPLYING THE WORD

- If you were to evaluate your daily activities based on love for God and neighbor, how would you fare? Explain.

- What steps can you take to make the love of God and love of neighbor a higher priority in your life?

- What implications does the example of the widow have for our giving to the Lord's work?

༒ RESPONDING IN PRAYER

Ask God to give you the attitude of the widow in your love both for him and for others.

MARK 13 *Keep Watch*

WAITING FOR CHRISTMAS can keep some children excited and on their best behavior for weeks. But what if Christmas never came? To many of us the second coming may seem like a Christmas that never comes. In this passage Jesus answers some questions about the future, both near and far off, but above all he encourages an attitude we all need to develop.

✍ WARMING UP TO GOD

When is it hard for you to wait for God? Ask him to give you insight and courage as you watch and wait.

✍ DISCOVERING THE WORD

1. *Read Mark 13.* Jesus doesn't seem to answer the disciples' question directly, at least not at first. What is he concerned about (vv. 5-8)?

2. How would Jesus' warnings and encouragements (vv. 5-13) have helped the disciples in the early years of the church?

3. Christians have sometimes disagreed about how to interpret Jesus' words in verses 14-23. Some think Jesus is talking about the destruction of the temple in A.D. 70 and the events leading up to that. Others think these events are still in the future. What evidence is there to support each view?

4. How is the distress described in verses 24-27 different from that described in verses 5-23?

5. Many people throughout the ages have tried to make precise predictions about the return of Jesus. How does watching, as Jesus urges, differ from making such predictions?

✍ APPLYING THE WORD

• What relevance do the warnings and encouragements in verses 5-13 have for us today?

• In what area of your life do you need to "be on guard"?

• In what practical ways can we be alert for Jesus' return?

✍ RESPONDING IN PRAYER

Spend some time in praise and thanksgiving for the promises in this passage.

MARK 14:1-42   *The Betrayer Approaches*

IF YOU'VE EVER caught yourself yawning at a critical moment or felt spiritually asleep when the Lord was calling you to a task, you'll have little difficulty in empathizing with the disciples in this account. We enter clearly now into the last few days of Jesus' earthly ministry. The mood is somber as more and more people begin to fail and desert him.

➷ WARMING UP TO GOD

What task has God been calling you to? Spend some time prayerfully considering what God has for you.

➷ DISCOVERING THE WORD

1. *Read Mark 14:1-42.* What different motives are present in the conflict that arises at the home of Simon the Leper (v. 3-11)?

2. During the Passover feast Jesus tells the Twelve that one of them will betray him. What do you think they were feeling as they responded to his announcement (v. 19)?

3. Few words have spawned as much debate regarding their meaning as those Jesus spoke in verses 22-24. Regardless of how literally we take them, what are the bread and cup of the Lord's Supper to symbolize for us?

4. How might verses 32-36 help those who struggle with the question of whether Jesus is the only way to God?

➷ APPLYING THE WORD

- How can the exhortations in verses 34 and 38 make the difference in your own life between resisting or falling into temptation?

- When have you felt like the disciples must have felt in verse 40?

- What consolation and encouragement can you draw from the disciples' experience?

➷ RESPONDING IN PRAYER

Thank God for his wonderful provision of forgiveness in Christ.

MARK 14:43-72 *Betrayed!*

THE PERSECUTION OF enemies is one thing, the abandonment of friends, another. In this study we find Jesus not only betrayed by one of his disciples but also abandoned by all the others and ruefully denied by one of his closest friends. All this added to the cruel and unlawful treatment by the Sanhedrin. This account reveals how intense pressures can test the quality of our discipleship.

⚜ WARMING UP TO GOD

We all betray Christ in the things we say or do. How have you betrayed him recently? Spend time in sincere confession. Hear the words of forgiveness.

⚜ DISCOVERING THE WORD

1. *Read Mark 14:43-72.* How does Jesus respond to his betrayal?

2. What aspects of Jesus' trial before the Sanhedrin (vv. 53-65) does Mark emphasize?

3. Up until this point Jesus has regularly disguised his identity, but in verse 62 he openly confesses his identity as the Christ. Why do you think he does this now?

4. How is the charge against Jesus both justifiable and unjustifiable?

5. What mix of motives brings Peter into the high priest's courtyard yet keeps him from acknowledging his relationship to Jesus (vv. 66-72)?

⚜ APPLYING THE WORD

• How are your motives mixed in following Jesus?

• In what circumstances are you most tempted to be ashamed of Jesus or to deny him?

• What warnings and encouragement can you draw from Peter's experience?

⚜ RESPONDING IN PRAYER

Ask God to keep you from betrayal.

MARK 15:1—16:8   *Victory Snatched from Defeat*

TRUE GREATNESS, Jesus taught, is found in being a servant: "Whoever wants to be first must be slave of all. For even the Son of Man did not come to be served, but to serve, and to give his life as a ransom for many" (Mt 20:28). Recorded here is the vivid testimony to Jesus' greatness and glory. Nearly all scholars agree that Mark's writing ends at verse 8. Some hold that Mark's original ending was lost and replaced with verses 9-20, but many believe that Mark stopped at verse 8 as an appropriate ending to the gospel story.

✧ WARMING UP TO GOD

What about death is intimidating to you? Reflect on how Jesus would have felt going to the cross. Spend time responding in prayer.

✧ DISCOVERING THE WORD

1. *Read Mark 15:1—16:8.* What kind of man is Pilate (vv. 1-15)?
2. What keeps him from doing what is right?
3. What ironies are present in the charges and jeers directed toward Jesus on the cross (vv. 25-32)?
4. Why do you think it was Joseph and the women who had followed Jesus, and not the eleven, who were present when Jesus died and his body needed a tomb (15:42—16:8)?
5. Why is it significant that Peter is mentioned by name in 16:7?

✧ APPLYING THE WORD

- How can we keep from succumbing to the temptation Pilate faced?
- How can this passage reinforce our commitment to sharing the good news of Christ with others?

✧ RESPONDING IN PRAYER

Spend time in praise and thanksgiving for Christ's sacrifice and for his victory over death.

INTRODUCING
THE GOSPEL OF LUKE

᪣

Master the facts and implications of Jesus' earthly life and mission: that is how the first disciples came to see who Jesus of Nazareth really was—a divine Messiah, the Son of God, the universal Savior.

Of the four Gospel writers, Luke was the only Gentile. As an initial outsider to God's chosen community, he was intrigued by Jesus' compassionate attention to foreigners and social outcasts. No other biblical author includes as many women as Luke does. No other writer talks about children and describes family life as he does. This is delightfully surprising for one who apparently was a bachelor.

Luke addresses his Gospel (and Acts) to Theophilus. His name, "lover of God," was a common aristocratic Roman one; he could have been an actual person or a literary representative of this upper class of Gentile readers. He was either a seeker or a new Christian in need of historical substantiation of the good news (1:4).

Luke claims to follow the principles for writing dependable history: (1) acquaintance with similar accounts, (2) interviews with eyewitnesses and leading personages, (3) investigation of reported events, (4) orderliness in arranging materials and (5) a stated aim. But Luke employs prose and poetry, dialogue and description. In his choice of events and people, he uses rhythm of emphasis, comparisons and contrasts. His book overflows with worship, prayer and praise, hope and joy. Luke's portrait of Jesus is strong, warm, compassionate and cosmopolitan—like the writer himself.

Ada Lum

LUKE 1

People of Hope

LUKE BEGINS HIS story by introducing some ordinary people in a small, second-rate country occupied by imperial Rome. It is around 4 B.C. For over four hundred years their nation, Israel, has not heard from God. Has God forgotten his chosen people? Has he left them to be the pawns of aggressive neighbors? Is he going back on his promises to send his Messiah to save them?

No. God is about to break into Israel's dark history with new light, and he chooses to do this through an elderly couple and a teenage girl.

❧ WARMING UP TO GOD

Think back on a time you were the only hopeful voice in a group of pessimistic people. Write down what helped you to stay hopeful.

❧ DISCOVERING THE WORD

1. *Read Luke 1.* Gabriel announces some astounding facts to Zechariah about his son, who is to be born (vv. 11-17). Do you find yourself sympathetic or critical of Zechariah's response of unbelief (vv. 18-22)? Explain.

2. How is Gabriel's second birth announcement (vv. 26-56) even more extraordinary than the first?

3. The visit to Elizabeth bolsters Mary's faith. As expressed in her response, what kind of God does she believe in (vv. 46-55)?

4. Note the effects of John's birth on neighbors and relatives (vv. 57-66). Why might Luke describe their response in such detail?

5. In Zechariah's prophecy he sees (1) the great acts that God's Redeemer will do (vv. 68-75) and (2) his child's unique relation to this Redeemer (vv. 76-79). Suppose you were listening to Zechariah. Which part would have stirred you as a devout Jew? Explain.

❧ APPLYING THE WORD

- When is it difficult for you to hope in God?
- Zechariah and Mary expressed their hope in God differently. What in their interaction with God gives you hope as you seek to trust God?

❧ RESPONDING IN PRAYER

Thank God for being the only source of true hope.

LUKE 2
Child of Hope

DID YOU HEAR the one about the woman shopper at Christmas who came upon a nativity scene in the store window? In disgust she exclaimed, "Now look what they're dragging into Christmas. Religion!"

ᕧ WARMING UP TO GOD

Write down the things that are most meaningful for you at Christmas.

ᕧ DISCOVERING THE WORD

1. *Read Luke 2.* As with other strategic events, Luke gives the historical setting of the birth of Jesus (vv. 1-4). What implications does this setting suggest about the world into which Jesus came?

2. Luke gives us few details of Jesus' birth in verses 6-7. But what impression does he leave with you?

3. We like shepherds on Christmas cards. But back then they were an outcast group. So, what in the angels' message would be incredible to the shepherds (vv. 9-14)?

4. The second and third prophetic events (note that the naming of Jesus was a prophetic event) are closely tied together (vv. 22-28). In what ways are Simeon and Anna similar?

5. How are their prophetic messages about Jesus similar yet different?

ᕧ APPLYING THE WORD

• Compare your development with Jesus' (vv. 40, 49, 51-52). In which area do you think you need more growth?

• What can you begin to do to experience that growth?

ᕧ RESPONDING IN PRAYER

Ask God to mold you into the person he wants you to be.

LUKE 3:1-20   *Public Preparation*

SEVERAL YEARS AGO, before Queen Elizabeth II arrived in a British Commonwealth country, its people feverishly prepared a royal welcome. They gave special attention to the highway running from the airport to the capitol. Each house along the way received from the government a fresh coat of paint—but only on the front of the house.

Superficial changes that people can notice—that's all some Christian leaders seem to ask for. Not so the preaching of John the Baptizer. He asked for radical moral changes, reversals of lifestyle.

ᴥ WARMING UP TO GOD

Think about the difference between superficial changes you've made to your life and the more radical changes you've made.

ᴥ DISCOVERING THE WORD

1. *Read Luke 3:1-20.* Reflect on John's dominant preaching theme in verses 3-9. How would you paraphrase this theme with contemporary relevance?

2. John gladly answers three distinct groups asking about the practical fruits of repentance. What basic sin does John attack in each case (vv. 8-14)?

3. In verses 15-20 John introduces Jesus the Christ. He has been uncompromising about the need for repentance. Now he also refuses to let the crowds think he is the expected Christ. In warning them, what picture of the Christ does he paint?

4. Like repentance, judgment is not a popular topic today among many Christians. Yet how is this also part of "the good news" (v. 18)?

ᴥ APPLYING THE WORD

• What injustices in your society would John attack?

• John's message and ministry show what repentance should be. How would you explain repentance to inquirers in terms that make sense to them?

ᴥ RESPONDING IN PRAYER

Pray for a friend who needs this explanation.

LUKE 3:21—4:13 *Personal Preparation*

"THE BEST WAY to get rid of temptation is to give in to it," said Oscar Wilde. He was the brilliant, flamboyant Irish writer of the second half of the nineteenth century. He died young, gifted and dissipated by his unbridled passions.

Jesus also died young and gifted, but disciplined by his passion for God. His discipline began in childhood, where we have already observed an early consciousness of his life mission. Now, at thirty, he submits himself to more tests to prepare him further for this goal.

✍ WARMING UP TO GOD

What would you like to have achieved ten years from now? Make a short list.

✍ DISCOVERING THE WORD

1. *Read Luke 3:21—4:13.* Jesus did not have to be baptized for the forgiveness of his sins (3:3). But by this public act he identified with our human race in need of repentance and forgiveness. What do Luke's details emphasize about Jesus' baptism?

2. Luke's genealogy of Jesus begins with his father, Joseph, and passing Abraham moves all the way back to "Adam, the son of God" (3:23-38). What does Luke want to bring out about Jesus?

3. Temptations are strong appeals to satisfy legitimate desires in wrong circumstances or by wrong means. What natural desire is the devil trying to get Jesus to satisfy in each appeal?

4. God created these desires. Why then would it become sin if Jesus were to satisfy each desire in his circumstances?

✍ APPLYING THE WORD

• What do you learn from Jesus about dealing with temptations?

• If we want to serve God wholeheartedly, we too must undergo tough training. In which area do you feel the greatest need for discipline?

• What should be your first step in that direction?

✍ RESPONDING IN PRAYER

Pray that God would work in your life to prepare you for the ministry he has for you.

LUKE 4:14—5:16   *Promising yet Dangerous Beginnings*

SOMETIMES PEOPLE SAY, "Everything has been going so well that I feel something awful coming." They know enough about life not to expect good things to continue forever. But we need not be fatalistic. We can be both realistic and positive about expectations in life. We have seen how well Jesus began. We shall also see how realistic he was about fickle human nature and how he drew out the best in people who wanted to follow him.

✧ WARMING UP TO GOD

What scares you most about rejection? Recall an experience of rejection and how you got past it.

✧ DISCOVERING THE WORD

1. *Read Luke 4:14—5:16.* What link do you see between Jesus' temptations and the beginning of his mission (4:14-15)?

2. Watch the people's changing attitudes toward Jesus (vv. 14-15, 20-22, 28-29). What has caused the radical change?

3. What prejudices can make people today object to Jesus' good news or perhaps to Jesus himself? How would you respond to these objections?

4. Having been rejected by Nazareth, Jesus now makes Capernaum his base of operations. Here Luke describes what may be a typical workday for Jesus. Identify his activities during that period (4:31-44).

5. Read 5:1-16. Note the progressive steps by which Jesus persuades Simon Peter to leave everything and follow him. When you met Jesus, what tensions arose as you recognized the need to leave everything to follow him?

✧ APPLYING THE WORD

• What can you learn from Jesus' example of dealing with rejection?

• In its context Jesus' healing of the leper appears to be a personal encounter, typical of his opening ministry. As such, then, what do you observe about Jesus as a people helper?

• Think of your ministry to others. Which of Jesus' ministering qualities do you want to have added to or reinforced in your life?

✧ RESPONDING IN PRAYER

Praise God for such a practical Teacher and Lord!

LUKE 5:17—6:11   *Radical Authority*

GOD IS ALWAYS full of surprises. Those who know him delight in this. However, surprises upset people who feel secure only with neatly structured beliefs that are left untouched. One problem for them is that every now and then God chooses to do something new and fresh. Then packaged religions and secure traditions fall apart. This often happened when Jesus came on Israel's religious scene with surprising teaching and authority.

☙ WARMING UP TO GOD

Do you wish you had more or less authority in your life? Why?

☙ DISCOVERING THE WORD

1. *Read Luke 5:17—6:11.* Imagine yourself a part of the religious establishment mentioned in 5:17. How would you have viewed Jesus' growing popularity?

2. Compare the Pharisees' questions in 5:21, 30, 33 and 6:2, 7—criticisms that climax in 6:11. What pattern(s) do you observe?

3. What skills in answering religious critics can you learn from Jesus?

☙ APPLYING THE WORD

- Jesus was relentless in his battle with the religious legalists of his day. He clearly saw that in distorting God's laws they also distorted God's image. What religious legalisms can keep you from enjoying the Lord and his true sabbath?

- Over which area of your life do you see Jesus exercising authority?

- Over which area of your life do you sense an absence of Jesus' authority?

☙ RESPONDING IN PRAYER

Ask Jesus to rule over your whole life.

LUKE 6:12-49 *Radical Lifestyle*

MAHATMA GANDHI was India's leader in the fight for national independence. As a child in India, a student in England and a lawyer in South Africa, he was exposed to Christianity and indeed was inspired to follow Jesus' example. But after years of observing Christians, he sadly concluded, "For me to believe in their Redeemer, their lives must show they are redeemed." He never became a Christian.

A Christian's lifestyle matters—not only correct words. The teaching and example of Jesus demand a lifestyle noticeably different from the average person's.

ᴄ⳾ WARMING UP TO GOD

Describe someone who has a truly Christlike lifestyle.

ᴄ⳾ DISCOVERING THE WORD

1. *Read Luke 6:12-49.* In verses 17-19 Luke has carefully given us the setting for the Sermon on the Plain. What kinds of people are in Jesus' audience?

2. Jesus begins with attitudes that shape one's lifestyle. What contrasts does he draw between his way of fulfillment and the world's way (vv. 20-26)?

3. Jesus knows that loving one's enemies is impossible without strong motivation. How does he argue that his disciples can have that motivation (vv. 31-36)?

4. It is impossible not to judge others. Rather we are to judge with good sense. What guidelines does Jesus give to judge in this way (vv. 37-42)?

5. Jesus warns his listeners of the long-term results of their lifestyle (vv. 43-49). How do his logic and illustrations sharpen his argument?

ᴄ⳾ APPLYING THE WORD

• In what ways have you found Jesus' road to happiness the right one—or an unsatisfactory one?

• Loving one's enemies is another aspect of a radical Christian lifestyle. In what ways does your enemy make it hard for you to love her or him?

• What in this study gives you hope that you can maintain the kind of radical lifestyle Jesus expects of his followers?

ᴄ⳾ RESPONDING IN PRAYER

Pray for the strength and wisdom you need to love your enemies.

LUKE 7   *Five People of Faith*

IS JESUS REALLY the only way to God? Growing up in a pluralistic society had conditioned an artist to resist such an intolerant position. Because she was still interested, some Christians pressured her to "accept Jesus as your Savior and Lord." She could not. But she privately pursued the Gospels. She began to note how differently people approached Jesus and how personally he treated each of them. Gradually she saw a distinction: There is only one way to God—through Jesus Christ—but there are many ways to Jesus. Today we meet five people with diverse backgrounds and varying approaches to Jesus—all different in expressing faith in Jesus.

✎ WARMING UP TO GOD

Write down what's hard to accept about there being one way to God.

✎ DISCOVERING THE WORD

1. *Read Luke 7*. Note the distinctive background of each of the individuals who met Jesus. What do they have in common as they relate to Jesus?

2. Picture the two processions in verses 11-13, meeting just outside the town gate. There is no request for help, no sign of faith from the widow. But look at Jesus himself in verses 13-15. What does this focus suggest about another dimension of faith in God's power?

3. Despite the Pharisees' public rejection of Jesus, one of them invites him to dinner. A drama unfolds (vv. 36-50). The woman's faith in Jesus is obvious. But Simon shows signs of some kind of faith in Jesus (vv. 36, 39, 40). How does Jesus proceed to draw out his faith?

4. Jesus' interaction with the woman is vastly different from his interaction with Simon. What does this indicate about his understanding of each?

✎ APPLYING THE WORD

- By touching the dead man, Jesus ritualistically contaminated himself. What comparable risks might you have to take to help needy people?

- Which of the five people you have looked at can you more readily identify with? How does that person challenge your faith in Jesus?

✎ RESPONDING IN PRAYER

Pray for courage in reaching out to those who are open to learning about Christ.

LUKE 8:1-21   *Taking Care How You Listen*

WHEN THE BERLIN WALL fell in 1989, Christians heard much of "tremendous openness," "thousands accepting Christ," "demand for Bibles." This was probably true. Then we began hearing about growing materialism and power struggles among some Christian leaders. Journalists began to report that many who came to meetings were mainly eager for Western contacts to worldly opportunities.

Wherever the gospel is preached, results vary, because people have different motives for listening and responding. Jesus knew this about his contemporary audience, and he dealt with it in a graphic way.

☞ WARMING UP TO GOD

What were the two most significant factors that influenced your response to the Christian gospel?

☞ DISCOVERING THE WORD

1. *Read Luke 8:1-21.* Luke's description of the women in verses 2-3 is unique among the Gospels. What do these verses say about the changing nature of Jesus' ministry?

2. In Jesus' first parable (vv. 5-8), the seeds sown are the same, but the soils are different. How are they different?

3. Jesus interprets this opening parable. What is his main point (vv. 11-15)?

4. As the crowds grow, Jesus increasingly teaches in parables. He gives his reason in verses 8-10. How are parables useful for testing a listener's sincerity?

5. Luke uses the family episode as a live illustration of listening to God (vv. 19-21). What does Jesus highlight by this illustration?

☞ APPLYING THE WORD

• Think over verse 15, where Jesus spells out what good soil is. How do you aim to cultivate your good soil?

• Reflecting on the parable of the lighted lamp (vv. 16-18), consider your habits of listening to God's truth. How can you be more open to God?

☞ RESPONDING IN PRAYER

Ask God to make you more open to what he has to say to you.

LUKE 8:22-56 *Four Signs of Power and Identity*

WHEN IS GOD present among people? Worshipers in Portugal, Yugoslavia and more recently Illinois all claimed the Virgin Mary had appeared to them, sometimes instructing or comforting and sometimes healing them. These locations drew thousands of people either seeking the physical reality of God or simply curious.

Visions, healing and deliverance services draw crowds all over the world. Believers and skeptics alike want to experience God's power—if it's there.

✦ WARMING UP TO GOD

To what extent do we today need unusual displays of God's power?

✦ DISCOVERING THE WORD

1. *Read Luke 8:22-56.* Jesus' Galilean disciples were used to sudden storms on their sea, but this one was ferocious. What emotions do they experience from the beginning to the end of this event (vv. 22-25)?

2. What unusual elements do you observe in the interchange between the man and Jesus (vv. 26-39)?

3. We should not get morbidly curious about the subject of demons. But from this text what can you know about them?

4. How is the healing of the woman different from other Bible healings you know of (vv. 40-56)?

5. What signs of God's power in your world move you most to worship and obey Jesus Christ as Lord of the universe?

✦ APPLYING THE WORD

- Jesus insists on knowing who touched him. How has it helped to witness publicly to what God has done for you?

- What signs of God's power in your world move you most to worship and obey Jesus Christ as Lord of the universe?

✦ RESPONDING IN PRAYER

Be thankful that you may worship God, who is all-powerful and all-loving.

LUKE 9:1-50 *Training for the Twelve*

"SUPERIOR PEOPLE ARE attracted only by challenge. By setting our standards low and making our life soft we have, quite automatically and unconsciously, assured ourselves of mediocre people," wrote Ambassador MacWhite in *The Ugly American,* referring to his observations in the diplomatic corps. Looking at Jesus' corps of twelve, we might wonder about *his* standards. The Gospels tell us much about how Jesus trained them.

✦ WARMING UP TO GOD

Think about a way that you are currently growing in your spiritual life. Thank God for giving you the growth.

✦ DISCOVERING THE WORD

1. *Read Luke 9:1-50.* For two years Jesus has been teaching, training and testing the Twelve. In what ways has he prepared them for this mission without him (vv. 1-9)?

2. The apostles have just returned from an intense and successful evangelistic mission. Their reluctance to help the crowd is understandable. But Jesus is insistent. What progressive steps do you see him take to involve them in feeding the people (vv. 10-17)?

3. Peter's "Great Confession" of Jesus' true identity is followed by two hard teachings from Jesus—the first prediction of his ignominious death (vv. 21-22) and the costs of commitment to him as Lord (vv. 23-27). But what does Jesus say are the long-term benefits of these short-term costs?

4. Luke links Jesus' transfiguration to his final trip to Jerusalem, where death awaits (9:30-32, 51). How then is the transfiguration important to Jesus himself and to the disciples?

5. On the plain with the mixed crowd, we can sense Jesus' deep feelings. How can he be at once both compassionate and impatient?

✦ APPLYING THE WORD

• When have you felt both God's compassion and his impatience?

• What is one area of spiritual immaturity that you need to work on?

✦ RESPONDING IN PRAYER

Talk to God about how you want to grow into spiritual maturity.

LUKE 9:51—10:24   *Short-Term Costs for Long-Term Benefits*

I THOUGHT ALL my problems would be solved when I became a Christian. But they have increased. Cost? Pain? Sacrifice? These elements don't fit into the American way of life of avoiding discomfort and inconvenience. Instant gratification is the order of the day. No goal could be further from Jesus' way of life for his disciples while here on earth.

⚘ WARMING UP TO GOD

Reflect on what following Jesus has cost you.

⚘ DISCOVERING THE WORD

1. *Read Luke 9:51—10:24.* This is the beginning of Jesus' final, yearlong journey to Jerusalem. What impressions of Jesus do the opening statements (9:51-53) leave with you?

2. In 9:56-62 Jesus interviews three would-be disciples. Each encounter reveals the person's inadequate understanding of what it means to follow Jesus. What issues are at stake for each of these people?

3. From Jesus' response to each, what do you learn about some specific costs of discipleship in his kingdom?

4. How is the mission of the seventy-two in 10:1-16 different from the mission of the Twelve in 9:1-6?

5. Luke records a post-mission report and evaluation (10:17-24). Of course celebration is in order! For Jesus the success of the seventy-two is a preview of the ultimate overthrow of Satan. But as one of them, how would you have felt on hearing Jesus' words in verse 20?

⚘ APPLYING THE WORD

• Jesus' every instruction reveals a deep sense of urgency. How do we develop an urgency for mission and evangelism?

• Jesus' demands in discipleship and mission are indeed serious (9:57-62; 10:2-12). But he accompanies them with positive appeals—explicit and implicit (9:60, 62; 10:2, 16, 18-24). Which of his appeals inspires you to pursue discipleship on his terms?

⚘ RESPONDING IN PRAYER

Ask for strength to bear the real cost of discipleship.

LUKE 10:25—11:13　　　　　　　*Marks of Jesus' True Disciples*

IT IS SOMETIMES hard to tell who is a real Christian. This is not necessarily because people indiscriminately claim to be Christians. Many people sincerely live by inherited Christian values and even show fruit of the Spirit. But they have no personal relationship with God. On the other hand, some claim such a relationship with God but do not live by his standards. Among the many who followed Jesus were those who were not clear about true discipleship. So Jesus makes it clear what marks a true follower of his.

✎ WARMING UP TO GOD

Reflect on what you would consider evidence that a person is a Christian.

✎ DISCOVERING THE WORD

1. *Read Luke 10:25—11:13.* The conversation begins with a man who had been listening to Jesus teach. What other facts about this man can you pick up in 10:25-29?

2. What does Jesus perceive about the man's understanding of the law (10:25-28)?

3. Jesus portrays the hero in his parable as a Samaritan—a despised outsider who proves obedience to God's law by his actions (the first mark of a true Christian). Note the ways he "took pity" on the victim (10:33-35). What could be Jesus' reasons for including such details?

4. In verse 36 Jesus reverses the expert's original question in verse 29. If you were the expert, what effect would this have on you?

5. Martha displays both positive and negative qualities (10:38-42). What (second) mark does her sister Mary show?

6. In 11:2-4 Jesus is not giving a prayer merely to be recited. Rather he is giving prayer headings. What basic needs do these headings cover?

✎ APPLYING THE WORD

* What qualities do you observe in people who choose "what is better"?
* We can dare to be bold because of who God is—our Father and our King (11:2, 13). How should trust in such a God radicalize your praying?

✎ RESPONDING IN PRAYER

Speak to God boldly and with trust.

LUKE 11:14—12:12 *Jesus the Controversialist*

AL WAS A remarkably effective missionary. Yet he stirred up controversy with almost everyone near him—his board, his colleagues, the local church leaders. They didn't know what to do with him, or what to do without him. But those he was evangelizing loved him.

Some people seem to be born controversialists. They're only half alive when the atmosphere is congenial. Jesus was a controversialist. But it was not for his ego that he debated the most highly trained Bible scholars of his day. He engaged in controversy because he loved the truth and hated lies.

ᴄᴆ WARMING UP TO GOD

Think back on a controversy that you handled well.

ᴄᴆ DISCOVERING THE WORD

1. *Read Luke 11:14—12:12.* In what two ways do Jesus' critics attack him (11:15-16)?

2. In 11:17-20 Jesus answers the first attack. How does he point out their illogical position?

3. Jesus answers his critics' second attack in 11:29-36. In what way is Jesus comparing himself to Jonah and Solomon?

4. In 11:37-38 the host is surprised that Jesus has not washed his hands after contact with public "uncleanness." Jesus counters that criticism, then adds six more attacks on their religious practices. Which of these reminds you of a contemporary practice (11:42, 43, 44, 46, 47, 52)? In what ways?

5. Jesus must now prepare his disciples for persecution by these same leaders (12:1-12). How does he help his disciples to distinguish between the wrong kind of fear and the proper kind (12:4-7)?

ᴄᴆ APPLYING THE WORD

• Few of us would engage in public religious controversy as Jesus did. But we all have occasions when we need to stand against lies and speak the truth. What are your opportunities to do this?

• In what ways is it difficult for you?

ᴄᴆ RESPONDING IN PRAYER

Ask the Lord Jesus to give you the help you need to take a stand.

LUKE 12:13—13:21 *Greed, Need and Judgment*

IS IT POSSIBLE to be Jesus' disciple with material values and the latest exotica as priorities? One such Christian yuppie described her experience: "For ten years I skillfully juggled both sets of values—Jesus' and Madison Avenue's. Then I collapsed." We are constantly tested in our value system, because we live between earth and heaven, time and eternity. Jesus gives us guidelines and solemn warnings on how to live productively in this creative tension.

↔ WARMING UP TO GOD

Think about the past few days. In what ways have you been enticed by materialism? Confess them before the Lord.

↔ DISCOVERING THE WORD

1. *Read Luke 12:13—13:21.* From 12:15, 22-23 and 31, how would you summarize Jesus' teaching about life and material goods?

2. The parable in 12:35-48 illustrates priorities Christians should have in view of Jesus' return after his departure—or in any crisis situation. What are these priorities that apply to all servant disciples?

3. All three parables in this passage speak of or hint at God's judgment on the choices we make (12:20, 40, 46-48). In the midst of these warnings, what hope does Jesus offer to the wise (12:57-59)?

4. Provoked by Jesus' teaching on judgment, some people raise a question about a well-known atrocity (13:1). In reply, how does Jesus both correct their wrong assumption and still extend hope?

5. This is the last time we see Jesus teaching in a synagogue (13:10-21). In what ways does this sabbath conflict with the synagogue ruler summarize the priorities and values of Jesus' total ministry?

↔ APPLYING THE WORD

- The obviously rich are not the only ones in danger of being fools. How do poor and middle-class people also face the same dangers?

- Recall again your past week's activities and personal concerns. To what extent do they reflect the priorities and values of God's kingdom?

↔ RESPONDING IN PRAYER

Ask God to mold your values and priorities into his own.

LUKE 13:22—14:35   *Are Only a Few Going to Be Saved?*

ANOTHER NEW GROUP has come to our town, attracting scores of disaffected members of other churches. The leaders have convinced them that they alone know "who is really saved." People in Jesus' day also wanted to be sure about salvation: "What must I do to inherit eternal life?" "How can a man be born again to enter the kingdom of God?" "Who then can be saved?" Even secular people ask, "Which life goal is right?" No matter the form, it is still an essential question for anyone to ask.

ᣅ WARMING UP TO GOD

When are you likely to question your salvation? Give some thought to what challenges your trust in God.

ᣅ DISCOVERING THE WORD

1. *Read Luke 13:22—14:35.* What in Jesus' parable (13:22-23) would startle his Jewish listeners or perhaps you?

2. The Pharisees' motive for warning Jesus is not clear. They are now allied with the Herodians, their political enemies, against Jesus. But he is fearless (13:31-33). Then he expresses other emotions (vv. 34-35). Why do you think Jesus is so deeply passionate about Jerusalem?

3. What explains the Pharisees' double silence to Jesus' questions (14:4, 6)?

4. How does this third parable climax Jesus' answer to our study question, "Who ultimately will be saved" (14:15-24)?

5. Travelers nearing Jerusalem passed by old crosses used for criminal execution. So how would Jesus' fellow travelers understand his words in 14:27?

ᣅ APPLYING THE WORD

- Jesus teaches guests about true honor (14:7-11) and his host about true hospitality (14:12-14). How should Jesus' lessons affect your social life?

- Jesus lays down his conditions for discipleship by calling into question powerful loyalties—to family and to self (vv. 26-27). What would be a contemporary example of Christians "hating" their family?

- Imagine not following Jesus on his terms. What to you is most sobering?

ᣅ RESPONDING IN PRAYER

Talk with God about how you've experienced the cost of discipleship.

LUKE 15 *The God Who Likes to Throw Parties*

THE TITLE OF Rembrandt's painting *The Return of the Prodigal Son* focuses on the younger son in Jesus' well-known parable. But by composition and lighting, the artist causes us to focus on the father—his face weathered by suffering, his hands lovingly embracing the ragged boy, his whole body bent to his returned son. Some people focus more on sin and repentance than on God's compassion and purposes. Repentance is necessary. But Jesus' rejoicing Father completes, indeed dominates, the picture.

⟨ WARMING UP TO GOD

How have you recently experienced the joyful side of God's nature? Praise God for who he is.

⟨ DISCOVERING THE WORD

1. *Read Luke 15.* What provoked Jesus' parables (vv. 1-2)?
2. In the first two parables (the lost sheep and the lost coin), the theme of an owner searching for something lost and rejoicing when it is found begins to answer Jesus' critics. The third parable (the prodigal son), repeats the basic theme. But how is it different from the first two?
3. What steps do you perceive in the young man's 180-degree turnaround?
4. The drama grows as Jesus describes the father in verses 20-24. In the light of verse 2, what does Jesus want his critics to see about this man?
5. In the interaction with his older son, what other dimensions of the father's character and motives appear (vv. 28-32)?
6. The rejoicing nature of God is foreign, if not offensive, to some religious people (see vv. 2, 6-7, 9-10, 22-24, 32; see also 14:16-17). Why?

⟨ APPLYING THE WORD

- How do these parables move you to believe in the possibilities of new or fresh changes in your relationship to family members and with God?
- Which of your friends have an inadequate or wrong view of God?

⟨ RESPONDING IN PRAYER

Pray for opportunities to share with your friends this appealing portrait of God.

LUKE 16   *Managing Your Money*

IN 1985 STOCK speculator Ivan Boesky was commencement speaker at a school of business administration. He said to the graduating class, "I want you to know that I think greed is healthy. You can be greedy and still feel good about yourself." The young men and women laughed and applauded. A year and a half later Boesky was in prison. The two parables in our present chapter show Jesus' judgment on the improper use of money.

☙ WARMING UP TO GOD

What do you like about money? Write down its benefits.

☙ DISCOVERING THE WORD

1. *Read Luke 16.* Jesus' parable in verses 1-18 is quite straightforward. His application, however, seems not as clear (vv. 8-9). At first reading, how does he seem to be applying the parable to his disciples?

2. Where in the context could you show that Jesus is not condoning greed and dishonesty?

3. According to Jesus in verses 10-15, what does our management of money have to do with our standing before God?

4. In the first part of the parable recorded in verse 19-31, Jesus contrasts the earthly statuses of Lazarus and the rich man, and then their different eternal states. What does Jesus want the Pharisees to see about the relationship of money in this life to the life after death?

5. In the second part of the parable we learn more about life after death (vv. 26-31). What facts and implications do you observe about this dimension of existence?

☙ APPLYING THE WORD

• How should these parables affect your current use of money?

• What would help you to use your money more effectively?

☙ RESPONDING IN PRAYER

Our relatives and friends are not all skeptics. Pray that Jesus' teaching on life after death may spur you to more personal evangelism with those who are open.

LUKE 17:1—18:14   *How to Grow Mustard-Seed Faith*

AS JESUS, his disciples and the crowds draw near Jerusalem, he knows disillusion will set in for them. No one understands his predictions of death by the hands of the nation's leaders. Their faith is in a political Messiah come to overthrow the Roman rulers. They had to learn faith is not a complete package we receive at conversion. Our trust is not to be in a set program but in a dynamic Person. Faith is a growing response to God, and it grows best in the adversities of life.

✍ WARMING UP TO GOD

Think back on a time you were disillusioned with Jesus and his way of life.

✍ DISCOVERING THE WORD

1. *Read Luke 17:1—18:14.* What caused the disciples' reaction in 17:1-5?

2. In the story of the lepers, Jesus seems surprised that only one of the ten returns in gratitude for his healing. What relation can you see between faith and gratitude in his final words (17:17-19)?

3. For the Pharisees, what emphasis about the kingdom of God does Jesus make (17:20-21)? Why?

4. Jesus stresses the need to be prepared for the coming of the Son of Man. He uses two examples of warning in the Old Testament. Why were those people unprepared for God's judgment (17:22-37)?

5. To encourage us to persist in praying, Jesus draws a portrait of a judge. In what ways is God different from the judge (18:6-8)?

6. In the second parable (18:9-14), both men address "God." But how do their prayers reveal different concepts of God and of each man's relation to him?

✍ APPLYING THE WORD

• What might your prayers reveal about your concept of God and how you relate to him?

• In this study, how has Jesus made faith more concrete and attainable for you?

✍ RESPONDING IN PRAYER

Pray from your heart to the God who desires to hear you.

LUKE 18:15—19:10   *The Nobodies God Wants*

"ONLY THE LITTLE people pay taxes." This quote comes from the very rich hotel "queen," Leona Helmsley, who is now paying dearly for tax evasion. What a contrast of attitude with God's compassion for "the little people." Our study introduces us to three groups or individuals whom society considered insignificant: little children, a blind beggar and a tax collector. They represent the kind of people he wants in his messianic community.

✌ WARMING UP TO GOD

Reflect on the past week. Is it possible that you have treated someone as insignificant? If so, confess your sin to the Lord.

✌ DISCOVERING THE WORD

1. *Read Luke 18:15—19:10.* The disciples represent their society's attitude—children are insignificant (18:15). How does Jesus give significance to them?

2. In contrast, 18:18-30 is about a "somebody" who disqualifies himself from the kingdom. He has everything society considers admirable and desirable. But what condition for eternal life does he lack (18:22)?

3. In 18:31-34 Jesus' fourth prediction to the Twelve about his coming violent death again meets with lack of understanding. Their presuppositions about riches and their political agenda (19:11) deafens them to Jesus' intent. Then in 18:35-45 Luke introduces us to someone who represents another group of nobodies. What is unusual about the beggar's attitude and how he address Jesus that catches his attention?

4. Jericho was a popular resort for royalty and priests. What kind of character would a chief tax collector in such a town likely develop?

5. What other side of Zacchaeus surfaces in 19:3-6, 8?

✌ APPLYING THE WORD

• How does Jesus' example with Zacchaeus show how you might share the gospel?

• Which outsider from your circle could you introduce to Jesus?

✌ RESPONDING IN PRAYER

Pray for those who are considered insignificant in your community.

LUKE 19:11-48   *False Hopes About the Kingdom of God*

IF WE RESPECT and like our bosses, we are often willing to work hard and even overtime. If we don't respect or like them, we usually are not willing. Then we probably become unproductive. Likewise our personal view of God affects our working relationship to him. In this case, productivity has not just temporal but also eternal consequences.

✺ WARMING UP TO GOD

How has work been for you this week? Talk to God about any frustrations you have experienced.

✺ DISCOVERING THE WORD

1. *Read Luke 19:11-48.* Jesus' key words in verse 10 inflamed the crowd's messianic expectations. His parable aims to counter false hopes. In verses 12-15, what comparisons between the nobleman and himself does Jesus highlight?

2. Consider the hour of accountability when the master returns as king (vv. 15-26). The reward of the first two (representative) servants is simple. But the king's dialogue with the third servant is detailed. With this emphasis, what point is Jesus making (keep in mind v. 11)?

3. The adversaries are mentioned only at the beginning and the end (vv. 14, 27). Whom does Jesus intend them to represent?

4. How does he smash the false hopes of this group?

5. In verses 28-40 we see Jesus in various aspects of his messianic role. What concern of Jesus do you see as he approaches Jerusalem?

6. What concern do you note as Jesus reflects on Jerusalem (vv. 41-44)?

✺ APPLYING THE WORD

• In this panoramic view of Jesus the Messiah, what do you find hard to understand about him?

• What about Jesus here can you positively respond to? Why?

✺ RESPONDING IN PRAYER

Worship Jesus the Messiah-King with praise, awe and thanksgiving.

LUKE 20:1—21:4 *Final Debates—Clear Rejection*

A HUMANIST BRANDED the Christians on campus a bunch of losers. He claimed he did not need religion for a crutch as they did. I was reduced to wordlessness by his hostile tone. I thought of three perfect responses—late that night in bed.

Most of us are not as quick to think on our feet as Jesus. We have seen him as a fearless controversialist in Galilee. Now we will see him in the capital, taking on four distinct authority groups as each mounts attacks on him.

✌ WARMING UP TO GOD

How would you defend your faith? Write down what challenges to your faith you find most difficult to answer.

✌ DISCOVERING THE WORD

1. *Read Luke 20:1—21:4.* By the end of the debate on Jesus' authority, what has each side achieved (20:1-8)?

2. By parable and commentary Jesus pronounces final judgment on the leaders (20:9-18). How do you respond to his characterization of God?

3. Sadducees accepted only the first five Old Testament books, which they (wrongly) presumed said nothing about life after death. What do they expect their story to do to belief in the resurrection (20:27-33)?

4. Again Jesus points to wrong assumptions behind their question. What error does he identify in their view of life after death (vv. 34-36)?

5. How refreshing this widow must have been to Jesus after the controversies! What does this tell you about the kind of faith Jesus values (21:1-4)?

✌ APPLYING THE WORD

- All four groups reject Jesus as God's Messiah-King. After this, there are no more debates—only arrest and death. Besides valid debates, how can we maintain biblical truth against the enemies of Christianity?

- What is a political/religious tension for you as a Christian?

- In what way would you like to be bolder in defending your faith?

✌ RESPONDING IN PRAYER

Pray now for faith like the widow's.

LUKE 21:5-38

Getting Ready for the End

SENSATIONAL INTERPRETATIONS of "the last days" can stir up some people, especially when the Middle East is in the news. Others react against what they perceive as scare tactics by avoiding any consideration of biblical prophecies. In today's study the Lord Jesus shows us how to keep a balance by being properly informed and obedient to his instructions.

৩ৡ Warming Up to God

What feelings does talk about the last days create in you? Ask God for guidance in processing those feelings.

৩ৡ Discovering the Word

1. *Read Luke 21:5-38.* What are your general impressions of Jesus' discourse on the end of the age?

2. At least three important events are evident. The first is Jesus' delivery of this discourse to his disciples in A.D. 30 in Jerusalem. What are the other two (vv. 20-24 and 27-28)?

3. But Jesus also says some positive things will happen during this time (vv. 12-19). (These activities can also be applied between the second and third events.) What in Jesus' message gives you hope for an otherwise uncertain future?

4. In verses 8-9 Jesus has said that certain activities are not signs of the end. But what does he say will be signs of his return (vv. 25-28, and probably vv. 10-11)?

5. How is Jesus' parable of the fig tree (vv. 29-31) related to his preceding teachings (for example, 19:41-44; 20:16)?

৩ৡ Applying the Word

• Earthly preoccupation can keep us insensitive to spiritual realities and unprepared "to stand before the Son of Man" (see vv. 5, 34-36). What aspects of modern living tempt you this way?

• Which one of Jesus' promises gives you strong incentive to be well prepared (vv. 14-15, 19, 24, 28, 31, 33)?

৩ৡ Responding in Prayer

Pray that you would be made ready.

LUKE 22:1-46   *Jesus' New Passover*

NOW WE ENTER deeply into the saddest days of history. With Judas' help, the religious leaders, considered the most enlightened men in their nation, complete their plot to kill the Son of God. But these days are also the greatest days on earth for Jesus. He is about to complete his life mission, and he confirms to the eleven remaining that they will carry on that mission. So with them he privately establishes his new Passover to supersede the old Passover.

✎ WARMING UP TO GOD

Recall your most moving celebration of the Lord's Supper.

✎ DISCOVERING THE WORD

1. *Read Luke 22:1-46.* What do verses 1-6 tell you about the authorities?

2. Looking at verses 7-23, contrast Jesus' plans with the authorities' plans. As you examine his plans, what impresses you about Jesus himself?

3. Jesus chides the disciples for their preoccupation with power and prestige. What lesson does he teach about the kind of leaders he wants to carry on his work (vv. 26-27)?

4. Jesus further prepares them for coming tests. The first preparation is immediately ahead for Peter. The second is for all the apostles in the long run. Like him they would have to face official hostility (vv. 36-38). In either testing, what should help them to persevere (vv. 28, 29-30, 31-32, 35)?

5. What guidelines for praying do you see in each verse of 39-46, showing Jesus' example?

✎ APPLYING THE WORD

• Jesus' institution of his new Passover was interspersed with human weakness and failure. In redeeming his disciples, he used their shortcomings. What weaknesses and failures do you want to acknowledge as you contemplate afresh eating Jesus' new Passover?

• What new, or renewed, truths about prayer do you discover in Jesus' example (vv. 39-46)?

✎ RESPONDING IN PRAYER

Follow the guidelines for prayer in Jesus' example.

LUKE 22:47—23:56   *The Message of the Cross*

THE SYMBOL OF the cross is used as jewelry even by non-Christians. But they would never think of wearing a burnished gold miniature of an electric chair around their necks. In the first century the cross meant capital punishment for criminals. Jesus died as a criminal to be the substitute for us sinners. Approach this study with prayer for a deeper understanding of the cross of Jesus.

↫ WARMING UP TO GOD

Think back to your first understanding of the Christian cross. Reflect on what's changed in your understanding over time.

↫ DISCOVERING THE WORD

1. *Read Luke 22:47—23:56.* In a word or phrase, what describes the way Jesus relates to each individual or group during his arrest (22:47-62)?

2. Only a few hours after Peter swore loyalty to Jesus, he makes an about-face (22:57-60). In what kind of situation are you tempted to avoid identification with Jesus and his cause?

3. Three times Pilate says he finds no valid charge against Jesus, and he seeks to release him (23:4, 13-16, 22). Why then does he ultimately pronounce the death penalty on Jesus?

4. Luke gives few details of Jesus' physical death. Instead he focuses on people's attitudes. What attitude to the man on the center cross does each group or individual reveal (23:32-49)?

5. Throughout his six hours on the cross, Jesus is in touch with his Father. What do his brief words to the Father reflect about their relationship (23:34, 46)?

↫ APPLYING THE WORD

• How can you make the message of the cross relevant to your needy world?

• How can the cross become more relevant to you as an individual?

↫ RESPONDING IN PRAYER

Praise God for giving his Son over to death on the cross for your sake.

LUKE 24 *God Has the Last Word*

HOW MIGHT YOU destroy Christianity? Explain away Jesus' resurrection. For instance, you could say the women at the tomb were deluded, or argue that they went to the wrong tomb. You might insist that the resurrection was spiritual, not physical, or that the disciples had hallucinations. From that first Easter till now, the enemies of the church have tried to get rid of the historical facts (Mt 28:11-15). None have succeeded.

૮ళ WARMING UP TO GOD

Think about what the world would lose if Jesus did not rise from death.

૮ళ DISCOVERING THE WORD

1. *Read Luke 24.* The women are a personal link between the cross and the empty tomb. Suppose you are one of them. How do you feel when the men respond with something akin to "Nonsense!" (vv. 1-12)?

2. What strikes you about the stranger's dialogue with the disciples (vv. 13-35)?

3. We can sympathize with the disciples' struggle between despair and hope. In his rebuke Jesus identifies the cause of their despair: their reluctance to believe the Scriptures about a suffering Messiah (v. 25). How have the Scriptures moved you from despair to new hope?

4. Which facts and implications in verses 36-53 help you to believe that Jesus really was resurrected?

5. For three or so years Jesus has been preparing his disciples to carry on his world mission. He climaxes this mission training by stressing systematic, in-depth Bible understanding (vv. 25-27, 32, 44-47). In what ways can you testify to this importance?

૮ళ APPLYING THE WORD

- We have been studying the life and mission of Jesus. What would you say are your three greatest incentives to be his witness of these things?

- Jesus has come to bring new hope and joy to the world. How can you (and your church or fellowship group) take Jesus' message to your community?

૮ళ RESPONDING IN PRAYER

Pray that you will be a source of joy to many as you bring Jesus' message.

Introducing
the Gospel of John

The most significant fact in history can be summed up in four words: Jesus Christ is God. The great declaration of the Bible is that God in human flesh was born in Bethlehem. It was God in the person of Jesus Christ who astonished people with his miracles and amazed them with his teaching. It was God who lived a perfect life and then allowed himself to be put to death on a cross for humanity's sins. It was God who, three days after he died, came out of the grave alive. The deity of Jesus—the fact that he was God in human flesh—is the bottom line of the Christian faith.

John's book is not a biography; it's a theological argument. He tells us in 20:30-31: "Jesus did many other miraculous signs in the presence of his disciples, which are not recorded in this book. But these are written that you may believe that Jesus is the Christ, the Son of God, and that by believing you may have life in his name." John wants to convince us that by believing in Jesus Christ as the Son of God we find life—a whole new kind of life!

John never mentions himself by name in the Gospel. He refers to himself simply as "the disciple whom Jesus loved." We have in this Gospel the memories of an intimate friend about the Lord Jesus. Jesus Christ had transformed John's life. You are about to begin a fascinating study focused on the greatest person who ever lived—Jesus Christ. If you will respond in faith and obedience to what John writes, you—like John—will experience a whole new kind of life.

Douglas Connelly

JOHN 1 *The Master and Five Who Followed*

IT WAS A GREAT day in our history when a man first walked on the moon. But the Bible declares that a far greater event took place two thousand years ago. God walked on the earth in the person of Jesus Christ. John opens his Gospel with a beautiful hymn of exaltation to Christ. It is one of the most profound passages in the entire Bible. It is written in simple, straightforward language, yet in studying the depths of its meaning, it is a passage where we never reach bottom. It is an ocean-sized truth, and we have to be content to paddle around in shallow water.

❧ WARMING UP TO GOD

Consider the miracle of God becoming human. Give him your praise and worship for what he has done for you.

❧ DISCOVERING THE WORD

1. *Read John 1.* John records more than a dozen names or descriptions of Jesus in this chapter. What are some of these?

2. In verses 1-3, what facts does John declare to be true of the Word?

3. According to verses 14-18, what specific aspects of God's character are revealed to us through Jesus?

4. What steps did John the Baptist take to guarantee that people would not look at him but at Christ?

5. In verses 35-51 we are introduced to five men: Andrew, Simon, Philip, Nathanael and one unnamed disciple (John). How did each man respond to the testimony he heard about Jesus?

❧ APPLYING THE WORD

• Which of the names of Jesus has the most significance to you personally? Explain why.

• What do you hope will happen in your life as a result of studying the Gospel of John?

❧ RESPONDING IN PRAYER

Ask God to bring the light and life of Jesus to you as you study his Word.

JOHN 2 *Wine and a Whip*

"WHAT PROOF DO you have that Jesus really was who he claimed to be?" People have been asking that question for two thousand years! For John the convincing proof of Jesus' deity was found in his words and deeds. No one but God could say the things Jesus said, and no one but God could do the things Jesus did. In this chapter are two signs that demonstrate that Jesus was the fullness of God clothed in humanity.

☙ WARMING UP TO GOD

Thank God for revealing himself to you personally.

☙ DISCOVERING THE WORD

1. *Read John 2.* When the groom's parents ran out of wine for their guests, Jesus' mother asked him to help (v. 3). What do you think Mary expected Jesus to do (Jesus had not yet performed any miracles; see v. 11)?

2. What did Jesus mean by his reply to Mary in verse 4?

3. The purpose of Jesus' miracle was not to save the groom from embarrassment but to display Christ's glory, according to verse 11. What aspects of Christ's glory does this miracle reveal to you?

4. How does John's picture of Jesus in verses 15-16 fit with today's popular concept of him?

5. Only the Messiah had the authority to cleanse the temple. The people recognized that and asked Jesus for a miraculous sign to confirm his identity (v. 18). To what "sign" did Jesus point them (vv. 19-22)?
   Why do you think that particular sign was so significant in Jesus' mind?

☙ APPLYING THE WORD

• In what practical ways can you demonstrate the same concern that Jesus does toward the holy character of God?

• How do Jesus' presence and actions at this party serve as a model for you?

☙ RESPONDING IN PRAYER

Ask God to help you to be his representative in everything you do.

JOHN 3 *The New Birth*

THE MOST BEAUTIFUL explanation of the new birth is found in John 3. It's a passage that children can understand, and one that the greatest saints of God have never fully grasped. It's a message not so much to be analyzed and dissected as it is to be received with joy.

✑ WARMING UP TO GOD

Do you remember your spiritual birthday? Reflect on what that time meant for you.

✑ DISCOVERING THE WORD

1. *Read John 3.* What is your impression of Nicodemus (vv. 1-21)?
2. Why do you suppose Nicodemus responds to Jesus' explanation of new birth with such amazement (v. 9)?
3. How does the story of Moses lifting up the snake in the desert (vv. 14-15; see Num 21:4-9) illustrate our need and Christ's offer?
4. How and why does our response to God's Son determine our destiny (vv. 18-21)?
5. How would you summarize John's view of the character and ministry of Jesus (vv. 22-36)?

✑ APPLYING THE WORD

- John made it clear that Jesus was superior to him. What is one way you can demonstrate Christ's superiority in your life?
- Who do you know that needs to know the truth about God?
- How can you help that person see God?

✑ RESPONDING IN PRAYER

Ask God to make you ready to testify of the role of Jesus in your life.

JOHN 4 *Soul and Body—Savings and Healing*

"I LOVE HUMANITY; it's people I can't stand!" Those well-known words from a character in the *Peanuts* comic strip still make us chuckle. But our smiles hide the fact that we sometimes feel exactly like that. John says very little about Jesus' contact with the multitudes. But long sections of the Gospel are devoted to conversations Jesus had with individuals. In John 4 we see Jesus reach out first to a woman, then to his disciples, and finally to a grieving father. Watching Jesus give himself to people with love and compassion will help us care for those God puts in our paths.

✎ WARMING UP TO GOD

When have you felt mobbed by the multitudes? Ask God to help you to take care of yourself even as you try to help others.

✎ DISCOVERING THE WORD

1. *Read John 4.* What is surprising about Jesus' question to the woman (vv. 8-9)?

2. Why does the woman suddenly change the subject and begin talking about the controversy over the proper place of worship (vv. 16-20)?

3. From verses 27-42, do you think the Samaritan woman genuinely believed? What do you see in the passage that supports your position?

4. After his encounter with the Samaritan woman, what specific lessons does Jesus apply to his disciples and to us (vv. 34-38)?

5. What does the "second miraculous sign" Jesus performs (vv. 43-54) reveal about him?

✎ APPLYING THE WORD

- What has Jesus taught you in this chapter about meeting the specific needs of those around you?

- What present-day situations might arouse the same racial, religious and sexual prejudices as the Samaritan woman did?

- How could you reach someone rejected by the world, as Jesus did?

✎ RESPONDING IN PRAYER

Ask God to help you be aware of the "Samaritans" around you. Ask him to help you reach out to them.

JOHN 5 *Deity on Trial*

TELEVISION LAWYERS always find the missing piece of evidence that will rescue the innocent and convict the guilty. In reality, however, sometimes judges and juries are wrong.

In John 5 Jesus is on trial. A group of people is forced to make a decision about him in their hearts. They hear all the evidence but make a disastrously wrong decision. Judgments are still made for and against Jesus. Whenever he is presented as Savior and Lord, people decide in their hearts to believe his claims or to turn and walk away.

ᑌ WARMING UP TO GOD

How has God recently revealed the truth of his claims as Savior to you? Thank him for his powerful works in your life.

ᑌ DISCOVERING THE WORD

1. *Read John 5.* Based on the scene and conversation around the pool, how would you describe the feelings and attitudes of the invalid (vv. 1-15)?

2. The seventh commandment says, "Remember the Sabbath day by keeping it holy" (Ex 20:8-11). In their zeal to apply this command, what were the Jews failing to see (John 5:9-15)?

3. What insights do verses 19-23 give us into (a) the Father's devotion to the Son and (b) the Son's dependence on the Father?

4. What "witnesses" does Jesus call on to testify on his behalf (vv. 31-47)?

5. What counteraccusations does Jesus make against those attacking him?

6. According to this chapter, what influences our verdict for or against Jesus?

ᑌ APPLYING THE WORD

• When have you been more concerned about a religious activity than about the reality behind it? Explain.

• How can you avoid the kind of religion that is outwardly pious but inwardly bankrupt?

ᑌ RESPONDING IN PRAYER

Ask God to help you discover true religion.

JOHN 6 *Jesus, the Bread of Life*

DURING YOUR LIFETIME you will probably spend more than thirty-five thousand hours eating. That's the equivalent of eight years of nonstop meals, twelve hours a day! The problem, of course, is that even after a big meal we get hungry again. At best, food only satisfies us for a few hours. Yet in this chapter Jesus offers us food that satisfies our hunger forever. You can't buy it in a grocery store. It is found only in Jesus himself.

✑ WARMING UP TO GOD

Think back on a problem in your life that didn't seem to have a solution. Reflect on what brought you through it.

✑ DISCOVERING THE WORD

1. *Read John 6.* Read verses 1-15. How would you characterize Philip's and Andrew's responses to the problem of feeding this enormous crowd (vv. 5-9)?

2. Imagine you are one of the disciples rowing the boat (vv. 16-21). How would your concept of Jesus be altered by seeing him walk on water?

3. The next day the people were hungry again, so they came seeking Jesus (vv. 22-25). How does he try to redirect their thinking (vv. 26-33)?

4. Based on the remarks of some in the crowd (vv. 41-42), do you think they finally understood what Jesus was saying? Explain.

5. What do you think it means to eat Jesus' flesh and drink his blood (vv. 53-59)? Is this something we do once, or is it an ongoing process? Explain.

6. In verses 60-71 Jesus turns away from the crowd and focuses on his disciples. How would you describe their responses to his "hard teaching"?

✑ APPLYING THE WORD

• Which response in question six best describes your current attitude toward Jesus? Explain.

• Jesus has contrasted the two appetites found in every person: the appetite for food that perishes and the appetite for food that endures. In what ways has Jesus satisfied the spiritual hunger in your heart?

✑ RESPONDING IN PRAYER

Praise God for satisfying all your needs.

JOHN 7:1-52 *Confusion over Christ*

IN THE EARLY chapters of John's Gospel, men and women responded to Jesus with belief. Then some of those who were following him turned away. Now open warfare breaks out between Jesus and his enemies—and yet, some still seek the truth. This chapter will help you respond positively to the wide variety of attitudes toward Jesus today.

✑ WARMING UP TO GOD

In what way do you need Jesus' spiritual refreshment? Be quiet before him and experience the "streams of living water."

✑ DISCOVERING THE WORD

1. *Read John 7:1-52*. The first blast of hostility toward Jesus comes from his family (vv. 1-13). How would you characterize the statements made by Jesus' brothers (vv. 3-5)?

2. When Jesus makes his presence in Jerusalem known, people begin to challenge the origin (and, therefore, the authority) of his teaching. According to Jesus, how can we verify the truth of his teaching (vv. 16-18)?

3. What other opinions or questions do people have about Jesus in verses 20-36?
   How does Jesus respond to each one?

4. On the last day of the Feast of Tabernacles, large vats of water were poured out on the pavement of the temple court as a reminder of God's provision of water in the wilderness. With that custom in mind, how would you explain the significance of Jesus' remarks in verses 37-39?

✑ APPLYING THE WORD

• What counsel would you give believers who face spiritual opposition from their family?

• Which of the opinions about Jesus you have identified in this chapter are still expressed today, and in what way?

• Based on Jesus' example, what should our response be to such reactions?

✑ RESPONDING IN PRAYER

Pray for wisdom as you face various reactions to Jesus.

JOHN 7:53—8:11   *Caught in Adultery*

NOTHING IS MORE humiliating than being caught in an act of disobedience. Whether it's a child with his hand in the cookie jar or an adult driving over the speed limit, we all know the sinking feeling of being caught. In John 8, a woman is caught in the most awkward of situations—in the very act of adultery. The way Jesus responds to her may surprise you.

☙ WARMING UP TO GOD

Think of a time when you hurt someone and that person was willing to forgive you. How did it feel to be forgiven? Thank God for extending forgiveness to you.

☙ DISCOVERING THE WORD

1. *Read John 7:53—8:11.* What do we know about the character and motives of those who bring this woman to Jesus?

2. While it is obvious that the woman is guilty, what elements of injustice can you find in this situation?

3. The Pharisees and teachers were often very self-righteous. Why do you think they went away rather than stoning the woman (vv. 7-9)?

4. How would you describe Jesus' attitude toward the woman (vv. 10-11)?

☙ APPLYING THE WORD

- What can we learn from this passage about Christ's attitude toward us— even when we feel awful about ourselves?

- What does it teach us about forgiving and accepting others?

- Who do you need to offer your forgiveness to?

☙ RESPONDING IN PRAYER

Ask God to show you what it means to forgive.

JOHN 8:12-59 *Jesus, the Light of the World*

JESUS NEVER SPOKE in public without creating controversy. In fact he was constantly in trouble. Rather than retreating behind the safety of a pulpit, Jesus spoke in settings where people were bold enough to talk back. In this portion of John's story, Jesus makes a series of claims about himself. Each claim is met by a challenge from his enemies. Each challenge is then answered, and the answer leads to the next claim. Throughout this interchange, Jesus shows us how to speak the truth in the face of hostility. He also reveals some amazing things about himself.

ᗑ WARMING UP TO GOD

Have you ever tried to talk about Christ with a family member or coworker who was hostile to your message? How did you feel at the time? Thank God for giving you a Savior who understands everything we experience.

ᗑ DISCOVERING THE WORD

1. *Read John 8:12-59.* The Pharisees challenge the validity of Jesus' claim (v. 13). How does Jesus answer their challenge (vv. 14-18)?

2. Jesus' reference to his Father leads to his second claim—that he came from God. How does this claim heighten the tension between Jesus and the Jews (vv. 19-30)?

3. Jesus makes another startling claim in verses 31-32: "If you hold to my teaching . . . then you will know the truth, and the truth will set you free." Why does holding to Jesus' teaching lead to true knowledge and freedom?

4. Jesus' opponents also claim to have both Abraham and God as their father. According to Jesus, how does their conduct contradict their claim (vv. 39-47)?

ᗑ APPLYING THE WORD

• Why is our conduct the truest test of our beliefs?

• In what ways does your lifestyle validate (or invalidate) your claim to be a follower of Christ?

ᗑ RESPONDING IN PRAYER

Ask God to help you change the parts of your life that don't match your beliefs.

JOHN 9   *A Blind Man Sees the Light*

OUR SIGHT IS A wonderful gift from God. We marvel at the fiery colors of a sunset, the rich pastels of spring and the delicate beauty of a flower. How tragic it must be to never see the light of day. Yet there is a far greater tragedy than physical blindness. In this passage Jesus meets a man who has been blind from birth. The man illustrates that those who are blind often see clearly, while those with sight see nothing at all.

✍ WARMING UP TO GOD

Before you begin this chapter about various kinds of blindness and sight, ask God to open your eyes so that you can see what he has for you.

✍ DISCOVERING THE WORD

1. *Read John 9.* Based on the question the disciples ask Jesus (v. 2), how do they view the relation of sickness to sin?

2. What is Jesus' view of the same issue (vv. 3-5)?

3. Why do you think Jesus goes through the process of making mud and instructing the man to go wash, instead of simply healing him instantly?

4. On what grounds do the Pharisees object to this miracle (vv. 16, 22, 24, 29)?

5. How do the Pharisees react when the genuineness of the miracle becomes undeniable (vv. 28-34)?

✍ APPLYING THE WORD

• When might Christians today exhibit the Pharisees' attitude toward a marvelous work of God's grace or power?

• What principles in this chapter could help you improve your spiritual eyesight?

✍ RESPONDING IN PRAYER

Ask God to strengthen your faith so that you might respond as the man did: "Lord, I believe."

JOHN 10 *The Shepherd and His Sheep*

JESUS WAS A master at using simple, everyday objects or events to illustrate profound spiritual truths. Farmers scattering seed, vines sustaining the branches and sparrows falling to the earth all took on a new dimension in Jesus' eyes. In John 10 Jesus uses the scene of a shepherd enclosing his sheep in a sheepfold to give us one of the most moving pictures of salvation and security in Christ found in the Bible. If you've ever doubted the love of Christ, Jesus will give you a healthy dose of assurance in this chapter.

WARMING UP TO GOD

What usually prompts you to have doubts about your salvation or your walk with Christ. Is it your own sin? Feelings of unworthiness? Personal failures? Be honest with Christ about your doubts.

DISCOVERING THE WORD

1. *Read John 10.* What spiritual truths is Jesus trying to convey in verses 1-5?

2. In verses 11-15 Jesus talks about the shepherd's care for his sheep. What can you learn from those verses about Jesus' care for and relationship with you?

3. According to Jesus, how are the Jews in this passage different from his sheep (vv. 22-27)?

4. When Jesus claims that he and the Father are one, the Jews pick up stones to stone him (vv. 30-33). Do you think his defense is a denial of his deity (vv. 33-36)? Explain.

APPLYING THE WORD

- How do you respond to promises and assurances Jesus gives his sheep in verses 28-29?

- Which promise from Jesus in this chapter is most encouraging to you?

- How can Jesus' promise help you when you have doubts?

RESPONDING IN PRAYER

Praise God for giving you such a good Shepherd.

JOHN 11   *Resurrection and Life*

EVER SINCE GOD judged Adam and Eve, death has plagued humanity. It separates us from those we love and looms over our own lives like a menacing spirit. In this chapter Jesus reaches out to a family struggling with the pain of death. He shows us why we need never fear death again.

❧ WARMING UP TO GOD

When is it difficult for you to feel that God is with you? Talk to God about your feelings of abandonment.

❧ DISCOVERING THE WORD

1. *Read John 11.* How can we resolve the apparent conflict between Jesus' love for Lazarus and his deliberate delay in helping him (vv. 4-5)?

2. What additional insight into God's purposes can we gain from Jesus' statement in verse 15?

3. What elements of doubt and faith do you see in Martha's statements to Jesus (vv. 17-27)?

4. How should Christ's statement in verses 25-26 radically alter our views of life and death?

5. Why do you think John emphasizes that Jesus was deeply moved by Mary's grief and the anguish of those with her (vv. 28-38)?

6. How would you explain the fact that the people who see the same miracle respond in two totally different ways (vv. 45-57)?

❧ APPLYING THE WORD

- How can those verses help us when we feel abandoned by God in a time of great need?

- In what ways will this chapter change the way you respond to personal difficulty or the apparent delay of God?

❧ RESPONDING IN PRAYER

Thank God for his personal presence with you.

JOHN 12   *The King's Last Acts*

IF YOU HAVE ever felt rejected or misunderstood, you know how Jesus felt as his public ministry came to an end. The hostility against him had risen to a fever pitch. His gentle compassion and abundant miracles were met with oppression and violence. Jesus knew what none of his friends knew—that he was about to die. In spite of the fleeting attempts of the crowd to make him king, Jesus chose the way of the cross.

✎ WARMING UP TO GOD

If you knew for sure that you had only one week to live, what would you do with that week? Make a list of the priorities that come to you.

✎ DISCOVERING THE WORD

1. *Read John 12.* What motivates Mary to pour expensive perfume on Jesus' feet?

2. Judas objects to Mary's extravagance. What motives and wrong thinking lie behind his objection (vv. 4-8)?

3. What do the shouts of the crowd tell us about their expectations of Jesus (vv. 12-13)?

4. How do Christ's statements about his mission clash with the crowd's expectations (vv. 23-28)?

5. When we stubbornly refuse to believe, what happens to our spiritual senses, and why (vv. 37-41)?

6. Jesus' last public message to his people is recorded in verses 44-50. What indications do you find that he is still reaching out in love and grace to those who have rejected him?

✎ APPLYING THE WORD

- In what ways should we be extravagant in our devotion to Jesus?

- How can you apply the example of Jesus to people who reject you or your testimony about Christ?

✎ RESPONDING IN PRAYER

In your own life, are you interested in earthly acclaim and glory or are you willing to lose your life for Christ's sake? Examine your direction and life goals in the light of Jesus' commitment to do the will of the Father.

JOHN 13:1-17 *The Son as a Slave*

THERE WERE TWO things on Jesus' heart the night before his crucifixion: his Father and his disciples. In John 13—17, we have the privilege of listening to his conversations with them both. However, before Jesus can instruct his disciples about his death, he has to act out a lesson in servitude. Jesus also shows us the spirit he expects in those who follow him. Greatness in his eyes does not come from having many servants but from being the servant of many.

✎ WARMING UP TO GOD

Have you ever been asked to do a demeaning, lowly job? What thoughts went through your mind at that time? Praise God for a Savior who was willing to take on the lowliest task of all.

✎ DISCOVERING THE WORD

1. *Read John 13:1-17.* According to John, what did Jesus know about himself (vv. 1-3)?
   In light of that knowledge, what is remarkable about what Jesus did next (vv. 4-5)?

2. Footwashing was normally done by servants or slaves. Why do you think Jesus washed his disciples' feet instead of just talking to them about love?

3. Was Peter simply being humble when he refused to allow Jesus to serve him (vv. 6-8)? Explain.

4. What spiritual truth was Jesus trying to communicate to Peter (and to us) in verses 8-10?

5. Based on Jesus' words in verse 17, how would you describe the relationship between knowledge, action and joy in the Christian life?

✎ APPLYING THE WORD

- What has this chapter revealed to you about your attitude toward serving?

- In what specific ways can you model the humility of Jesus toward those with whom you live or work?

✎ RESPONDING IN PRAYER

Ask God to give you a humble spirit.

JOHN 13:18-38 *The Betrayer and the Boaster*

THERE ARE SOME people we just don't like to be around. They aren't necessarily our enemies; they simply have the uncanny ability to irritate us. If we had been one of Jesus' disciples, we would probably have found it difficult to be around Peter. He was blunt and, at times, arrogant. On the other hand, we might have regarded Judas with trust and respect. The only one who saw deeply enough to discern the true character of these men was Jesus.

⊱ WARMING UP TO GOD

Has someone in your life ever hurt you deeply? How have you responded to that hurt? Tell God how you feel about what happened. Allow him to speak to your pain.

⊱ DISCOVERING THE WORD

1. *Read John 13:18-38.* Jesus takes this opportunity to predict his betrayal. How would his prediction dispel any doubts the disciples might have and strengthen their faith (v. 19)?

2. Evidently the disciples did not know who would betray Jesus (v. 22). What does this tell us about how Jesus had treated Judas?

3. Why does the kind of love Jesus describes convince all of humanity that we are Jesus' disciples (v. 35)?

4. Do you think Peter's declaration in verse 37 comes from pride or from sincerity? Explain.

5. Three people stand out in this passage: Jesus, Judas and Peter. What one character quality of each—good or evil—impresses you the most?

⊱ APPLYING THE WORD

• How would you have treated Judas if you knew he would eventually betray you?

• John later wrote, "This is how we know what love is: Jesus Christ laid down his life for us. And we ought to lay down our lives for our brothers" (1 Jn 3:16). In what practical ways can you exhibit this sacrificial love?

⊱ RESPONDING IN PRAYER

Pray for a strong faith that won't lead you into betrayal when times are tough.

JOHN 14 *Comfort for a Troubled Heart*

THE CALL COMES late at night. A broken sob is followed by these words: "Our son is dying. Will you please come to the hospital?" What can you say to bring comfort to broken hearts? Jesus faced that challenge too. In this chapter he comforts eleven disciples who feel that their world is coming unglued.

᪐ WARMING UP TO GOD

What is troubling you? Give it to God, and wait before him to receive his comfort.

᪐ DISCOVERING THE WORD

1. *Read John 14.* How would the promises Jesus makes in verses 1-4 bring comfort to his disciples?

2. In light of verses 5-14, why is it crucial for our focus to be on Jesus himself?

3. According to Jesus, how will the Spirit bring comfort and help to his followers (vv. 15-27)?

4. What is the relationship between our love and obedience to Jesus and his love and presence in our lives (vv. 15-24)?

5. How does the peace Christ offers differ from that which the world offers (vv. 25-31)?

᪐ APPLYING THE WORD

• Think of a friend who is going through a personal crisis. How could this chapter help you to minister to that person?

• How can Jesus' words help you in a personal crisis or when you have a troubled heart?

᪐ RESPONDING IN PRAYER

Ask God to comfort someone you know who is troubled.

JOHN 15:1-17 *The Secret of Remaining*

THE FINAL WEEKEND before Christmas is not the time to visit a shopping mall. The press of people makes shopping almost impossible. One mother gave instructions to her young son before plunging into the crowd: "Stay close to me and hold my hand all the time. We won't get separated if we hold on to each other."

As Jesus prepared his disciples to face life without his visible presence, he impressed on them the importance of staying close to him spiritually. He said, "Remain in me." If you've ever longed to understand the secret of spiritual growth, you will find it in Jesus' words to us in John 15.

☙ WARMING UP TO GOD

Have you ever felt far from Christ since becoming a Christian? What circumstances made you feel that way? Be still before God and feel his presence with you now.

☙ DISCOVERING THE WORD

1. *Read John 15:1-17.* Jesus' instructions to his disciples in this passage revolve around three symbols: the vine, the gardener and the branches. What is Jesus trying to communicate by calling himself the true vine?

2. What does it mean to remain in Christ (v. 4)?

3. The Father prunes fruitful branches to make them more fruitful (v. 2). In what ways have you experienced the Father's "pruning"?

4. What spiritual benefits result from remaining in Christ (vv. 7-11)?

5. What are the requirements and benefits of friendship with Christ (vv. 14-17)?

☙ APPLYING THE WORD

• There are three categories of branches described in this passage: those bearing no fruit, those bearing some fruit and those bearing much fruit. In which category would you place yourself and why?

• If you are not bearing fruit, what is Jesus' counsel to you in these verses?

☙ RESPONDING IN PRAYER

Picture yourself as a tree laden with plump, healthy fruit. Ask God to help you become the person he wants you to be.

JOHN 15:18—16:4   *The Cost of Friendship with Jesus*

WHILE ON EARTH, Jesus did not surround himself with a group of students or even a group of followers. He placed himself in the company of friends. To admit that we need friends is a sign of maturity, not immaturity. Close relationships are Christlike! In this passage Jesus shows us what friendship with him is really like. There's both comfort and cost.

⚘ WARMING UP TO GOD

Are you ready to face the cost of following Christ? Talk openly with God about your fears—and excitement.

⚘ DISCOVERING THE WORD

1. *Read John 15:18—16:4.* If love is to characterize our relationship with other believers, hate will characterize our relationship with the world. What reasons does Jesus give for the world's hatred (15:18-21)?
2. What does Jesus mean when he says that without his coming, his words and his miracles, the world "would not be guilty of sin" (15:22-25)?
3. In what specific ways will the Counselor and the disciples themselves continue the ministry begun by Jesus (15:26-27)?
4. What kind of treatment can the disciples expect from those who do not know Christ (16:1-4)?

⚘ APPLYING THE WORD

• What kinds of persecution are more probable for us in our society? Explain.
• If we as Christians are not persecuted in some way, what might that imply about our spiritual commitment?
• How are you experiencing the world's hatred as a Christian?

⚘ RESPONDING IN PRAYER

Pray for those around the world who face persecution for their faith.

JOHN 16:5-33 *Secrets of the Spirit*

A LOVELY WOMAN knew for almost a year that, unless the Lord intervened, the cancer in her brain would kill her. That year brought wonderful interactions with her husband and family. They had the opportunity to express their love for her, and the dying woman had the privilege of passing on her godly wisdom.

In John 16 Jesus knows that he will die in less than twenty-four hours. When his disciples are faced with that reality, Jesus responds to their concerns by talking about the coming Holy Spirit.

❧ WARMING UP TO GOD

Think about the important people in your life. What would you tell them if you had only a short time to live? Ask God to make you ready to hear what Jesus had to say in his last days.

❧ DISCOVERING THE WORD

1. *Read John 16:5-33.* Jesus said that it was for the disciples' good that he go away and that the Counselor come. Why was the Spirit's presence more profitable to the disciples than Jesus' presence?

2. What would the Spirit's ministry be toward the world (vv. 8-11)?

3. The Spirit's ministry is one of communication. What specific things did Jesus say the Spirit would communicate to the disciples (vv. 13-15)?

4. Jesus answers the disciples' questions in verses 17-18 not by giving an explanation but by making a promise (vv. 19-22). What was the promise?

5. Why would Jesus' promise bring joy in the midst of grief and confusion?

6. How would Jesus' assurance of the Father's love help the disciples in the days just ahead of them (vv. 25-33)?

❧ APPLYING THE WORD

- How can this incident help us when our questions to the Lord seemingly go unanswered?

- How do you respond to the promise in verses 23-24?

❧ RESPONDING IN PRAYER

Give God the desires of your heart, knowing he wants to make your joy complete.

JOHN 17   *The Master's Final Prayer*

THE APPROACH OF death has a way of bringing our priorities into focus. People who know death is imminent also know what is really important in life and who they really care about. In Jesus' final prayer with his disciples, he prays for himself, for them and for you. Every believer is on Jesus' mind as he faces the greatest trial of his life—the cross.

๛ WARMING UP TO GOD

Spend some time reflecting on God's glory. To what extent is God's glory foremost in your mind on a daily basis? Explain.

๛ DISCOVERING THE WORD

1. *Read John 17.* Jesus makes only one request for himself: that the Father would glorify him so that he might glorify the Father. In what way would each one glorify the other (vv. 1-5)?
   Why do you think that was so important to Jesus?

2. According to verses 6-19, what specific ministries did Jesus have toward his disciples?

3. Twice Jesus asked the Father to protect his disciples from the evil one (vv. 11, 15). Why would that protection have been so important in Jesus' mind as he faced the cross?

4. Jesus prayed that those who believe in him would be one "so that the world may believe that you have sent me" (v. 21, see also v. 23). Why is our unity a powerful argument for the reality of Jesus?

๛ APPLYING THE WORD

- Jesus also asked the Father to sanctify his disciples through his word (v. 17). How can we allow God's Word to have that kind of effect on our lives?

- Jesus obviously prayed this prayer out loud to bring comfort and assurance to his disciples. In what particular ways do Jesus' words encourage or assure you?

๛ RESPONDING IN PRAYER

Ask God to bring unity to your church or fellowship.

JOHN 18:1-27 *"Jesus, You're Under Arrest!"*

MOST OF US would hate the thought of being arrested and brought to trial. If we were guilty of a crime, being arrested would be humiliating. But if we were innocent, it would be devastating. Yet in what should have been a demeaning experience for Jesus, we see again his majesty and glory. Jesus uses an experience of attack, betrayal and abandonment to demonstrate his confident trust in the Father. His calm assurance will help us face life's hurts and injustices with the same trust in the same Father.

✎ WARMING UP TO GOD

Think about a time when you realized you had committed a deep sin. How did you feel when you took it before Christ? Thank him for his grace to you then and now.

✎ DISCOVERING THE WORD

1. *Read John 18:1-27.* Why would Jesus go to a place where Judas knew he might be found (vv. 1-3)?

2. When the soldiers say they are seeking Jesus of Nazareth, Jesus replies, "I am he" (literally "I am"; v. 5). How would you explain the reaction of the soldiers (v. 6)?

3. What insight do Peter's action and Jesus' rebuke (v. 11) give you about our attempts at times to "help God out" in our own strength and wisdom?

4. Think back to the deepest sin of your life. How does a look at your own sin change your attitude toward Peter's denial of Jesus?

5. What specific events in this passage display (a) Jesus' courage, (b) his power and (c) his obedience to the Father?

✎ APPLYING THE WORD

- What can we learn from Peter's failure about being ready to stand against the world's challenges?

- How will this study change the way you will face a time of testing in your own life?

✎ RESPONDING IN PRAYER

Ask God to make you ready to face difficulties with grace.

JOHN 18:28—19:16   *Pilate on Trial*

"CHRIST KILLERS." Someone had spray-painted the words and a series of swastikas on a Jewish synagogue. Anti-Semitism had raised its ugly head again.

The New Testament does blame Jewish leaders for condemning Jesus to die. But they weren't acting alone. The Roman governor, Pontius Pilate, also condemned Jesus to die. There is also a sense in which we all killed Jesus. He died for our sins. But the most amazing answer to the question of who killed Jesus is that no one did. Jesus said, "No one takes my life from me, but I lay it down of my own accord" (Jn 10:18).

☞ WARMING UP TO GOD

What temptation to compromise your Christian faith are you facing? Ask the One who faced deep trials to give you strength.

☞ DISCOVERING THE WORD

1. *Read John 18:28—19:16.* A Roman trial included four basic elements: the accusation (18:29-31), the interrogation (search for evidence; 18:32-35), the defense (18:36-37) and the verdict (18:38). What events or statements from the text are included in each?

2. Pilate obviously was trying to release Jesus. What specific attempts did he make (18:39; 19:4, 6, 10, 12, 15)?

3. The true charge against Jesus comes in verse 7: "He claimed to be the Son of God." Why do you think Pilate reacted to that statement as he did (vv. 8-9)?

4. Why didn't Jesus say more to Pilate (vv. 9-11)? Shouldn't he have defended himself more vigorously?

5. What can you conclude about Pilate's character after reading this passage? What kind of man was he?

☞ APPLYING THE WORD

- How can you respond appropriately to Christ's grace to you?

- How does this passage speak to how you should respond when treated unjustly?

☞ RESPONDING IN PRAYER

Ask God to help you follow his example of grace when you are under pressure.

JOHN 19:17-42   *Obedient to Death*

THE ACCOUNT OF the crucifixion is not easy to read. You may be tempted to think that Jesus' death was a cruel mistake. It wasn't. Jesus' life was not taken from him; he laid it down willingly. It was part of his plan—a plan that included you and me. His cross was truly our cross.

✎ WARMING UP TO GOD

When you think about death, what feelings and thoughts come to mind? Ask God for help in making sense of death.

✎ DISCOVERING THE WORD

1. *Read John 19:17-42.* Three groups were involved in Jesus' death: the soldiers, the Jewish leaders and Pilate. How would you characterize each one's attitude toward Jesus?
   In what ways do their attitudes toward Jesus parallel those of men and women today?
2. How is Jesus' care for Mary evident even while he is dying (vv. 26-27)?
3. What was the significance of Jesus' cry "It is finished" (v. 30; see Jn 17:4)?
4. What evidence does John give that Jesus really died?
5. Why was it so important for John to establish the certainty of Jesus' death?

✎ APPLYING THE WORD

- The disciples are not mentioned at the crucifixion; they probably were not there. When it comes to public identification with Jesus, under what circumstances are you tempted to respond in the same way?
- What aspect of Jesus' death has made the deepest impression on you, and why?

✎ RESPONDING IN PRAYER

Thank God for providing salvation to you through Christ's death.

JOHN 20   *The Son Is Up!*

AN ORDERLY WAS told to take a body to the morgue. Simply out of habit, the orderly felt the man's wrist for a pulse. When he realized his mistake, the orderly quickly dropped the arm, but not before his sensitive fingers told him there was a pulse! The doctors were called, and the man revived.

That story may or may not be true. But one man certainly came back to life. The man lived for years after the event. In fact, he is still alive.

☞ WARMING UP TO GOD

Imagine how you would feel if you were with Joseph of Arimathea and Nicodemus preparing Jesus' body for burial (vv. 38-42).

☞ DISCOVERING THE WORD

1. *Read John 20.* John records three witnesses to the empty tomb: Mary Magdalene, Peter and "the other disciple" (John himself). What important details do we learn from each one (vv. 1-9)?

2. John also records three appearances of the risen Christ: to Mary, to his disciples and to Thomas. Why do you think Mary doesn't immediately recognize Jesus (vv. 10-15)?

3. After she does recognize him, what impresses you most about their encounter (vv. 16-18)?

4. When Jesus appears to his disciples, what specific gifts and promises does he give them (vv. 19-23)?

5. How does Thomas's attitude—both before and after Jesus appears to him (vv. 24-29)—add credibility to the resurrection?

☞ APPLYING THE WORD

• What do you learn from Jesus' encounter with Thomas about dealing with people who have doubts about Christianity?

• Who could you help to understand and believe the claims of Christ?

• In verses 30-31 John tells us why he has written his Gospel. Of all the "miraculous signs" he has included, which have been most convincing to you? Why?

☞ RESPONDING IN PRAYER

Praise God for what he has done in Christ.

JOHN 21 *A Walk with a Resurrected Man*

MOST OF US find it easier to forgive than to forget. We may be ready to forgive someone who has hurt us deeply, but we have a hard time trusting that person again. Peter failed Jesus miserably. He promised to give up his life if necessary to protect Jesus, but denied him a few hours later. Peter knew Jesus had forgiven him. But would Jesus still trust him? Could Jesus still use him to bring glory to God? Will Christ still use us after we've failed?

✒ WARMING UP TO GOD

How do you feel when someone you have hurt refuses to forgive you? Write down the name of someone who needs your forgiveness.

✒ DISCOVERING THE WORD

1. *Read John 21.* What was Jesus trying to show the disciples by allowing them to catch such a large number of fish (vv. 4-6; see Lk 5:4-11)?
2. When Peter hears that "it is the Lord," he jumps into the water and begins swimming ahead of the boat (vv. 7-8). What does this reveal about Peter and his relationship with Jesus?
3. What subtle differences do you notice in Jesus' three questions and Peter's responses (vv. 15-17)?
4. Why do you think Jesus chose this particular time to predict the kind of death Peter would die (vv. 18-19)?
5. What does Jesus' rebuke to Peter (v. 22) reveal about the danger of comparing ourselves with other Christians?

✒ APPLYING THE WORD

- What can we learn from this passage about the steps involved in restoring a Christian who has sinned?
- How does it help to know that you can still serve and glorify God no matter what your past failures have been?

✒ RESPONDING IN PRAYER

Respond to God with your heart and life for what you have learned about Jesus in your study of John.

Introducing Acts

✑

The book of Acts should come with a warning label reading, "If you are open to God, this book will call you to new life." In essence it is the story of transformed lives—and the difference these lives made in the world.

By the second chapter of Acts, the same men who abandoned Jesus at Gethsemane have become irrepressible dynamos, preaching with utter conviction—and at great personal risk—"the mighty acts of God." Acts is an important book for us today because it confirms that the power that transformed the disciples' lives is the same power that can transform our lives today. That power is, of course, God himself—coming to us through the Holy Spirit.

In the book of Acts we will see the dynamics of the earliest church, the nature of their fellowship, the intensity of their prayer life and their out-and-out zeal to declare the saving gospel of Jesus Christ. Through this example, our own situation will be called into question. What does it mean to be the church today—and what are we to be doing?

In Acts we see the entire formative process of calling, healing, empowering and sending people forth to love and obey Jesus Christ. Speaking the gospel is only part of the task; Acts will challenge us to a holistic-community spirituality that can renew our churches today.

Jesus promised power to the disciples after the Holy Spirit came upon them. Acts reveals the Holy Spirit as the driving force behind all meaningful ministry in Jesus' name. Where do we look for spiritual power? Education? Work? Religious heritage? Acts calls us to a Spirit-filled life.

The explosive power of this living document will touch you. As you work through these quiet times, may you experience the calling, healing, empowering and sending dynamic of the Holy Spirit.

Phyllis J. Le Peau

ACTS 1   *You Will Be My Witnesses*

DURING THE DAYS between his resurrection and ascension, Jesus built the confidence of his disciples. He demonstrated and spoke truth about himself. And then he left them with a clearly defined task and the promise of the power to carry out that task. Thus Luke was able to write with confidence to Theophilus about Jesus.

✺ WARMING UP TO GOD

Have you had days when you did not feel confident, but fearful? Let God encourage you this day with the power and strength contained in his Word.

✺ DISCOVERING THE WORD

1. *Read Acts 1.* What did Luke, the author of Acts, report to Theophilus about Jesus' last days on earth (vv. 1-11)?
2. Put yourself in the shoes of the apostles. How would you feel if you were the first to be given the task described in verse 8?
3. How are we equipped for this task, according to the passage?
4. How did the disciples respond to all that they had seen and heard (vv. 12-26)?
5. Peter goes to Scripture immediately when he speaks. How do you think these words of David affect their confidence as well as give them direction (v. 20)?

✺ APPLYING THE WORD

- When has your faith in Jesus Christ been encouraged by the words of others?
- How is your hope and confidence in Jesus affected by what you learn about him in this passage?
- How are you affected when you pray with other believers, especially as you consider your part in God's mission for the church (v. 14)?

✺ RESPONDING IN PRAYER

Thank God for giving you a task to carry out, and tell him about the fears and joys you feel as his servant.

ACTS 2 *Receiving the Power*

A GROUP OF college students wanted to communicate the message of Jesus to the incoming class of freshmen. They realized there was only one source to accomplish this task: the power of the Holy Spirit. So they decided to pray for the new students by name weeks before they arrived. As a result, many who did not know Jesus when they arrived graduated as maturing Christians.

✎ WARMING UP TO GOD

Although at times we do not sense him, the Holy Spirit is always there to help us. Let him quiet you now and open your heart to what he wants to tell you about himself.

✎ DISCOVERING THE WORD

1. *Read Acts 2.* How do the Jews in verses 5-12 respond to the power of the Spirit that they witness?

2. Scripture is the foundation of Peter's proclamation of truth. What message does the Old Testament book of Joel have for the bewildered crowd (vv. 17-21)?

3. What is there in Peter's sermon that would reassure Theophilus about his faith and help him "know the certainty of the things" (Lk 1:4) he'd been taught?

4. What does Peter have to offer to those who are responsive to his message (vv. 37-39)?

5. Describe the fellowship of the believers in this young church (vv. 42-47).

✎ APPLYING THE WORD

- Imagine you were there on the day of Pentecost. What do you think it would have been like for you as one of the crowd looking on?

- How has your life been affected by the gift of the Holy Spirit?

- How does the life and purpose of your church or Christian fellowship group compare to that of this group?

✎ RESPONDING IN PRAYER

Ask God to make the power of the Holy Spirit come alive in your life, and pray that God will use you through that power.

ACTS 3 *Healing Power*

THE POWER OF the Holy Spirit is demonstrated not only in physical healing but also in the "complete healing" that includes every aspect of our life.

৫ৈ WARMING UP TO GOD

Recall a time when you felt broken and in need of healing. Thank God for the ways he has transformed and healed you since then.

৫ৈ DISCOVERING THE WORD

1. *Read Acts 3.* How does the response of the people to the miracle in verses 6-8 contrast with the beggar's response (vv. 8, 11-12)?

2. When Peter noticed how the crowd reacted, he saw his opportunity and talked to them about Jesus. According to Peter's message, what had God done to Jesus (vv. 13-15)? What had the people done to him?

3. How is the authority of Jesus demonstrated in this miracle (v. 16)?

4. How did Peter explain that all that had happened to Jesus was a part of God's plan (vv. 17-26)?

৫ৈ APPLYING THE WORD

• What healing do you need in your life?

• How do you respond when you have opportunities like Peter's to talk about Jesus?

• The "completely" healed man was a powerful testimony to the power of God and the truth of Peter's words. How have you seen the power of God demonstrated in your life and in the lives of others?

৫ৈ RESPONDING IN PRAYER

Thank God for working so powerfully to change your life, and ask him to give you the opportunity to talk about Jesus to one person this week.

ACTS 4:1-31 *Called into Question*

A DISABLED PERSON becomes abled. A one-time burden to society, a beggar, becomes a contributing citizen. How do the religious leaders respond to these miraculous events? Instead of expressing gratitude, they become extremely upset. The two men responsible for the healing are arrested.

✐ WARMING UP TO GOD

Let the distractions around you—the voices and restless thoughts—slip away. As the Spirit of God comes to dwell with you, allow yourself to enjoy his presence in quietness and gratitude.

✐ DISCOVERING THE WORD

1. *Read Acts 4:1-31.* What has upset the religious leaders (vv. 1-2)?
2. What action did they take (vv. 3-7)?
3. Just a few weeks have passed since Annas and Caiaphas had been involved in the condemnation of Jesus. In his response to their question, "By what power or what name did you say do this?" Peter is forcing them to encounter Jesus again. What does Peter say about him (vv. 10-12)?
4. In verses 13-22, what made it so difficult for the opposing religious leaders to bring this unacceptable behavior to a halt?
5. How did the believers react to John and Peter's account (vv. 24-30)?
6. What does their prayer tell you about their faith in the character, power and faithfulness of God (vv. 24-30)?

✐ APPLYING THE WORD

• When has your faith been challenged by others?
• Imagine that you were in a group of believers John and Peter returned to and told of what had happened. What would have been your reaction?
• "After they prayed, the place where they were meeting was shaken. And they were all filled with the Holy Spirit and spoke the word of God boldly" (v. 31). In what ways do you need the power of the Holy Spirit to face the world today?

✐ RESPONDING IN PRAYER

Ask God to fill you with the Spirit and empower you for the task of experiencing and communicating the gospel.

ACTS 4:32—5:16 — *Oneness of Heart*

NEXT TO THE Vietnam memorial in Washington, D.C., is a statue of three soldiers standing very close together. One is black, one is Hispanic and one is white. In Vietnam American soldiers learned, like never before, how very much they needed each other. In this study we will see that when the battle is spiritual, our need for each other is even more critical.

☙ WARMING UP TO GOD

Who has God given you that meets a need in your life? Thank God for giving you such a valuable and loving gift.

☙ DISCOVERING THE WORD

1. *Read Acts 4:32—5:16.* How is oneness of heart and mind demonstrated in 4:32-37?
2. What have Ananias and Sapphira done that is not consistent with Christian community (5:1-2)?
3. Pretend you are watching the interaction between Peter and Ananias and Sapphira (5:3-9). How would you report this incident?
4. Verse 11 states that "great fear seized the whole church and all who heard about these events." How do you think the church was affected by this fear?
5. What are the tangible evidences of the power of the Holy Spirit in this community in 5:12-16?

☙ APPLYING THE WORD

- How does this story demonstrate the high value that God places on truth and unity within the body of Christ?
- In what ways do we lie to each other today within our Christian communities?
- How could you help others in your church or fellowship understand what Christian community is about?

☙ RESPONDING IN PRAYER

Ask God to uphold truth in his church and to help you speak the truth before others.

ACTS 5:17—6:7 *Persecution and Expansion*

IN 1956 FIVE MEN were massacred by a tribe of the Auca people in Ecuador. The men had taken the good news of Jesus Christ to the Aucas. Opposition to this endeavor cost them their lives.

Over the years that same tribe was transformed as the loved ones of those five men took the message of Jesus to them. Many others have gone into the world with the gospel, inspired by these missionaries. The church continues to expand in spite of persecution, even as it did in the day of the apostles.

✑ WARMING UP TO GOD

Although we know God is in control of the universe, we often forget he has specific plans for our individual lives. Thank him for being sovereign everywhere, including in the secrecy of your own heart.

✑ DISCOVERING THE WORD

1. *Read Acts 5:17—6:7.* List the expressions and causes of emotion throughout 5:17-42.

2. Describe the apostles' response, motivation and source of strength throughout this whole episode.

3. What was Gamaliel's message to the religious leaders (5:34-39)?

4. How was his influence in saving the apostles' lives an example of the truth he spoke?

5. As the number of disciples increased, what practical needs began to present themselves (6:1-6)?

6. How did the Twelve respond to those needs (6:2-6)?

✑ APPLYING THE WORD

• When have you encountered internal or external opposition when you have attempted to proclaim the message of Jesus?

• Is it more difficult to deal with internal or external opposition? Why?

• As you observe the Holy Spirit, how do you think you or your church can ensure his ministry among you?

✑ RESPONDING IN PRAYER

Tell God about the struggles you have been facing as a believer. Ask him to give you strength and to remind you that his ways are higher than your own.

ACTS 6:8—7:60 *Full of the Spirit and Wisdom*

SOME people make you long to know God better. God's character in them makes you hunger and thirst for him. Stephen is described as "full of faith and of the Holy Spirit" (6:6). He was a gift to the early church but could not be tolerated by its enemies.

⌘ WARMING UP TO GOD

Think of a person who makes you want to know God better. Reflect on the qualities you see in her or him.

⌘ DISCOVERING THE WORD

1. *Read Acts 6:8—7:60.* What do you learn about Stephen throughout this passage?
2. What do the accusations against Stephen tell us about why the Jewish religious leaders were so upset (6:13-14)?
3. Sometimes the speech in chapter 7 is called "Stephen's defense," although it is actually a defense of pure Christianity as God's appointed way to worship. What are the main points of this defense?
4. What did God tell Abraham would happen to his descendants, the Hebrews (7:1-7)?
5. What direct application does Stephen make concerning the religious leaders from 7:39-43 (see 7:51-53)?

⌘ APPLYING THE WORD

• God told Abraham what would happen to the Hebrews years before it all happened, even before he had a son. How are you affected when you see all that unfolds in history?
• Throughout this whole passage, we see in Stephen the evidence of being full of the Spirit and wisdom. What are the evidences today of being full of the Spirit and wisdom?
• In what aspect of your life would you like to reflect more of the Spirit and wisdom?

⌘ RESPONDING IN PRAYER

Ask God to fill you with the Spirit and with wisdom.

ACTS 8   *The Power of Suffering*

STEPHEN IS DEAD. The church has experienced the tragedy of its first mar-
tyr. Saul approves of Stephen's death. He is putting all his energy into destroying the rest of Jesus' followers. In contrast, Philip is one of the seven,
full of the Spirit and wisdom. His energy goes into the proclamation of the
truth about Jesus. People respond. And so both the persecution and the ex-
pansion of the church continue.

◈ WARMING UP TO GOD

Has there been a time you were confused about God's intentions behind
events he placed in your life? Ask him to give you understanding and peace.

◈ DISCOVERING THE WORD

1. *Read Acts 8.* In this passage the command to be witnesses in all of Judea
   and Samaria (Acts 1:8) is fulfilled. What are the causes and extent of the
   spread of the gospel at this time?

2. How does Simon the sorcerer (vv. 9-25) attempt to get spiritual power?
   What is his motivation for wanting this power (vv. 18-19)?

3. What is God's way for people to receive spiritual power (vv. 20-23)?

4. What are the factors involved in the eunuch's coming to know the Lord
   (vv. 26-39)?

5. How was Philip's ministry to the eunuch the beginning of the witness "to
   the ends of the earth" (1:8)?

◈ APPLYING THE WORD

- The story of Simon the sorcerer demonstrates that becoming a Christian
  does not instantly resolve all problems and character flaws. What do you
  learn from Peter concerning nurturing young believers?

- What principles of evangelism have you observed in this passage?

- What lessons from Acts 8 might make you a more effective witness for
  Jesus?

◈ RESPONDING IN PRAYER

Ask God for the guidance of his Holy Spirit, and ask him to help you follow
the model of evangelism that Philip provides.

ACTS 9:1-31 *Saul's Conversion*

WHEN CHUCK COLSON became a Christian in prison, the whole nation reacted with skepticism—Christians and non-Christians alike. Of all the leading characters in the Watergate scandal, he was one of the most notorious. Could such a calculating man sincerely come to God?

ᵉᵃ WARMING UP TO GOD

Think back to what your life was like before you met Christ. Thank God for the transformation that he has made in your life—both your instant rebirth into his kingdom and the gradual remolding of your character since then.

ᵉᵃ DISCOVERING THE WORD

1. *Read Acts 9:1-31.* Review what you know about Saul (7:58—8:3). What further insights do you get about him from 9:1-2?

2. Describe Saul's encounter with Jesus Christ in verses 3-9. (What is the emotional, spiritual, physical and social climate?)

3. Ananias is the second person in three days to have a direct encounter with the Lord. Compare and contrast his encounter (vv. 10-16) with that of Saul.

4. What is the significance of Ananias addressing Saul as "brother" (v. 17)?

5. What is the response of both believers and nonbelievers to Saul and his ministry (vv. 19-30)?

6. What role does Barnabas play in Saul's life and ministry?

ᵉᵃ APPLYING THE WORD

• What do you learn about obedience to God through Saul and Ananias?

• What does Saul's conversion teach us about those in our lives who are most likely not to believe?

• Consider the people in your life who are most antagonistic to Christianity. How might God use you to bring them to Christ?

ᵉᵃ RESPONDING IN PRAYER

Pray for the salvation of someone you consider an unlikely convert. Ask God to increase your faith.

ACTS 9:32—10:48 *Salvation for Every Nation*

ONCE THE BERLIN WALL seemed impenetrable, and Communism, powerful and indestructible. For seventy years Christians wondered if Christmas would ever be openly celebrated in Russia. Then, dramatically, the wall fell. Communism collapsed. Nations that had been closed to the gospel for years began to welcome Christians, their help and their message with open arms. That historic breakthrough was like the one the early Christians experienced in this passage. A seemingly impenetrable spiritual wall was broken down. In both situations we see that, from God's perspective, there is always the potential for reaching every person in all the corners of the world with the wonderful news of Jesus Christ.

✍ WARMING UP TO GOD

Think of an impossible feat you have seen God accomplish. Thank him and allow him to show you again that he truly is almighty.

✍ DISCOVERING THE WORD

1. *Read Acts 9:32—10:48.* How is God's power demonstrated in 9:32-43?
2. This is the first time Peter has been involved in raising someone from the dead. How might this prepare him for what happens in chapter 10?
3. How did God prepare Cornelius for Peter (10:1-8)?
4. In what ways did God prepare Peter for Cornelius (10:9-33)?
5. What evidence is there that Cornelius expected God to work (10:24-26)?

✍ APPLYING THE WORD

- What lessons do we learn from Cornelius's life?
- In summary, how do you see God's purpose, as stated in Acts 1:8 ("You will receive power when the Holy Spirit comes on you; and you will be my witnesses in Jerusalem, and in all Judea and Samaria, and to the ends of the earth"), being fulfilled in this passage?
- In what ways could you grow in relating to people of other cultures and races?

✍ RESPONDING IN PRAYER

Ask God to use your experiences in life and your knowledge of him to bring others to Christ.

ACTS 11 *The First Jewish-Gentile Church*

LUKE SET UP the stories of Peter with Cornelius and Ananias with Saul with amazing symmetry. The Holy Spirit simultaneously prepared the hearts of Ananias and Saul as he simultaneously prepared those of Peter and Cornelius. Peter doubted whether he could be friends with Gentiles; Ananias, whether he could approach an enemy of the church. Both obeyed without hesitation when God made his divine will known.

These stories come together in today's study. Peter defends his ministry to Cornelius to the church at Jerusalem, convincing them of God's work in the Gentiles. Here also Saul, the one-time enemy of the church, reappears as a minister to a church filled with both Jew and Gentile Christians.

⚕ WARMING UP TO GOD

In the face of change, how do you handle the need for a new perspective? With resistance? Excitement? Uncertainty? Do you face a change now? Take time to put your response, whatever it is, in God's hands.

⚕ DISCOVERING THE WORD

1. *Read Acts 11.* What kind of reception awaited Peter when he went back to Jerusalem (vv. 1-3)?

2. What seemed to be the final and most convincing proof to Peter of God's working in the Gentiles (vv. 15-17)? Why?

3. In the meantime the gospel is spreading to Gentiles at a tremendous rate in Antioch. What kind of care is provided for new believers (vv. 22-30)?

4. What was the reason for, and what were the results of, Barnabas's trip to Antioch (vv. 22-30)?

⚕ APPLYING THE WORD

• What can we learn from the way Peter responded to his critics?

• How does our care for new believers compare to the care given here?

• How do you see in this passage the true meaning of "Christian" being more fully discovered and lived out in a multicultural church?

⚕ RESPONDING IN PRAYER

Ask God to help you be more open and flexible to the changes that he desires to bring about in your life.

ACTS 12   *Miraculous Escape*

HUDSON TAYLOR, a well-known missionary to China, said, "Man is moved by God through prayer alone." We see the power of God demonstrated in this passage in response to the prayers of his people.

✎ WARMING UP TO GOD

Recall a time when God answered one of your prayers. Thank him for the joy and encouragement you received from his gracious blessing upon you.

✎ DISCOVERING THE WORD

1. *Read Acts 12.* Describe the main characters in this passage.
   How do they respond to what is happening to and around them?
2. What seems to motivate Herod's actions (vv. 1-5)?
3. What does the church's response to James's death and Peter being in prison (vv. 5, 12) demonstrate about prayer?
4. Why was Herod struck down (vv. 21-23)?
5. Contrast Herod's end with what happened with the Word of God (vv. 19-24).

✎ APPLYING THE WORD

- How have you seen God respond to a group of people who were earnestly praying?
- Why do you think the praying Christians reacted as they did to Peter's return (vv. 14-15)?
- The earnest prayer of the church significantly affected the outcome of the events of this chapter. How is your motivation to pray influenced by this truth?

✎ RESPONDING IN PRAYER

Think of an "impossible" prayer request or need you have. Place it before God and ask him to give you the faith to believe that he will answer your prayer and give you "the desires of your heart" (Ps 37:4).

ACTS 13—14   *Paul's First Missionary Journey*

PETER HAS DISAPPEARED. Luke is ushering him from the stage while Paul steps to the forefront. Peter, the apostle to the Jews, has played his part well and prepared the way for Paul, the apostle to the Gentiles. Paul and Barnabas have completed their mission of mercy in Jerusalem on behalf of the church in Antioch (11:29) and have returned to Antioch with John Mark. In this study we will look at Paul's first missionary journey.

✒ WARMING UP TO GOD

Do you feel distant from God as you try to approach the Scriptures? Remember that God wants to meet us here.

✒ DISCOVERING THE WORD

1. *Read Acts 13—14.* Antioch was the second greatest metropolis of the church and the mother of Gentile Christianity. What role did the church of Antioch play in Paul's first missionary journey (13:1-3; 14:26-28)?

2. Review Paul's message in the synagogue in Pisidian Antioch (13:16-41). What truths of the gospel are communicated?

3. How does Paul's message show sensitivity to audience and context?

4. List the different responses to the gospel (13:7-8, 13, 42-45, 48, 52; 14:1-5) that you see throughout this passage.

5. How did Paul respond to those who rejected the gospel (13:9-11, 46, 51)? To those who believed (14:9-10, 21-23)?

✒ APPLYING THE WORD

- In what ways are you tempted to be "God" in another's life or to take credit for what God has done?

- How can we help one another when in the midst of such temptations?

- Consider the qualities that made Paul and Barnabas effective in their ministry. Which of these qualities do you want God to develop in you?

✒ RESPONDING IN PRAYER

Is there a way God wants to change you? Talk to him about it.

ACTS 15   *Conflict in the Church*

BELIEVERS SHOULD be able to talk, pray and work through conflict—just the way it was worked through by the church at Jerusalem. However, as Kenneth Strachen of Latin American Mission said, "We all need to live and serve in the constant recognition of our own humanity." Paul and Barnabas, who were used by God to keep a church from splitting, could not resolve their own differences and ended up going separate ways.

✎ WARMING UP TO GOD

Has there been a time when you were in conflict with someone? Tell God about it and let his peace and compassion wash over you as he teaches you.

✎ DISCOVERING THE WORD

1. *Read Acts 15.* Describe the conflict that arises between the Christians (vv. 1-35).

2. Describe the spirit of those involved and the steps that were taken to resolve this conflict. What were the results?

3. In what ways do you see (or can you assume) unity between Paul and Barnabas (vv. 36-41)?

4. Paul and Barnabas came to the point of "agreeing to disagree" and going their separate ways. What were the benefits of this temporary solution?

✎ APPLYING THE WORD

- What principles do you observe that are vital to follow as we face conflict with others in our Christian community?

- Which of these principles do you struggle with implementing the most?

- Both Paul and Barnabas seemed to have strong cases for their points of view. Under what kinds of circumstances should we surrender deep convictions when they are challenged by another?

- No matter how strongly we feel about an issue, we do not see the whole picture. How should that affect the way we respond to people with whom we are in conflict?

✎ RESPONDING IN PRAYER

Ask God to give you discernment as you face conflict in both the church and your personal life.

128

ACTS 16

What Must I Do?

THE MEMORY IS still vivid. Susan looked up from the booklet she was reading and said, "I would like to become a Christian. Will you help me?" This dormitory setting was not quite as dramatic as a Philippian jail. But it was just as exciting to hear Susan's words as it was for Paul and Silas to hear the jailer's cry, "What must I do to be saved?"

ᴥ WARMING UP TO GOD

Think back to the time you uttered those words, either to a friend or to God himself. Praise God for creating a desire for him in you, and thank him for giving his precious salvation to you.

ᴥ DISCOVERING THE WORD

1. *Read Acts 16.* How is Paul directed about where he should go (vv. 6-10)?

2. What principles of guidance do you see in verses 6-10?

3. Paul responded immediately to God's message. How was his obedience confirmed on arriving in Macedonia (vv. 11-15)?

4. The slave owners had Paul and Silas jailed. Their response to being in jail and beaten was to pray and sing hymns. Describe the events that led up the jailer's question, "What must I do to be saved?" (vv. 23-30).

5. It is clear in the book of Acts that God is concerned about the world and the nations being reached with the gospel. But he is also concerned about reaching individuals. What individuals were affected by Paul's obedience to God's leading, and how (vv. 14, 18, 30-31)?

ᴥ APPLYING THE WORD

- How does your response to opposition to and suffering for the gospel compare and contrast to that of Paul and Silas (v. 25)?

- Paul and Silas speak the truth of the gospel as well as live it out. How do you give both a verbal and a living witness to Jesus?

- Is there a person or task to which God is calling you? What steps do you need to take for immediate and unreserved obedience?

ᴥ RESPONDING IN PRAYER

Ask God to give you courage as you step in faith to obey him, to tell those around you about the good news that has transformed your life.

ACTS 17
An Unknown God

ONLY A FEW decades ago, Christians in the West could assume that most people they met belonged to a church or based their lives on Judeo-Christian values. Today Christians in the West face what Christians in the East have had to cope with for centuries—a variety of religious beliefs and practices that often have little in common with Christianity. How do we cope with a world that knows or cares so little about the truth of Jesus Christ? Paul left a helpful model when he visited the center of pagan philosophy and religion—Athens.

ᴄᴏ WARMING UP TO GOD

Do you feel overwhelmed by the spiritual condition of the world? Remember that the sin and pain around us are subject to Jesus' will.

ᴄᴏ DISCOVERING THE WORD

1. *Read Acts 17.* Compare and contrast Paul's ministry in Thessalonica and Berea. (What approach did he take? How did the people receive his message? What kind of results did he have?)

2. In most places, Paul makes contacts in the synagogues and speaks almost exclusively from Scripture. How does his ministry in Athens differ?

3. How do the people respond to his teaching in Athens?

4. Though Paul approaches people differently, some points in the content of his message are very consistent. Identify these (vv. 3, 18, 24-28, 30-31).

ᴄᴏ APPLYING THE WORD

• In his lecture in Athens, Paul mentions "the objects of your worship" (v. 33). What are some of the objects of worship for people in our culture?

• Paul begins with an inscription from an altar: "to an unknown god." What "points of truth" can you communicate the gospel from in your world?

• What are ways you might be tempted to compromise the message of the gospel as you communicate it to certain people?

• How can you better prepare yourself to effectively communicate the gospel of Jesus Christ to those to whom God has called you to minister?

ᴄᴏ RESPONDING IN PRAYER

Ask God what you have in common with non-Christians in your life.

ACTS 18 *Companions in Ministry*

I ENJOY THINKING about the people who have touched my life and who have been companions in ministry. I am thankful for those who have prayed for me, walked along with me, listened to me, loved me and cared about my walk with God and my service to others, who have encouraged me and corrected me. I am not alone in this need for companionship. In this study we will look at some of the people in Paul's life who were his companions in ministry.

⌘ WARMING UP TO GOD

Think about one person who profoundly affects your life. Thank God for loving you through that person.

⌘ DISCOVERING THE WORD

1. *Read Acts 18.* List the people in Paul's life that you see in this passage.
2. What did Silas and Timothy contribute to Paul's life and ministry (v. 5)?
3. In verses 18-23, what do you learn about Paul's relationships?
4. Describe Apollos (vv. 24-26).
5. How was Apollos's ministry affected by his relationship with Aquila and Priscilla (vv. 27-28)?

⌘ APPLYING THE WORD

- When has someone encouraged you with good news of God's work elsewhere, entered into your ministry, shared themselves or their home with you, or supported you financially or in other ways?

- What keeps you from allowing others to enter into your life and ministry in such ways?

- As you review this passage, what ways do you recognize in which you need to develop, build and nurture relationships that will contribute to your spiritual growth and outreach?

⌘ RESPONDING IN PRAYER

Who are your companions in ministry? Thank God for their presence in your life as good gifts from him.

ACTS 19:1—20:12 *In the Name of Jesus*

WE LEFT PAUL, in chapter 18, traveling throughout Galatia and Phrygia "strengthening all the disciples." In this passage he returns to Ephesus, where he settles for two and a half years. Great work is done there during this time, and it radiates out to other cities in the province of Asia. Luke vividly portrays the effect of Paul's ministry in just a few scenes in this section.

✒ WARMING UP TO GOD

Often we feel that reading the Bible is our time to give to God. But he dearly wants to come to us as we study Scripture and pray. Lay aside your effort right now and commit yourself to accepting God's grace. Let God be your companion while you study the Word.

✒ DISCOVERING THE WORD

1. *Read Acts 19:1—20:12.* Scan chapter 19. Where do you see God's power revealed?

2. In 19:1-7 Paul encounters some disciples. What did he do to interact with them effectively?

3. Throughout this entire passage it is evident that Paul has a strategy for communicating the gospel. Specifically what strategy does Paul have for his ministry in Ephesus (19:8-10)?

4. What was the cause of the riot in Ephesus (19:23-41)? How was it settled?

5. Paul continued to travel and encourage believers as he preached the gospel. What effect did the episode in 20:7-12 have on the crowd?

✒ APPLYING THE WORD

• What do you see in Paul's relationship with the disciples that might help you in relating to young Christians or your non-Christian friends?

• What kind of plan for communicating the gospel would be helpful in your world?

• How can you prepare yourself for both positive and negative responses as you are a part of communicating the gospel of Christ?

✒ RESPONDING IN PRAYER

Thank God for the amazing fact that he uses us, sinful humanity, to spread the gospel and advance his kingdom. Thank him for using you.

ACTS 20:13-38 *Paul's Farewell*

"I WILL SEE you in heaven." In this study we will enter into weeping as Paul says his final goodbye to the elders at Ephesus. He knows that more hardship and prison await him in Jerusalem. And he will never see the faces of these elders again.

❧ WARMING UP TO GOD

Is the busyness of the world around you crowding you as you seek the face of God? Thank God that he has given you the grace that brought you to his Word right now, and ask him to still your restless heart as he comes to sit with you.

❧ DISCOVERING THE WORD

1. *Read Acts 20:13-38.* What does Paul say about his ministry to the Ephesians (vv. 18-21, 26-27, 31, 33-35)?
2. What are Paul's priorities (vv. 22-25)?
3. What instructions did Paul give to the leaders of the church at Ephesus (vv. 28-31)?
4. According to verse 32, why can Paul leave them with confidence?
5. In summary, according to this passage, why might Paul be able to say with integrity and humility to these leaders, "Follow my example. Do as I have done"?

❧ APPLYING THE WORD

- Who is in your spiritual care?
- How are you preparing those whom you nurture spiritually so you can leave them with this same confidence?
- Paul and the Ephesian elders were given the rare and special gift of being able to say goodbye. What would you want to say to those in your spiritual care if you knew you were going to die? Take time to express your hope and your love to that person in the near future.

❧ RESPONDING IN PRAYER

Ask God for the courage to say these most important words to those you love and for whom you care deeply.

ACTS 21:1—22:21 *Facing Opposition*

FIVE YOUNG MEN sang as they went to their death, taking the gospel of Jesus Christ to the Auca tribe. Like Paul, knowing that death was a very real possibility, they did not turn aside from what they knew God wanted them to do. And they died doing it.

☙ WARMING UP TO GOD

There are times when we question our faith. However, God is just as real when we doubt or fear as when our faith is strong. Let him come to you now in the midst of your fear, and allow him to stretch your vision of how powerful he truly is.

☙ DISCOVERING THE WORD

1. *Read Acts 21:1—22:21.* Describe the warnings to Paul concerning going to Jerusalem (21:4, 10-12).

2. How did Paul respond to these warnings (21:5, 13)?

3. Paul arrives in Jerusalem, is greeted by the elders and reports what God has done through his ministry. What are the elders concerned about for Paul (21:20-25)?

4. How does Paul demonstrate his desire to be at one with the Jewish Christians (21:26)?

5. Note how Paul was treated with mob hysteria, assumption and false evidence (21:27-36, 38). How does he respond to all of this (21:37—22:21)?

☙ APPLYING THE WORD

• Think of a person you know who is focused on obeying God. How are you affected by that person's obedience?

• How do you usually respond when you find yourself in conflict with others as a result of your obedience to God?

• What have you seen in this passage that will help you become more single-minded in your obedience to God's will?

☙ RESPONDING IN PRAYER

Tell God of your desire to be obedient, but admit the difficulties you face because of your sin. Ask him again to cleanse you and help you run the race with fervor.

ACTS 22:22—23:35 *God at Work*

BEING UNDER GOD'S protection is not a guarantee of physical safety. Being under his protection does guarantee that our Father has a purpose for us and that nothing happens to us that does not come through his hands. We can live with confidence that our life on earth will not end until that purpose for us is complete; ultimately we will end up safe and protected in heaven. Paul was so sure of God's hand in his life that he continued to move out boldly with the message of Jesus Christ in spite of intensifying physical danger.

✎ WARMING UP TO GOD

The protection of the Father's strong arms is always around us. Thank him for his mighty but unseen acts that keep you safe and secure.

✎ DISCOVERING THE WORD

1. *Read Acts 22:22—23:35.* Throughout this passage, we can see God's hand in the circumstances of Paul's life, protecting and directing him. In 22:22-29, what is the source of the conflict?
   What is it that protects Paul?

2. In 23:1-10, what is the source of the conflict? How is Paul protected?

3. Why was Paul struck on the mouth for saying, "My brothers, I have fulfilled my duty to God in all good conscience to this day" (23:1)?

4. In 23:12-25 the Jews are frustrated because they cannot get rid of Paul through the law, so they decide to kill him. How is Paul protected?

5. We have observed God's protection of Paul. How do we see God's care for Paul in a more direct and supernatural way in 23:11?

✎ APPLYING THE WORD

• Think about God's hand in your life and ministry. How have you seen him work to protect and direct you toward his will?

• In what ways do you need to grow in humbly acknowledging God's hand in your life?

• How has your hope for God's will to be done in you been affected by looking at his hand in Paul's life?

✎ RESPONDING IN PRAYER

Ask God to show you his active hand in your life.

ACTS 24:1—25:12   *Falsely Accused*

GEORGE WAS FALSELY accused of heresy. Andy prayed fervently that God would shut the accusers' mouths and bind their efforts, and that truth would prevail and bring freedom. God chose to do what Andy asked, and George was exonerated in dramatic fashion. The words of the accusers brought condemnation on them. The defense did not even have to present its case.

The pain of being falsely accused is great. And the damage was not easily repaired. But George's consistent godly response throughout the whole ordeal is reminiscent of when Jesus and Paul were falsely accused.

᪥ WARMING UP TO GOD

Remember that whatever comes, today has been given to you by God and he desires to be with you as you walk through it.

᪥ DISCOVERING THE WORD

1. *Read Acts 24:1—25:12.* What are the accusations brought against Paul by the Jews (24:1-27)?

2. How would you describe Paul's defense? (Consider content, attitude and tone.)

3. What do you think is the significance of the fact that Felix was "well acquainted with the Way" (v. 22)?

4. In 25:1-12 two years have passed since Paul's trial. Festus has become the new governor. The Jews continue to plot to kill Paul, and they ask Festus to have him transferred to Jerusalem. Festus tells them to come to Caesarea. What evidence is there that Festus knows Paul is innocent?

5. Why does Festus suggest that Paul go back to Jerusalem to be on trial?

᪥ APPLYING THE WORD

• When have you known someone to respond to the proclamation of the gospel as Felix did? What might this mean?

• Describe a time you have been falsely accused because of your faith.

• What can you learn from the way Paul responded to his accusers?

᪥ RESPONDING IN PRAYER

Ask God to give you patience and a heart of love for the people who surround you—people you can show the example of Christ.

ACTS 25:13—26:32 *Testimony Before Agrippa*

THOUGH HIS INNOCENCE has been clearly stated many times, Paul remains a prisoner. He repeatedly has to face the unfair charges of the Jewish leaders. He has made his defense with integrity and power, and in return he gets only threats of death. In it all Paul's witness remains consistent. His greatest desire is that his accusers and those in judgment over him will become Christians.

☙ WARMING UP TO GOD

How do you respond to the unfairness in the world around you—poverty, homelessness, unfairness in your own life? It is difficult to assume an attitude like Paul's in the face of injustice. But God sees and knows what is right, and he understands the anger we feel. Express your thoughts and feelings to him. Let him calm the stirring in your heart with his gentle words.

☙ DISCOVERING THE WORD

1. *Read Acts 25:13—26:32.* Describe the nature and content of Festus's report to Agrippa (25:13-22).
2. What are the main points about himself that Paul presents in his defense (26:1-23)?
3. Why does Paul say he is on trial (26:6-8)?
4. Contrast the commission of the Sanhedrin (26:9-11) to the commission of Christ (26:15-18).
5. Describe Paul's final interaction with King Agrippa (26:26-29).

☙ APPLYING THE WORD

- What motivates you to tell non-Christians about Jesus?
- How does Paul's desire for King Agrippa compare or contrast to your desire for those around you who do not know Christ?
- How might you move closer to where Paul was in this desire?

☙ RESPONDING IN PRAYER

Ask God to give you the proper response to injustice and a heart that is soft toward those who do not know him.

ACTS 27—28 *Paul in Rome*

ROME AT LAST! Paul was innocent. He could have been a free man. But he had appealed to Caesar—and to Caesar he was to go. As we look at these last two chapters of Acts and complete our study of the life of this marvelous servant of God, it might be worthwhile to ask the questions "Who was really free, and who were the real prisoners?"

๛ WARMING UP TO GOD

Sit quietly for a few moments, without trying to force your thoughts to move in any direction. Let silence reign in your heart before you look to Scripture.

๛ DISCOVERING THE WORD

1. *Read Acts 27—28.* Though Paul had every reason by this time to become very self-centered, how do you see him continuing to minister to others throughout these two chapters (27:9-10, 21-25, 31-38, 42-43; 28:3, 8-9, 17-20, 23-31)?

2. What do you see of Paul's compassion as he ministers?

3. What do you think it says about Paul that Julius let him go see his friends (27:3)?

4. What do you see of Paul's confidence in God throughout this passage?

๛ APPLYING THE WORD

• What are the situations or relationships in your life with non-Christians in which you are tempted to give up on your proclamation of the gospel?

• What truths from this study of Acts encourage you not to give up?

• The words "boldly and without hindrance he preached the kingdom of God and taught about the Lord Jesus Christ" (28:31) summarize not only Paul's two years in Rome, but his whole Christian life. To what degree would you like this to be a summary of your life? Explain.

• In conclusion, what from the book of Acts motivates and equips you to be a witness "to the ends of the earth" (1:8)?

๛ RESPONDING IN PRAYER

Thank God for the ways he has taught you through the book of Acts. Ask him to continue to teach you as you try to live out the lessons you have learned.

Introducing Romans

I n our day, many are preaching a gospel that lacks clarity and substance. People are told to "invite Jesus into their heart" or simply "follow Christ" without understanding the meaning of his death and resurrection. We cannot correct this problem merely by memorizing gospel outlines or canned presentations. We need to immerse ourselves in Scripture through diligent study and thoughtful reflection.

Paul probably wrote Romans between A.D. 57 and 58 while he was at Corinth in the home of his friend and convert Gaius. He planned to go first to Jerusalem to deliver a gift of money from the Gentile churches to the poor in Jerusalem. Then he hoped to visit Rome on his way to Spain. His hopes were later realized, but not as he had expected. When he finally arrived in Rome in early A.D. 60, he was a prisoner under house arrest (Acts 28:11-31).

Romans may be the most important letter you will ever read. It is Paul's masterpiece, the clearest and fullest explanation of the gospel in the Bible. John Calvin said that "if a man understands it, he has a sure road opened for him to the understanding of the whole Scripture."

As you study Romans, may you be encouraged and challenged by the new life and the new lifestyle we have in Christ.

Jack Kuhatschek

ROMANS 1:1-17 *Good News from God*

WHAT IS OUR immediate response to good news? We tell others! We feel we will burst unless we share our joy with those around us.

Paul felt that way about the gospel, the good news about Jesus Christ. As we read these opening verses in his letter to the Romans, we find his excitement is contagious.

✎ WARMING UP TO GOD

Our days and weeks are often filled with bad news. Think of all the good news you can, and praise God for it.

✎ DISCOVERING THE WORD

1. *Read Romans 1:1-17.* Imagine that verses 1 and 5 are the only information you possess about Paul. Describe everything you would know about him.
2. In verses 1-5 Paul gives a summary of the gospel for which he had been "set apart." What do we learn about the gospel from these verses?
3. What do verses 8-13 reveal about Paul's attitude toward the Romans?
4. Paul says we can be eager to preach the gospel or be ashamed of it (vv. 15-16). What might lead us to adopt one attitude or the other?

✎ APPLYING THE WORD

• Because he was an apostle ("one who is sent"), Paul felt obligated to preach the gospel to everyone (v. 14). Who do you have the greatest opportunity of reaching with the gospel?
• What steps can you take to reach them?

✎ RESPONDING IN PRAYER

Pray that God will use Romans to give you Paul's attitude toward the gospel and toward those who need its message.

ROMANS 1:18-32 *The Wrath of God*

"HOW ARE YOU?" someone asks. "I'm fine," we reply. But are we really, or do our words mask our true condition? In this passage Paul tells us that we are not fine—neither we nor our friends nor society. Something is dreadfully wrong.

᨞ WARMING UP TO GOD

Usually we have to admit we need help before we can be helped. Why do we often find it so difficult to admit a need? Give your needs to God's care.

᨞ DISCOVERING THE WORD

1. *Read Romans 1:18-32.* John Stott, speaking to the Urbana Student Mission Convention in 1979, defined God's wrath (v. 18) as "his righteous reaction to evil, his implacable hostility to it, his refusal to condone it, and his judgment upon it." According to this definition, how would God's wrath differ from the sinful anger or violent temper condemned by Scripture?

2. What does everyone know about God, according to verses 19-20?

3. Verses 21-32 describe the downward spiral of sin experienced by people who rebel against God. How would you summarize each level of their descent? How might each level lead to the next?

4. People often raise the question of how God could condemn those who have never heard of him. How does this passage address this question?

᨞ APPLYING THE WORD

- What evidence do you see of this moral and spiritual degeneration today?

- How might this passage make you less ashamed of the gospel and more eager to preach it?

᨞ RESPONDING IN PRAYER

Pray that God would be revealed powerfully to those who are rejecting him.

ROMANS 2 *The Judgment of God*

PROSTITUTES, DRUG ADDICTS, thieves—it's easy to see why these people need the gospel. But what about "respectable" people: doctors, business executives, the family next door? They seem so contented, so fulfilled, so . . . nice!

In Romans 1:18-32 Paul described the depravity of those who reject God. Now he imagines someone saying, "You're absolutely right. Such people are wicked and deserve everything that's coming to them! But we would never do such things." In this passage Paul shows why even nice people need the gospel.

✺ WARMING UP TO GOD

Have you ever wondered whether some non-Christians really need the gospel? Ask God to open your heart to understand what place he has in each of our lives.

✺ DISCOVERING THE WORD

1. *Read Romans 2*. When people are judgmental, how do they reveal both an understanding and a misunderstanding of God's judgment (vv. 1-4)?

2. Verses 5-16 describe a day of judgment known as "the day of God's wrath" (v. 5). What will God consider important and unimportant on that day?

3. How are God's standards of judgment both similar and different for the two groups described in verses 12-16?

4. In verses 17-29 Paul focuses his attention on a hypocritical Jew. How does such a person view himself and others (vv. 17-20)?

5. Jews placed great value on circumcision because it was the visible sign that they were God's people. How had some of them confused the sign with what it signified (vv. 25-29)?

✺ APPLYING THE WORD

- How has religious hypocrisy hurt the cause of Christ in our day?

- Many non-Christians have high moral standards. How can we use their own standards to help them see their need of Christ?

- How can this chapter help you to more effectively share the gospel with respectable, religious or moral non-Christians?

✺ RESPONDING IN PRAYER

Ask God to make you bold in talking with a non-Christian.

ROMANS 3:1-20 *The Verdict*

IF YOUR ETERNAL destiny were decided by the quality of your life and the level of your obedience to God, how would you fare? There is one sure way to find out. Take your case to the divine court. The Bible assures us that we will all have our day in court (Rom 2:5-6; 14:10-12). But we need not wait until then to find out the verdict. Paul tells us in advance in this passage.

ᑎᐧᕳ WARMING UP TO GOD

Describe the thoughts and feelings you might have if you were on trial for committing a crime—and you knew you were guilty. Reflect on how it feels to know that Christ has set you free despite your guilt.

ᑎᐧᕳ DISCOVERING THE WORD

1. *Read Romans 3:1-20.* Why might some Jews have accused God of unfaithfulness and injustice (vv. 3-8)?
   How does Paul respond to these accusations?

2. In the role of prosecutor, Paul charges that "Jews and Gentiles alike are under sin" (v. 9). How does Scripture support his charge (vv. 10-18)?

3. In verses 13-18 Paul describes how the various parts of our bodies are involved in sin. How does this illustrate our condition as fallen people?

4. How would you reconcile verses 10-18 with the fact that some non-Christians seem to seek after God and lead exemplary lives?

5. Imagine a courtroom scene with God as the judge and the world on trial. From what you have learned in Romans 1:18—3:20, summarize the charges against us, the supporting evidence and the verdict.

ᑎᐧᕳ APPLYING THE WORD

- Paul discusses God's grace (3:21—5:21) only after he has discussed God's judgment (1:18—3:20). He proclaims the good news after we have understood the bad news. Why does he follow this order?

- How should Paul's example affect our evangelism? (Be specific.)

ᑎᐧᕳ RESPONDING IN PRAYER

The letter to the Romans could have ended with 3:20. God would be perfectly just to condemn us and leave us awaiting his wrath. Let this fact sink in, then thank God for being not only just but also merciful and gracious.

ROMANS 3:21-31 *The Righteousness from God*

LIKE PRISONERS on death row, people are guilty and await the execution of God's wrath. They sit in their cell, all hope extinguished.

Then abruptly the door swings open and darkness becomes light, death becomes life, and bondage becomes freedom. "You are pardoned," a voice tells them. But how? Why? This passage answers these questions.

✺ WARMING UP TO GOD

Imagine you are a judge and someone you love is on trial. Would you be more tempted to compromise justice or love? Explain.

✺ DISCOVERING THE WORD

1. *Read Romans 3:21-31.* How is righteousness from God (3:22-24) different from righteousness by law (2:5-13)?

2. The word *redemption* (v. 24) means to buy someone out of slavery. From what types of slavery has Christ delivered us?

3. The phrase "sacrifice of atonement" (v. 25) is borrowed from the Old Testament. Animal sacrifices turned away God's wrath from the sinner. Why does Christ's death turn away God's wrath from us?

4. How should we respond, emotionally and spiritually, to the fact that Jesus experienced God's wrath for us?

5. Some people find it difficult to understand how God can be perfectly just and gracious at the same time. How do the justice and grace of God meet at the cross (vv. 25-26)?

6. How does boasting about ourselves betray a fundamental misunderstanding of the gospel (vv. 27-31)?

✺ APPLYING THE WORD

- At times do you still feel unacceptable to God? Explain.

- In what ways might you feel or act differently if you more fully grasped what Jesus has done for you?

✺ RESPONDING IN PRAYER

Take time to praise and thank God for Jesus Christ.

ROMANS 4 *The Example of Abraham*

"IT'S HOPELESS." No words are more discouraging than these. Yet some-times situations appear beyond hope, beyond help. Our natural response during such times is despair and depression. Abraham knew what it meant to face insurmountable obstacles. He too was hopeless, yet somehow he found renewed reason to hope. For this reason he has become a timeless ex-ample and encouragement to us.

☞ WARMING UP TO GOD

Recall a situation in which you felt hopeless. Write down what restored you to hope.

☞ DISCOVERING THE WORD

1. *Read Romans 4.* According to Paul, how were Old Testament saints, such as Abraham and David, justified (vv. 1-8)?

2. What are some of the differences between justification by faith and by works (vv. 4-8)?

3. It's easy to feel that God accepts us only when we are good. When we feel this way, how can the examples of Abraham and David give us hope?

4. Some people today claim that unless we are baptized we have no hope of being saved. How might Abraham's experience refute this claim?

5. God promised that Abraham and his offspring would inherit the world (v. 13). Who are Abraham's offspring (vv. 13-17)?

6. How does Abraham illustrate our own hopeless predicament as non-Christians and the solution provided in Jesus Christ (vv. 18-25)?

☞ APPLYING THE WORD

• What situation are you currently facing that requires faith in the God of resurrection and creation?

• How can you demonstrate faith and hope in that situation?

☞ RESPONDING IN PRAYER

Know that God wants you to have hope. Pray with that assurance.

ROMANS 5 *Reasons to Rejoice*

WE ALL LONG to be joyful, to experience the pure delight that life sometimes offers. But life's joys are elusive, momentary, gone as quickly as they
come. How can we have an abiding, enduring joy, especially when suffering
intrudes into our lives? In Romans 5 Paul gives us several firm and lasting
reasons to rejoice.

☙ WARMING UP TO GOD

What kinds of things make you joyful? If you are in a place where you feel
comfortable, sing a short song of praise to God.

☙ DISCOVERING THE WORD

1. *Read Romans 5.* How has faith in Jesus Christ changed our relationship
   with God (vv. 1-2)?
2. In verses 2-11, what reasons does Paul give for rejoicing?
3. How does suffering for Christ's sake produce the character change mentioned in verses 3-4?
4. How do verses 5-8 emphasize the love God has for us?
5. Read verses 12-21. How are Adam and Christ similar (vv. 12, 18-19)?
6. How is Christ's gift different from Adam's trespass (vv. 15-21)?

☙ APPLYING THE WORD

- In what area of your life are you experiencing suffering?
- How can a knowledge of the process of character change help us to rejoice in our sufferings?

☙ RESPONDING IN PRAYER

This passage gives us many reasons for rejoicing. Spend time thanking and
praising God for all we have in Christ Jesus.

ROMANS 6:1—7:6 *New Life, New Lifestyle*

SUBTLE ALLURE, persistent urges, passionate desires. Sin entices us in many ways. A thought enters our mind that we dare not acknowledge: "If I give in, I can always be forgiven." Sound familiar? Such thinking can become an excuse for immoral practices. But it betrays a fundamental misunderstanding of God's grace in our lives. In Romans 6:1—7:6 Paul explains why the idea of sinning "so that grace may increase" is unthinkable for Christians.

✎ WARMING UP TO GOD

When you became a Christian, was the change in your life dramatic, gradual or imperceptible? Explain. Whether it has taken place slowly or quickly, praise God for the change he has worked in your life.

✎ DISCOVERING THE WORD

1. *Read Romans 6:1—7:6.* In what sense was our baptism both a funeral and a resurrection?
2. Our "old self" (v. 6) refers to everything we were as non-Christians. When our old self was crucified with Christ, in what sense was sin rendered powerless (vv. 5-7)?
3. What does it mean to "count yourselves dead to sin but alive to God" (6:11)?
4. Paul compares both our old life and our new to slavery (6:15-18). Why is this analogy appropriate in each case?
5. How is the principle "the law has authority over a man only as long as he lives" illustrated by marriage (7:1-3)?
6. In 6:1—7:6 Paul uses baptism, slavery and marriage to illustrate the differences between our old life and our new life. What common themes are emphasized in these illustrations?

✎ APPLYING THE WORD

- What sins are you particularly struggling to free yourself of?
- What assurance and encouragement is Paul giving you in your struggle against sin?

✎ RESPONDING IN PRAYER

Thank God that you are no longer a slave to sin. Pray that you will live as a slave to righteousness.

ROMANS 7:7-25 *Our Struggle with Sin*

ARE YOU EVER baffled by your behavior? You know the right thing to do, but you fail to do it. You resolve to avoid certain things, and they become even more attractive and enticing. Why? What keeps us from translating our desires into actions? In Romans 7 Paul explores his own inner struggles to do good and avoid evil. As we look into his mind and heart, we see a reflection of ourselves and the power that opposes us.

☙ WARMING UP TO GOD

Think back on a recent struggle to do what you knew you should do. Did you do it?

☙ DISCOVERING THE WORD

1. *Read Romans 7:7-25.* How did the law create in Paul a vivid awareness of sin (vv. 7-12)?

2. Why would it be wrong to blame the law for Paul's spiritual death (vv. 13-14)?

3. According to verses 14-20, why does Paul feel so wretched?

4. In chapter 6 Paul stated that Christians are no longer slaves to sin. Yet here he claims he is a slave to sin (v. 14). How would you explain this difference?

5. How can a person's anguish and frustration with sin be beneficial (vv. 24-25)?

☙ APPLYING THE WORD

• To what extent can you identify with Paul's struggles in these verses? Explain.

• Why is it important to realize that only Christ can rescue you from the power of your sin?

☙ RESPONDING IN PRAYER

When Paul realized that Jesus could rescue him from his wretched condition, he cried out, "Thanks be to God!" If this is your response too, spend time thanking him.

ROMANS 8:1-17   *The Spirit Brings Life*

IF WE WERE unable to obey God as non-Christians, then how can we as Christians? What has happened to turn our slavery into freedom, our sin into righteousness and our spiritual death into life? The struggle described in Romans 7 does not end when we become Christians. But there is a new dimension to that struggle that totally changes its outcome. In chapter 8 Paul describes the life-giving effects of the Spirit.

✧ WARMING UP TO GOD

This chapter is one of celebration. Think about what the Holy Spirit has done recently in you that gives you reason to rejoice.

✧ DISCOVERING THE WORD

1. *Read Romans 8:1-17.* Romans 7 described how the law of sin brought about our spiritual death. What has God done to free us from the law of sin and death (vv. 1-4)?

2. In verses 5-8 Paul divides humanity into two categories: those who live according to the sinful nature and those who live according to the Spirit. In your own words, what are some characteristics of each group?

3. There are many professing Christians whose lives seem very different from Paul's description of life in the Spirit. How do you think Paul would account for this fact?

4. In verse 12 Paul concludes that we have an obligation. Describe in your own words the negative and positive aspects of that obligation (vv. 12-14).

5. How do we experience the reality and privileges of being God's children (vv. 15-17)?

✧ APPLYING THE WORD

- What evidence do you see of your life being controlled by the Spirit?

- Practically speaking, how can we put to death by the Spirit the misdeeds of the body?

✧ RESPONDING IN PRAYER

Spend time thanking God for the gift of the Spirit and the difference he makes in our lives.

ROMANS 8:18-39   *Glorious Conquerors*

AT THE END of the movie *Patton,* the general reflected on the procession of a freshly victorious Roman conqueror. "A slave stood behind the conqueror, holding a golden crown and whispering in his ear a warning: that all glory is fleeting." In Romans 8 Paul describes Christians as glorious conquerors who by God's grace overcome all forces arrayed against us. But the glory we receive is eternal.

ᙆ WARMING UP TO GOD

Think back on a time you felt like a glorious conqueror. What brought you back to earth?

ᙆ DISCOVERING THE WORD

1. *Read Romans 8:18-39.* What words and vivid images in these verses underscore the difficulties of the present time?

2. Explain why these difficulties don't compare with the glory that will be revealed in us (vv. 18-25).

3. How can the Spirit's help encourage us (vv. 26-27)?

4. In verse 28 Paul speaks of "the good" and "his purpose." What is God's good purpose for us (v. 29)?

5. How might trouble, hardship, persecution, famine, nakedness, danger or the threat of death cause us to question God's love for us (vv. 35-36)?

6. In spite of these things, why does Paul proclaim that we are "more than conquerors" (vv. 37-39)?

ᙆ APPLYING THE WORD

• How can eager expectation of glory help us cope with our present problems and sufferings?

• Look again at the powerful words of verses 38-39. How does this give you courage to persevere?

ᙆ RESPONDING IN PRAYER

Ask God to make you ready for his future glory.

ROMANS 9:1-29   *The Potter and His Clay*

"I DON'T BELIEVE in Christ." It grieves us to hear these words. But when they come from close friends or family members, the pain can be unbearable. Why doesn't God open their hearts to the gospel? Why did he save us and not them? Paul felt great pain and perplexity over Israel's unbelief. Their Messiah had come, and they had rejected him. In chapters 9—11 Paul wrestles with these questions.

✎ WARMING UP TO GOD

Whose unbelief grieves you? Talk openly with God about your concerns.

✎ DISCOVERING THE WORD

1. *Read Romans 9:1-29.* Why does Paul have great sorrow for the people of Israel?

2. How do verses 6-13 demonstrate that God has not failed in his promises and purposes for Israel?

3. Many people feel it is unjust for God to choose some and not others (v. 14). In reply, why does Paul speak of God's mercy rather than his justice or injustice (vv. 15-18)?

4. How does the illustration of the potter and his clay help us gain a proper perspective (vv. 20-23)?

5. How is God's mercy and justice revealed in his treatment of the Gentiles and Jews (vv. 24-29)?

✎ APPLYING THE WORD

- How do you respond to the idea of election (v. 11)—God choosing certain people to be the objects of his mercy?

- When do you feel uncertain about your own salvation?

- What would help you to feel more secure?

✎ RESPONDING IN PRAYER

Thank God for the fact that although he would have been perfectly just to condemn us all, he mercifully chose to save some.

ROMANS 9:30—10:21   *Misguided Zeal*

THE WORLD IS full of religious people: Jews, Christians, Muslims, Hindus, Buddhists and many others. Many of these people are zealous, dedicated and sincere. But are zeal and sincerity enough? Are there many paths to God, or just one? In this passage Paul continues to wrestle with the problem of Israel's unbelief. He now focuses on Israel's and on our own responsibility to believe the gospel.

❧ WARMING UP TO GOD

Have you ever known a sincere and devout non-Christian? How would you respond to such a person's beliefs?

❧ DISCOVERING THE WORD

1. *Read Romans 9:30—10:21.* Why was Jesus Christ more of a stumbling stone to the Jews than to the Gentiles (9:30-33)?

2. Many people believe religious zeal and sincerity are all a person needs to be saved. How would Paul respond to this belief (10:1-4)?

3. How do verses 6-8 stress the simplicity of righteousness by faith?

4. First-century Christians publicly confessed "Jesus is Lord" at their baptism. Why is public confession important in addition to the belief in one's heart (10: 9-13)?

5. William Carey, the father of modern missions, once proposed to a group of ministers that they discuss the implications of the Great Commission. Dr. John C. Ryland retorted, "Young man, sit down. When God pleases to convert the heathen, he will do it without your aid or mine!" How does Ryland's understanding of God's sovereignty mesh with verses 14-15?

❧ APPLYING THE WORD

• Realizing the implications of verses such as 10:14-15, William Carey responded to God's call and went to India. Where do you feel called to go with the gospel?

• What steps can you take (or have you taken) to be obedient to that call?

❧ RESPONDING IN PRAYER

Israel's unbelief did not stop Paul from praying for them (10:1). Spend time praying for those with whom you have the opportunity to share the gospel.

ROMANS 11   *The Future of Israel*

FOR CENTURIES the people of Israel awaited their Messiah. But when he came, very few believed in him. This situation has persisted to the point that Christianity is now considered a Gentile religion. What happened to God's promises and plans for Israel? Has God rejected his people? In this chapter Paul answers these questions.

༖ WARMING UP TO GOD

We all have expectations of how God will work in our lives that come out of our desires rather than God's. In what way do you feel that God has failed to follow your plan? Express to God any feelings of disappointment or discouragement you might have.

༖ DISCOVERING THE WORD

1. *Read Romans 11.* How does Paul know that God has not rejected his people (vv. 1-6)?

2. What were the spiritual consequences for those Israelites who rejected Jesus Christ (vv. 7-10)?

3. Why are these consequences inevitable for anyone who persistently rejects the gospel?

4. Why is Paul convinced that even greater blessings will come from Israel's acceptance of Christ (vv. 11-16)?

5. Why should Paul's illustration of the olive tree prevent Gentiles from feeling superior to unbelieving Israelites (vv. 17-24)?

6. In this chapter Paul has argued that Israel's unbelief is partial (vv. 1-10), purposeful (vv. 11-16) and temporary (vv. 25-32). How does this make him feel about God (vv. 33-36)?

༖ APPLYING THE WORD

• Why is it foolish for Christians today to feel superior to non-Christians?

• How can Paul's description of God in verses 33-36 also encourage us to trust and praise him?

༖ RESPONDING IN PRAYER

Thank God that his plans are greater than anything we can conceive.

ROMANS 12 *Living Sacrifices*

IN THE FIRST eleven chapters of Romans, Paul has described God's gift of righteousness. In Christ we who were condemned are justified. We who were sinners are sanctified. And we who had no hope will be glorified. But what is our proper response to God's mercy, love and grace? Paul tells us in this and the following chapters.

❧ WARMING UP TO GOD

Jesus once told a Pharisee that a person who is forgiven little loves little, but a person who is forgiven much loves much (Lk 7:47). Write down what that statement means to you.

❧ DISCOVERING THE WORD

1. *Read Romans 12.* Why do you think Paul uses the imagery of "living sacrifices" to describe our proper response to God's mercy?

2. Sometimes we view God's will as something to be avoided rather than desired. How can the last part of verse 2 correct this distortion?

3. How can the realization that we are members of a body prevent us from thinking too highly of ourselves (v. 3-8)?

4. How would the kind of love Paul describes in verses 9-16 transform our relationships with other Christians?

5. How would Paul's advice in verses 17-21 help us to overcome our enemies?

❧ APPLYING THE WORD

- What are some ways we can renew our minds and so be transformed (v. 2)?

- As you think "with sober judgment" about yourself, what gift (or gifts) do you think God has given you (vv. 3-8)?

- In what ways do you need to begin living more sacrificially before God, other Christians or the world?

❧ RESPONDING IN PRAYER

Ask God to use you in serving the body of Christ.

ROMANS 13 *Submitting to Authorities*

THE SERGEANT GLARES at a delinquent recruit. "That's an order!" he barks. "Do you understand?"

"YES, SIR," screams the recruit, who has just had his first lesson in military authority.

For many people the word *authority* conjures images like the one just described. Those in authority are viewed as oppressors, and too often the impression is correct. Paul was no stranger to abuse of authority. He had experienced persecution at the hands of civil and religious authorities all around the Mediterranean. In light of this, Paul's view of authority may be surprising.

౼ Warming Up to God

What comes to mind when you hear the word *authority?* Why?

౼ Discovering the Word

1. *Read Romans 13.* What is Paul's view of authority and those who exercise it (vv. 1-5)?

2. How would Paul's view of governing authorities apply to wicked and perverse rulers such as Nero or Hitler?

3. What are some reasons Paul gives for submitting to those in authority (vv. 1-5)?

4. In verses 11-14 Paul uses several vivid images to describe "the present time." How does each one give us a picture of how we should (or shouldn't) live?

౼ Applying the Word

• In verses 6-7 Paul suggests some practical ways we should submit to those in authority. What other examples can you think of?

• Is it ever appropriate to resist rather than submit to authority? Explain.

•. Think back over this chapter. In what ways do you need to "clothe yourselves with the Lord Jesus Christ" (v. 14)?

౼ Responding in Prayer

Submission does not come to us naturally. Pray that you will learn to submit.

ROMANS 14 *To Eat or Not to Eat*

IN THE LATE 1800s some Christians considered robed choirs worldly. More recently, going to movies, watching television and drinking wine or beer have been viewed as sinful. The Bible contains many clear commands. But it is also silent or ambiguous about many moral issues. Gray areas have always been a source of dispute and conflict among Christians, even though the specific areas of dispute change from time to time. What principles should guide us when others criticize our actions or when we feel critical toward others? Romans 14 helps us answer these questions.

✑ WARMING UP TO GOD

List some types of behavior Christians disagree about today.

✑ DISCOVERING THE WORD

1. *Read Romans 14.* What are some areas of dispute between the "weak" and the "strong" in verses 1-6?

2. What attitudes do the weak and the strong tend to have toward each other (vv. 1-4)? Why?

3. What types of Christians are you most likely to judge or look down on? Why?

4. Why is it wrong to pass judgment on other Christians (vv. 1-13)?

5. When we are not around those whose faith is weak, what principles should govern our Christian liberty (vv. 5-23)?

6. When we are around those whose faith is weak, what principles should guide our actions, and why (vv. 13-21)?

✑ APPLYING THE WORD

• What practices offend you?

• Which of your own practices might distress or destroy another brother or sister in Christ?

✑ RESPONDING IN PRAYER

Ask God for wisdom to know how to respond in areas in which you are causing offense.

ROMANS 15:1-13 *Unity, Hope and Praise*

YOU DESERVE the best. Look out for number one. Pamper yourself. These are the watchwords of our age. But in this chapter Paul urges us to stop gazing at our own reflection. For the first time in Romans he holds up the example of Christ, the one who embodies all the qualities God desires in us.

✎ WARMING UP TO GOD

Think about a time when your self-concern turned into selfishness. Reflect on what made the difference.

✎ DISCOVERING THE WORD

1. *Read Romans 15:1-13.* What personal attitudes might hinder or help us in bearing with the failings of the weak (vv. 1-2)? Explain why.

2. If we follow Christ's example in this and other areas of our lives, why will we need endurance, encouragement and hope (vv. 4-5)?

3. In contrast to the discord and possible verbal abuse hinted at in Romans 14, what does God desire of us (vv. 5-6)?

4. In verses 9-12 Paul quotes from four different Old Testament passages. What words and phrases express the dominant mood of these verses?

5. Why is this mood appropriate for all who hope in Jesus? .

✎ APPLYING THE WORD

• Keeping in mind the context of verses 1-12, how can we become those whose lives overflow with joy, peace and hope (v. 13)?

• Paul concludes this passage with a vivid prayer (v. 13). Consider these words, and try to picture this reality. How do you feel?

✎ RESPONDING IN PRAYER

Spend time praising God for the joy, peace and hope we have in Christ.

ROMANS 15:14—16:27 *Brothers and Sisters in Christ*

IN CHRIST WE have a bond that is stronger than flesh and blood. We are now and will always be brothers and sisters in Christ, members of God's family. This passage introduces us to some of our first-century relatives. As you read about them, notice the care they had for each other.

ᗷ WARMING UP TO GOD

Imagine what it would have been like to be a part of the first-century church.

ᗷ DISCOVERING THE WORD

1. *Read Romans 15:14—16:27.* What do we learn about Paul's apostolic ministry from 15:22?

2. What are Paul's immediate and future plans (15:23-33)?

3. What does 15:23-33 teach us about relationships among first-century Christians?

4. Use your imagination. From what we know about Paul and the Romans, how might the people in 16:1-16 have "risked their lives," "worked very hard" and "been a great help" to Paul and others?

5. How do the final words of this letter summarize the scope of our salvation from beginning to end (vv. 25-27)?

ᗷ APPLYING THE WORD

- In what ways can we share material blessings with other Christians?

- What can you do to strengthen relationships in your spiritual family?

- In what practical ways might we imitate the example of those Paul describes in 16:1-16?

ᗷ RESPONDING IN PRAYER

Pray for your church and the needs of specific people you know.

Introducing 1 Corinthians

᪥

Are there cliques and power struggles in your workplace? Are you plagued by people who think they are spiritually or intellectually superior? How do you handle the immorality that seems so prevalent in the world, especially when it invades the church? What is the proper way to exercise your rights, especially when a friend wrongs you or a matter of principle is at stake? How do we regulate marriage and singleness in the face of so many attacks on the health of both these life situations? How are we going to solve the battle of the sexes? How do we respect one another's personality and gifts? Can eternity make a difference in how we live today? If these questions are relevant to your life and communities, 1 Corinthians has something to say to you.

Both comedy and tragedy are found in the story of the Corinthian church. A dynamic, gifted Christian community composed of uneducated, uninfluential people is plucked out of one of the greatest centers of trade, political authority, pagan religion and immorality in the Roman Empire. The existence of a church in such a setting was a reason for comic rejoicing.

However, there was also the tragedy of the Corinthians forgetting their humble roots and placing themselves as kings over one another—even over Paul, their founder and friend. The resulting tensions and schisms would boil over with even greater heartache for Paul in 2 Corinthians.

As always, Paul is interested not only in correcting practice but also in grounding his instruction in theological principles. In fact the Corinthians had two root problems: premature spirituality (they thought they had everything heaven could offer) and immature spirituality (they forgot that the heart of the gospel is love, servanthood and the cross). Perhaps our communities also need correction in both practice and theology.

Paul Stevens and Dan Williams

1 CORINTHIANS 1 *Called in Christ*

HAVE YOU EVER found a Christian group that doesn't have any problems? If so, don't join it—you'll ruin everything!

The church in Corinth was far from perfect. Paul had heard a long list of complaints about this eager but misguided flock. As he attempted some long-distance pastoring, where would he begin? Paul's starting point is very relevant for problem groups and individuals today.

ᕼ WARMING UP TO GOD

Think back on a time you were hurt by division within a church or Christian group you were a part of. What brought you through it?

ᕼ DISCOVERING THE WORD

1. *Read 1 Corinthians 1.* Before discussing the problems in Corinth, Paul affirms his readers (vv. 1-9). Why is he thankful for them?

2. Why do you think cliques had formed around Paul, Apollos and Cephas (v. 12)?

3. How did Paul conduct himself in Corinth to try to avoid the problem of a personality cult (vv. 14-17)?

4. The Corinthians boasted in worldly wisdom and those who taught it. How does the message of the cross destroy all such boasting (vv. 18-25)?

5. The Corinthians also felt intellectually and spiritually superior to others. What had they forgotten about their past and the reason God chose them (vv. 26-29)?

6. What does it mean to "boast in the Lord" (vv. 30-31)?

ᕼ APPLYING THE WORD

• As you reflect on your own past, what reasons do you have for being humble rather than proud?

• How can genuine humility promote unity in your church or fellowship?

ᕼ RESPONDING IN PRAYER

Take time to thank the Lord for all he has done for you.

1 CORINTHIANS 2

Mind of Christ

MANY PEOPLE THINK Christianity is for the mindless and dull. Someone has said, "I feel like unscrewing my head and putting it underneath the pew every time I go to church." Unfortunately this chapter has been used to support an uneducated, unthinking approach to Christianity. But this misses the point. As Søren Kierkegaard, the Danish philosopher, once said, Christ doesn't destroy reason; he dethrones it.

✑ WARMING UP TO GOD.

List some particular areas of your life that could use some of God's wisdom.

✑ DISCOVERING THE WORD

1. *Read 1 Corinthians 2.* Greek philosophers were often polished orators whose eloquence and wisdom dazzled their audiences. How does this contrast with Paul's preaching in Corinth (vv. 1-5)?

2. How is God's wisdom different from the wisdom of this age (vv. 6-10)?

3. Why are *secret* and *hidden* appropriate words to describe this wisdom?

4. When it comes to understanding God's wisdom, how does the person without the Spirit contrast with the spiritual person (vv. 14-16)?

5. Based on this passage, how would you define spiritual maturity?

✑ APPLYING THE WORD

• Who has been an example of spiritual maturity to you?

• What can you do to become more spiritually mature?

✑ RESPONDING IN PRAYER

Ask that you would be given the true wisdom that comes from the Spirit.

1 CORINTHIANS 3 *Founded on Christ*

THE DUKE OF WINDSOR says that his father, then King of England, used to daily remind him, "Never forget who you are." As the spiritual father of the Corinthians, Paul reminds them in this chapter, "Never forget *whose* you are."

The Corinthians were worldly and quarrelsome because they misunderstood the message and the messengers of the cross. In chapters 1—2, Paul focused on the message. Now he looks at God's messengers. As he does so, Paul reminds the Corinthians and us of our true identity in Christ.

ᐸᕐ WARMING UP TO GOD

Think of a time someone who really cared for you confronted you. Praise God for people who care about your spiritual life.

ᐸᕐ DISCOVERING THE WORD

1. *Read 1 Corinthians 3.* Even though the Corinthians had the Spirit, why couldn't they be considered spiritual (vv. 1-4)?

2. In what ways is God's church like a field being planted (vv. 6-9)?

3. In verses 10-15 Paul changes the metaphor from farming to building. Describe the various ways the church is like a building under construction.

4. In verse 3 Paul accuses the Corinthians of being worldly. How can he say to the same people, "You . . . are God's temple" and "God's Spirit lives in you" (v. 16)?

5. The Corinthians had initially claimed, "I belong to Paul" or "I belong to Apollos" (1:12 RSV). In what sense do Paul, Apollos and everything else belong to the Corinthians—and to us (vv. 21-23)?

ᐸᕐ APPLYING THE WORD

- How does this chapter affect your view of your own ministry in the church and that of professional ministers?

- How does this way of evaluating our lives apply to our relationships, occupations, community involvement and so on?

- In what way are you challenged to "be careful" about how you build?

ᐸᕐ RESPONDING IN PRAYER

Everything we do must be founded on Christ. Before God, search your attitudes and actions, and pray that this would be true of you.

1 CORINTHIANS 4
Servants of Christ

ST. FRANCIS OF ASSISI walked through Muslim battle lines during the Crusades to preach to the Sultan. Mother Teresa bent down to care for a dying beggar in Calcutta. There is power in such actions, even though the "wise" ones of this age shake their heads in disbelief or wag their tongues in scorn. In 1 Corinthians 3 Paul called the Corinthians not to forget that they were God's holy temple. Now he calls them and all Christian communities to experience the power of radical servanthood for Christ's sake.

✑ WARMING UP TO GOD

Picture a radical Christian like St. Francis or Mother Teresa. Reflect on how your picture of them makes you feel.

✑ DISCOVERING THE WORD

1. *Read 1 Corinthians 4.* In contrast to the heroes worshiped in Corinth, how do Paul and his coworkers wish to be regarded (vv. 1-2)?

2. Paul fears the Corinthians are moving "beyond what was written"—probably a reference to the Old Testament. How might going beyond the authority of Scripture result in taking "pride in one man over against another" (v. 6)?

3. Scripture teaches that the suffering of this present age precedes the glory of the age to come. In their own minds, how had the Corinthians taken a shortcut to glory (vv. 8, 10)?

4. How did their "glorious" description of themselves contrast with the experiences of Paul and the other apostles (vv. 9-13)?

5. We receive the first hint in this section that some in Corinth were not only boasting about other leaders but were also putting down Paul. How does the apostle choose to combat these opponents (vv. 18-21)?

✑ APPLYING THE WORD

• How would imitating Paul's way of life (vv. 16-17) require changes in your thinking and actions?

• In what ways does this passage challenge you to become a "fool for Christ"?

✑ RESPONDING IN PRAYER

Thank God for leaders who have shaped your Christian faith and walk.

1 CORINTHIANS 5—6

Members of Christ

THE NEW TESTAMENT church has inspired both exciting and disastrous experiments down through history. Hoping to create the perfect New Testament community, some have tried to design groups where all the gifts are expressed, worship is spontaneous and fellowship is deep. But they forget the common element of all New Testament churches—problems!

❧ WARMING UP TO GOD

How do you react to serious moral and spiritual problems in your church? Ask God to open your heart to this study.

❧ DISCOVERING THE WORD

1. *Read 1 Corinthians 5—6.* In Greece there was no shame in having sexual relationships before or outside marriage. What made the sexual problem in this church loathsome to Paul?

2. How is Paul's strategy of discipline designed to bring health to both the church and the individual (5:2-5)?

3. Paul compares the Christian life to the Passover and Feast of Unleavened Bread. According to Paul, what do the yeast, the bread without yeast and the Passover lamb symbolize (5:6-8)?

4. What commands and guidelines does Paul give for settling disputes between Christians (6:1-8)?

5. Paul calls the body "a temple of the Holy Spirit" (6:18-20). How does the biblical view of the body presented here contrast with the modern view?

❧ APPLYING THE WORD

- Why do you think so few churches discipline those who commit immorality?

- How can we distinguish between people who should be put out of the church (5:2, 9-11; 6:9-10) and those who are simply "worldly" and immature (3:1)?

- How can understanding your body as a temple of the Holy Spirit (v. 19) lead to a healthy balance of bodily control and bodily celebration?

❧ RESPONDING IN PRAYER

Ask God to help you maintain both personal and corporate purity.

1 CORINTHIANS 7 *Devoted to Christ*

IN 1 CORINTHIANS 6 Paul dealt with those who justified a permissive lifestyle in the name of Christian freedom. In chapter 7 he battles on the opposite front. Some Corinthians claimed sex was sinful—or at least a second-class diversion—even in marriage. In response Paul answers questions about marriage, sexuality and singleness.

✑ WARMING UP TO GOD

How did you learn about sexuality? What attitudes did you learn that have been hurtful to you? Ask God to use this passage to help you better understand marriage and singleness.

✑ DISCOVERING THE WORD

1. *Read 1 Corinthians 7.* Although Paul agrees that celibacy is good (v. 1), why is it impractical for most people (vv. 2, 7)?

2. What practical advice does Paul give to the unmarried and the married for avoiding sexual immorality (vv. 2-9)?

3. According to Paul, what are some benefits of remaining in a marriage to a non-Christian (vv. 12-16)?

4. Under what circumstances would Paul seemingly allow for divorce, and why (vv. 15-16)?

5. Paul speaks of God calling us to a certain situation (vv. 17, 24) and of God calling us while we were in that situation (vv. 18-22). How are these two dimensions of calling different?

6. In verses 24-40 Paul addresses those considering marriage. Why does Paul call singleness a "better" way (v. 38) and a "happier" way (v. 40) when he has such a high view of marriage?

✑ APPLYING THE WORD

• What principles from this passage could help us care for Christians who are considering separation or divorce?

• Whether you are married or single, in what way do you struggle to be faithful to God's calling?

✑ RESPONDING IN PRAYER

Ask God to show you his calling for you.

1 CORINTHIANS 8—9 *Living for Christ*

INDIVIDUALS AND groups clamor and clash over rights: the right to free speech, the rights of the poor, the right not to be bothered by smokers (or nonsmokers), the rights of animals, the rights of blacks, the rights of whites. So many of the struggles over rights, both legitimate and bogus, seem to revolve around attaining freedom to change the status quo. The apostle Paul, however, appears to be on opposite ground. For him rights and freedoms are unimportant compared to the privilege of living for Christ.

◌ᗡ WARMING UP TO GOD

In what area are you struggling with a person or group in opposition to you? Ask God to show you how to be righteous.

◌ᗡ DISCOVERING THE WORD

1. *Read 1 Corinthians 8—9.* Sacrificial animals offered in temples were dedicated to a pagan god. Most of them were sold in the public market. Many Christians in Corinth wondered whether they should eat such meat. According to Paul, what do mature Christians know about food sacrificed to idols (8:4-6, 8)?

2. What warning does Paul give about this kind of knowledge (8:1-3)?

3. What does Paul say is more important than exercising freedom (8:9-13)?

4. What apostolic rights has Paul given up (9:4-5, 11-12, 14, 18-19)?

5. How and why has Paul given up the freedom to live whatever lifestyle he prefers (9:19-23)?

6. In giving up the rights mentioned in chapters 8—9, how are we like athletes in training (9:24-27)?

◌ᗡ APPLYING THE WORD

- How might our knowledge and freedom harm a weaker Christian?

- What distinguishes actions that challenge the immature to grow from actions that wound them?

- How might we adjust our lifestyles to reach various subcultures?

◌ᗡ RESPONDING IN PRAYER

Ask God to help you train more rigorously so you will not be disqualified but will receive the victor's crown.

1 CORINTHIANS 10:1—11:1 *Eating with Christ*

SHOULD CHRISTIANS GO to R-rated movies—or any movies, for that matter? Should they drink alcoholic beverages such as beer or wine? Should they wear expensive clothes, makeup and jewelry? Debates over such "questionable" practices are as old as the church. How can we resolve them?

The Corinthians were divided over such issues. Some would not sit down to a meal if the meat had been offered to a "god." Others were so "liberated" that they could eat the Lord's Supper and then commit sexual immorality. These liberated Christians regarded baptism and the Eucharist (Communion) as automatic protection against God's judgment. Paul finds a way of reaching both kinds of people: he calls them and us to do everything for the glory of God.

↶ WARMING UP TO GOD

Think back on a time you took a position on a "questionable" practice. How did you determine what you believed?

↶ DISCOVERING THE WORD

1. *Read 1 Corinthians 10:1—11:1.* What experiences did all the Israelites have in common when they left Egypt and headed for the Promised Land (10:1-10)?

2. Why does Paul remind us of these events (10:11-13)?

3. Why are some lifestyles incompatible with celebrating the Lord's Supper (10:14-22)?

4. According to verses 23-33, what principles should guide our behavior as Christians?

5. How does Paul apply these principles to meat offered to idols?

↶ APPLYING THE WORD

• Think of one or two areas where you are experiencing temptation. In which one of these are you least likely to believe there is a way of escape?

• In what way has God provided an escape for your temptation?

• How can the principles discussed in this passage guide your behavior in areas that might be "permissible" but not "beneficial" (6:12)?

↶ RESPONDING IN PRAYER

Ask God to give you courage to flee temptation.

1 CORINTHIANS 11:2-34
Headship of Christ

IN THE MOVIE *Tootsie* a male actor impersonating a woman romanticizes androgyny: "I was a better man with you when I was a woman than I am a woman with you now that I am a man." In contrast, Fritz Perls characterizes human potential as "I do my thing and you do your thing and if by chance we meet, it's beautiful." Both trends work against our newness in Christ. Followers of Jesus are neither independent nor dependent, but interdependent. We discover interdependence in Christian worship in this passage.

✺ WARMING UP TO GOD
When you enter a worship service, do you tend to think mainly of your relationship to God or your relationship with your fellow worshipers? Explain.

✺ DISCOVERING THE WORD
1. *Read 1 Corinthians 11:2-34.* What seems to be Paul's major concern for the church in this section?
2. The word *head* could mean "chief" and "ruler" or "source" and "origin." Which understanding best fits Paul's concern here? Explain.
3. In the culture of Corinth, a woman signaled she was in right relationship with her husband by wearing a veil or by wearing her hair up. What reasons does Paul give for continuing this practice (vv. 4-10, 13-16)?
4. Paul balances his previous statements by saying that "in the Lord" man is not independent of woman (vv. 11-12). Why is this balance important?
5. Why would eating and drinking "without recognizing the body of the Lord" be so dangerous (vv. 29-32)?
6. How can we take the Lord's Supper in a worthy manner (vv. 28-33)?

✺ APPLYING THE WORD
- How should male-female relationships be expressed in Christian community today?
- What has this chapter taught you about worship that is honoring or dishonoring to God?
- How do you need to change your pattern of worship?

✺ RESPONDING IN PRAYER
Thank God for making you part of a larger body.

1 CORINTHIANS 12 *Body of Christ*

THE CHURCH TODAY has enormous frozen assets. Only when we thaw these assets and release every member for ministry can the work of God be done in the world. After several decades of "gifts" teaching, however, we have made surprisingly little progress. One reason is that gifts have been co-opted by the human potential movement. We view our gifts as part of our development and fulfillment rather than as one more glorious way to be interdependent in Christ. This passage focuses on the true nature and purpose of spiritual gifts.

✧ WARMING UP TO GOD

Reflect on what God has shown you about your gifts and how you might use them in the church.

✧ DISCOVERING THE WORD

1. *Read 1 Corinthians 12.* What particular problem in the Corinthian church may have led Paul to offer the "test" in verse 3?

2. What clue does Paul's test give us about the ultimate goal of spiritual gifts?

3. What do verses 4-6 reveal about the unity and diversity of spiritual gifts?

4. What might make some members of your church feel useless or envious of other parts of the body (vv. 12-26)?

5. According to Paul, how can we make every part of the body feel special (vv. 21-26)?

6. Paul does not give us a complete list of gifts in this chapter. What might the words *first, second, third* and *then* in verse 28 indicate?

✧ APPLYING THE WORD

- What can you do to help others in your group or church to discover their giftedness?

- How would you like to develop and exercise your spiritual gifts?

✧ RESPONDING IN PRAYER

Pray that both you and those you know would use your gifts to God's glory.

1 CORINTHIANS 13

Love of Christ

PERHAPS THE MOST abused phrase in the English language is "I love you." Instead of communicating unselfish caring, it often expresses enlightened self-interest, manipulative affection or sheer lust. In 1 Corinthians 13 Paul not only defines love for us but shows us why this is the most excellent way to relate to anyone—especially to members of the family of God.

✑ WARMING UP TO GOD

Think of a person who has truly loved you. List the things that marked that person's way of relating to you.

✑ DISCOVERING THE WORD

1. *Read 1 Corinthians 13.* What is so tragic about using our gifts without love (vv. 1-3)?

2. How would you define each of love's qualities (vv. 4-7)?

3. In verses 8-13 Paul summarizes the supremacy of love. Compared with love, why do the spiritual gifts have limited value?

4. Some understand the "perfection" in verse 10 as the completed New Testament, thus eliminating the need for tongues or prophecy today. Others understand it as the perfection we will experience when Christ returns. In light of Paul's other comparisons (vv. 11-12), which interpretation seems more accurate? Explain.

5. Why is love greater than faith or hope (v. 13)?

✑ APPLYING THE WORD

- How can love lead to healthy interdependence in your relationships rather than unhealthy independence or dependence?

- Which aspect of love do you most need to develop?

- Besides telling us what love is, this passage gives us an incidental portrait of Jesus as the ultimate lover. Reread verses 4-7, replacing *love* with *Jesus*. What fresh picture of Jesus' care do you gain through this exercise?

✑ RESPONDING IN PRAYER

Ask Jesus Christ to teach you what it means to love.

1 CORINTHIANS 14 *Speaking for Christ*

WORDS ARE CHEAP TODAY. They can be digitized and processed. With one depressed button on a computer we can eliminate words forever, without even a trace remaining in memory. However, the Bible says words have great power because they are an extension of our personality. God's Word always accomplishes his purposes because it is spoken with his personal power. In this chapter Paul focuses on the exciting potential of God-inspired speech in the Christian community.

✎ WARMING UP TO GOD

Recall a time when you were encouraged by something you were told in a group setting. What made the remarks so encouraging?

✎ DISCOVERING THE WORD

1. *Read 1 Corinthians 14.* Evidently the Corinthians placed great value on the gift of tongues. Why does Paul prefer prophecy to uninterpreted tongues (vv. 1-5)?

2. What illustrations does Paul use to show why uninterpreted tongues do not build up the church (vv. 6-12)?

3. What remedy does Paul suggest (vv. 13-19)?

4. What does Paul say about the purpose of tongues and of prophecy (vv. 20-25)?

5. What guidelines does Paul give for when someone should speak in tongues and when that person should remain silent (vv. 27-28)?

6. How can Paul's statements in verses 33-35 be harmonized with his teaching about women praying and prophesying (11:5)?

✎ APPLYING THE WORD

- In what ways might we be guilty of meaningless or mindless worship today?

- How can Paul's counsel improve the quality of our worship?

✎ RESPONDING IN PRAYER

Ask that worship in your church might be meaningful and powerful for all who come.

1 CORINTHIANS 15—16 *Hope in Christ*

WHAT HAPPENS AFTER DEATH? Do we live on as disembodied souls, as the Greeks taught? Do we go through countless cycles of reincarnation, as the Hindus believe? Do both body and soul cease to exist, as naturalism maintains? Because of their Greek heritage, the Corinthians questioned the reality of the resurrection. In this passage Paul challenges their thinking by pointing out the absurd conclusions to which it leads. He reminds us that the resurrection is a crucial aspect of our hope in Christ.

✸ WARMING UP TO GOD

Have you ever pondered what death will be like? How do you feel about it? Express your feelings to Christ. Allow him to prepare you for this study.

✸ DISCOVERING THE WORD

1. *Read 1 Corinthians 15—16.* Paul reminds the Corinthians of the gospel he preached to them. What are the essential elements of the gospel (15:1-11)?

2. If there is no resurrection, what are the consequences for Christ, for Paul and for us (15:12-19)?

3. How does belief or disbelief in the resurrection affect a person's lifestyle (15:29-34)?

4. What illustrations does Paul use to explain why the resurrection is not illogical but makes good sense (15:35-41)?

5. Although the resurrection body is somehow related to the natural body, how is it also radically different (15:42-49)?

6. How does chapter 16 give several illustrations of "the work of the Lord" Paul referred to in 15:58?

✸ APPLYING THE WORD

- To which specific area of service will you give yourself this week, knowing that "your labor in the Lord is not in vain" (15:58)?

- What is the most substantial change that studying 1 Corinthians has brought about in your life?

✸ RESPONDING IN PRAYER

Praise God for what you have learned in 1 Corinthians.

Introducing 2 Corinthians

❧

Life is relational. We hope and hurt the most about relationships with people who matter to us. When a special relationship is hanging by a slender thread, we are often at a loss to know what to say or do. Should we tell the truth even if it hurts? Should we avoid confrontation? Should we share what is going on inside us even if it shows we are weak and struggling, far weaker than we would like others to know?

Second Corinthians is all about relationships—not perfect ones, but real ones. In this letter the apostle Paul reveals that he is struggling deeply in his relationship with the believers in Corinth. Though he founded this church, they have apparently rejected him. This letter is an attempt at reconciliation.

Paul chose to pour out his soul to them, trusting that in the process Christ would be revealed. This great Christian leader takes the enormous risk of telling how confused, upset and weak he is. Through his large heart we see into the heart of God and the heart of the Christian message. Against the false triumphalism of his opponents, Paul proclaims a gospel in which God's power is demonstrated best in human weakness. We have the Christ-treasure in jars of clay or, as Phillips powerfully paraphrases, "in a common earthenware jar" (2 Cor 4:7).

In a day when authentic Christianity seems less attractive than super-spirituality or the gospel of health, wealth and prosperity, Paul's searing honesty offers exactly what the world so deeply hungers for: it tells us how to be really real. As we walk through Paul's relationship with the Corinthians step by step, we discover how God in Christ is prepared to meet our deepest relational needs just as we are and where we are.

Paul Stevens

2 CORINTHIANS 1:1-11   *Our Comforting God*

"LIFE IS DIFFICULT!" With these three words Scott Peck begins his best-selling book *The Road Less Traveled.* In 2 Corinthians Paul says this and more. Just where life is difficult, where our relationships are strained, where our competence is questioned, where our health and security are threatened, God makes himself known in powerful comfort. We discover that one of the supreme greatnesses of Christianity is that it does not seek a supernatural escape from the difficulties of life. Instead it offers a supernatural use for them. Troubles become triumphs as God makes himself known in our weakness.

↩ WARMING UP TO GOD

What comfort do you need from God today? Sit and wait for him to visit you with his peace and reassurance.

↩ DISCOVERING THE WORD

1. *Read 2 Corinthians 1:1-11.* After his customary greeting and "signature," Paul breaks into praise. What evokes this spontaneous worship (vv. 3-7)?
2. What is the connection between the sufferings of Christ and the comfort of Christ (vv. 5-6)?
3. Paul's hardships in the province of Asia (modern-day Turkey) were evidently life-threatening. What did he discover about the meaning of such sufferings in the Christian life (vv. 8-11)?
4. How do you think Paul's openness in sharing the realities of his Christian experience affected his relationship with the Corinthians?

↩ APPLYING THE WORD

- In what ways have you experienced God's comfort in a difficult situation?
- How does your experience of God's comfort enable you to comfort others who are suffering?
- Based on what you have learned in these first eleven verses, how can hardships draw you closer to God instead of driving you away from him?

↩ RESPONDING IN PRAYER

Think of someone you know who needs to experience God's comfort. Ask God to comfort that person and to use you in offering comfort.

2 CORINTHIANS 1:12—2:11 *Always Yes in Christ*

CONTRARY TO WHAT some misguided Christian parents think, affirming children does not make them proud and self-centered. Rather it meets a fundamental need of the human personality. But often our attempts to affirm each other backfire. Such was Paul's experience with the Corinthians. Paul had promised to visit them again, twice in fact—first as he made his way to Macedonia and then on his way back. But he changed his plans, delaying his visit and deciding to visit only once. In the process of defending his actions, Paul pointed the Corinthians to the ultimate ground of our affirmation: the eternal yes spoken to us by God in Christ.

☜ WARMING UP TO GOD

Recall an experience of being affirmed by a parent or a good friend. What made that affirmation meaningful for you?

☜ DISCOVERING THE WORD

1. *Read 2 Corinthians 1:12—2:11.* Based on 1:12-22, what do you think Paul's opponents were saying about his motives and ministry style?

2. What reasons does Paul give for maintaining that his change of itinerary was not a change of mind about the Corinthians (1:12, 17)?

3. Why do you think Paul directs their attention away for his travel plans to the unqualified yes or "amen" of the gospel (1:18-20)?

4. What further reason does Paul give for his change of plans (1:23—2:4)?

5. In 2:5-11 Paul refers to the discipline of a member of the church (see 1 Cor 5:1). How does Paul's handling of this problem affirm his love not only for the Corinthians but also for the man who had sinned?

☜ APPLYING THE WORD

• What experiences have you had with church discipline?

• How would Paul's approach to discipline be one that would still allow the person confronted to hear God's affirmation in Christ?

• What have you learned about the conditions of receiving the affirmation Christ wants us to give?

☜ RESPONDING IN PRAYER

Praise God for his faithful promises and his yes in Christ.

2 CORINTHIANS 2:12—3:6 *A Letter from Christ*

CHRISTIANITY IS essentially a lay movement. But one would not think so while visiting the average church. Often the impression we get is that ministry is for the theologically trained, the polished and proficient. With the professionalism of ministry in our society, many of us question our ability to minister. Like Paul, we ask, "Who is equal to such a task?" (2:16). In this section Paul tells us why all believers are competent for ministry in Christ.

⚜ WARMING UP TO GOD

How do you feel about being told that becoming a Christian means becoming a minister? Talk to God about fears you have about being a minister.

⚜ DISCOVERING THE WORD

1. *Read 2 Corinthians 2:12—3:6.* Because Paul had no peace of mind in Troas, he couldn't take full advantage of the "door" the Lord had opened for him. How was he able to speak of his triumph in Christ (2:14) in the same breath as confessing his weakness?

2. What do you think Paul means in saying we are "the smell of death" to some and "the fragrance of life" to others (2:15-16)?

3. In contrast to those who boasted about their letters of recommendation, Paul says the Corinthians are his letter (3:1-3). What sort of letter are they?

4. In 2:16 Paul asked, "Who is equal to such a task?" What answer does he give in 3:4-6?

5. According to Paul, how does our ministry under the New Covenant contrast with ministry under the Old (3:3-6)?

⚜ APPLYING THE WORD

- When has Christ enabled you to triumph in the midst of a personal struggle?
- How does the thought that Christianity spreads like a fragrance challenge your church or Christian group?
- How has this passage encouraged you to feel competent to minister as a disciple of Jesus?

⚜ RESPONDING IN PRAYER

You are a letter from Christ. Pray that you would represent Christ to those around you.

2 CORINTHIANS 3:7-18 *Becoming Like Christ*

THE NEW COVENANT ministry is paradoxically this: as I look at Christ and as I reveal myself, it is not I who am revealed but Christ. I am like an X-ray photograph: if I am looked at, one will see almost no image at all. But if I am held to the light and looked through, a beautiful image begins to appear. In this passage Paul celebrates the revelation that comes with the New Covenant.

✍ WARMING UP TO GOD

Ask God to reveal that part of himself that is in you. Spend some time seeing yourself through his eyes. Praise him for the beauty he reveals.

✍ DISCOVERING THE WORD

1. *Read 2 Corinthians 3:7-18.* How does Paul demonstrate that ministry under the New Covenant is more glorious than under the Old (vv. 7-11)?

2. How are we contrasted with Moses (vv. 12-16)?

3. What does verse 18 reveal about the process and goal of our lives as Christians under the New Covenant?

4. Paul speaks of our boldness (v. 12) and freedom (v. 17). Why should each of these characterize our New Covenant ministry?

✍ APPLYING THE WORD

• What evidence do you see of the glorious transformation (metamorphosis) described in verse 18 in your life?

• Is it easy or difficult for you to recognize God's glory as it is revealed in you? Explain.

• In what area would you like to be made more like Christ?

✍ RESPONDING IN PRAYER

Praise God for the transformation he has worked and is working in you.

2 CORINTHIANS 4:1—5:10 *Jars of Clay*

"WHAT IS REAL?" Velveteen Rabbit asks Skin Horse in Margery Williams's delightful story *The Velveteen Rabbit.* The Skin Horse said, "Once you are real you can't become unreal again. It lasts for always."

The gospel treasure is contained by people marked by weakness, frailty and a kind of living death. Paradoxically, as we shall see, this life situation serves to enhance the message we bring, not detract from it. Once real in Christ, you can't become ugly or unreal again.

⚘ WARMING UP TO GOD

Talk to Christ about the parts of yourself you feel are shabby. Listen for his loving response.

⚘ DISCOVERING THE WORD

1. *Read 2 Corinthians 4:1—5:10.* How does Paul's ministry contrast with the practices of evangelists who discredit the gospel (4:2)?
2. What forces does Paul see at work behind those who reject and those who accept his gospel (4:4-6)?
3. In what ways does Paul contrast the glory of the gospel with the weakness of those who preach it (4:7-18)?
4. What images does Paul use to compare the shabbiness of life now with the glory of the life to come (5:1-5)?
5. How does Paul's wonderful destiny in Christ affect his view of life and death (5:6-10)?
6. Reviewing the entire passage, what do you now understand Paul to mean by saying "we live by faith, not by sight" (5:7)?

⚘ APPLYING THE WORD

- We often assume that our weakness will hinder the gospel and detract from it. On the contrary, how does our weakness reveal God's power?
- How can Paul's perspective help you come to terms with your own weaknesses and mortality?

⚘ RESPONDING IN PRAYER

Praise God for what you have learned about yourself through this passage.

2 CORINTHIANS 5:11—6:13   *Ambassadors for Christ*

DIETRICH BONHOEFFER describes the emergence of the super-leader under Hitler in Ray Anderson's *Minding God's Business*. "It is essential for the image of the Leader that the group does not see the face of the one who goes before, but sees him only from behind as the figure stepping ahead. His humanity is veiled in his Leader's form."

❧ WARMING UP TO GOD

Reflect on how you have tended to defend yourself in the context of a strained relationship.

❧ DISCOVERING THE WORD

1. *Read 2 Corinthians 5:11—6:13*. Paul defends his ministry and message of reconciliation in this passage. What accusations might Paul's opponents have made about his ministry (5:11-13)?

2. How does Paul explain his true motives and goals (5:11-14)?

3. In describing his message, Paul uses the words *reconciliation* and *reconciled* five times (5:18-20). What does it mean to be reconciled to God?

4. What would it mean for the Corinthians—or us today—to receive the grace of God in vain (6:1)?

5. To what further credentials does Paul point in order to commend himself to the Corinthians (6:3-10)?

❧ APPLYING THE WORD

• How might Paul's example help you be a more effective ambassador, especially to people who are "turned off" by Christianity?

• Who, specifically, would you like to be an ambassador to?

• How could you reach that person?

❧ RESPONDING IN PRAYER

Ask God to make you an effective ambassador.

2 CORINTHIANS 6:14—7:16 *Good Grief*

A GREAT THEOLOGIAN once said, "To be a sinner is our distress, but to know it, is our hope!" Paul would say, "Amen." We have nothing to lose and everything to gain if we are in Christ and walking into the light. But the Corinthians were tempted to cover up a scandal and not to call it sin. In response Paul patiently and effectively ministered to the Corinthians, urging them not to cover up the problem. The result was what Paul calls godly sorrow.

ᐊᔅ WARMING UP TO GOD

Recall an experience of significant loss, hurt or disappointment. What good things, if any, came after the sorrow had passed? Praise God for what you learned from that experience.

ᐊᔅ DISCOVERING THE WORD

1. *Read 2 Corinthians 6:14—7:16.* This passage is usually applied to marriages between believers and unbelievers. What other relationships or partnerships might Paul have in mind?

2. What reasons does Paul give for avoiding such unions (6:14-16)?

3. Although we may forfeit certain relationships, what positive promises does the Lord give us (6:16—7:1)?

4. What difference should our relationship with God make when we contemplate marriage or other close relationships (6:17; 7:1)?

5. Why is Paul so "confident" and "encouraged" (7:4) about the Corinthians?

6. Paul compares worldly sorrow with godly sorrow (7:9-10). What are some positive indications and constructive results of godly sorrow (7:10-11)?

ᐊᔅ APPLYING THE WORD

• It is often counterproductive to try to persuade someone not to marry a person they deeply love. What clues does this passage give us for ministering to someone who is tempted to marry outside the faith?

• If godly sorrow is so beneficial, why do you think Christians shrink from the discipline and tough love required to bring it about in others?

• In what areas of your life are you most in need of godly sorrow?

ᐊᔅ RESPONDING IN PRAYER

Ask Christ to teach you more about godly sorrow.

2 CORINTHIANS 8:1—9:15 *The Need to Give*

THE FIG LEAF has slipped from the genitals to the wallet. The privacy of the purse makes it extremely difficult for Christians to talk about their money. The problem is compounded by hard-sell media evangelists raising funds for their personal empire. Paul devotes two whole chapters to the grace of giving because both he and the Corinthians have a problem in this area.

✺ WARMING UP TO GOD
Reflect on what makes financial giving difficult.

✺ DISCOVERING THE WORD
1. *Read 2 Corinthians 6:14—7:16.* In what ways are the Macedonians excellent examples of generosity (8:1-5)?
2. Paul refrains from using the word *money.* Instead he speaks of *sharing* (8:4; 9:13), *service* (8:4, 18; 9:1, 12-13), *offering* (8:19), *grace* (8:6-7) and *gift* (8:12, 20; 9:5). What do these words tell us about the nature of giving?
3. Paul never raised money for himself, for his own missionary organization or even for Corinth Community Church. What is the primary goal that governs his appeal for gifts (8:10-15)?
4. What care does Paul take to avoid any suspicion of dishonesty or self-interest as he handles this large gift (8:16-24)?
5. Some people teach that giving money to God's work results in more money for you. What does Paul say about the personal benefits of giving (9:6-11)?

✺ APPLYING THE WORD
- What positive and negative feelings do you have about people raising money for a Christian cause?
- Paul encourages cheerful giving (9:7). The word is the root of our English *hilarious.* It is the opposite of giving under compulsion. According to these two chapters, how could you become a more cheerful giver?
- What difference will this study make in how you manage your resources?

✺ RESPONDING IN PRAYER
Pray for believers around the world, especially those who suffer persecution.

2 CORINTHIANS 10 *Spiritual Warfare*

SOMETIMES WHEN THINGS seem to be getting better we hear news that the situation is worse than we thought. While Paul was writing this letter (or perhaps after completing and sending chapters 1—9), he got news that some "super-apostles" had usurped his rightful place. Now Paul engages in spiritual warfare with principalities, powers and persons who oppose not only Paul but Christ himself. Unlike many of us, Paul wants to make peace, not keep the peace by covering over the problem.

ᴥ WARMING UP TO GOD

In what area do you feel that you are currently battling evil? Ask for help from God.

ᴥ DISCOVERING THE WORD

1. *Read 2 Corinthians 10.* What apparent disadvantages did Paul suffer in comparison to his opponents in Corinth? (See especially verses 1, 9.)
2. Paul says he is not waging war "as the world does" (v. 3). What types of worldly weapons and strategies do you think he has in mind?
3. What is Paul's strategy in this spiritual warfare (vv. 4-6)?
4. Trace, in verses 7 and 10, the arguments of Paul's opponents.
5. What is wrong with the boasting of Paul's opponents (vv. 7-18)?

ᴥ APPLYING THE WORD

- In what situations are we tempted to use worldly weapons and strategies today?
- What similar arguments and pretensions oppose the knowledge of God today?
- Which of your own thoughts need to be taken "captive" to obedience to Christ (v. 6)?

ᴥ RESPONDING IN PRAYER

Ask God to guard your words, that your boasting might be only in the Lord.

2 CORINTHIANS 11 *Super-Apostles, Super-Leaders*

IN HIS BOOK *Servant Leadership,* Robert K. Greenleaf wrote, "We live in the age of the anti-leader, and our vast educational structure devotes little care to nurturing leaders or to understanding followership."

✧ WARMING UP TO GOD

Whose leadership are you under? Reflect before Christ about the positive or negative impact of that leadership in your life.

✧ DISCOVERING THE WORD

1. *Read 2 Corinthians 11.* What are Paul's motives for challenging the so-called super-apostles who are winning over the Corinthians (vv. 1-6)?

2. Why do you think betrothal rather than marriage is a good image of the goal of Christian ministry (vv. 2-3)?

3. Why do you think Paul's decision to preach the gospel "free of charge" was so important in defending his ministry (vv. 7-12)?

4. Looking at the whole chapter, what marks of the super-apostles justified Paul's description of them as false, deceitful and masquerading?

5. In contrast, what does Paul boast about as the mark of his own leadership (vv. 16-33)?

✧ APPLYING THE WORD

• What kind of Christian leadership today might fall under the apostle's judgment?

• What have you learned from this study about the marks of true Christian leadership?

• What have you learned about being a healthy follower?

✧ RESPONDING IN PRAYER

Pray for your pastor and other Christian leaders.

2 CORINTHIANS 12 *My Burden Carries Me*

UNINTENTIONALLY, A GERMAN philosopher captured the genius of Paul's spirituality with these arresting words: "My burden carries me." Normally we think about the difficulty of carrying our burdens. But in reality our burdens carry us to Christ by convincing us that we are not self-sufficient. They are spiritual assets, not liabilities. "When I am weak, then I am strong" is Paul's final distinction between super-spirituality and the real thing.

✑ WARMING UP TO GOD

What burdens are you carrying today? Turn them over to Christ one by one. Feel the weight lifted from you.

✑ DISCOVERING THE WORD

1. *Read 2 Corinthians 12.* Paul describes his experience of being caught up to paradise by referring to "a man in Christ" (vv. 1-6). Why do you think he refrains from boasting about such an exalted experience?

2. While no conclusive answer can be given about the details concerning Paul's "thorn in my flesh" (v. 7), what do we know about this bitter reality Paul faced?

3. How does Paul view Satan's part and God's part in his "thorn" (vv. 7-9)?

4. In contrast to Paul's ecstatic experiences, the simple answer to his prayer (v. 9) gives us the most complete view of Paul's apostleship. What effect did this answer have on Paul himself?

5. To what credentials does Paul point while pleading for his rightful place in the Corinthians' hearts (vv. 11-21)?

✑ APPLYING THE WORD

- Reflecting on the whole chapter, what kinds of weaknesses or problems can we legitimately expect God to transform into a means of grace?

- What kinds of problems or weaknesses should we not expect God to transform?

- How does this help you to understand an ongoing problem in your life?

✑ RESPONDING IN PRAYER

Pray to be made strong in your weak places, that you might serve Christ.

2 CORINTHIANS 13 *Examine Yourselves*

IMAGINE LIFE WITHOUT a final examination. At first it strikes us as a wonderful vacation, like school without tests and report cards. But without accountability, life quickly loses its meaning. The whole Bible looks toward the final day with vibrant hope. Those genuinely in Christ have nothing to fear and everything to anticipate. But what of those who are not sure, or who like the Corinthians might have false confidence about the outcome of the final exam? Paul deals with this matter in his final passionate plea.

✙ WARMING UP TO GOD

Think back on a time when God's power was especially real to you.

✙ DISCOVERING THE WORD

1. *Read 2 Corinthians 13.* What can the Corinthians expect from Paul's third visit (vv. 1-3, 10)?

2. Verse 4 sums up the whole book. Why does the cross represent the heart of what Paul has been saying to the Corinthians?

3. Paul asks them to examine themselves not so much in their doctrine as in their experience (vv. 5-6). How could the Corinthians know experientially that they truly belonged to Christ?

4. In what ways does Paul show that he cares more for their passing the test than for his seeming to pass the test in the eyes of others (vv. 7-9)?

5. In what specific ways does Paul pray they will be built up (v. 11-14)?

✙ APPLYING THE WORD

- In what ways do you shrink from your daily cross and find your power elsewhere?

- If you are unsure of your position in Christ, what can you do about it in light of this chapter?

✙ RESPONDING IN PRAYER

Pray for courage to take up your cross and follow Christ.

Introducing Galatians

We all want to be accepted—by our family, by our friends and most of all by God. But so often people accept us only if we are attractive, smart, wealthy or powerful. So we work hard to project the right image and to conceal our faults.

We often transfer this attitude to our relationship with God. We feel we must earn his acceptance. If we could only work harder, live better, pray longer, witness to more people—then we might get on God's good side.

In Galatians Paul challenges this kind of thinking. He exposes the futility of trying to earn God's acceptance when we are already accepted in Christ. His message frees us from living out of a sense of guilt. We find fresh assurance of God's love and renewed power to serve him.

Paul and Barnabas visited Antioch, Iconium, Lystra and Derbe, which were located in the Roman province of Galatia, during their first missionary journey. In spite of opposition against Paul and Barnabas, people believed the gospel and churches were formed.

The real threat arose shortly thereafter. Certain people infiltrated the new churches with a different message. "Paul omitted an important part of the gospel," they claimed. "You must also be circumcised and keep the law of Moses if you want to be saved" (see Acts 15:1). Their arguments were impressive and the religious zeal was undeniable. The Galatians were almost persuaded when Paul received word of what was happening. Quickly he dictated this letter and sent it to be read in each of the churches. Centuries later it still radiates the heat of Paul's anger. These preachers were impostors. Their gospel was perverted. The Galatians were in grave danger!

Jack Kuhatschek

GALATIANS 1:1-10 *Good News and Bad*

THE CHURCH HAS always been plagued by false teachers, heretics and followers of various cults. Usually such people have an aggressive program for winning new converts. How are we to respond to those who preach or accept a twisted gospel? Paul gives us an example in this passage.

☙ WARMING UP TO GOD

Read and reflect on Galatians 1:3-5. Allow these verses to speak to you. Let them soak into your mind and heart. Praise God for what he has done in Christ.

☙ DISCOVERING THE WORD

1. *Read Galatians 1:1-10.* In three brief verses (3-5) Paul tells us an enormous amount about the gospel. What do we learn?

2. In verses 6-7 Paul summarizes the problem that caused him to write this letter. What was happening in the Galatian churches?

3. Verse 6 implies that if we desert the gospel, we also desert God. Why would this be true?

4. Why do you think Paul is so harsh in his judgment of those who preach a different gospel (vv. 8-9)?

5. How might the way we present the gospel be different if we were seeking the approval of people instead of God (v. 10)?

☙ APPLYING THE WORD

• What are some ways the gospel is being perverted today?

• According to this passage, how can we ensure that the gospel we believe and preach is the true gospel?

• What can you do to increase your understanding of the gospel?

☙ RESPONDING IN PRAYER

Confess before God the ways in which you are seeking the approval of others before him. Ask God to help you to turn your priorities around.

GALATIANS 1:11—2:10   *Why Believe the Gospel?*

YOU'RE TALKING with someone about the gospel when suddenly that person says, "But that's just your opinion!" If the gospel is merely our opinion, why should they listen to us? There are many other religions in the world, each one claiming to be a path to God. Who are we to assert that the gospel is the only true message of salvation? This objection isn't new. Paul's opponents questioned the authenticity of the gospel he preached.

✎ WARMING UP TO GOD

When is belief difficult for you? Don't be afraid to talk to God about it. Express your struggles and doubts to him.

✎ DISCOVERING THE WORD

1. *Read Galatians 1:11—2:10.* In 1:11-12 Paul claims he received the gospel from Jesus Christ, not people. How does his brief autobiography in 1:13-24 confirm this claim?

2. Paul obviously did not need human authorization to preach the gospel. Why then did he present his gospel to the leaders in Jerusalem (2:1-2)?

3. Why was it significant that Titus (a Gentile) was not compelled to be circumcised (the sign of becoming a Jew) (2:3-5)?

4. Paul refused to give in on the matter of circumcision "so that the truth of the gospel might remain with you" (2:5). How do you show your concern to preserve the gospel?

5. How did the leaders in Jerusalem respond to Paul's message and ministry (2:6-10)?

✎ APPLYING THE WORD

- The apostles were not simply zealous to preserve the gospel. They also felt called to proclaim the gospel (2:7-10). To whom do you feel called to bring the gospel?

- What step can you take this week to bring the good news to someone?

- How can Paul's testimony in this passage increase our confidence in the truth of the gospel?

✎ RESPONDING IN PRAYER

Ask God to help you be a bearer of the good news.

GALATIANS 2:11-21 *Accepting Others*

HAVE YOU EVER felt like avoiding certain types of Christians? Perhaps you don't like their theology. You may disapprove of their lifestyle. Or you may prefer to avoid people of their race, nationality or economic background. This passage helps us see why such attitudes conflict with the basic message of the gospel.

✍ WARMING UP TO GOD

How does God's acceptance help you feel good about who you are?

✍ DISCOVERING THE WORD

1. *Read Galatians 2:11-21.* How were Peter and the other Jews not "acting in line with the truth of the gospel" (vv. 11-14)?
2. How might their actions have forced "Gentiles to follow Jewish customs" (v. 14)?
3. Why is it wrong to make such customs a basis for fellowship (vv. 15-16)?
4. How does Paul refute the accusation that Christ promotes sin (vv. 17-19)?
5. How has Christ enabled us to die to the law and to live for God (v. 20)?

✍ APPLYING THE WORD

- What nonessential customs do Christians sometimes force on each other? (For example, certain ways of praying, certain dress at worship, certain lifestyle habits and so on.)
- Which of these are you most likely to be concerned about?
- How can God's acceptance of you help you to be more accepting of others?

✍ RESPONDING IN PRAYER

Pray for discernment about your own attitudes toward others, asking God to make you more accepting.

GALATIANS 3:1-14 *Why God Accepts Us*

WE ALL WANT to be accepted. We do everything we can to win people's approval and avoid their rejection. But if we work so hard to please people, then what about God? How can we possibly meet his standards? The Galatians felt these inner struggles. They wanted to be fully accepted by God. But they seemed to forget that God had already accepted them. They also forgot why.

ᗖ WARMING UP TO GOD

When have you felt unacceptable to God recently? Describe your feelings to God. Listen for his reassurance.

ᗖ DISCOVERING THE WORD

1. *Read Galatians 3:1-14.* From verses 1-5 try to reconstruct in chronological order the Galatians' spiritual biography.
2. In what ways did the Galatians' behavior seem "bewitched" and "foolish" according to verses 1-5?
3. When we follow the example of Abraham's faith, what are the results (vv. 6-9)?
4. How does Abraham's experience contrast with that of the person who seeks to earn God's acceptance (vv. 10-12)?
5. How does the gift of the Spirit affirm that God accepts us completely in Christ?

ᗖ APPLYING THE WORD

- In what ways do we sometimes try to earn God's favor by what we do?
- How can a vivid image of Christ's crucifixion (v. 1) guard us from this warped way of thinking?
- How have you been blessed by the Spirit's presence in your life?

ᗖ RESPONDING IN PRAYER

Spend some time thanking God for what Christ has done for us as described in these verses.

GALATIANS 3:15-29 *Exposing Our Needs*

"HONEY," JILL CALLS OUT, "you'd better call the repairman. Our TV is on the blink again."

"Who needs a repairman?" Ron replies confidently. "I can fix this myself."

Four hours later. "Uh . . . maybe you're right, dear," Ron says sheepishly. "I suppose calling a repairman couldn't hurt."

People must admit they need help before they can receive it. Yet often this is very difficult. In Galatians 3:15-29 Paul tells us how God exposes our need for Christ.

✎ WARMING UP TO GOD

What needs are pressing on you right now? Give them to God one by one.

✎ DISCOVERING THE WORD

1. *Read Galatians 3:15-29.* Why is the law unable to set aside or add to the promises spoken to Abraham (vv. 15-18)?

2. If the law did not set aside or add to the promises given to Abraham, then why was it given (vv. 19-25)?

3. How does a clear grasp of God's law help us to realize our need for Christ (vv. 22-25)?

4. In verse 28 Paul lists several ways in which people have been categorized. How have these categories sometimes functioned as barriers?

5. In light of the context, how have these barriers been broken down in Christ?

✎ APPLYING THE WORD

• When is it difficult for you to admit to God that you have a need or problem?

• When is it difficult for you to ask others for help?

• What would help you allow both God and others to help you?

✎ RESPONDING IN PRAYER

Ask God to help you put aside your pride and expose your needs to him and to your Christian friends and church family.

GALATIANS 4:1-20 *The Joys of Growing Up*

HAVE YOU EVER longed to be a child again—to be free from work, mortgage payments, bills and taxes? Remember the carefree days, when from morning till night your job was to play? The Galatians did. They longed to return to the spiritual childhood of the law. But aren't we forgetting something? Just think of all the things we couldn't do as children. In Galatians 4:1-20 Paul reminds us of the joys of growing up.

✎ WARMING UP TO GOD

What is frustrating you today? Take time to journal or talk to God about how you are feeling and why. Work at it until your mind is clear and you are ready to study.

✎ DISCOVERING THE WORD

1. *Read Galatians 4:1-20.* How was life under the law like spiritual childhood (vv. 3-7)?

2. Verse 4 states, "When the time had fully come, God sent his Son." How did things change because of his coming (vv. 4-7)?

3. In view of Paul's discussion in verses 1-7, how does the Galatians' behavior seem incredible (vv. 8-11)?

4. How and why had the Galatians' attitude toward Paul changed (vv. 12-20)?

5. What do these verses reveal about Paul's feelings toward the Galatians?

6. How do verses 12-20 illustrate the care and concern we should have for other members of God's family?

✎ APPLYING THE WORD

• In what ways do you sometimes act like a spiritual slave?

• How can you begin acting more like God's beloved son or daughter?

✎ RESPONDING IN PRAYER

Spend a few minutes of intimate prayer with the Father, thanking him for the privileges of being a member of his family.

GALATIANS 4:21—5:1 *Do-it-yourself Religion*

TRUSTING GOD can seem risky. What if he lets us down? Still worse, what if our faith is simply foolishness? When such thoughts enter our minds, we are tempted to take back what we have entrusted to God. Abraham felt these struggles while waiting for God's promise of a son. He rushed God's plan and had a son through his slave Hagar. Later, even though he and Sarah were very old, the promised son was born. This story has become a timeless illustration of do-it-yourself religion versus trust in the promises of God.

✦ WARMING UP TO GOD

What promises has God kept with you? Spend time in reflection, thanksgiving and worship.

✦ DISCOVERING THE WORD

1. *Read Galatians 4:21—5:1.* What does Paul mean when he says that the son of the slave woman was born the "ordinary way" but the son of the free woman was "the result of a promise" (v. 23; see also v. 29)?

2. In verse 24 Paul says that the story of Hagar and Sarah may be understood "figuratively." What do Hagar, the covenant from Sinai and "the present city of Jerusalem" have in common (vv. 24-25)?

3. How is Sarah (who, although unnamed, is the other woman in the story) similar to the new covenant and to the Jerusalem that is above (vv. 26-27)?

4. How does Paul describe the ultimate fate of the slave woman's and the free woman's spiritual descendants (v. 30)?

5. In 5:1 Paul states that Christ set us free so we could experience freedom. Given the thrust of Galatians 1—4, what does Paul mean by *free*?

✦ APPLYING THE WORD

• In what areas are you trusting in the promises of God and the power of the Spirit to accomplish the extraordinary?

• What are some present-day threats to our spiritual freedom?

• What are some practical ways we can "stand firm" against them?

✦ RESPONDING IN PRAYER

Ask God to help you stand against any threat to spiritual freedom.

GALATIANS 5:2-15

Heavenly Help

"HELP!" The man cried as he dangled helplessly from the edge of a cliff. "Can anyone up there help me?"

"Yes," answered a heavenly voice, "I'll help you. But first you must let go."

"Let go?!" gasped the man. "But then I'd fall!"

If we want Christ to save us, we must let go of the idea that we can save ourselves—even a little.

✍ WARMING UP TO GOD

In what area of your life are you ignoring God's offer of help? Humble yourself before the Lord and give him this area of concern.

✍ DISCOVERING THE WORD

1. *Read Galatians 5:2-15.* What were the Judaizers (those preaching against Paul) urging the Galatians to do and why (vv. 2-4)?

2. In verses 2-4 Paul gave stern warnings to those who desired to be circumcised. Now he says, "Neither circumcision nor uncircumcision has any value" (v. 6). How can both of these views be true?

3. Paul compares the Galatians to runners in a race and to a batch of dough (vv. 7-9). How do these comparisons illustrate the nature and perils of the Christian life?

4. In verses 10-12 Paul makes some severe statements about those who are troubling the Galatians (especially v. 12!). Even by today's standards they are harsh. Why was he so upset?

5. What is the difference between the two concepts of freedom described in verses 13-14?

✍ APPLYING THE WORD

- Are you running the good race? In what area do you need to ask God to help you stay on track?

- When have you "cut in on" someone and kept them from "obeying the truth" (v. 7)?

- How can you encourage someone you know to stay in the race?

✍ RESPONDING IN PRAYER

Ask God to help you to be a good runner and a good companion in the race.

GALATIANS 5:16-26 *Living by the Spirit*

IF CHRIST HAS set us free, then why not live as we please? Why not grab all the money, sex and power we can get? Afterward we can simply ask for forgiveness! Paul challenges this kind of thinking with the true meaning of Christian freedom.

✺ WARMING UP TO GOD

Spend some time in quiet before the Lord, opening yourself to what he wants to say to you in prayer and through the Scripture.

✺ DISCOVERING THE WORD

1. *Read Galatians 5:16-26.* What does it mean to "live by the Spirit" (v. 16)?
2. How is being led by the Spirit different from living under law (v. 18)?
3. Why is it so easy to recognize the acts of the sinful nature (vv. 19-21)?
4. How can Paul's warning in verse 21 be reconciled with his emphasis on justification by faith?
5. Why is fruit a good description of the Spirit's work in us (vv. 22-23)?

✺ APPLYING THE WORD

- Paul assumes that even though all Christians live by the Spirit, we do not always keep in step with the Spirit (vv. 25-26). In what ways do you struggle to keep in step with the Spirit?
- In what ways do you see the Spirit's fruit ripening in your life?
- What fruit would you like to cultivate more?

✺ RESPONDING IN PRAYER

Spend time thanking God for the Spirit's work in your life. Pray for the Spirit's help in those areas where you feel out of step.

GALATIANS 6:1-10 *The Law of Love*

THE FRUIT OF the Spirit is most clearly demonstrated in our relationships with others. They are a visible and practical measure of our spirituality. In this passage Paul describes how we should relate to the family of believers and to all people.

✎ WARMING UP TO GOD

This is a passage about relationships. Who are you having difficulty loving right now? Talk to God about it.

✎ DISCOVERING THE WORD

1. *Read Galatians 6:1-10.* What guidelines does Paul offer for dealing with a person who is "caught in a sin," and why is each important (v. 1)?

2. How does the law of Christ (v. 2) differ from the kind of law-keeping urged by Paul's opponents?

3. The sins or burdens of others can lead us to feel superior. How can proper methods of self-examination correct this attitude (vv. 3-5)?

4. What other application of the principle of sowing and reaping does Paul make in verses 9 and 10?

✎ APPLYING THE WORD

- What burdens are people you know carrying?
- What are some ways you can help a friend carry these?
- What are one or two new ways you could begin sowing to please the Spirit (a) personally, (b) in relationships with other Christians and (c) in relationships with non-Christians?

✎ RESPONDING IN PRAYER

Ask God to help you "do good to all people," especially to those in the family of God.

GALATIANS 6:11-18 *Getting Motivated*

PEER PRESSURE can exert a powerful influence on us. The style of our clothes, the kind of music we listen to, our vocabulary, even the soft drinks we buy are affected by what others do and say. We are often tempted to change our behavior so others will accept us. But such approval can have a high price tag. In this final passage Paul helps us to consider whose approval we desire most.

☞ WARMING UP TO GOD

In what areas are you feeling cultural pressure? Consider work, family, Christian and non-Christian friendships, how you dress, what you do or don't buy and so on. Bring each of these pressures to God.

☞ DISCOVERING THE WORD

1. *Read Galatians 6:11-18.* What do verses 12-13 reveal about the motives of Paul's opponents?

2. How will boasting in the cross affect our desire for the world's approval (v. 14)?

3. Why does the new creation have value in contrast to the worthlessness of circumcision or uncircumcision (v. 15)?

4. In Paul's closing blessing and benediction he mentions peace, mercy and the grace of our Lord Jesus Christ (vv. 16, 18). Why is each of these appropriate for those who follow the "rule" of verses 14-15?

☞ APPLYING THE WORD

• In what situations are you tempted to hide your Christianity in order to "make a good impression outwardly" (v. 12)?

• Paul bore on his body the marks of Jesus (the evidence of faithful service). What are the "marks of Jesus" in your life?

• How has this passage helped to purify your motives and goals in life?

☞ RESPONDING IN PRAYER

Ask God to make the marks of Jesus more evident in your life.

INTRODUCING EPHESIANS

Paul's letter to the Ephesians communicates the Christian vision more powerfully and succinctly than any of his other letters. Most of Paul's other letters are directed to the particular problems of a given church. But his letter to the Ephesians is blissfully free of turmoil.

Some believe the letter has this quality because it was not written solely for the church at Ephesus. Rather it was probably a circular letter sent to the Christian communities of Asia and other provinces, especially where Paul was not personally known. While most of his letters are full of personal greetings, no individuals are mentioned here or greeted by name. In fact the oldest and best manuscripts even lack the words *in Ephesus* (1:1). They are addressed generally "to the saints who are also faithful in Christ Jesus." But at an early date the letter became associated with the Ephesian church, so most later manuscripts have "to the saints in Ephesus, the faithful in Christ Jesus."

Ultimately, whoever the original readers were, this letter is written to us. It enables us to see the full sweep of God's program from before creation to the ultimate union of everyone and everything in Jesus Christ. It puts our problems and our entire lives in the context of eternity.

May Ephesians expand your vision of what God is doing in history and give you wholeness in this broken world.

Andrew T. and Phyllis J. Le Peau

EPHESIANS 1:1-14 *The Purpose of God*

WE HAVE A love-hate relationship with God's will. We dearly want to discover it and obey it, to be secure in knowing we are following the path he desires. On the other hand, we definitely don't want to find out what he wants, because deep down we suspect it may not be to our liking. In this study, we'll see what Paul says about God's will.

✒ WARMING UP TO GOD

Reflect on the ways God has revealed his will to you over the course of your life. What patterns do you see? Thank God for his guidance.

✒ DISCOVERING THE WORD

1. *Read Ephesians 1:1-14.* According to verses 3-6, what blessings are ours from the Father?

2. What other blessings, according to verses 7-12, do we have in Jesus Christ?

3. From the information given in verses 1-14 alone, try to formulate a clear statement of what it means to be chosen by God.

4. What additional blessings do we receive through the Holy Spirit (vv. 13-14)?

5. What does it mean to live "to the praise of his glory" (vv. 6, 12, 14)?

✒ APPLYING THE WORD

• How do you respond emotionally to knowing you are chosen by God?

• How has this passage increased your sense of participation in God's total purpose of the universe?

• How could your life be more in keeping with the phrase "to the praise of his glory"?

✒ RESPONDING IN PRAYER

Spend time in praise to the God and Father of our Lord Jesus Christ who has blessed us with every spiritual blessing.

DAY TWO

EPHESIANS 1:15-23   *"I Keep Asking"*

SOMETIMES PRAYER can be like pushing a full wheelbarrow with no
wheel. At other times it's like rushing down the rapids of a mountain river.
What makes the difference? In this passage, we'll see why Paul's prayers
overflow with praise and thanksgiving.

⌘ WARMING UP TO GOD

Talk to God about the times prayer has been hard for you. Describe your disappointment or pain. Take time to allow him to listen to you fully.

⌘ DISCOVERING THE WORD

1. *Read Ephesians 1:15-23.* How do Paul's prayers for his readers throughout
   this passage cover the past, the present and the future?
2. How does Paul emphasize the tremendous power available "for us who
   believe" (v. 19)?
3. How do verses 20-23 expand on Paul's discussion of Christ's headship begun in verses 9-10?
4. How is the church, the body of believers, central to God's plans for the
   universe (vv. 22-23)?

⌘ APPLYING THE WORD

• When you pray for fellow Christians, how do you usually pray for them?
• In what ways would you like your prayers to be more like Paul's?
• How could you make the church a more central part of your life?

⌘ RESPONDING IN PRAYER

Pray for Christ's church and individuals in your church, following Paul's example.

EPHESIANS 2:1-10   *Amazing Grace*

ONE OF THE best-known verses in the book of Ephesians is 2:8: "By grace you have been saved, through faith." Grace has often been defined by the acrostic God's Riches At Christ's Expense. With this passage, we'll consider some of the riches we have been given in Christ.

☙ WARMING UP TO GOD

Focus on God's graciousness to you in the past days, weeks and months. Allow yourself to experience the depth of his goodness. Respond to him in prayer and praise.

☙ DISCOVERING THE WORD

1. *Read Ephesians 2:1-10.* In verse 1 Paul says, "You were dead in your transgressions and sins." How does sin kill?

2. In verses 2-3 Paul mentions three negative influences on our lives, which are later put into the formula of "the world, the flesh and the devil." According to Paul, how did each of these affect our lives as non-Christians?

3. What does Paul mean when he says we have been "made alive," "raised" and "seated" with Christ (vv. 5-6)?

4. When Paul says that our salvation is not from ourselves (vv. 8-9), is he saying that we play no role in our salvation? Explain.

5. What do you learn about God's grace from verses 4-10?

☙ APPLYING THE WORD

• What good works has God prepared you to do?

• What has hindered you from doing these?

☙ RESPONDING IN PRAYER

Thank God specifically for some of the many ways he has been gracious to you. Ask him to remove the barriers to the good works he has created for you to do.

EPHESIANS 2:11-22 *We Are One*

MANY OF US have sung, "We are one in the Spirit; we are one in the Lord." But we also continue to find ourselves at odds with Christians who believe or live differently than we do. Such problems were just as common in Paul's day as in ours.

✒ WARMING UP TO GOD

Consider what groups of Christians you disagree with or have trouble getting along with. Reflect on what causes these tensions. Ask God to open your mind and heart so that you can develop understanding.

✒ DISCOVERING THE WORD

1. *Read Ephesians 2:11-22.* Paul uses vivid imagery in this passage. What are some of these images?

2. What divided Gentiles from Jews (vv. 11-13)?

3. How are the two reconciliations Christ achieves related (vv. 14-18)?

4. How do the images Paul uses in verses 19-22 emphasize the unity Christians have with one another?

✒ APPLYING THE WORD

• What kinds of name-calling (perhaps even using biblical terms) do Christians in your church engage in?

• What rules and requirements would you be inclined to enforce (like "the law" in verse 15) that might hinder people from coming into the kingdom?

• What practical first step toward unity with another Christian can you take in the next week?

✒ RESPONDING IN PRAYER

Pray for unity in the church, that people would not be turned away from Christ by Christians who don't get along with each other.

EPHESIANS 3   *Prisoner and Preacher*

WHAT DO YOU think of when you hear the word *church*? A building on the corner? A stuffy group of religious hypocrites? A vibrant fellowship? Paul's special ministry enables him to enlarge our conception of the church. In this passage he clarifies and exalts its place in God's plan.

✺ WARMING UP TO GOD

When have you had a particularly powerful experience in the church? It might have been worship, teaching or fellowship. Reflect on what made it special and thank God for it.

✺ DISCOVERING THE WORD

1. *Read Ephesians 3.* What gifts of God's grace does Paul say he has received (vv. 2-3, 8)?

2. Explain the meaning of the mystery revealed to Paul (vv. 2-6).

3. How is the mystery connected with the ministry given to him (vv. 7-13)?

4. Three times in verses 14-21 Paul mentions "love" and "power." What do we learn about power and love in these verses?

5. How does the benediction in verses 20-21 tie together the main themes that have run through the first three chapters of Ephesians?

✺ APPLYING THE WORD

- What is your attitude toward the church?
- What about your attitude matches Paul's?
- What about your attitude would you like to change?

✺ RESPONDING IN PRAYER

Choose at least one item from Paul's prayer and make it a prayer of your own, for yourself and your church.

EPHESIANS 4:1-16 *Unity and Uniqueness*

WHILE EPHESIANS 1—3 provides a doctrinal foundation, Ephesians 4—6 shows in practical detail how to give glory to God in the church. Paul now considers the quality of life that is demanded of believers individually and in the fellowship of Christ's church.

✿ WARMING UP TO GOD

Ephesians 4:2 reads, "Be completely humble and gentle; be patient, bearing with one another in love." Reflect on these words. Measure your recent behavior against them. Talk to God about what you discover.

✿ DISCOVERING THE WORD

1. *Read Ephesians 4:1-16.* What are the characteristics of a life that is worthy of our calling (vv. 1-3)?

2. Paul says we have one body, one Spirit, one hope, one Lord, one faith, one baptism and one God and Father of all (vv. 4-6). How do these seven "ones" contribute to actually living out true unity?

3. In verses 8-10 Christ is compared to a conquering hero whose victory parade fills "the whole universe," from the highest heaven to the lowest earth. He then generously distributes gifts (the spoils of victory) to his loyal followers. What is the nature and purpose of these gifts (vv. 11-13)?

4. How does spiritual infancy differ from spiritual maturity (vv. 14-16)?

✿ APPLYING THE WORD

- What spiritual gifts do you think you might have?

- How do they fulfill the purposes described in verses 11-13?

- In verse 16 Paul says that the body "grows and builds itself up in love, as each part does its work." What steps must you take to more fully work toward this goal?

✿ RESPONDING IN PRAYER

Pray that your spiritual gifts will be used to help others grow in Christ and to build the church.

EPHESIANS 4:17-32 *Something Old, Something New*

ALREADY AND NOT YET. That's how we experience Christ. Already we have come out of spiritual darkness and into his light. Already we have received his grace and come to know him. But not yet do we live completely the way God wants. We have not yet arrived. Still, Jesus is right beside us on this journey.

✎ WARMING UP TO GOD

When have you felt that you were lost in the darkness? What brought you into the light? Spend time praising God for his redemption.

✎ DISCOVERING THE WORD

1. *Read Ephesians 4:17-32.* How does Paul contrast the life of the Gentile (unbeliever) with that of a true believer throughout these verses?

2. What are the effects of hard-heartedness (vv. 17-19)?

3. What does it mean to put off the old self (v. 22)?

4. In verses 25-32, what does Paul tell us to "put off," what does he say to "put on" and what reason does he give (or imply) for doing these things?

✎ APPLYING THE WORD

- Which of the commands in verses 25-32 do you have the most difficulty following? Explain.

- What practical steps could you take this week to improve your relationships with others in this area of difficulty?

- Which of the commands in verses 25-32 have you seen God strengthen you to obey?

✎ RESPONDING IN PRAYER

Spend time praising God for his work in your life, and pray that he will give you grace in the areas needing improvement.

EPHESIANS 5:1-20   *Live in Love, Live in Light*

NOT DOING WHAT is wrong is one thing. But sometimes it can be even more difficult to do what is right. In Ephesians 5 Paul continues to outline what it means "to live a life worthy of the calling you have received" (4:1). He does this by considering ways we shouldn't act and ways we should.

❧ WARMING UP TO GOD

Spend some time singing and making music in your heart to the Lord with "psalms, hymns and spiritual songs" (5:19).

❧ DISCOVERING THE WORD

1. *Read Ephesians 5:1-20.* How is Christ the perfect example of what Paul asks of us (v. 2)?

2. How is thanksgiving an appropriate replacement for the behavior Paul condemns in verses 2-4?

3. Why will immoral, impure or greedy people be unable to inherit the kingdom (vv. 5-7)?

4. In verses 8-14 Paul contrasts light and darkness to say more about holy living. According to these verses, what does it mean to "live as children of light"?

5. Verses 19-20 describe several beneficial results of being filled with the Spirit. In your own words, explain the characteristics of those who are filled with the Spirit.

❧ APPLYING THE WORD

- Look again at verses 1-2. What have you observed about God that you have begun or could begin to imitate?

- Looking again at verses 3-4, how could you use thanksgiving to replace improper behavior in your life?

- According to the characteristics in verses 15-17, how could you live more wisely?

❧ RESPONDING IN PRAYER

Talk to God as a child to a father. Tell him how you would like to imitate him.

EPHESIANS 5:21-33 *Wives and Husbands*

A LOT OF EMOTION and misunderstanding surrounds the word *submit*. So try to come to this text as if you had never seen it before. Try to set aside your own biases and see what Paul really has to say on the subject of submission.

☞ WARMING UP TO GOD

How has God shown you that he is faithful and trustworthy? Express your thanksgiving for his care.

☞ DISCOVERING THE WORD

1. *Read Ephesians 5:21-33.* How does verse 21 set the tone for this passage?

2. Why is the church's submission to the Lord a helpful illustration of a wife's submission to her husband (vv. 22-24)?

3. How are husbands to show love for their wives (vv. 25-30)?

4. Why do you think Paul calls on wives to respect their husbands while he calls on husbands to love their wives (v. 33)?

5. How do verses 31-33 summarize his teaching on the unity that is to exist between wives and husbands?

☞ APPLYING THE WORD

• How do you react to the idea of being told to submit to someone?

• If you are married, how would you like to grow in your ability to love and submit to your spouse?

• Whether you are married or single, how would you like to grow in your submission to Christ?

☞ RESPONDING IN PRAYER

Tell Christ how you would like to more fully submit your life to him.

EPHESIANS 6:1-9 *Children, Parents, Slaves, Masters*

HOW MUCH OUR parents mean to us—yet how difficult they can be! How much we love our children—yet how exasperating they are at times! In nine packed verses Paul delves not only into these important relationships but also into those of the work world as well.

✧ WARMING UP TO GOD

Reflect on the finest qualities of your parents (or of parenting in general). Consider which of these qualities you have experienced in your relationship with God, and thank him.

✧ DISCOVERING THE WORD

1. *Read Ephesians 6:1-9.* What reasons are given for obeying and honoring parents (vv. 1-3)?

2. Why does Paul contrast making children exasperated with bringing "them up in the training and instruction of the Lord" (v. 4)?

3. What is implied about the way slaves normally worked for their masters (vv. 5-8)?

4. Paul says masters should treat slaves the way slaves should treat masters because both have the same Master in heaven. Why should this make a difference in how slaves are treated?

5. How do verses 1-9 contribute to the theme of the church glorifying God through visible unity?

✧ APPLYING THE WORD

- What are some practical ways you can obey or honor your parents?

- If you are a parent, what can you do this week to follow verse 4 more closely? (If you are not a parent, how have you seen verse 4 in action?)

- How could the principles Paul considers in verses 5-9 be lived out in situations you have been in or are in?

✧ RESPONDING IN PRAYER

Pray that in all you do you would serve "wholeheartedly, as if you were serving the Lord."

EPHESIANS 6:10-24 *Prayer Wars*

IN A WAR OF BULLETS, careful aim and heavy armor win battles. In a war of words, eloquent speech and sharp pens overcome the opposition. But if the fight is outside the realm of sight, sound and touch, how are victories won?

ᴦ WARMING UP TO GOD

Reflect on a time God protected you as you faced spiritual battles.

ᴦ DISCOVERING THE WORD

1. *Read Ephesians 6:10-24.* Four times in verses 10-14 Paul urges his readers to stand firm in the battle against the devil's stratagems. How are we as Christians susceptible to instability?

2. How does the "armor of God" (vv. 13-17) prepare us for spiritual battle?

3. In verses 18-20 Paul urges all kinds of prayers. How has he been a model prayer warrior throughout this letter?

ᴦ APPLYING THE WORD

• How do you sense a battle around you with more than physical forces and foes?

• Which piece of armor do you need most to fight your spiritual battles? Explain.

• What main obstacle do you face in fighting the battle of prayer more effectively?

ᴦ RESPONDING IN PRAYER

Take time now to pray about your fight in spiritual warfare.

Introducing Philippians

ᴄ❧

Rejoice in the Lord always," the author of Philippians exhorts us, "I will say it again: Rejoice!" (4:4). Coming from most people, such words might sound trite and simplistic, but this is the apostle Paul speaking, a prisoner awaiting news—perhaps news of his death. As we study Philippians, we discover Paul's secret: a life lived for the glory of God will overflow with joy. What a message for our hurting world!

Philippi was an important city because it straddled the great east-west highway known as the Egnatian Way. The population of this city was cosmopolitan, being made up of Tracians, Greeks, Romans and a few Jews. In the center of the city was a large forum surrounded by temples, a library, fountains, monuments and public baths.

We know Paul was writing to the Philippians from prison (1:12-14). Unfortunately it is not clear which prison he was writing from. If he was writing during his imprisonment in Rome, the letter can be dated sometime between A.D. 61 and 63. However, many scholars have pointed out that the conditions Paul describes seem much harsher than what we know of the Roman imprisonment (Acts 28:16, 30-31). It could be there was an earlier imprisonment not recorded in Acts. A good case has been made for Ephesus. If this is true, Philippians would have been written about A.D. 54. Paul had several reasons for writing this letter. He wanted to explain why he was sending a man named Epaphroditus back to Philippi. He also wanted to thank the Philippians for the gift of money they had sent and to reassure his friends of his condition. Also, the news Paul had received concerning the Philippians made him long to encourage and advise a church he loved.

May these quiet times help you learn and apply Paul's secret to joyful living.

Donald Baker

PHILIPPIANS 1:1-11 *Paul's Prayer for the Philippians*

HAVE ANY OF your good friends ever told you what they appreciate about you? Have you ever listened while others prayed for you? If so, you know what a warm feeling it is to be assured that others care. In Philippians 1:1-11 Paul prays and thanks God for his friends in Philippi. As you read the passage, try to imagine yourself sitting with the Philippian Christians as this letter is read for the first time. You might be meeting in the home of Lydia, a Christian businesswoman. Perhaps you would be seated next to the jailer who heard about Christ while guarding Paul and Silas.

✎ WARMING UP TO GOD

Write down the names of people you know pray faithfully for you.

✎ DISCOVERING THE WORD

1. *Read Philippians 1:1-11.* What are Paul's feelings toward the Philippians (vv. 3-8)?
2. Why does he feel this way about them?
3. What do verses 3-8 reveal about healthy Christian relationships?
4. What are Paul's prayer requests for the Philippians (vv. 9-11)?
5. Why would each of these qualities be essential to spiritual maturity?

✎ APPLYING THE WORD

- How can your present relationships be strengthened to become more like what is described in verses 3-8?
- What does Paul's prayer teach about how we should pray for others?

✎ RESPONDING IN PRAYER

Using Paul's prayer as a model, spend a few minutes thanking God and praying for someone you love in Christ.

PHILIPPIANS 1:12-30   *A Joyful Imprisonment*

IN THIS PASSAGE we discover that Paul is writing to the Philippians from prison. This puts a whole new perspective on the joyful mood of the letter. While Paul is writing, he is experiencing what most of us would describe as awful circumstances. Yet even at a time like this, Paul's first concern is that Christ is praised. This passage can teach us how to honor Christ in a difficult situation.

✎ WARMING UP TO GOD

What people or things in life bring you the greatest joy? Thank God for these.

✎ DISCOVERING THE WORD

1. *Read Philippians 1:12-30.* What does Paul say has happened as a result of his imprisonment (vv. 12-14)?

2. Compare the motives of the two groups described in verses 15-18.

3. What are Paul's considerations in choosing between life and death (vv. 20-26)?

4. What does it mean to conduct ourselves in a manner worthy of the gospel (vv. 27-30)?

✎ APPLYING THE WORD

• To what extent have you adopted Paul's attitude toward life and death?

• What are the most difficult circumstances you are currently facing?

• How can Christ be exalted in that situation?

✎ RESPONDING IN PRAYER

Pray that you would learn to experience the joy that can emerge amid sorrow.

PHILIPPIANS 2:1-18 *The Path of Humility*

IS IT POSSIBLE to have a good self-image and still be humble? Can a person want to be the best without being conceited? In Philippians 2:1-18 Paul directs us to Jesus Christ, a person equal with God yet whose incarnation and life are the supreme example of humility. This passage urges us to imitate Christ's attitude.

⟡ WARMING UP TO GOD

List the differences between humility and a poor self-image.

⟡ DISCOVERING THE WORD

1. *Read Philippians 2:1-18.* How can our experience of Christ and his Spirit (v. 1) help us to achieve the unity Paul desires in verse 2?

2. How do verses 3-4 help us to understand the nature of humility?

3. How did each of Christ's actions illustrate humility and a concern for the interests of others (vv. 6-8)?

4. In your own words, describe God's response to Jesus' humility (vv. 9-11).

5. In verses 12-13 Paul says you are to "work out your salvation" because God "works in you." How are these ideas related?

⟡ APPLYING THE WORD

- Who might you be tempted to impress during the next few days?
- What act of humble service could you do for this person instead?

⟡ RESPONDING IN PRAYER

Pray for the opportunity to serve others as Christ has served you.

PHILIPPIANS 2:19-30 *Servants of Christ*

WHEN THE PHILIPPIANS heard that Paul was in prison, they sent one of their members—a man named Epaphroditus—to Paul with a gift of money. It was his job to help Paul in any way necessary. Epaphroditus returned home, carrying the letter to the Philippians. In this section of the letter, Paul outlines his future plans and explains why he is sending Epaphroditus back. The passage gives several beautiful examples of Christian service as displayed in the lives of Timothy, Epaphroditus, Paul and the Philippians.

✺ WARMING UP TO GOD

Think about what you enjoy most and least about serving others.

✺ DISCOVERING THE WORD

1. *Read Philippians 2:19-30.* Imagine that Timothy is being sent to visit your church or fellowship group. What might he do to help you?

2. Why is Paul sending Epaphroditus back to Philippi (vv. 25-28)?

3. How is Christ's attitude evident in the relationships among Paul, Epaphroditus and the Philippians (vv. 25-30)?

4. Why is it important to honor people like Epaphroditus, especially in light of Christ's exaltation (2:9-11)?

✺ APPLYING THE WORD

• Examine your plans and goals for the coming week. How can you bring your own interests into closer harmony with those of Jesus Christ?

• What are some practical ways you can serve those around you during the coming week?

✺ RESPONDING IN PRAYER

Pray that Christ will continue to give you the heart of a servant.

PHILIPPIANS 3 *Rejoice in the Lord*

HAVE YOU EVER become excited about an idea only to be deflated by the realities of making it work? Sometimes trying to live a Christian life is like that. We start off very excited about knowing the Lord, but it isn't long before the pressure of keeping "all the right rules" drains us of our joy. Unfortunately we can then swing too far in the other direction and decide, "I'm not going to be concerned about Christian conduct. If Jesus has saved me, then it doesn't matter how I live." This attitude will destroy our joy as quickly as the first. So what is the solution? Paul tells us in this passage.

෯ WARMING UP TO GOD

List some of your most important goals in life.

෯ DISCOVERING THE WORD

1. *Read Philippians 3.* How does rejoicing in the Lord (v. 1) differ from other reasons for joy?

2. Why were the people Paul warns against in verses 2-3 so dangerous?

3. Contrast Paul the Pharisee (vv. 4-6) with Paul the Christian (vv. 7-11). How have his reasons for confidence changed?

4. In verses 12-14 Paul compares himself to an athlete who is running a race. Why is this such an appropriate description of the Christian life?

5. In verses 17-21 Paul contrasts Christians with "enemies of the cross." What are the concerns and destiny of each group?

෯ APPLYING THE WORD

• Have you ever placed your confidence in something, thinking it would bring you closer to God, that you now consider to be rubbish? Explain.

• In verse 6 Paul speaks of "legalistic righteousness." What legalisms are today's Christians pressured to keep?

• How do these legalisms get in the way of knowing Christ and rejoicing in the Lord?

෯ RESPONDING IN PRAYER

Reflect on Paul's words "We eagerly await . . . the Lord Jesus Christ" (v. 20). Worship Christ with your anticipation of his return.

PHILIPPIANS 4:1-9   *Stand Firm in the Lord*

TAKE A MOMENT to think of the people you care about most. What is your greatest desire for these people? As Paul thinks of the Philippians, his greatest desire is that they will stand firm in what they have been taught. But he is also aware of some problems that may cause their faith to weaken. He writes to warn them that, in order to stand firm, they must put an end to disagreements, rejoice always and fill their thoughts with good things.

ᴥ WARMING UP TO GOD

Do you find your stand in the Lord to be firmer or weaker than it was a year ago? Reflect on what has made the difference.

ᴥ DISCOVERING THE WORD

1. *Read Philippians 4:1-9.* Paul opens this chapter with the statement "that is how you should stand firm in the Lord." Look back at 3:12-21. How are we to stand firm in the Lord?

2. In verse 2 Paul pleads with Euodia and Syntyche "to agree with each other in the Lord." Why do you think he is so concerned about their relationship?

3. How can each of the promises and commands listed in verses 4-7 help you to be joyful, peaceful and free from anxiety?

4. How can improper thoughts rob us of the peace God desires for us?

5. How can true, noble, right, pure, lovely, admirable, excellent or praiseworthy thoughts help to cleanse our minds and restore our tranquility (v. 8)?

ᴥ APPLYING THE WORD

• What should be your response to disagreements within your church or fellowship group?

• In verse 9 Paul tells us that "the God of peace" will be with us as we practice what we have learned. What have you learned in this passage that you need to put into practice?

ᴥ RESPONDING IN PRAYER

Ask God to show you the thoughts and attitudes that are robbing you of joy and weakening your faith.

PHILIPPIANS 4:10-23 *Paul's Thank-You Note*

WE'VE ALL WRITTEN thank-you notes for gifts received for a birthday or for Christmas. Such notes usually include rather conventional phrases about the thankfulness of the recipient and the thoughtfulness of the giver. In Philippians 4 Paul thanks the Philippians for a gift of money they sent. However, it is a most unusual thank-you note. First he breaks the conventional rules by waiting until the very end of the letter to say thank you. Then he writes as though he didn't really need the gift!

☙ WARMING UP TO GOD

Have you thanked God for his many gifts to you lately? Take time to do so before you begin.

☙ DISCOVERING THE WORD

1. *Read Philippians 4:10-23.* Paul thanks the Philippians not for the money but for the concern they have shown (v. 10). Why would this have been more important to Paul?

2. Many people believe they can only be content once they have reached a certain level of economic prosperity. How does their view differ from Paul's secret of contentment (vv. 11-13)?

3. How had the Philippians helped Paul in both the past and the present (vv. 14-18)?

4. What benefits does Paul expect the Philippians to receive from their giving (vv. 17-19)?

☙ APPLYING THE WORD

• Many people complain that missionaries are always asking for money. How does this passage provide a model for both missionaries and those who support them?

• How will this passage affect your giving?

☙ RESPONDING IN PRAYER

Pray for Christian workers you know, that they would have the emotional and financial support they need.

INTRODUCING COLOSSIANS

Our culture is on a search for more: more power, more money, more knowledge—more everything! Books on self-improvement and success flood the market. Gurus gain eager followers by offering enlightenment, power and secret wisdom. Millions read horoscopes every day.

We cry for more in the church as well. If only we had more wisdom, more maturity, more power, more faith. To fill these needs we attend seminars, hear celebrity speakers and read their latest books.

Colossians was written to Christians with similar longings. They didn't know who and what they already had. False teachers urged them to add rules, ascetic practices and new philosophies to their Christian faith. Then they would have fullness of life. Paul writes to satisfy their desire for more by showing that they already have fullness in Christ.

While in prison in Rome, Paul learned from Epaphras about the Colossian church and the pressures threatening their peace and stability. Paul's warm letter affirms their positive qualities and the changes in their lives. But he warns them against being deceived by "fine-sounding arguments" (2:4) or by "hollow and deceptive philosophy, which depends on human tradition and on the basic principles of this world rather than on Christ" (2:8).

Colossians is Paul's strongest declaration of the uniqueness and sufficiency of Christ, his authority over all powers and the fullness of life he gives. Paul spells out the implications of this fullness of life throughout the letter.

Like the Colossians, we are bombarded by longings for something more. But Paul thunders in Colossians, You already have fullness in Christ. Enjoy it! "For in Christ all the fullness of the Deity lives in bodily form, and you have been given fullness in Christ" (2:9-10).

Martha Reapsome

COLOSSIANS 1:1-14 *Thanks and Prayer*

"GOD BLESS JENNIFER TODAY" may be a typical prayer for a friend as she comes to mind. But what am I specifically asking for? How will I know if my prayer is answered? What difference would it make in Jennifer's life? Paul begins his letter by telling the Colossians why he is thankful for them and what he asks God to do in them. Paul's example gives us a model for encouraging and praying for one another.

✑ WARMING UP TO GOD

How does it make you feel when friends tell you specific things they appreciate about you?

✑ DISCOVERING THE WORD

1. *Read Colossians 1:1-14.* What characteristics of the Colossians cause Paul to always be thankful for them (vv. 3-6)?

2. What impresses you about how the gospel was spreading (vv. 5-8)?

3. After affirming their strengths, Paul tells the Colossians what he prays for them. What are Paul's requests for how they think and act?

4. How might spiritual wisdom and understanding help us to understand God's will (v. 9)?

5. According to Paul, true knowledge leads to "a life worthy of the Lord" (v. 10). What qualities does such a life include (vv. 10-12)?
   How are these qualities related to each other?

✑ APPLYING THE WORD

• In what specific ways do you see the qualities in verses 10-12 developing in your life?

• Reread verses 12-14, putting your name in each sentence. How would meditating on these verses help you to appreciate what God has done for you?

✑ RESPONDING IN PRAYER

Take time to pray for your church or fellowship group, using verses 9-14 as your model.

COLOSSIANS 1:15-23 *Jesus Is Supreme*

WE FREQUENTLY HEAR, "All roads lead to God. Everyone is trying to get to the same place. That belief is fine for you, but I don't buy it for myself. Only bigots and fanatics label belief true or false." The Colossians heard, "Worship Jesus, but not exclusively. Jesus is just one spirit among many to be worshiped." In this passage we'll study Paul's adamant declaration of Christ's supremacy over every being and idea that invites our attention.

✎ WARMING UP TO GOD

Think back on problems you encountered when you've tried to help someone understand why Jesus is the only way to God.

✎ DISCOVERING THE WORD

1. *Read Colossians 1:15-23.* Make as many statements as you can about why Jesus is supreme (vv. 15-18). Begin each with "Christ is . . ."

2. What does it mean that Christ is the "head of the body, the church" (v. 18)?

3. What actions was God pleased to take to reconcile us to himself (vv. 19-22)?

4. How does understanding God's actions help you explain why Jesus is the only way to God?

✎ APPLYING THE WORD

• How do the words "reconciled" and "holy in his sight, without blemish and free from accusation" (vv. 22-23) motivate you to continue firm in your faith in Christ?

• How might those words appeal to unspoken needs of the friends you want to introduce to Jesus?

• How did some recent choice you made about your time or money reflect Christ's supreme place in your life?

✎ RESPONDING IN PRAYER

Spend some time worshiping Jesus Christ for who he is and what he has done for you and your friends who don't yet know him.

COLOSSIANS 1:24—2:5 *Struggles for Maturity*

FOR A WHOLE YEAR a young man lived in isolation on a remote Arctic mountain. He risked his life on the flight in and on trails over thin ice (which gave way when he struggled under a heavy backpack). He shared his cold tent with mice and mosquitoes. He experimented with a diet of boiled, fried or charred mice. Why would anyone willingly subject himself to such hardships? Farley Mowat had a goal. He wanted to learn the relationship between the wolves and the diminishing caribou herds. In this study Paul describes his own compelling goal, and his struggles and his resources to reach it.

☙ WARMING UP TO GOD

Recall a time when a goal was compelling enough to cause you to suffer for it. Think about what helped you to keep going.

☙ DISCOVERING THE WORD

1. *Read Colossians 1:24—2:5.* How does Paul define God's commission to him (1:24-29)?

2. In the New Testament the term *mystery* refers not to something mysterious but to something previously hidden that God now wishes to make clear. What is the mystery that represents the "word of God in its fullness" (1:26-27; 2:2-3)?

3. According to Paul, what are the marks of Christian maturity (2:2-5)?

4. The Gnostics taught that their secret knowledge was the key to salvation. How would Paul's description of Christ (2:3-4) protect the Colossians from the "fine-sounding arguments" of the Gnostics?

☙ APPLYING THE WORD

• What "fine-sounding arguments" today lure us away from Christ and hinder our spiritual maturity?

• What can you do to refocus your attention on Christ and on his goals for you?

☙ RESPONDING IN PRAYER

Thank God for the people who labored to help you mature in Christ. Pray for friends who need to be encouraged in heart and united in love. Ask God to increase your awareness of the wisdom and knowledge in Jesus Christ.

COLOSSIANS 2:6-23   *No Additions Needed*

KIM YENG AND his family celebrated the day they became American citizens. Now they were no longer refugees but free citizens with full privileges and endless opportunities. But soon the neighbors began to question Kim. "Why are you making your kids super-patriots? They don't have to wear flags on their shirts every day." "Why did you spend all that money installing a tall flagpole in your yard?" "Don't you know that making your family eat hamburgers instead of egg rolls doesn't make you a better citizen?" In this study Paul questions the Colossians about the foolish human additions they are trying to add to all they have in Christ.

ᘓ WARMING UP TO GOD

How would you finish the following sentence? "I would feel fulfilled if . . ."

ᘓ DISCOVERING THE WORD

1. *Read Colossians 2:6-23.* How does each of the images "rooted," "built up," "strengthened" and "overflowing" (v. 7) help us understand how we should continue to live in Christ?

2. In verse 8 we get the first real glimpse of the heresy being taught to the Colossians. What do we learn about it?

3. How would Paul's two statements about fullness in Christ (vv. 9-10) protect the Colossians from those deceptive ideas?

4. In verses 11-15 Paul describes some of what "fullness in Christ" includes. Which of our basic needs did Jesus' death, burial and resurrection meet?

5. What "shadows" were the Colossians adding to the "reality" they had found in Christ (vv. 16-17, 20-23)?

ᘓ APPLYING THE WORD

• Silently reread verses 9-15, inserting your name every time Paul says "you" or "us." How do these facts affect your view of yourself?

• What "shadows" are we tempted to add today?

ᘓ RESPONDING IN PRAYER

Consider the fact that we are made complete in Christ. Allow your prayer and praise to arise out of that fact.

COLOSSIANS 3:1-11 *New Life, New Lifestyle (Part 1)*

HAVE YOU SEEN pictures of marathon runners? Concentration and determination seem to ooze from every pore. These people set their hearts and minds on one thing: finish this race. They focus on the next step, the next checkpoint, until the race is complete. They shed pounds, unnecessary clothing or anything else that might slow them down. As Christians, we are to live like marathon runners. We are to take off anything that slows us down and set our hearts and minds on the finish line.

☙ WARMING UP TO GOD

Think back on your favorite toy or gift. How did your anticipation of it affect how you acted and what you thought about?

☙ DISCOVERING THE WORD

1. *Read Colossians 3:1-11.* What do you think Paul means by "things above" and "earthly things" (vv. 1-2)?

2. How can we set our hearts and minds on things above rather than on earthly things?

3. What do the things we are to "put to death" have in common (v. 5)?

4. Why is each type of behavior in verses 8-10 inconsistent with our new life in Christ?

5. Although we may still struggle with these sins, what resources for change do we now have (vv. 9-11)?

☙ APPLYING THE WORD

- How can we keep God's perspective on immorality and greed when our culture accepts them as the norm?

- What has been the effect on you and others when you have fallen back into these old motives or actions (vv. 5, 8-9)?

- How would becoming aware of Christ in other Christians help us to eliminate our cultural divisions?

☙ RESPONDING IN PRAYER

Paul has shown how our emotions, mind and will are blended in a life raised with Christ. Pray for help in the area where you feel weak. Spend time thanking God for the changes he has already made in you.

COLOSSIANS 3:12-17   *New Life, New Lifestyle (Part 2)*

MARATHON RUNNERS not only shed anything that might slow them down, they also dress carefully. They choose the best running shoes and the most comfortable shorts and shirt possible. Paul, after telling us what to get rid of, now speaks about the new clothes we are to wear because of our new life in Christ.

ᗌ WARMING UP TO GOD

List the behaviors that your parents expected "because you are a member of this family."

ᗌ DISCOVERING THE WORD

1. *Read Colossians 3:12-17.* Why does Paul begin by reminding us of who we are in God's sight (v. 12)?

2. Why is the description "God's chosen people, holy and dearly loved" not dependent on our feelings or efforts (1:12-14; 2:9-10)?

3. Paul recognizes that grievances occur even in the church. How are his instructions for handling grievances different from the way our culture handles them (vv. 13-14)?

4. Paul also recognizes that Christians conflict with each other. How could conflicts be better managed with peace ruling (literally, functioning like an umpire) in our hearts (v. 15)?

5. What does it mean to let Christ's words "dwell" in us richly (v. 16; see also Eph 5:18-20)?

ᗌ APPLYING THE WORD

- What new clothes (v. 12) would you like to put on?
- How would doing everything "in the name of the Lord Jesus" transform what you have to say and do today (v. 17)?

ᗌ RESPONDING IN PRAYER

Let your prayer grow out of the need to put on specific new clothes. If there is someone you need to forgive, confess that and ask for power and determination to forgive.

COLOSSIANS 3:18—4:1   *At Home and on the Job*

FACTORY WORKERS in the Philippines had been meeting for months for a lunch-hour Bible study. One day the supervisor came to the leader and asked, "Could you start some more Bible studies in the factory? The men in the study have become the best workers on my shift." That wouldn't have surprised the apostle Paul. In this section he instructs us about the distinctive attitudes and behaviors that should mark Christians at home and on the job.

☙ WARMING UP TO GOD

When is it easiest for you to have a "Christian" attitude toward your work?

☙ DISCOVERING THE WORD

1. *Read Colossians 3:18—4:1.* How do Paul's commands to wives/husbands, children/fathers and slaves/masters address our tendency to do the opposite?

2. The wife is to submit to the husband "as is fitting in the Lord" (3:18). From what you learned in Colossians 3:5-17, what would that kind of submission include? What would it not include?

3. The husband is to love his wife and not be harsh with her (v. 19). How would 3:12-17 help him understand what that love should be like in actions and attitudes?

4. What attitudes and actions of parents embitter or discourage their children?

5. When and how are slaves to obey their masters (vv. 22-25)? With what motives?

6. What would it demand of a master to "provide your slaves with what is right and fair" (4:1)?

☙ APPLYING THE WORD

- How could the motivations of pleasing the Lord and not discouraging others (3:20-21) improve relationships in your family?

- How would obeying these instructions change how you do your job as employee or employer (3:22—4:1)?

☙ RESPONDING IN PRAYER

Ask God to show you any attitudes or actions toward your family or at work that you need to change. Ask for grace to begin making one small change today.

COLOSSIANS 4:2-18 *Making the Most of Opportunities*

NO ONE EVER becomes a Christian by just watching how a Christian lives. An observer might think Christians earn their way to heaven by trying to be good. How could anyone ever guess how to become a Christian?

Debating whether what we say or how we live is more important in witnessing is like asking which leg is more important for walking. In this study Paul shows that witnessing is an interplay among prayer, living and speaking. His closing greetings illustrate many ways Christians help and encourage each other.

✎ WARMING UP TO GOD

Write down the advice about witnessing you would give to a younger Christian.

✎ DISCOVERING THE WORD

1. *Read Colossians 4:2-18.* In verses 2-6 Paul teaches us how to speak to God about people and how to speak to people about God. Why would he tell us to devote ourselves to prayer (v. 2)?

2. Paul might have asked the church to pray for his release from prison. What requests does he make instead (vv. 3-4)? Why?

3. What advice does Paul give us about the way we live and converse with non-Christians (vv. 5-6)?

4. Paul concludes this letter with numerous personal messages and greetings. What qualities in people does Paul affirm, and why (vv. 7-18)?

✎ APPLYING THE WORD

• In what ways might you "be wise in the way you act toward outsiders" and "make the most of every opportunity" (v. 5)?

• How could you encourage or comfort a fellow Christian this week by following the example of someone named here?

✎ RESPONDING IN PRAYER

Use verses 3-4 to pray for yourself, your church leaders and missionaries. Ask God to make you aware of every opportunity to influence nonbelievers to consider Jesus.

INTRODUCING
1 THESSALONIANS

W ouldn't you like to be sure about where you stand with God? That's what the Thessalonians were looking for, and Paul's letters to them can help you find that assurance as well.

In A.D. 50 Paul entered Thessalonica while on his second missionary journey. He preached there for three weeks and was able to establish a church. However, a group of jealous Jews interpreted Paul's message to mean that he was proclaiming another ruler in opposition to the Roman emperor, and he was forced to leave town (Acts 17:1-10).

Because of Paul's concern for this young church, he sent his coworker Timothy to learn how the Thessalonians were doing. Timothy reported that the Christians' faith remained strong but that they continued to be persecuted by those who had banished Paul. Timothy also brought back questions that Paul had not had time to answer during his short stay. First Thessalonians was Paul's first attempt at offering encouragement and answering questions; in fact it was probably the first of Paul's epistles. It was written from Corinth only a few months after Paul had left Thessalonica.

In 1 Thessalonians Paul offers encouragement in four areas: (1) How can I be sure I will be with Jesus after death? (2) How can I be sure Jesus is coming again? (3) How can I be sure Jesus hasn't forgotten me when I am suffering persecution? (4) How can I be sure my life is pleasing to God?

Through your study of these letters, you will become sure of your faith and of your salvation. As a result, you will be able to "encourage each other with these words" (1 Thess 4:18).

Donald E. Baker

1 THESSALONIANS 1 *Faith That Shows*

A LIGHTHOUSE has become a common analogy for a church. Just as a lighthouse stands in a dark and dangerous spot, flashing its message of warning and pointing to safe harbor, a church should also be a prominent and unmistakable sign to the community in which it exists. How can you help your church or fellowship group become such a shining light? This passage describes how the church in Thessalonica was able to do it.

✆ WARMING UP TO GOD

Give some thought to the reputation of your church or fellowship group throughout the community.

✆ DISCOVERING THE WORD

1. *Read 1 Thessalonians 1.* Paul writes that he remembers the Thessalonians' "work produced by faith," "labor prompted by love" and "endurance inspired by hope" (v. 3). How do you think he could tell that faith, love and hope were behind their actions?

2. What role has the Holy Spirit played in the Thessalonians' faith (vv. 5-6)?

3. What role did Paul, Silas and Timothy have in the Thessalonians' conversion (v. 6)?

4. When is it wise and when is it unwise to imitate another Christian (vv. 6-7)?

5. What were the results of the Thessalonians' strong faith (vv. 8-10)?

✆ APPLYING THE WORD

• What do you think your reputation is with non-Christians?

• How can your faith (and the faith of your church or fellowship group) become more of a witness to others?

✆ RESPONDING IN PRAYER

Ask to be made a genuine witness, and pray for the witness of your church.

1 THESSALONIANS 2:1-16   *Gentle Evangelism*

WHAT THOUGHTS COME to your mind when you hear the word *evangelism?* Pushy people trying to get others to see things their way? Guilt for not saying enough about your Savior? People swarming down the aisles at a gigantic rally? Or friends sharing the excitement of the good news with each other? For Paul, evangelism was always delightful and exciting. In this passage he tells us why talking about Christ is such a positive experience for him.

✍ WARMING UP TO GOD

How do you feel about telling others about your faith? Talk with God about any fears or guilt you experience.

✍ DISCOVERING THE WORD

1. *Read 1 Thessalonians 2:1-16.* What excuses might Paul have had not to preach to the Thessalonians (vv. 1-2)?

2. What attitudes enable Paul to continue preaching despite opposition (vv. 3-6)?

3. What does this teach you about proper and improper reasons for witnessing to others?

4. Paul claims to have been "holy, righteous and blameless" (v. 10) among the Thessalonians. If this is important, how can imperfect people dare to do evangelism?

5. How is a father dealing with his children a good example of an evangelist (vv. 11-12)?

✍ APPLYING THE WORD

• In what specific ways can gentleness and caring become more a part of your evangelistic efforts?

• In what ways have you found evangelism to be difficult?

• What ideas and encouragement from this passage can help you to overcome these difficulties?

✍ RESPONDING IN PRAYER

Ask God to give you encouragement to be a gentle evangelist.

1 THESSALONIANS 2:17—3:13 *Unmistakable Love*

IN THEIR BOOK *Who Cares About Love?* Win Arn, Carroll Nyquist and Charles Arn show that more people leave their churches today for lack of love than for any other reason. It is indeed sad that even those who are committed to the Lord of love are unable to offer that love to others. How can your church become a place where love will "increase and overflow for each other and for everyone else" (3:12)? This passage provides some practical examples.

⌘ WARMING UP TO GOD

On a scale of one to ten, how loving are you to the members of your church or fellowship group?

⌘ DISCOVERING THE WORD

1. *Read 1 Thessalonians 2:17—3:13.* What evidence do you find in this passage that Paul really did love the Thessalonians (2:17, 20; 3:2, 5, 10)?
2. What phrases does Paul use to express his love (2:17-18; 3:5)?
3. What fears caused Paul to send Timothy to Thessalonica (3:2-5)?
4. What are Paul's desires for the Thessalonians (3:10-13)?
5. How do these desires reflect Paul's love and care?

⌘ APPLYING THE WORD

- How do you most often express your love for others?
- What ideas from this passage can help you become even better at expressing love?
- How can you (as an individual or group) help love increase within your church or fellowship group?

⌘ RESPONDING IN PRAYER

Ask God to help you show love to someone in your church this week.

1 THESSALONIANS 4:1-12   *A Life That Pleases God*

ALL OF US WANT to please the people we love the most. That is why a husband will plan a special evening at a concert he knows will excite his wife or a child will pick a bouquet of dandelions to present to Mom and Dad. What can Christians do to please God, whom they love so dearly?

ᘒ WARMING UP TO GOD

Write down what you would tell a Christian brother or sister who asked you for advice on how to be more pleasing to God.

ᘒ DISCOVERING THE WORD

1. *Read 1 Thessalonians 4:1-12.* Why would Paul give these instructions on holy living to people whom he says are already living a life that pleases God (vv. 1, 10)?

2. What clues does this passage give as to how Paul would define sexual immorality (vv. 3-6)?

3. How does sexual immorality "wrong" or "take advantage of" others (v. 6)?

4. Scholars agree that verses 11 and 12 were directed toward members of the church who had quit working and were relying on the kindness of their fellow Christians to provide them with necessities. Why would Paul have been concerned about the effect this attitude was having on outsiders?

ᘒ APPLYING THE WORD

- What work habits detract from your Christian witness?

- How can this passage help you to resist sexual temptation?

- Paul has given commands in this passage concerning sexual immorality, love for fellow Christians and work. What can you do this week to become more obedient in one of these areas?

ᘒ RESPONDING IN PRAYER

Give your life to the Lord, praying that it will be made pleasing to him.

1 THESSALONIANS 4:13—5:11   *Hope of Christ's Coming*

A CRISIS OCCURRED in the Thessalonian church when one of their members died. Because they had expected to all be alive when Christ returned, they were now confused. Did this mean their friend would miss out on Christ's coming? Had this person died because God was angry with him? How much longer would it be before Christ finally did return? Maybe you have fears about what will happen when you die or when Christ returns. In this passage, Paul seeks to calm our fears and encourage us to look forward to the day we meet our Maker.

✎ WARMING UP TO GOD

List some of the fears you have about death.

✎ DISCOVERING THE WORD

1. *Read 1 Thessalonians 4:13—5:11.* In what ways is grief different for a Christian than it is for a non-Christian (4:13)?

2. What sequence of events does Paul say will occur when Christ returns (4:16-17)?

3. Why are the examples of a thief and labor pains (5:2-3) good analogies of what will happen on the day of the Lord?

4. What dangers are associated with living in darkness (5:5-7)?

5. What instructions does Paul give for living in the light (5:8)?

✎ APPLYING THE WORD

- How do Paul's words help you to face your own fears about death?

- Paul tells us that our defensive weapons against darkness are faith, love and hope (5:8). What are some practical ways in which these virtues can defend you?

✎ RESPONDING IN PRAYER

Pray that you will be made ready for the day of the Lord.

1 THESSALONIANS 5:12-28 *Life Among Friends*

ANY GROUP OF people needs rules for getting along, and the church is no exception. Paul so wants the Thessalonians to "live in peace with each other" (5:13) that he closes his first letter to them with several instructions on how they can do this. These instructions have never gone out of date and can still be used to end the quarrels, hurt feelings and resentments in your church or fellowship group.

⁶ WARMING UP TO GOD

If you had the power to make one rule for helping people get along, what would it be? Why?

⁶ DISCOVERING THE WORD

1. *Read 1 Thessalonians 5:12-28.* What does it mean for someone to be "over you in the Lord" (v. 12)?

2. How can you warn people about something they are doing wrong (v. 14) or prevent them from taking revenge (v. 15) and still live in peace with them?

3. What does it mean to "be joyful *always;* pray *continually;* give thanks *in all circumstances*" (vv. 16-18, emphasis added)?

4. How can you test things like prophecy or teaching to find out if they are good or evil (vv. 19-22)?

5. Look through the passage again and pick out the actions and attitudes (stated or implied) that are displeasing to God. What are they?

⁶ APPLYING THE WORD

• When have you found God faithful in keeping you from sin (v. 24)?

• In what way do you currently need God's faithfulness to keep you from sin?

⁶ RESPONDING IN PRAYER

Follow the discipline of giving thanks in all circumstances by finding as many things in your life as you can to be thankful for.

INTRODUCING
2 THESSALONIANS

Second Thessalonians was written a short time after 1 Thessalonians to clear up misconceptions about the second coming that the first letter had failed to answer. Although the letter was written to Gentiles, it assumes some knowledge of the Old Testament. According to Donald Guthrie's *New Testament Introduction,* this was typical of early Christian teaching.

Paul most likely wrote the letter from Corinth. In addition to clarifying the Thessalonians' understanding about Christ's return, he addressed some ongoing problems in the church in dealing with idleness. This book offered its readers comfort and insight about faith and end times, as well as a call to take responsibility. May it both challenge and encourage you.

Donald E. Baker

2 THESSALONIANS 1   *Evidence of Faith*

CAN I KNOW for sure that I will go to heaven? This is a question that plagued the Thessalonians to such an extent that even after the comfort of his first letter, Paul has to write again and give further encouragement. It was difficult for these young Christians to believe that the suffering of their present life would really be followed by the eternal joy of heaven. Perhaps you also wonder if heaven really exists and if you can be sure of going there. If so, you will find Paul writing this passage directly to you.

☙ WARMING UP TO GOD

Have you ever met a person and gone away thinking, "They must be a Christian"? Reflect on what gave you that impression.

☙ DISCOVERING THE WORD

1. *Read 2 Thessalonians 1.* What good things does Paul notice about the lives of the Thessalonians (vv. 3-4)?

2. Why do you think that, in times of persecution, some people's faith and love grow while others' fail (v. 4)?

3. Paul proclaims that "God is just." How does he describe God's justice (vv. 5-10)?

4. According to this passage, what makes a person "worthy of the kingdom" (v. 5) or "worthy of [God's] calling" (v. 11)?

5. In light of his teaching about God's judgment, why does Paul pray as he does in verses 11-12?

☙ APPLYING THE WORD

- How can God's justice encourage you when things are "just not fair"?
- If someone were to pray for you as Paul did in verses 11-12, what is one specific way in which you would want God to change your life?

☙ RESPONDING IN PRAYER

Pray that God's justice would be done in your life and throughout the world.

2 THESSALONIANS 2   *Lawlessness on the Loose*

HOW WILL THE world end? Will there be nuclear war? An evil empire? The destruction of civilization? Paul advises us that Satan has yet to attack us with the worst he has, and when he does, it will be a fearful time to be alive. However, Paul also promises that God will always be in control.

ᛊ WARMING UP TO GOD

What potential threats to the safety of the world do you see right now (for example, attitudes, weapon building, prejudice and so on)? Think about how those threats affect you personally.

ᛊ DISCOVERING THE WORD

1. *Read 2 Thessalonians 2.* In 1 Thessalonians 4:13-18 Paul responded to the fears of the Thessalonians that if they died before Christ returned, they would miss the joy Christ had for them. Apparently, after Paul sent the first letter, someone tried to convince the Thessalonians that the day of the Lord had already come. What is Paul's proof that the day of the Lord has not come (vv. 3, 9)?

2. What can you learn about the "man of lawlessness" from this passage (vv. 3-4, 7-10)?

3. In what ways have you noticed the "secret power of lawlessness" (v. 7) to be already at work?

4. What contrasts do you find between those whom God condemns (vv. 10-12) and those whom he chooses for salvation (vv. 13-17)?

ᛊ APPLYING THE WORD

• Even for Christians, the lawless one will bring fear and testing. What can you do to prepare yourself to withstand him?

• How can this passage encourage you about facing the future?

ᛊ RESPONDING IN PRAYER

Talk with God about any fears or concerns you have regarding the future.

2 THESSALONIANS 3   *Lazy Christians*

MEMBERS OF THE Thessalonian church were refusing to take responsibility. Some had quit working because they thought Jesus would be back any moment and they didn't see any reason to exert themselves. Others relaxed because there were plenty of wealthier members in the church who were always willing to share. Regardless of the reason, Paul abhorred such laziness and set the rule "If a man will not work, he shall not eat" (v. 10). How can our laziness affect the work of Christ? What can we do about the laziness of others? Paul addresses those questions in this study.

✒ WARMING UP TO GOD

When is it hard for you to feel motivated to do the work of your church?

✒ DISCOVERING THE WORD

1. *Read 2 Thessalonians 3.* In what ways did Paul expect that his ministry could be enhanced because of the Thessalonians' prayer (vv. 1-2)?

2. How is Paul's confidence in the Lord expressed in this request for prayer (vv. 3-5)?

3. How would you describe the problem the Thessalonian church was experiencing (v. 11)?

4. How did Paul make himself an example of the proper attitude toward work (vv. 7-9)?

5. What actions are to be taken against those who refuse to work (vv. 12-15)?

✒ APPLYING THE WORD

• What encouragement and ideas do these verses give you concerning your own prayer life?

• In what ways do lazy Christians still continue to take advantage of the work of others?

• What principles for discipline that could be applied in the church today do you find in this passage?

✒ RESPONDING IN PRAYER

Pray that like Paul you will be a good example to others in your attitude toward work.

INTRODUCING 1 TIMOTHY

Ephesus, a key seaport for Asia Minor, was a swinging commercial center. Dominating the economy of Ephesus was the temple of Artemis, "goddess of the Ephesians"—a thirty-seven-breasted fertility goddess who stood for bringing prosperity out of constant change.

Various cultures mixed in Ephesus. Its heritage was Greek, but Romans pushed in when it became part of the empire. A sizeable Jewish community took root, as well as smaller communities of many ethnic groups. Different religions, philosophies and ethics coexisted while everybody sought some piece of the economic action.

Paul saw Ephesus as a great place to preach the gospel. He began with preaching to his fellow Jews on his second missionary journey. On his third journey, he invested two solid years evangelizing and developing Christian leaders. Christian faith became so popular that the magic trade and temple business fell sharply.

Paul turned over the leadership of the church in Ephesus to Timothy, a bright, sensitive associate. Timothy was about forty years old at that time, which was considered young for such leadership. Timothy's mission was to deal with false teaching, and it seems he was a capable teacher. In these letters we can see Paul coaching the younger leader. In the process he raises issues that bear on us all—leaders or not.

Pete Sommer

1 TIMOTHY 1 *What Difference Does It Make?*

"CHRIST CONSCIOUSNESS—Mystical Teaching in the Bible," advertises a poster. "The mystical core of Christ's teaching has been obscured by centuries of dogma," it announces, inviting Christians to come to lectures by a young lady who follows a Hindu sect. And at the other extreme, some Christian leaders, dismayed by a low level of commitment, create special teachings and extra rules to regulate the social lives of their members. These modern examples are the kinds of thing that were rampant in the church at Ephesus; Paul sent Timothy to Ephesus to deal with them.

✐ WARMING UP TO GOD

What helps you distinguish between true and false spirituality?

✐ DISCOVERING THE WORD

1. *Read 1 Timothy 1.* How does Paul describe Timothy's job (vv. 3-5)?
2. Finding hidden meanings in the Old Testament was big business in first-century religion. False teachers mixed "secret teachings" with the gospel. What results were the false teachers getting for their efforts (vv. 4-6)?
3. From what Paul says about the proper use of the law, how does it seem that the false teachers use it (vv. 8-11)?
4. In what ways was Paul himself like the false teachers before his conversion (vv. 12-17)?
5. Note the places where *conscience* comes up (vv. 5, 19). When we speculate and theorize instead of dealing with sin, what happens to conscience?

✐ APPLYING THE WORD

- How can the kind of faith Paul shows in verse 15 help you face your own issues of conscience?
- Christians can wander into groups that make unusual claims and demands. A lot of energy goes into keeping faith and conscience apart in these groups. Are you involved with some "spiritual" activities that bother your own conscience? (Be as honest as possible.)

✐ RESPONDING IN PRAYER

Close in prayer by putting your own name in place of the general word *sinners* in verse 15. Now read verses 16-17 as your own prayer of thanks to God.

1 TIMOTHY 2 *Barriers to Renewal*

DO YOU EVER have difficulty approaching God in prayer? The Christians in Ephesus did. The barriers to prayer described here are anger, an overemphasis on appearance and an inappropriate role for women. Having sized up the situation and reminded Timothy of his mission, Paul outlines first steps to dealing with the needs of the church.

❧ WARMING UP TO GOD

Think back on a time when you found prayer difficult. Reflect on what made it so difficult.

❧ DISCOVERING THE WORD

1. *Read 1 Timothy 2.* Find all the times Paul says "all" and "everyone" (vv. 1-6). What does the use of these terms communicate about God?

2. Why do you think Paul emphasizes the word *one* in verse 5?

3. This entire chapter deals with worship. The church in Ephesus was probably a network of house churches. Their worship may have been patterned after the Jewish synagogues, which separated men and women. What problem hindered the worship by men (v. 8)?

4. What problem hindered the worship by women (v. 9)?

5. In verses 11-12, Paul forbids women to teach men. But in 1 Corinthians 11:5, he tells them how to dress when they preach (or "prophesy"). How do you reconcile these texts?

❧ APPLYING THE WORD

• According to this passage, what could hinder worship and sharing the gospel?

• Consider which of those are problems for you. How can you better deal with them?

❧ RESPONDING IN PRAYER

Pray for your church's worship and for your personal worship.

1 TIMOTHY 3   *Who Can Lead?*

SOME CHURCHES AND fellowships have a few people who are willing to lead. Those people may end up feeling burdened and alone. Other churches have people who are willing to lead but are not ready. If there are not enough leaders, however, the work of the church will not get done. The church of Ephesus was in the latter category. Those who were willing to lead were immature. And Timothy could not hope to carry out his mission against false teachers unless the leadership was healthy.

✥ WARMING UP TO GOD

Reflect on your best and worst experiences of Christian leadership.

✥ DISCOVERING THE WORD

1. *Read 1 Timothy 3.* Consider two categories of qualification: character and ability. How do the qualities mentioned in these verses divide into these two categories?

2. What do you think is Paul's reason for insisting that a leader's relationships must work in the spheres of both church and family (vv. 5-6)?

3. How have you seen the principle in verse 7 obeyed or disobeyed?

4. *Deacon* simply means "servant." In the passage it seems that deacons deal with the more practical affairs of church life, rather than with teaching. Given that, why do you think the point about doctrine in verse 9 is made with so much emphasis?

5. What do verses 14-16 tell us about Paul's purpose in writing this letter?

✥ APPLYING THE WORD

• Verse 16 was probably a hymn sung in the church at Ephesus. The word translated as "deep truths" in v. 9 is rendered "mystery" here. We can say that the result Paul wanted from good Christian leadership was that these truths would be revealed. Therefore, when people look at our fellowship, what should they see?

• How can you serve your church through leadership, or encourage others who lead?

✥ RESPONDING IN PRAYER

Pray for your pastor and church leaders.

1 TIMOTHY 4   *True and False Ministry*

PAUL'S STRATEGY FOR Timothy starts to emerge clearly in 1 Timothy 4. Paul sees that fighting false teachers with ideology alone is fruitless. The real mission is that the church be healthy so that Jesus Christ is communicated through it. So he spoke of prayer and leadership first. With that foundation in place, Timothy will be able to turn his attention directly to the problems at hand.

✋ WARMING UP TO GOD

List the best advice you've been given by older Christians in your family or church.

✋ DISCOVERING THE WORD

1. *Read 1 Timothy 4.* What is the nature of the teachings described in verses 2-3?

2. Why is this teaching—which could seem to be "super-spiritual"—really a doctrine of demons (vv. 3-4)?

3. When you think of "false teaching," do you think of teachers who are morally too loose or too strict? Explain.

4. What was Timothy's personal life to be like (vv. 7-16)?

5. How was it to differ from that of the false teachers?

✋ APPLYING THE WORD

• Why do you think you are motivated at some times and not motivated at other times for training in godliness (v. 7)?

• Timothy's primary ministry was teaching. What in this passage encourages you to develop and use your ministry gifts?

✋ RESPONDING IN PRAYER

Pray for those who might be under the hold of false teachers, that the truth would be revealed to them.

1 TIMOTHY 5:1—6:2 *Implementing Spiritual Teaching*

AT ONE TIME or another all of us have probably been in a situation in which we felt that someone in our church or fellowship was sinning. Whether or not we act on the situation and how we communicate to that person has a big effect on the outcome. Often when we rebuke others about their lifestyles, we come off as being judgmental and self-righteous. When Paul tells Timothy about specific persons and groups he needed to confront about certain issues, he is careful to show how to do so in love. Paul's teaching here gives us valuable guidance on being both direct and loving with other Christians.

ᴥ WARMING UP TO GOD

Recall a time you observed or experienced rebuke. What good came out of it?

ᴥ DISCOVERING THE WORD

1. *Read 1 Timothy 5:1—6:2.* Paul touches on the different age and gender groups Timothy must lead. How is Timothy to regard the people he ministers to?

2. How is a godly widow to be distinguished from an ungodly one (5:3-8)?

3. What criteria did a widow need to meet to secure a place on the list of those who received financial aid from the church (5:9-10)?

4. Why do you think Paul gives these specific instructions about rebuking an elder in 5:19-20?

5. How have you found 5:24-25 to be true?

6. From 6:1-2, what do you think has been happening as slaves became believers?

ᴥ APPLYING THE WORD

- How can you rebuke someone in ways that are clear but also affirm the other person as a member of God's family?

- In affluent Ephesus, like twentieth-century America, many elderly people evidently were abandoned. What obligations do you have to your own parents?

- What ideas does this passage give you for new areas of ministry?

ᴥ RESPONDING IN PRAYER

Pray for those in your church who are needy and who may be without family.

1 TIMOTHY 6:3-20   *Find Your Riches in Christ*

SOME WELL-KNOWN Christian teachers and authors tell us that being a Christian means success and prosperity—that if we are faithful, God will bless us with wealth. Other Christians advocate a simple lifestyle without interest in material possessions. What does Scripture say about how we are to regard money? In this chapter Paul concludes his agenda of how to lead the powerful and the powerless by addressing the wealthy members of the church.

ᜦ WARMING UP TO GOD

What do you believe is the place of money in the life of a Christian?

ᜦ DISCOVERING THE WORD

1. *Read 1 Timothy 6:3-20.* What do you think Paul means by an "unhealthy interest" (v. 4)?

2. According to verses 6-8, how are we to find contentment?

3. In your own words, how would you explain Paul's teaching on riches in verses 9-10?

4. What was Paul commanding Timothy to do in this context (vv. 11-14)?

5. How is Christ pictured in verses 13-16?

6. Why do you think Paul told Timothy to turn away from "godless chatter" (v. 20)?

ᜦ APPLYING THE WORD

• In what ways does your Christian life feel like a fight?

• Describe how you have seen Christians use riches to do good work.

• What has God entrusted to your care, and how do you guard it?

ᜦ RESPONDING IN PRAYER

Pray that you would be a good steward of what you have been given.

INTRODUCING 2 TIMOTHY

Second Timothy is Paul's last letter. He is in prison in Rome again—under Nero. He is an older man and does not expect to get out, but to die in prison (contrast with Phil 1:23-25).

Opposition to Paul both inside and outside the church had intensified. Many former associates had deserted him. His loneliness and desire to see Timothy came through clearly. Further, Nero's persecution was underway, and many Christians were facing the choice of suffering or leaving the faith. Much of what Paul built was at risk. When his personal resources were at their lowest, he faced the greatest test. In this context he reflects on his own life and gives his final counsel.

This letter has fantastic value for us. It gives us insight into facing persecution and supporting others who are persecuted. It also shows both how to give away leadership and how to assume it at the right time. Finally, it provides encouragement to us in facing our own death.

Pete Sommer

2 TIMOTHY 1   *Rejected but Not Ashamed*

SHAME MEANS BEING revealed to others as weak and inadequate. Rejection is cause for shame unless we are sure of both our ideas and our approach. We are prone to believe what others say about us, especially if they are more successful or in authority. We often need support from our own friends to maintain our dignity in the face of unjust charges.

When Paul was imprisoned, the church in Rome did not come to his defense. Only one believer came looking for him. The rest probably held back from fear or considered the imprisonment something shameful. But although he has been rejected, Paul tells us he is not ashamed.

❧ WARMING UP TO GOD

Think back on a time non-Christian friends or pressures from the world caused you to feel ashamed of the gospel.

❧ DISCOVERING THE WORD

1. *Read 2 Timothy 1.* What are we told about the relationship of Paul and Timothy (vv. 2-6)?
2. What is Paul's situation (vv. 1, 8, 11-12, 15-16)?
3. Find the references to shame (vv. 12, 16). Why would shame be a response to Paul's imprisonment?
4. How did Paul reject shame in this situation (vv. 3, 8-12)?

❧ APPLYING THE WORD

- How can we apply Paul's example of resisting the shame that arises from situations that severely restrict our freedom and separate us from people?
- Timothy's mentor has been disgraced; his associates have deserted the ministry; his church's members are drifting from the faith or cowed by the threat of persecution. How have you struggled with similar situations?
- How is God calling you to testify about him in your situation?

❧ RESPONDING IN PRAYER

With your call to witness in mind, pray through what the text affirms about God in verses 8-12. As you pray, think especially about how you might be ashamed of sharing your faith, and ask for God's help.

2 TIMOTHY 2   *Pass It On*

BARBARA BOYD once said, "Paul had no dead-end disciples." The essence of Paul's ministry was to be certain that the gospel was handed on to other people in such a way that they came to regard this task as their own. This approach, which was very radical in its time, puts the power of the movement into the hands of thousands. Having been deserted by many, Paul wants to make sure the gospel won't die when he does—or when Timothy does.

✥ WARMING UP TO GOD

Recall a time when an older Christian entrusted some aspect of ministry to you. How did this create growth and maturity in your life?

✥ DISCOVERING THE WORD

1. *Read 2 Timothy 2.* Paul begins with the call to Timothy to "be strong in grace" (v. 1). Why does he give that instruction rather than "be strong in your gifts," "be strong in knowledge" or "be strong in willpower"?

2. What do each of the three images in verses 3-7 illustrate about the ministry of entrusting the gospel to others who can pass it on?

3. Why does Paul cite these specific aspects of Christ that Timothy should remember (v. 8)?

4. How does this explain Paul's own confidence even while he is imprisoned (v. 9)?

5. Why does Paul say he endures (vv. 10-13)?

6. What do verses 18-19 say is both the potential and the limitation of false teaching?

✥ APPLYING THE WORD

- Which of the images in verses 3-7 seems most applicable to your life right now? Why?

- How should the "trustworthy saying" in verses 11-13 motivate us?

✥ RESPONDING IN PRAYER

Where is your own character being tested as you try to entrust the gospel to others? Pray that God will encourage you and strengthen you in those areas.

2 TIMOTHY 3 *How to Recognize God's Voice*

MOST OF US GO through stages when we are vulnerable to false teachers. Campus cults make their biggest outreaches during the opening days of school and during finals week—when students are under the greatest stress. Life crises are doors of change for good or evil. In addition, guilt, greed and other lusts distort judgment and give false teachers their opportunity.

Philetus and Hymanaeus represent a tradition of potent religious falsehood Timothy fought against his whole career. We can expect the same kind of struggle. In spite of the power and appeal of such groups, however, Paul had great confidence in both Scripture and those who live by it. In this chapter he encourages Timothy to have confidence in God's teaching as well.

ᘓ Warming Up to God

What factors do you think would make a person particularly susceptible to heresy?

ᘓ Discovering the Word

1. *Read 2 Timothy 3.* What evidence do we have in this chapter that these people are religious?
2. Notice the way those controlled by these religious leaders are described (v. 6). Why are we vulnerable to spiritual manipulation when we are "weak-willed," "loaded down with sins" and "swayed by . . . evil desires"?
3. Why could Timothy trust Paul's spiritual influence (vv. 10-13)?
4. Paul does not expect blind faith from Timothy. What does he expect, and what two reasons does he give for it (vv. 14-15)?
5. Where does Scripture come from, and what is its power (vv. 15-17)?

ᘓ Applying the Word

- What would enhance your own trustworthiness among those you influence (children, students, coworkers or employees, friends)?
- In Hebrew (conceptually) to hear is to obey and do God's will. During this study, how have you sensed that God wants you to change in order to hear his voice more clearly?

ᘓ Responding in Prayer

Pray that you would hear God's voice and be kept safe from false teaching.

2 TIMOTHY 4 *It's Your Turn Now*

THE STORY IS told of the umpire who called a strike on Babe Ruth. The Babe turned around and angrily shouted, "Hey, meathead! Me and forty thousand people here know that pitch was a ball!" The umpire replied, "Yeah, and mine is the only opinion that matters."

The gospel is not often popular. As he gears up for ministry, Timothy needs to know that only God's opinion matters. In this passage, the last written words of Paul we have, Paul instructs Timothy to think of eternity.

☙ WARMING UP TO GOD

How do you respond (inwardly and outwardly) when you see friends turning away from the faith?

☙ DISCOVERING THE WORD

1. *Read 2 Timothy 4.* What charge was Timothy to keep (vv. 3-5)?
2. Paul is seeing a big part of what he labored so hard to build under God's power dissolve. How can he still feel such satisfaction about his life (vv. 6-8)?
3. What do verses 9-13 reveal about Paul's situation?
4. Rome had a big Christian community, but they shunned Paul when he came to trial (vv. 16-17, see also 1:8, 12, 16-18). Paul could have chosen to burn with resentment. What clues in the passage show why he was not bitter?
5. The names in verses 19-20 denote men, women, Romans, Greeks, nobles and commoners. What comfort would that fact give both Paul and Timothy?

☙ APPLYING THE WORD

- What life tasks do you need to finish in order to share Paul's satisfaction?
- Who is taking a public stand for the gospel in your community, and how can you support them?

☙ RESPONDING IN PRAYER

Pray for the spread of the gospel locally and around the world.

INTRODUCING TITUS

꧁

Titus was no stranger to conflict. Titus was a Gentile, and he was essentially "tried" (and acquitted) by the leaders in Jerusalem over the question whether Gentiles should have to comply with Jewish ceremonial rites (circumcision, diet restrictions and so on) in order to be full members of the Christian community.

Titus had the unwelcome job of delivering what we call the "severe letter" referred to by Paul in 2 Corinthians 2:1-4 and 7:5-13. Then he delivered the letter we now call 2 Corinthians, in which Paul takes on his critics and calls the church to honor an unfulfilled financial pledge.

At the time Paul wrote to him, Titus was in Crete, a sleazy port of call for cargo ships traversing the Mediterranean. Paul had preached in Crete and was giving Titus the job of following through with developing a healthy church. This letter shows Titus as a forceful personality and skilled administrator.

Paul's letter to Titus gives us two very valuable things: (1) a showcase of Paul's strategy for leadership in the midst of chaos, and (2) a model of hope in the face of a very messy situation. Paul's confidence in the power of the gospel shines throughout the letter.

Pete Sommer

TITUS 1—3 *Great Expectations*

GREAT EXPECTATIONS is the well-known title of a novel by Charles Dickens, the story of a young man's early experiences out in the "real world" as he seeks to gain the fortune he has inherited. Similarly the book of Titus tells of Paul's expectations for Titus during his first ministry experience on his own. Paul's promise to Titus is that he will become an heir of eternity.

❧ WARMING UP TO GOD

Think of a person in your life who expects great things from you. How do you feel about that person's expectations? Are they realistic?

❧ DISCOVERING THE WORD

1. *Read Titus 1—3.* Note all you can from the book about the social situation (family, public and private morality).

2. What do you learn about the economic situation (work, wealth and poverty)?

3. What is revealed about the religious situation (spirituality, doctrine, church life)?

4. Paul expected enormous things of Titus. And he wanted Titus to meet him in Nicopolis in about eight months (3:12). When it comes to what others expect of us, our first response is often to question whether they are fair. How fair do you think Paul's expectations of Titus were?

5. Paul's expectations were built not only on his knowledge of Titus but also on solid theological grounds. What were they (1:1-3; 2:11-14; 3:3-7)?

6. Do you think Paul's expectations helped Titus to accomplish his mission? Why or why not?

❧ APPLYING THE WORD

- Do your own Christian leaders expect too much or too little of you? What effect does that have on your own walk with Jesus Christ?

- At work, home, school or church, whether you are a follower or a leader, you have a responsibility to communicate your expectations. Name one step you could take to do this more effectively.

❧ RESPONDING IN PRAYER

What expectations are you wrestling with? Ask God for insight to know which come from him and which do not.

Introducing Philemon

ᥫᩣ

The little book of Philemon is the only surviving letter of Paul to an individual friend and convert about a private matter. In it we learn that Onesimus, one of Philemon's slaves, had stolen from his master and run away to Rome. In that great city he met Paul and became a Christian. Under Roman law, Philemon had the right to brand a returned slave or even kill him. Paul applies what he wrote in Colossians: "Here there is no Greek or Jew . . . slave or free, but Christ is all, and is in all" (Col 3:11). Philemon and Onesimus are given the chance to participate in a revolutionary new process for reconciliation.

Martha Reapsome

PHILEMON 1-25 *Mending Fractured Relationships*

DAVE AND ANDY enjoyed a prosperous business partnership for several years. Their families became closest friends, sharing vacations made possible by their growing computer business. Then one day Andy disappeared, along with the company bank account. Dave lost his friend, his business and his home. Three years later Andy returned, having squandered the money but having found Christ. Could Dave forgive him? Could they ever be friends again?

In Paul's letter to Philemon, you'll find principles for bringing reconciliation between two Christians who know the pain of wronging another and being wronged.

✎ WARMING UP TO GOD

Recall a time when you wanted to restore a broken relationship. What were some of your fears in approaching the situation?

✎ DISCOVERING THE WORD

1. *Read Philemon 1-25.* Based on what you have read, how would you reconstruct the events that led up to this letter?

2. Having described Philemon's loving character, Paul appeals to him "on the basis of love" (v. 9). Why is love so essential for mending a fractured relationship?

3. In what ways has Onesimus changed since running away from Philemon (vv. 10-16)?

4. What will it require of Onesimus to return to Philemon?

5. What will it require of Philemon to do what Paul asks?

✎ APPLYING THE WORD

- What principles in this letter could you use for mending a fractured relationship?

- Paul intervened to restore these two brothers in Christ. When might we need the help of a friend or counselor?

✎ RESPONDING IN PRAYER

Pray for God's grace for you to follow these principles in a situation where you may be an Onesimus or Philemon or Paul.

Introducing Hebrews

❧

In his book *Rebuilding Your Broken World*, Gordon MacDonald quotes a former Olympic distance runner and veteran missionary, who wrote the following to a friend in crisis: "Whatever the difficulty, the blow, we must keep on. God will lead to the result that will glorify him."

Throughout the letter to the Hebrews, the author emphasizes this chief concern for the readers: that they finish their faith-race with Jesus Christ gloriously and triumphantly. After convincingly showing how Jesus meets all of our needs, the writer devotes an entire chapter (11) to draw the readers to the stories of great heroes who finished the race to glory, people like Moses, Abraham, Noah, Jacob and Joseph. These witnesses are summoned to inspire us onward in our own faith-race.

Scholars speculate about the identity of the author of Hebrews. Paul, Silas, Titus, Mark, Clement, Luke, Aquila, Priscilla and Barnabas are all candidates. Whoever the author was, the readers were knowledgeable Jews who had converted to faith in Jesus Christ. They were being taunted by Jews as apostates from God and renegades from Moses. They were accused of abandoning their law and forfeiting the Old Testament promises.

Today's readers likely will not have come to faith in Christ out of such a deeply embedded cultural and religious tradition. But every Christian at some time or other is tempted to ask, "What's the use?" As problems mount, as faith seems unproductive, we think about quitting our own faith-race.

We need reminders about the supremacy of Jesus Christ. There is no stronger enticement to stay in the race than to "fix your eyes on Jesus" (12:2). As the pioneer of our salvation, he brings us to glory (2:10).

James Reapsome

HEBREWS 1 *Starting the Race*

WHEN JOHN CHRYSOSTOM, bishop of Constantinople, was threatened by Emperor Arcadius, he responded, "I defy you, because you can do me no harm." Such conviction grows out of a firm grasp of who Jesus Christ really is. Hebrews 1 will get you started on the race with a look at the majesty, power and glory of Jesus Christ.

⚘ WARMING UP TO GOD

Focus on what you have experienced of the majesty, power and glory of Jesus Christ. Praise Jesus for who he is.

⚘ DISCOVERING THE WORD

1. *Read Hebrews 1.* How do verses 1-3 reveal the essential truth of Christ's supremacy and sufficiency?

2. Based on what we learn in verses 2-3, how would you answer the question "Who is Jesus Christ?"

3. To drive a point home, the author uses seven Old Testament citations. What characteristics or attributes of Jesus does the writer find in the Old Testament to prove his claim that Jesus is superior to angels (vv. 4-14)?

4. Who is the source of all these astounding statements (vv. 5-8, 10, 13)?

5. What do you learn about angels from these verses?

6. Based on what you have observed in verses 5-14, how would you expand your answer to the question "Who is Christ?"

⚘ APPLYING THE WORD

• What needs in your life do these qualities of Jesus address?

• What kind of life should you have because all this is true of Jesus?

⚘ RESPONDING IN PRAYER

Pray that your life will reflect your knowledge of Jesus.

HEBREWS 2 *Warning Signs*

"WARNING!" A black-and-white lettered sign on the Fox River in St. Charles, Illinois, alerts boaters to a dam ahead. Cigarette packs, cans of weed killer and fences around nuclear power plants all carry impressive warnings, designed to steer us from life-threatening perils. In Hebrews 2, the writer erects the first of six prominent warning signs in the letter. The first, in effect, alerts us to the danger of drifting off the course of our faith-race. It tells us to concentrate on staying in the race.

✍ WARMING UP TO GOD

List what would have to happen in your life before you would find your faith slipping away.

✍ DISCOVERING THE WORD

1. *Read Hebrews 2.* In verse 1 we read, "pay more careful attention," and in verse 3 we are told not to "ignore." What is it that we are to focus our lives on?

2. What logic does the writer use in verses 2-3 to further focus our attention on the peril of drifting away?

3. How does the writer strengthen the warning that God's salvation in Christ is well worth our most intense obedience (vv. 3-4)?

4. To prove that Jesus is too great and too valuable to neglect, the writer tells us more about him (vv. 5-9). What major facts does the writer cite here?

5. Why did Jesus have "to be made like [you and me] in every way" (vv. 16-18)?

✍ APPLYING THE WORD

• How does Jesus help you when you are tempted?

• What helps you to maintain a warm, life-changing relationship with Jesus?

• "Be sure your seatbelts are securely fastened," the aircraft's captain warns you because of approaching turbulence. How can you help other believers to be "securely fastened" into Jesus?

✍ RESPONDING IN PRAYER

Ask God to keep you securely fastened to Jesus.

HEBREWS 3 *Winning the Race*

COACHES TELL US that what distinguishes average from superior athletes is the will to win. Endowed with equal physical strengths, one reaches the heights of stardom while the other slips into obscurity. In this chapter, the writer describes two equally endowed Christian runners in the faith-race. One succeeded and the other failed. What made the difference? The will to win. One held firmly to Christ, but the other fell by the wayside because of a hard heart.

✎ WARMING UP TO GOD

What makes the difference between vibrant, growing Christians you know and those who appear to be dull and uninterested in the implications of their profession of faith?

✎ DISCOVERING THE WORD

1. *Read Hebrews 3.* What does the writer emphasize about Jesus in verses 1-6 that would encourage us to "fix [our] thoughts" on him (v. 1) and "hold on" to our courage and hope (v. 6)?

2. In verses 7-11 the writer hoists a second warning—against unbelief and disobedience. These verses describe the nation of Israel after they crossed the Red Sea. They refused to obey God's command to take the Promised Land because they were afraid of the military might they would face. So they were forced to wander forty years till that whole generation died off. How does the psalmist describe God's perspective on the Israelites?

3. In what ways might Christians "test and try" God (v. 9)? Why?

4. How did God judge the Israelites whom Moses led out of Egypt (vv. 15-19)?

5. Why did he judge them in this way?

✎ APPLYING THE WORD

- Review the facts about the hardhearted (vv. 8, 10, 12-13, 15-18). Which aspects of this lifestyle come closest to your experience?

- What are you doing to avoid the peril of "falling in the desert" (v. 17)?

✎ RESPONDING IN PRAYER

Pray for your own salvation.

HEBREWS 4:1-13 *Receiving God's Blessings*

AMERICAN BUSINESS tycoon Roger Babson once observed, "Opportunities are greater today than ever before in history. Young people have greater chances for health, happiness, and prosperity than had the children of any previous generation." The same is true for Christians in God's faith-race. It was true for God's people, Israel, yet they missed the opportunity to live in God's land of blessing and perished in a wilderness of unbelief and disobedience. This chapter tells Christians in the race that there is something to fear, but also something to strive for: experiencing God's promised rest now.

ᙙ WARMING UP TO GOD

Think about areas of your life where you need more rest.

ᙙ DISCOVERING THE WORD

1. *Read Hebrews 4:1-13.* What do you think "the promise of entering [God's] rest" means in verse 1?

2. The fate of the Israelites who perished in the desert serves as the basis of God's warning to those who have heard the gospel. Why did some who had the gospel preached to them not receive God's rest (v. 2)?

3. From what you have observed in Hebrews thus far, how would you describe the faith that is required to receive God's rest?

4. We are told to do our best to reach God's rest (3:11, 18; 4:1, 3, 5-6, 9-11). How do you picture such rest?

5. Verses 6-8 refer to the Israelites. How did they refuse to receive God's rest?

6. The "word of God" that judges our thoughts and attitudes (vv. 12-13) is the specific promise of God's rest. How can God's Word show you the condition of your heart?

ᙙ APPLYING THE WORD

- God rested from his work (v. 4), and he offers us a "Sabbath-rest" each week. What does it mean to you to rest from your work?

- What role does Scripture have in your life right now?

- How would you like to deepen or change that relationship?

ᙙ RESPONDING IN PRAYER

Praise God for the gifts in this passage—of Scripture and of rest.

HEBREWS 4:14—5:10 *Overcoming Weakness*

THE PULITZER prize-winning book *City of Joy* tells about the intense suffering of a Polish priest in a Calcutta slum. His superiors offered him comfortable lodging, but he chose to live just like the slum-dwellers. By his suffering he learned what it was like to be a slum-dweller. He could not have learned that any other way. Likewise the Hebrews needed to be reminded of their God-appointed, suffering high priest, Jesus Christ, so they would hold firmly to him.

⟨❧ WARMING UP TO GOD

Recall an experience that helped you to better understand another person.

⟨❧ DISCOVERING THE WORD

1. *Read Hebrews 4:14—5:10.* What commands are given in 4:14 and 16?

2. What is there about the character of Jesus that encourages us to obey these commands?

3. Jesus, as our merciful and faithful high priest, made atonement for our sins. The writer reminds the Hebrews of their earthly high priest in Judaism. What was the high priest like (5:1-4)?

4. How would you compare Jesus' high appointment with the life he lived (5:7-8)?

5. What was the result of Christ's suffering (5:8-10)?

⟨❧ APPLYING THE WORD

• When you are tempted, what difference does it make to know that Jesus was likewise tempted and therefore sympathizes with your weakness?

• How does Christ's suffering help you to take a positive attitude toward suffering?

⟨❧ RESPONDING IN PRAYER

Pray that your life would reflect your high appointment as the adopted son or daughter of God.

HEBREWS 5:11—6:20   *The Race to Maturity*

PETER SNELL, former Olympic gold medalist, said that the only way to win a race is to get in front and go flat out. Prior to that, he said, it takes a whole lot of hard training and self-discipline. The Hebrews were in desperate danger of quitting the race, so the writer urged them to go forward. This is a section with four strong appeals: "Let us . . . go on to maturity" (6:1). "Show . . . diligence" (6:11). "Do not . . . become lazy" (6:12). "Take hold of the hope" (6:18).

✎ WARMING UP TO GOD

When are you most tempted to drop out of the faith-race? Why?

✎ DISCOVERING THE WORD

1. *Read Hebrews 5:11—6:20.* How would you describe the failures of the Hebrews (5:11-14)?

2. In view of their resources and opportunities for growth, how do you account for their problems?

3. According to 6:6, why is it absolutely essential to develop Christian maturity?

4. What hope does the writer see for better things to come (6:9-10)? Why?

5. What essential part of God's nature encourages the Hebrews to be positive and hopeful about their future (6:13-18)?

✎ APPLYING THE WORD

- Two kinds of land production vividly portray the reason to go on to maturity (6:7-8). How does each characterize your life?

- As you reflect on your track record of both diligence and laziness (6:11-12), how can you improve?

- In 6:19-20 the writer returns to the Hebrews' familiar religion of priests and their temple with its holy place curtained off. In other words, it was a picture of a more profound spiritual reality in Christ. How does Jesus fulfill your deepest aspirations and help you to go on to maturity in your faith-race?

✎ RESPONDING IN PRAYER

Ask God to firmly anchor your soul with hope in Christ.

HEBREWS 7 *Eternal Companion*

IN THE OLD TESTAMENT, religion and priests go hand in hand. Hebrew Christians had departed from their old religion centered on priestly functions. Yet some hankered to return to their old ways. "Don't turn back," the writer appeals. "You have something far better in Christ." In chapters 7—10 the author tells of Christ's superior priestly origin, his better covenant and his sufficient-for-all-time sacrifice of himself. Regardless of whether we have left behind old traditions to find Christ, we all need confidence builders like chapter 7 so we will stick with Jesus no matter what.

✎ WARMING UP TO GOD

What relationships strengthen your knowledge of Christ and build you up? Thank God for those relationships.

✎ DISCOVERING THE WORD

1. *Read Hebrews 7.* "Think how great he [Melchizedek] was," commands the writer (v. 4). What about Melchizedek made him so great (vv. 1-3)?

2. One incident proved Melchizedek's superiority to the Hebrews: Their patriarch Abraham tithed (gave one-tenth of his income) to him (v. 4). According to verses 5-10, why does this prove that Jesus' high priesthood is superior to that of Levi (Aaron's son)?

3. Jesus inaugurated a new era because he was not of the priestly tribe (vv. 11-14). On what does his priestly authority rest (vv. 15-17)?

4. In what sense were the ancient rules "weak and useless" (vv. 18-19)?

5. God's oath set aside Jesus as a distinctive high priest (vv. 20-21). How does Jesus guarantee our faith-agreement (covenant) with him (vv. 22-25)?

6. What about Christ sets him above earthly priests (vv. 26-28)?

✎ APPLYING THE WORD

- Twice the writer tells us to come to God through Christ's high priesthood (vv. 19, 25). Why do you need to do this?

- How can you practice it in your faith-race?

✎ RESPONDING IN PRAYER

Praise God for giving you a high priest over all in Jesus Christ.

HEBREWS 8   *God's "New Deal"*

BACK IN 1932, President Franklin Roosevelt sought to rescue the country from the pit of the Great Depression by launching the New Deal. The concept caught the imagination of the people. The time was ripe for a radically new economic and social program. In this chapter, the writer of Hebrews announces God's "new deal"—a covenant, or agreement, between God and humanity. It offers far superior promises to those of the "old deal" (Old Testament laws and regulations).

✦ WARMING UP TO GOD

Write down what knowing you are God's child means to you.

✦ DISCOVERING THE WORD

1. *Read Hebrews 8.* "We do have such a high priest" (v. 1) refers to the description of Jesus in 7:23-28. What additional facts do you learn about him (vv. 1-2)?

2. What is Christ's heavenly ministry (vv. 3-6)?

3. Verse 6 looks back to prove Christ's superior ministry and ahead to prove that we have a superior covenant with God. The key is "better promises." What was the problem with the first covenant (vv. 7-12)?

4. What guarantees God's "new deal" (v. 12)? (See also vv. 1-3; 9:14.)

✦ APPLYING THE WORD

• Do you function better under external restraint (the law) or inner constraint (God's Spirit) (v. 10)? Why?

• What happens to you when you say to God, "Thank you for forgiving and forgetting my sin"?

• A magazine ad offers dishwashers with more power, more pizzazz and more performance. How could your understanding and application of God's new deal offer all of that to you in your walk with him?

✦ RESPONDING IN PRAYER

Ask God to forgive your sins, naming those you can think of specifically.

HEBREWS 9 *The Runner's Power*

IN VIEW OF the problems besetting us—drugs, divorce, depression, to name a few—it seems like a gross oversimplification to say the blood of Jesus is the solution. But, in a different context, the Hebrews faced similar problems of neglect, unbelief and immaturity. They were in danger of turning back to their old ways. Seemingly they lacked the power and purpose to press on in their faith-race. What was the solution given to them? The blood of Jesus. Only a full and perfect knowledge of what Jesus is and does can bring us to a full and perfect Christian life.

❧ WARMING UP TO GOD

Recall a time you wanted to drop out of the faith-race. What got you through?

❧ DISCOVERING THE WORD

1. *Read Hebrews 9.* Contrast what Jesus did (vv. 11-14) with the old system (vv. 1-10).

2. Why was the shedding of sacrificial blood required even under the old covenant (vv. 16-22)?

3. The writer explains why the offering of Jesus' blood is not only necessary, but also a superior sacrifice. Why is it important to direct our attention to "heavenly things" (v. 23)?

4. What difference would it make to those steeped in Old Testament religion to know that Jesus once-for-all offered his own blood rather than offering animal blood (vv. 25-26)?

❧ APPLYING THE WORD

• How can you deepen your understanding of and appreciation for Christ's self-sacrifice?

• Death and judgment are certain. In view of that, how would you encourage someone to face eternity with hope and peace, based on what you have learned in this chapter?

• Also certain is Jesus' second coming (v. 28). In light of his blood offering, how should you spend your time waiting for him?

❧ RESPONDING IN PRAYER

Pray that you will use your time to serve Jesus even as you wait for him.

HEBREWS 10 *Staying in the Race*

FACED WITH seemingly endless years of schoolwork and a multitude of rules to obey, children get discouraged. When that happens, parents say, "Look at your great opportunities. Take advantage of what you have now. Don't throw it away." The writer of Hebrews, in chapter 10, offers his readers encouragement with a picture of Jesus and calls us to warm up to God, hold our faith in him and stir up one another in Christian faith and practice.

ᗡ WARMING UP TO GOD

Recall an opportunity you missed because it sounded too good to be true. What did you miss by not believing the evidence?

ᗡ DISCOVERING THE WORD

1. *Read Hebrews 10.* The writer continues to discuss Jesus and the Old Testament offerings. How do verses 1-4 prove that the Old Testament system was a shadow, not the real thing?

2. Contrast Jesus' sacrifice (the reality) with the shadow (vv. 5-10). Why is his sacrifice better?

3. As you meditate on verses 11-18 and the awesome love and power of Jesus to take away your sins, what are the responses in your heart and mind?

4. In light of what God has done for us in Christ (vv. 19-21), what three commands does the writer feel compelled to issue (vv. 22-24)?

5. If we fail to draw near to God, hold fast our faith and stir up one another, what is likely to happen (vv. 25-26, 38-39)?

ᗡ APPLYING THE WORD

• How can you help hold someone you know "unswervingly" to faith?

• What purposes could be achieved in your life by both this strong encouragement and this stern warning?

ᗡ RESPONDING IN PRAYER

Pray for your church, that you would support and encourage one another.

HEBREWS 11 *Models of Faith*

PROBABLY NO SUBJECT is so glibly misunderstood as faith. Nearly everyone professes to have some of it. Many people would like to have more. The writer to the Hebrews takes faith out of religious theory and clothes it with flesh and blood. The author does this with what we today call role models. These models inspire us to go on believing in Jesus.

᪣ WARMING UP TO GOD

Complete this sentence: "Faith is . . ."

᪣ DISCOVERING THE WORD

1. *Read Hebrews 11.* Look for both assured confidence and calm expectation (v. 1) in the role models of faith in this chapter. How did Abel, Enoch and Noah express their faith (vv. 4-7)?

2. Considering the foolishness of his choices by human standards, what do you think Abraham's emotions were like (vv. 8-10)?

3. How does the promise of a heavenly country help us to keep our faith, even when we don't see our hopes fulfilled immediately (vv. 13-16)?

4. Why do you think Abraham's faith triumphed when he was asked to give up Isaac (vv. 17-19)?

5. How would you compare the faith of the named heroes and heroines who achieved greatness (vv. 20-34) with those unnamed persons who suffered grievously (vv. 35-38)?

6. Some Christians believe that faith always leads to material and physical blessing. What does this passage tell you about the role of both blessing and suffering?

᪣ APPLYING THE WORD

- In tough circumstances, what connection do you make between your faith and the certainty of resurrection (v. 35)?

- What unseen certainties have guided you in making fundamental, life-changing decisions?

᪣ RESPONDING IN PRAYER

Pray for the faith you need in your life right now to do God's will.

HEBREWS 12   *The Runner's Discipline*

WE OFTEN WONDER why thousands of marathoners seem to enjoy punishing themselves in grueling races. Certainly, for most, it's not the hope of
winning. What is it then? Explaining it to his readers, writer Art Carey said,
"The real joy of the Boston Marathon is just finishing, just winning the con-
test with yourself—doing what you have set out to do." That's the attitude
the Hebrews were supposed to have: Stay in the faith-race to the end.

✎ WARMING UP TO GOD

Who has been a model of perseverance and endurance for you? Thank God
for that person.

✎ DISCOVERING THE WORD

1. *Read Hebrews 12.* Of what value is it to keep your eyes on Jesus (vv. 2-3)?

2. What discipline of the Hebrews do you think the writer alludes to (vv. 3-
   4, 7; 11:35-38)?

3. How do the values of God's discipline cited here help us to respond positively to discipline (vv. 10-12)?

4. Identify the writer's specific instructions in verses 14-17. On what principles are they based?

5. How could you identify a "bitter root" or a "godless Esau" in your life (vv.
   15-16)?

6. We've all been tempted to drop out of the race. Why would the warning
   of verses 25-29 cause us to reconsider?

✎ APPLYING THE WORD

• What hindrances and entanglements get in the way of your Christian
  faith-race (v. 1)? Why?

• What encouragement do you find in verses 18-24 to run the faith-race
  with perseverance?

✎ RESPONDING IN PRAYER

Let your prayer be one of worship for the God who is a "consuming fire."

HEBREWS 13   *Running by the Rules*

BEN JOHNSON OF Canada was stripped of the Olympic gold medals he
won at Seoul in 1988 because he broke the rules about drug use. Similarly
the Christian's faith-race is much more than a sprint to the finish line. It's a
race that brings glory to God by the way the runners behave. In the concluding chapter, the writer to the Hebrews sketches a variety of duties to
God and humanity. Together they reveal an exalted level of personal morality and duty.

✎ WARMING UP TO GOD

Consider your attitude toward God's law. At what times do you find it a burden? When does it help you?

✎ DISCOVERING THE WORD

1. *Read Hebrews 13.* Verses 1-3 tie in with verse 16. In what sense should
   loving others, doing good, sharing, entertaining strangers and helping
   the prisoners and the mistreated be considered "sacrifices" to God?

2. Sexual purity is one of God's absolutes (v. 4). How do you account for
   sexual impurity among professing Christians—some of them well-
   known public figures?

3. What facts about God help to keep you from loving money (vv. 5-6)?

4. Obligations to spiritual leaders are laid out in verses 7 and 17-18. What
   is here that we should follow?

5. In what sense is our praise a sacrifice to God (v. 15)?

✎ APPLYING THE WORD

• Which of these exhortations do you need to apply to yourself?

• On the basis of your study of Hebrews, what do you think God would
  like to "work" in you that would please him?

✎ RESPONDING IN PRAYER

Verses 20-21 are a benediction, a summary prayer. Make it your prayer for
yourself.

Introducing James

W ho is this fellow James? There are several people in the New Testament called James, including two apostles. Though they have never been completely certain, most church scholars have believed that a third man, James the brother of Jesus (Mt 13:55; Mk 6:3), wrote this letter. While he probably joined the others in Jesus' family in rejecting Jesus during his earthly ministry, James certainly started following Jesus after his resurrection. In fact James soon became the head of the church in Jerusalem.

James knows nobody's perfect, so he doesn't tell us how to live trouble-free. He tells us how to live when troubles hit. James helps us use words, money and time more carefully, more positively. James is practical—maybe too practical! Expect these quiet times to be challenging—not because they will be hard to understand but because they will be all too easy to understand.

James addresses his letter to "the twelve tribes scattered among the nations" (1:1) "Twelve tribes" could refer to Jewish Christians who through exile, enslavement and trade were spread throughout the entire Mediterranean basin. More likely it refers simply to Christians, because the New Testament compares the church to Israel (Gal 6:16 RSV; 1 Pet 2:9-10). In any case, the letter is not addressed to one specific congregation, as Paul's letters were. James calls each of us to a consistent Christian life, a practical faith—a faith that works.

Andrew T. and Phyllis J. Le Peau

JAMES 1:1-18 *Dependable or Double-Minded?*

NO PAIN, no gain. Or so the saying goes. Athletes remind themselves of this to get their best possible performance. Sometimes they have to go through grueling training. Without it there is no improvement. James suggests it is the same for Christians.

✍ WARMING UP TO GOD

Enduring pain is not pleasant. What fears do you have as you think about what it means to face trials? Be honest with yourself. Describe your fears to God. Allow him to comfort you.

✍ DISCOVERING THE WORD

1. *Read James 1:1-18.* How are perseverance and maturity developed in us by enduring trials (vv. 3-4)?

2. Under pressure, how does the faithful Christian (described in vv. 5-6) contrast with the person described in verses 6-8?

3. In the context of trials and perseverance, why does James contrast rich and poor Christians (vv. 9-11)?

4. How are temptations different from trials (vv. 2-16)?

5. How is God the ultimate example of goodness and dependability (vv. 16-18)?

✍ APPLYING THE WORD

• What difficult experiences have increased your perseverance and maturity?

• In what ways do you tend to rely on your possessions?

• Think of trials or temptations you are currently facing. How can this passage encourage you to depend on God?

✍ RESPONDING IN PRAYER

Take time now to talk to God about your needs. Ask him to help you be like him in his goodness and dependability.

JAMES 1:19-27   *Words, Words, Words*

WE ALL DO IT. It's as common as flies around a horse. While someone else is talking, we're thinking about what we're going to say next instead of about what is being said to us. We know others are worth more care and attention. But the habit is hard to break.

God wants us to slow down and listen to him too. But even when we've really listened to him, we're still not done. This study gives us practical help on listening and more.

☙ WARMING UP TO GOD

There's so much to listen to all around us. What different voices and messages are on your mind? Tell God about them and ask him to help you clear your mind and focus on his Word.

☙ DISCOVERING THE WORD

1. *Read James 1:19-27.* How can being quick to listen and slow to speak help us to be slow to become angry (v. 19)?

2. James tells us that God's Word was planted in us. What weeds can choke that Word and keep it from growing (v. 21)? Explain.

3. In your own words explain how the person who merely listens to God's Word is different from the one who puts it into practice (vv. 22-25).

4. According to verses 26-27, how do people who think they are religious differ from those who are truly religious?

5. Based on what you've read in this chapter, do you think James would be satisfied with good works apart from our listening to and receiving God's Word? Explain.

☙ APPLYING THE WORD

- When is it hard for you to listen to God?

- Sometimes we do listen to God's Word, but we still don't follow it. How is this true for you?

- How would you like your religion to be more "pure and faultless" (v. 27)?

☙ RESPONDING IN PRAYER

Ask God to help you become a better listener and doer of his Word.

JAMES 2:1-13

Who's the Judge?

LABELS AREN'T JUST found on soup cans. We put them on people all the time. Funny or dull. Smart or thickheaded. Friendly or cold. There are all kinds of ways we can categorize people. And our categories can have a profound influence on the way we treat people. As you might suspect, James has a few words to say about favoritism.

⟨⟩ WARMING UP TO GOD

Reflect on judgmental words and thoughts you have had this week. Confess them to God. Allow yourself to experience his mercy.

⟨⟩ DISCOVERING THE WORD

1. *Read James 2:1-13.* How would you react if someone came into your church who wore sloppy clothes, was dirty or had body odor (vv. 2-4)?

2. Why is it wrong to give preferential treatment to those who have money (vv. 5-7)?

3. Verse 5 says God has chosen the poor to be rich in faith. Is God guilty of showing favoritism in this way? Explain.

4. How can "the royal law" (v. 8) guide our treatment of both poor and rich?

5. In what sense is violating one law as serious as breaking every law (vv. 9-11)?

⟨⟩ APPLYING THE WORD

- Toward what people or groups do you show favoritism?
- How can you change your attitude and actions?

⟨⟩ RESPONDING IN PRAYER

Ask God to work in your heart and mind to help you see beneath the surface as you relate to people.

JAMES 2:14-26 *Just Works*

"IT IS EASIER said than done" is a cliché that certainly applies to our Christian life. It is much easier to talk about God than to obey him. James said that even the demons believe there is one God. But that certainly does not make them Christians! That's why someone can have all his or her doctrine perfectly straight and still miss out on God's will. James helps us to stay on target.

❧ WARMING UP TO GOD

What has God been asking you to do that you have been ignoring? Talk to him about it.

❧ DISCOVERING THE WORD

1. *Read James 2:14-26.* According to James, what good is faith without deeds (vv. 14-17)? Explain why he says this.

2. How does James answer the objection "You have faith; I have deeds" (vv. 18-19)?

3. James gives two Old Testament examples of faith in action. The first is the familiar story of God testing Abraham by asking him to sacrifice his son Isaac. Abraham obeyed but was stopped by an angel at the last minute. How was Abraham's faith made complete by what he did (vv. 21-24)?

4. The second Old Testament example is Rahab, the prostitute who hid two Israelite spies sent to Jericho before Israel's attack. How did Rahab's belief affect her (v. 25)?

5. How does James's closing analogy (v. 26) summarize his teaching on faith and actions?

❧ APPLYING THE WORD

- How do your actions demonstrate the reality of your faith?

- In what ways can you bring your actions more in line with your beliefs?

❧ RESPONDING IN PRAYER

Ask God to help you follow through with the works that will reveal your true faith.

JAMES 3:1-12 *Preventing Forest Fires*

ONE OF THE most distressing crises is a fire out of control. The pain of seeing the destruction can be almost unbearable. Personal belongings going up in smoke. The beauty of nature destroyed. Even loss of life itself. In this passage James compares the destructive power of the tongue to that of a forest fire.

✥ WARMING UP TO GOD

How have you been hurt by someone's destructive words recently? Give your pain to God. Let him comfort you.

✥ DISCOVERING THE WORD

1. *Read James 3:1-12.* James compares the tongue (the words we speak) to a bit and a rudder (vv. 3-4). Why do you think the tongue has such control over our lives?

2. James also compares the tongue to a fire and to "a world of evil" (vv. 5-6). What is the point of these two comparisons?

3. Verses 7-8 emphasize what a challenge it is to control the tongue. What makes this so difficult?

4. In what ways can the tongue poison people and relationships?

5. In verses 9-12 James uses a series of analogies from nature (springs, trees, vines). How do they highlight the inconsistencies of the tongue?

✥ APPLYING THE WORD

• What damage has your tongue done recently?

• What in this text gives you added strength and motivation to be more careful with your words?

• What can you do to give God more praise? Be specific.

• How can you give more affirmation to those you come in contact with each day?

✥ RESPONDING IN PRAYER

Ask God to help you to be self-controlled about how you speak to others.

JAMES 3:13—4:10   *Keeping the Peace*

WHY DO PEOPLE who love each other the most often fight the most too? Husbands and wives, parents and children, brothers and sisters—it's all too common. James offers a valuable remedy for this sickness.

☙ WARMING UP TO GOD

How have you gotten caught up in fighting recently? If that conflict continues to be a concern to you, talk to God about it. Ask God to clear your mind of anger and distrust so you can focus on his healing Word.

☙ DISCOVERING THE WORD

1. *Read James 3:13—4:10.* In 3:13-18 James discusses earthly and heavenly wisdom. What are the characteristics of each?

2. What does James say is the source of quarrels (4:1-2)?

3. What does James say is necessary to come to God in prayer? (vv. 3-10)?

4. What does it mean to be humble, to submit to God (vv. 6-7)?

5. In verses 7-10 James gives several suggestions for humbling ourselves before God. How does each contribute to a humble spirit?

☙ APPLYING THE WORD

• As you look at 4:3, what might be examples of right and wrong motives in your prayer?

• In what area are you an enemy of God (see 4:4 and consider your attitude toward material possessions, friends, study or work, and leisure time)? How can you restore your relationship to him?

• In what situations could humility help you become a source of peace? Explain.

☙ RESPONDING IN PRAYER

Take a few minutes to quietly humble yourself before God. Ask him to help you become a peacemaker.

JAMES 4:11-17   *Getting Perspective*

"I AM THE master of my fate. I am the captain of my soul." How subtly we convince ourselves that we control our lives. Sometimes only a crisis or even death itself convinces us otherwise. If we are truly wise and humble, we will listen carefully when James says, "You are a mist that appears for a little while and then vanishes" (v. 14).

✎ WARMING UP TO GOD

How have you been trying to control your life? Confess it to God and experience the freedom of giving him control.

✎ DISCOVERING THE WORD

1. *Read James 4:11-17.* Why does James say we shouldn't slander or speak against a Christian brother or sister (vv. 11-12)?

2. If we judge the law, what does this say about our attitude toward the law-giver (v. 11)?

3. How can a proper attitude toward God (v. 12) enable us to have a proper attitude toward others?

4. How would you describe the two attitudes toward the future found in verses 13-17?

5. If our life is like a mist, what should be our attitude toward tomorrow?

✎ APPLYING THE WORD

• If you knew you were going to die tomorrow, how would your attitude toward life today be different?

• What future plans do you often dwell on?

• In what area of your life do you need to turn your plans over to God's will?

✎ RESPONDING IN PRAYER

Ask God to help you love those around you rather than judge them. Humbly commit your future plans to the Lord.

JAMES 5:1-11   *What Awaits*

YOU HAVE PROBABLY heard of the young man who cried out, "Lord, I want patience and I want it now!" James encourages us in this passage to wait on God, to be patient, and he warns us against wanting it all now.

✎ WARMING UP TO GOD

God wants to know your concerns and frustrations. Tell God what has been making you impatient lately.

✎ DISCOVERING THE WORD

1. *Read James 5:1-11.* James declares that misery awaits rich people. What crimes have they committed (vv. 1-6)?
2. Is James condemning all rich people? Explain.
3. James goes on to give three examples of patient people: a farmer, the prophets and Job. How is each an example of patience (vv. 7-11)?
4. What different reactions would you expect the rich and those who suffer to have to the prospect of the Lord's return (vv. 7-9)?
5. How is piling up riches the opposite of patience that waits in faith for God to provide?

✎ APPLYING THE WORD

• When are you tempted to hoard rather than to give and to wait on God?
• In what areas of your life are you impatient?
• What do you learn about patience from the examples James mentions?

✎ RESPONDING IN PRAYER

Pray that God would make you a person who can wait for God to answer prayer.

JAMES 5:12-20 *Making Others Whole*

BROKEN HOMES, shattered relationships, damaged emotions—we live in a fragmented and hurting world. As we see all the wounded people around us, we long to help, to offer a healing touch. James gives us very practical suggestions for helping people become whole.

❧ WARMING UP TO GOD

God wants you to be whole. In what area are you struggling with emotional pain? Tell God how you want him to help you.

❧ DISCOVERING THE WORD

1. *Read James 5:12-20.* What different types of prayer are mentioned in verses 13-18?

2. In verses 14-16 James discusses physical and spiritual healing. What are the steps in this process?

3. How is physical healing connected with the forgiveness of sins?

4. How does the Old Testament prophet Elijah illustrate the effectiveness of prayer (vv. 17-18)?

5. According to verses 19-20, how, if at all, are we our brother's keeper?

❧ APPLYING THE WORD

- Do you pray more when you are in trouble or when things are going well? Explain.

- How could you make one of the types of prayer James describes more a part of your life?

- How can you help others become whole physically, emotionally or spiritually?

❧ RESPONDING IN PRAYER

Ask God for grace as you minister to others.

INTRODUCING 1 PETER

It was a shaky time for Christians in the Roman Empire. In A.D. 68 Emperor Nero saw himself surrounded by political enemies and committed suicide. Three emperors in rapid succession took his place but couldn't hold the job. So in A.D. 69 troops proclaimed the military leader Vespasian as emperor—and saw that he stayed there.

Vespasian hated Jews, and he counted Christians among them. His oldest son, Titus, put Jerusalem under siege for three months. Troops leveled buildings to the ground. The temple became a crumble of stones. Jerusalem fell. Jews (and Christians) became Roman captives.

Aftershocks vibrated throughout the Roman Empire, blending with the general persecution against "atheists" (people who refused to worship Roman gods) that Nero had begun. Christians were driven from their homes, deported to the outer borders of the empire and forbidden to worship openly. It was a dark season for Christians. How were they to endure?

Through God's inspiration, Peter sensed this coming darkness. Many scholars date Peter's first letter to about A.D. 64, written probably from the city of Rome—referred to as Babylon in 1 Peter 5:13. Yet this is not a bleak letter. It is full of hope and practical counsel on how to endure. It tells us to balance holy living with correct doctrine, to nurture spiritual growth, to work within existing authority structures and to take care of each other.

This letter, sent with prophetic love to first-century Christians, still lives today. It provides a compass for our own dark road.

Carolyn Nystrom

1 PETER 1:1-12   *Strangers in the World*

CHRISTIANS IN South Korea have a right to feel nervous. South Korean newspaper clippings hint of takeover by the North. Will they still have a church five years from now? Will they still have Bibles? Will they have to shutter their windows and lower their voices when they pray with their children? How can a believer prepare for that kind of suffering? And what is it, anyway, that makes Christians strangers to the rest of the world?

☞ WARMING UP TO GOD

If you knew you were about to enter a difficult set of circumstances that would test your faith, how would you prepare yourself?

☞ DISCOVERING THE WORD

1. *Read 1 Peter 1:1-12.* Study Peter's description of the people who were about to receive his letter (vv. 1-2). How does his description of them help explain why they were "strangers in the world"?

2. Peter says in verse 6, "Now for a little while you may have to suffer grief in all kinds of trials." If you were to hear that kind of message, what information in this paragraph might help you through the suffering (vv. 3-9)?

3. What did Peter believe to be true of genuine faith (vv. 7-9)?

4. By what different routes did news of salvation come to the readers of Peter's letter (vv. 10-12)?

☞ APPLYING THE WORD

• How does the future, as Peter describes it here, offer you hope in your own setting?

• When have you seen Jesus (through a person or event) in a way that increased your faith?

• Peter refers to new birth, or salvation, throughout this passage as a central difference between Christians and the world. What tensions have you experienced because of this difference?

☞ RESPONDING IN PRAYER

Praise God for his gift of salvation that can help us cope with tensions with the world.

1 PETER 1:13-25   *Called to Be Different*

ITS POSSIBLE THAT some of our attempts to be separate and holy do more to close people out of our beliefs than to invite them in. Yet God does call his people to be different; different from what they would be if they did not believe in Jesus and different from the unbelievers around them.

☞ WARMING UP TO GOD

Think of a Christian you admire. In what ways does that person resemble Christ? Praise God for what you learn about him through others.

☞ DISCOVERING THE WORD

1. *Read 1 Peter 1:13-25.* Peter lists several ways that followers of Jesus ought to respond to his gift of salvation. Define each of these responses more fully (vv. 13-16).

2. Select one of these responses. If you were to put that response on the "front burner" of your priorities, what changes would you have to make in your life?

3. What events from the past would help the recipients of Peter's letter to appreciate God's concern for them (vv. 18-21)?

4. How could the conditions that Peter describes in verses 21-25 promote sincere love among Christians?

5. Peter links the Word of God with salvation and new birth. (Compare verses 10, 12, 23, 25.) What do you think Peter meant when he said that this Word is "enduring" and "stands forever" (vv. 23, 25)?

☞ APPLYING THE WORD

- How might an honest attempt to "be holy" improve your relationships with people close to you?

- In what situations might it make you, as verse 17 says, more like a stranger?

- Jot a quick list of all you have to do today (or tomorrow). How could you begin to tackle this list with the goal "Be holy in all you do"?

☞ RESPONDING IN PRAYER

Pray specifically from your list that you would be holy and would improve relationships with those around you.

1 PETER 2:1-12   *Do I Want to Grow Up?*

"I DON'T WANT to go to school and learn solemn things," Peter implored in James M. Barrie's *Peter Pan.* He resisted the offer of a home and a normal childhood extended to him by Wendy's mother. "Keep back, lady, no one is going to catch me and make me a man."

☙ WARMING UP TO GOD

In what ways are you tempted to follow Peter Pan's approach to life?

☙ DISCOVERING THE WORD

1. *Read 1 Peter 2:1-12.* Peter speaks here of two aspects of Christian growth: individual and corporate. How might the five sins of verse 1 damage relationships with other believers?

2. What does the metaphor in verses 2-3 contribute to your understanding of how to nurture spiritual growth?

3. How does belief or unbelief influence the way a person understands Jesus, the "living Stone" (vv. 4-8)?

4. What reasons do the people here have to praise God (vv. 9-10)?

5. Verse 11 repeats a now familiar theme in 1 Peter: Christians are "aliens and strangers in the world." How might living up to the description of verse 9 cause a Christian to be alienated from the world?

☙ APPLYING THE WORD

- The *New Bible Commentary* interprets verse 12, "the day [God] visits us," as "the day God will visit the earth and search out man's hearts in judgment." If this were to occur in your lifetime, what evidence would you want God to find of your own spiritual growth?

- How could today's passage help you to overcome a tendency to become a spiritual Peter Pan?

☙ RESPONDING IN PRAYER

Ask God to rid you of "all malice and all deceit, hypocrisy, envy, and slander of every kind" (v. 1).

1 PETER 2:13—3:7 *In His Steps*

IN THE LATE 1800s a young social worker, disguised as an unemployed printer, begged for food, work, hope. He was a believer in Jesus and knew the giving, caring moral code that Jesus lived and taught. He assumed that fellow Christians would be among the first to help. He was wrong. He found that a tramp's life was tough—and that Christians didn't make it any easier.

Charles Sheldon went home to write a book about his experience—a novel that introduced a dying tramp to the Reverend Henry Maxwell and his congregation. In it, a body of believers begins to see the submissive suffering of Jesus and what it means to walk *In His Steps*.

⚘ WARMING UP TO GOD

If you were to rate your submissiveness on a scale of one to ten, where would you place yourself and why?

⚘ DISCOVERING THE WORD

1. *Read 1 Peter 2:13—3:7.* According to Peter, why should Christians treat their governing leaders with respect (2:13-15)?
2. How could the teachings of 2:16-17 keep you from becoming a "muddy doormat" to your government?
3. How might being a Christian bring some meaning to the suffering that comes from being a slave (2:18-21)?
4. Jesus "entrusted himself to him who judges justly" (2:23). How might a similar trust in God help you submit to suffering in your own life?

⚘ APPLYING THE WORD

- Acting responsibly for healthy change or submitting to authority is a constant tension for the Christian who wants to obey this passage. How can you draw together both ends of this tension? (In what situations would you take action? At what point would you submit?)
- How do you balance the tension of submission versus responsible action in your job? In your marriage? In other relationships?

⚘ RESPONDING IN PRAYER

Pray for courage to walk "in his steps" even in the face of suffering.

1 PETER 3:8-22   *If I'm Living Right, Why Do I Hurt?*

WE OFTEN ASSUME a direct connection between "right living" and "easy living." It's an added pat on the back when life runs smoothly. But it is an unspoken accusation when trauma strikes. Peter contemplated this connection—even added a link or two to the chain. Sure, there are ways to live that will decrease our chances for unjust conflict, but Peter made no promises of easy living. Sometimes suffering comes—whether or not we earn it. It came to Jesus.

ᓂ᠊ WARMING UP TO GOD

Recall a time when suffering was hard to understand.

ᓂ᠊ DISCOVERING THE WORD

1. *Read 1 Peter 3:8-22.* Find as many phrases as you can that describe what a Christian ought to be and do in verses 8-12.

2. What do you find difficult about the way of life described in verses 8-12?

3. Peter knew that Christians may encounter hardship in spite of godly living. What counsel does Peter offer for coping with suffering (vv. 13-17)?

4. Why might unbelievers be willing to listen to reasons for hope from a person who is living the way Peter describes (vv. 15-17)?

5. Verse 18 is a capsule description of Christ's work and purpose. What all can you know from this verse about why Jesus came and what he accomplished?

ᓂ᠊ APPLYING THE WORD

- How could setting apart Christ as Lord, as verse 15 commands, help you endure suffering?

- Our world is often unjust. Bring to mind some of your past or current sufferings. In the context of these sufferings, how can the picture of Christ portrayed by this passage bring you hope?

ᓂ᠊ RESPONDING IN PRAYER

Thank God for the hope we have been given in Christ.

1 PETER 4 *The Christian Path of Nails*

SHUSAKO ENDO, the Japanese novelist, tells the story of two missionary priests in *Silence*. The priests came from Portugal in the mid-1600s. At that time the Christian faith in Japan had some 300,000 followers, but persecution had struck. A fragmented government united under a single cause: erasing foreign religion. Christians suffered horrible deaths.

Endo's book asks, Why did God sit through it in silence? This question is just as relevant for us today as we continue to suffer because of our beliefs.

✑ WARMING UP TO GOD

When you learn of Christians suffering because of their faith, what questions come to your mind? Voice your questions to God.

✑ DISCOVERING THE WORD

1. *Read 1 Peter 4.* According to this passage, how are Christians different from pagans (vv. 1-6)?

2. Our doubts may sometimes taunt us, "God does not protect you. When your time comes, you die like the rest." How might the information in verses 4-6 help us to deal with those doubts?

3. What specific instructions does Peter give suffering Christians who are aware that the end of all things is coming (vv. 7-11)?

4. Of what spiritual and practical value are these instructions?

5. Verse 11 speaks of two forms of leadership: those who speak (teach) and those who serve. How would the purpose of church leadership as described here prevent a misuse of power between Christians?

6. According to verses 12-19, what are some right and wrong ways for a Christian to suffer?

✑ APPLYING THE WORD

• Think back to the questions you posed above, under "Warming Up to God." How do Peter's teachings help you deal with these questions?

• How might verse 19 become both a comfort and a challenge to you when you suffer because of your faith?

✑ RESPONDING IN PRAYER

Pray for Christians around the world who suffer for their beliefs.

1 PETER 5 *TLC for Trying Times*

RELATIONSHIPS BRING color to life. Sure, the mountaintop hermit has a spectacular view outside the window. But the colors inside the cabin are browns and grays. It is people who bring sparkle and fire to existence. When Peter concluded his first letter, a work frequently pointing to suffering, he did not tell his readers to escape to the isolation of a spiritual or literal mountaintop. Instead he pointed to their relationships and said, "Here's how to take care of each other."

↷ WARMING UP TO GOD

What has been one of your most valuable relationships, and what made it valuable?

↷ DISCOVERING THE WORD

1. *Read 1 Peter 5.* Peter speaks, in verse 1, to his fellow elders. In what ways did Peter see himself as like the elders he was writing to (vv. 1-4)?

2. When have you appreciated a person who acted toward you as a spiritual elder?

3. With what different beings or groups do these verses describe a Christian's relationships (vv. 5-11)?

4. What reasons did Peter give for following each of the commands in verses 5-9?

5. Peter points out three sets of relationships for all Christians: relationships with other believers, relationship with Satan, relationship with God. How would you summarize Peter's ideal for each of these?

↷ APPLYING THE WORD

• God's Word speaks to us in a variety of ways. What joy, comfort or warning do Peter's instructions in verses 5-11 point to in your own experience?

• How could Peter's teachings about relationships in this chapter help you to stand fast in your own faith?

↷ RESPONDING IN PRAYER

Ask God to comfort you, and wait before him to experience his care.

INTRODUCING 2 PETER

Peter's second letter refers appreciatively to Paul's letters (3:15-16), but bears no hint that Paul is dead. On the other hand, Peter seems to anticipate his own death soon (1:13-14). Scholars therefore date this letter in the same decade (A.D. 60s)—but closer to the end.

This letter does not tell us how to escape suffering, but instead to expect it. It shows us that throughout suffering we can enjoy our fellowship with other believers and look forward to a new heaven and a new earth, a "home of righteousness," with an end to pain.

Carolyn Nystrom

2 PETER 1:1-11 — *The Long Way Home*

HOW DOES A person get to heaven? Is it by proper knowledge of Christian doctrines? Or by godly living? Is it by faith in Christ's gift of salvation? Or by working according to Christ's goals and principles? Is it by God's call to us to be his own? Or by our own endurance with God until the day we die? Weighty issues. And with them, Peter opens his second letter.

✎ WARMING UP TO GOD

Reflect on your life. What qualities of godliness is God developing within you?

✎ DISCOVERING THE WORD

1. *Read 2 Peter 1:1-11.* In verses 1-2 we are promised gifts of faith, grace and peace through Christ's righteousness and the knowledge of God. How does your spiritual well-being depend on Christ's righteousness and your knowledge of God?

2. Think of the balance between knowledge of Jesus and holy living you have seen in Christians (v. 3). What happens if one area or the other is weak?

3. Peter writes in verse 4 that because of God's promises, Christians "may participate in the divine nature and escape the corruption in the world." How does he expect believers to nurture their own holy living (vv. 5-7)?

4. How are godly living and knowledge of Jesus related (vv. 8-9)?

5. What do you think it means to be called and elected by God (vv. 10-11)?

✎ APPLYING THE WORD

- Select one of the Christian qualities mentioned in verses 5-7. If you were to practice this quality more faithfully, how would it help you escape the pollution of evil influences around you?

- Verse 3 says the divine power of Jesus has given us all we need for godliness now and for eternal life. If you were to draw more fully on this power, what changes would you hope to see in yourself?

✎ RESPONDING IN PRAYER

Pray for the inner changes you think God is calling for within you.

2 PETER 1:12-21

If I Should Die . . .

IN 1976 JOE BAYLEY lay on a gurney outside an operating room at the Mayo Clinic's Methodist Hospital. He was scheduled for a minor operation. He'd probably be shuffling through the hospital hallway in a couple of days. But what if he just didn't wake up?

Joe's musings on that possibility left readers with a small, thought-provoking book titled, appropriately, *Heaven.* In it he speaks of his faith in Jesus Christ and his hope here—and hereafter. It has influenced children and adults, believers and nonbelievers to follow Christ.

Ten years later, Joe again lay on a gurney outside the operating room. The operation was a little more serious this time—his heart. But in 1986, when Joe woke up, it was hereafter.

⌘ WARMING UP TO GOD

As you think back over why you believe what you believe, who or what were the major influences in your life? Praise God for the privilege of knowing him.

⌘ DISCOVERING THE WORD

1. *Read 2 Peter 1:12-21.* What phrases here create a picture of Peter's view of death (vv. 13-15)?

2. Based on these phrases, how would you describe Peter's attitude about death?

3. What difference would it make to those who knew Peter that his teachings about Jesus came from an "eyewitness of his majesty" (v. 16)?

4. What do verses 19-21 show about the origin and purpose of Scripture?

⌘ APPLYING THE WORD

- What do you hope will be your own feelings when you approach death?

- What could you be doing during your lifetime to build toward a "good death"?

- Peter did not want his readers to be so dependent on him that their faith would fall apart after his death. Who would you like to influence with your faith in your lifetime, and how can you best go about it?

⌘ RESPONDING IN PRAYER

Thank God for the gift of Scripture and the ways in which it increases our faith.

2 PETER 2

Follow Which Leader?

"I HUGGED HER, and it was like hugging a statue. I looked into her eyes, and I felt that the lights were on, but no one was home. She had been my best friend in a Christian college! What happened?" For months this woman puzzled over this strange reunion with her college housemate. Later the puzzle pieces fell into place. A cult. "Someone got to her," she said later. "That person had to be very persuasive, and very tricky. My friend knew the Bible, and she wasn't dumb. I wish I knew what happened."

❧ WARMING UP TO GOD

Jesus Christ is always faithful to his promises. Reflect on that fact and allow praise to well up within you in response.

❧ DISCOVERING THE WORD

1. *Read 2 Peter 2.* Why are false teachers dangerous (2:1-3; also 1:20-21)?

2. Study verses 4-9. What did Peter want his readers to learn from these Old Testament events?

3. What characteristics should alert us that we are encountering a false teacher (vv. 10-19)?

4. Why might some people be attracted to teachers with these characteristics?

5. Why might it be better if a false teacher had never known the truth (vv. 20-22)?

❧ APPLYING THE WORD

• How can you protect yourself from the influence of false teachers?

• What cautions can you institute to keep from becoming a false teacher yourself?

❧ RESPONDING IN PRAYER

Pray for those who are victims of false teachers.

2 PETER 3   *The Fire Next Time*

WHEN I WAS a teen and young adult, when someone mentioned the end of the world, I shuddered and hoped, "Not yet." I wanted to graduate, fall in love, get married, raise children, work at a career—not necessarily in that order. At the very least I wanted to see how the weekend's date turned out. My sunsets looked like sunrise. And God's promised end of the world seemed a cruel interruption.

But at this writing, my twenty-two-year-old daughter and her unborn child lie cold in a country cemetery, a teenage son struggles with severe depression in a nearby psychiatric ward, my husband's colleague of over twenty years just revealed a secret life that includes distributing drugs to teens. My sunrises long for sunset. And the end of the world promises welcome relief.

✧ WARMING UP TO GOD

When are you likely to wish the world would end? Explain.

✧ DISCOVERING THE WORD

1. *Read 2 Peter 3.* What reasons did Peter give his readers to pay attention to this writing? (Look especially at verses 1-3, 15-18.)

2. What mistakes will the last-day scoffers make (vv. 4-7)?

3. What reasons does Peter offer for a delay in Christ's return (vv. 8-9, 15)?

4. Compare and contrast the use of fire and water in this passage. What is the significance of each?

5. Notice the question of verse 11, "What kind of people ought you to be?" What answers can you find through the remainder of the chapter?

✧ APPLYING THE WORD

- If the day of the Lord were to come in your lifetime, what would you like to accomplish beforehand?

- In what condition would you like God to find your work?

- How would you like God to find your relationships?

✧ RESPONDING IN PRAYER

Pray that you will be always ready for Christ's return.

INTRODUCING 1 JOHN

How can we tell the difference between genuine Christians and those who merely profess to know Christ? John's letters were written for that very purpose. John writes to expose those whose conduct contradicts their claims. He also provides strong assurance to those whose lifestyle is consistent with their Christian faith.

First John was written between A.D. 85 and 95 by the apostle John. Evidently the letter was circulated among a number of churches in Asia that were threatened by false teachers embracing an early form of heresy known as Gnosticism. They taught that matter was entirely evil and spirit was entirely good. This teaching resulted in two fundamental errors:

1. Because God could not be contaminated by a human body, God did not become a man in Jesus Christ.

2. "What might be sin for people at a less mature stage of inner development," as F. F. Bruce summarizes in his *Epistles of John*, "was no longer sin for the completely 'spiritual' man."

John provides a series of tests for distinguishing genuine Christians from those who falsely claim to know Christ. In response to the "new" theology, he provides us with a doctrinal test: What does the person believe about Christ? In response to the "new" morality, he provides us with a moral test: How does the person respond to the commandments of Christ? Finally, he provides us with a social test: Does the person love other Christians?

Ron Blankley

1 JOHN 1 *Fellowship and Forgiveness*

CHRISTIANS EVERYWHERE seem to be interested in fellowship. They gather in fellowship halls, attend fellowship dinners and participate in well-organized activities with fellow believers. But what really constitutes biblical fellowship? Perhaps more than any other passage of Scripture, these opening verses of 1 John establish the basis of true fellowship that is to be enjoyed and experienced by all Christians. More important, they enable us to understand how we can know we have fellowship with God.

✑ WARMING UP TO GOD

What comes to mind when you think of Christian fellowship?

✑ DISCOVERING THE WORD

1. *Read 1 John 1.* John begins this chapter by announcing an apostolic message. What is the content of that message (vv. 1-2)?

2. What are John's reasons for announcing his message (vv. 3-4)?

3. John provides a test by which we can know if we have fellowship with God (vv. 5-10). Describe it in your own words.

4. The first part of John's test concerns the way we live or "walk" (vv. 6-7). What is the relationship between our conduct and our claim to have fellowship with God?

5. The second part of John's test concerns our attitude toward sin (vv. 8-10). What does our denial or confession of sin reveal about the reality of our relationship with God?

6. Based on your study of this passage, what does it mean to have fellowship with God—and each other?

✑ APPLYING THE WORD

• Does John's test strengthen or weaken your assurance of fellowship with God? Explain.

• How can we enjoy a greater fellowship with those who know the Father and the Son?

✑ RESPONDING IN PRAYER

Pray that the fellowship in your church would be deepened and enriched.

1 JOHN 2:1-11 *Talking and Walking the Truth*

FROM THE VERY beginning of Jesus' ministry, he emphasized that it is not what we profess but what we possess that counts for eternity. In his first major message he declared, "By their fruit you will recognize them." He then went on to teach, "Not everyone who says to me, 'Lord, Lord,' will enter the kingdom of heaven, but only he who does the will of my Father who is in heaven" (Mt 7:20-21). In the same way, John emphasizes that our claim to know Jesus must be backed by our conduct. This is necessary if we are to be certain about the reality of our faith.

✎ WARMING UP TO GOD

When have you been impacted by someone saying one thing and doing another?

✎ DISCOVERING THE WORD

1. *Read 1 John 2:1-11.* According to John, how can we tell whether we truly know Christ or merely claim to know him (vv. 3-6)?

2. Practically speaking, what does it mean to "walk as Jesus did" (v. 6)?

3. In verses 7-11, John focuses on one of the commands. How can this command be both old and new (vv. 7-8)?

4. Why would love for our brother and sister rather than love for God serve as a test of being in the light (vv. 9-11)?

5. In view of the overall context of this passage, what does it mean to live in the light (v. 10)? To live in Christ (v. 6)?

✎ APPLYING THE WORD

• Although John does not want us to sin, he knows that we sometimes do (vv. 1-2). How does the realization that Jesus speaks "in our defense" provide comfort and assurance when you sin?

• How does this passage encourage you to obey Christ and love other members of his body?

✎ RESPONDING IN PRAYER

Ask that your life would reflect the integrity of Christ.

1 JOHN 2:12-17   *Encouragement and Warning*

PILGRIM'S PROGRESS is the classic tale of Christian's escape from the City of Destruction to the Heavenly City. It is true to experience because all of us can identify with his encounters along the way. In the Valley of Humiliation he enters into combat with Apollyon, his fiercest foe. At the Hill of Difficulty he meets Adam-the-First and his three daughters: the Lust-of-the-Flesh, the Lust-of-the-Eyes and the Pride-of-Life. In the town of Folly he narrowly escapes its greatest attraction, Vanity Fair. These encounters are John Bunyan's well-known descriptions of the threefold arena of all Christian conflict: the world, the flesh and the devil. They are the same three foes that appear here in 1 John.

⚑ WARMING UP TO GOD

How far did you progress as a Christian before you became aware of these three foes? Explain.

⚑ DISCOVERING THE WORD

1. *Read 1 John 2:12-17.* Who is represented by the three groups being addressed (vv. 12-14)?

2. What is the source of our victory over the evil one (vv. 13-14)?

3. Why can there be no middle ground between our love for God and love for the world (vv. 15-17)?

4. What are the reasons we are to resist such temptations (vv. 15-17)?

5. How does the realization that the world is passing away (v. 17) lessen its appeal in your life?

⚑ APPLYING THE WORD

• How does this passage help us gain a better understanding of our spiritual battle?

• On a daily basis, how can that truth help us overcome the tactics and schemes of the evil one?

⚑ RESPONDING IN PRAYER

Praise God for giving you the strength you need to overcome the evil one.

1 JOHN 2:18-27 *How Important Is Theology?*

THERE IS AN increasingly popular mindset within the church today that seeks to divorce Christian teaching from Christian living. "We don't want more theology," we are told, "just more about Jesus." But how can we learn more about Jesus apart from a proper understanding of who he is and what he has accomplished? The fact is, there is nothing more basic to Christianity than the person and work of Christ. Apart from understanding Christ, there can be no real Christian living. That is why John goes to great lengths to protect his "dear children" from false views about Christ and to instruct them in the truth.

ᜃ᠊ WARMING UP TO GOD

What have you been learning about the person and work of Christ recently?

ᜃ᠊ DISCOVERING THE WORD

1. *Read 1 John 2:18-27.* What characteristics of false teachers and their teaching is John exposing in these verses?

2. All the New Testament authors viewed the first coming of Christ as the event that marked the beginning of the end—"the last hour." What are some of the signs of the last hour (vv. 18-19)?

3. To deny that "Jesus is the Christ" (v. 22) is to deny that the man Jesus is the eternal, divine Christ—the God-Man. Why is John so harsh toward those who believe and teach such a denial (vv. 22-23)?

4. Why is remaining in the truth so important in the Christian life (vv. 24-25)?

5. How does his instruction (v. 27) help us understand what it means to remain in Christ?

ᜃ᠊ APPLYING THE WORD

• What does this passage teach us about the Holy Spirit's ministry of preserving us from error?

• What does it teach about our responsibility to persevere in the truth?

ᜃ᠊ RESPONDING IN PRAYER

Ask God to fill your heart and mind with truth about himself.

1 JOHN 2:28—3:10 *Like Father, Like Son*

A 1976 *NEWSWEEK* article commented on the phenomenon of "50 million adult Americans who claim . . . a personal commitment to Jesus Christ as their Savior." How would we go about discovering if the results of that survey were true? Without question, 1 John 2:28—3:10 provides one of the clearest tests in Scripture for determining whether one who claims to be a Christian has truly been born of God.

☙ WARMING UP TO GOD

List some of the ways your local community would change if one third of everyone who lived there was born again.

☙ DISCOVERING THE WORD

1. *Read 1 John 2:28—3:10.* Based on John's emphasis at the beginning and the end of the passage (2:28-29; 3:9-10), what test is he using to validate a person's claim of being born again?

2. Throughout this passage John teaches that God's children resemble their Father. In what ways does he reinforce this principle (2:29—3:10)?

3. How does John's definition of sin (v. 4) compare with some of the viewpoints people have today?

4. Although Christians can and do sin, how does knowing Christ change our relationship to sin (v. 6)?

5. Why does the new birth make it impossible for God's children to have a life characterized by sin (v. 9)?

☙ APPLYING THE WORD

- As one who has been born of God, what are some ways you see the family traits of obedience and love developing in your life?

- In what area would you like to be more obedient?

☙ RESPONDING IN PRAYER

Pray that your family resemblance to God and to Christ would be increased.

1 JOHN 3:11-24

Blessed Assurance

WITHOUT QUESTION, doubt and fear have robbed many of the joys of Christian assurance. That is why 1 John 3:11-24 is so important for Christian living. It overflows with the confidence and assurance that ought to characterize every member of God's family.

✍ WARMING UP TO GOD

Have you ever questioned whether you were a member of God's family? Explain.

✍ DISCOVERING THE WORD

1. *Read 1 John 3:11-24.* John begins this passage by talking about love and hate. How do Cain and Abel illustrate the two basic categories of humanity (vv. 11-15)?

2. Why is Christ's death on the cross the supreme example of love (v. 16)?

3. How can John's assurances in verses 19-20 help us to deal with times of doubt?

4. Why would our obedience to God's commands affect our confidence in prayer (vv. 21-22)?

5. Why do you think John reduces the commandments to a single command to be obeyed (v. 23)?

✍ APPLYING THE WORD

• In verse 17 John mentions one specific way we can follow Christ's example. How have you and those in your church sought to love those with material needs?

• In what other practical ways might we "lay down our lives" for each other?

• Based on this passage, how would you counsel someone who lacked assurance that he or she was a Christian?

✍ RESPONDING IN PRAYER

Pray about the needs on your heart with confidence before God.

1 JOHN 4:1-12   *Discernment and Devotion*

EVERY CHRISTIAN VIRTUE bears within itself the seeds of its own destruction. A zeal for the truth, for example, if not tempered by love and compassion, can cause us to become arrogant, harsh and cold. Likewise love for others, if unchecked by the truth, can cause us to be wishy-washy and even tolerant toward sin. If one of these virtues is not governed by the other, it can become a liability and not a strength. As in everything else, obtaining a proper balance is of utmost importance. In this passage, both doctrinal discernment and devotion to other Christians are held before us in perfect balance. They are not either-or but both/and. One without the other is not enough.

◌ WARMING UP TO GOD

Which of these two aspects of the Christian life (truth and love) do you tend to emphasize above the other? Why?

◌ DISCOVERING THE WORD

1. *Read 1 John 4:1-12.* Why is there such a great need for Christians to be discerning (v. 1)?

2. What test does John give us for determining whether a person's teaching is from "the Spirit of God" or the "spirit of the antichrist" (vv. 2-3)?

3. As Christians, how can we overcome the doctrinal errors that continually confront us (vv. 4-6)?

4. Why must we be diligent in our devotion to one another (vv. 7-8)?

5. How does our love for each other make the invisible God visible in our midst (v. 12)?

◌ APPLYING THE WORD

• How does God's love for you motivate you to love others (v. 11)?

• In what practical way can you show love this week to a brother or sister in Christ?

◌ RESPONDING IN PRAYER

Ask that you would be filled with love.

1 JOHN 4:13-21

Fear's Remedy

IN THE SEQUEL to *Pilgrim's Progress,* Mr. Great-Heart and Father Honest engage in a conversation about an old friend, Mr. Fearing. At one point in the dialogue he is portrayed in the following way: "He was a man that had the root of the matter in him, but he was one of the most troublesome Pilgrims that I ever met with in all my days." That is Bunyan's way of describing many who are on the road to heaven: thoroughly sincere (the root of the matter is in them) yet so overloaded with doubts and fears that their pilgrimage is indeed "troublesome." How is Mr. Fearing to fare in this life? How does he, and how do we, overcome this kind of problem? The answer, in part, lies within this passage in 1 John.

❧ WARMING UP TO GOD

In what ways do you feel burdened by fear? Pause to voice your fears to God and listen for his assurance.

❧ DISCOVERING THE WORD

1. *Read 1 John 4:13-21.* What three tests does John give for determining whether "we live in him and he in us" (vv. 13-16)?

2. How is our experience of God's love related to our ability to love others (vv. 16, 19)?

3. What insights does verse 18 give us into why we sometimes fear God and others?

4. Why is it impossible to love God and yet hate one of the members of his family (vv. 19-21)?

❧ APPLYING THE WORD

- How can the principle "perfect love drives out fear" (v. 18) help you overcome your fears?

- In what ways can this passage strengthen our confidence before God?

❧ RESPONDING IN PRAYER

Ask God to fill you with love for someone you find difficult to love.

1 JOHN 5:1-12 *Faith Is the Victory*

CHRISTIANS WITH A variety of theological views have wholeheartedly sung the words to the well-known hymn: "Faith is the victory! Faith is the victory! O glorious victory, That overcomes the world." But in light of the daily battles in the Christian life, not all agree on what this victory is, when it is accomplished or how we go about achieving it. In this passage John clears up some of our confusion by focusing our attention not only on the victory we have in Christ, but also on Christ himself. For, first and foremost, an overcoming faith is one centered in a correct understanding of who Christ is.

☙ WARMING UP TO GOD

What spiritual battles are the focus of your attention?

☙ DISCOVERING THE WORD

1. *Read 1 John 5:1-12.* What are some inevitable results of the new birth (vv. 1-2)?

2. Why is obedience to God's commandments not burdensome for Christians (v. 3)?

3. How then can we explain the struggle we sometimes have in obeying?

4. Reflect for a moment on the two major characteristics of the world described earlier (2:15-17; 4:1-6). What then does it mean for us to "overcome the world" (vv. 4-5)?

5. The heretics of John's day taught that the divine Christ descended on Jesus at his baptism but left before his death (v. 6). What is wrong with this view?

6. The Old Testament law required two or three witnesses to prove a claim. Who are John's three witnesses, and what do they testify (vv. 7-8)?

☙ APPLYING THE WORD

• What evidence of the victory over the world do you see in your life?

• How does your own experience confirm the truth that eternal life is found in Jesus (vv. 10-12)?

☙ RESPONDING IN PRAYER

Take time to thank God for his Son and for the victory and eternal life we have in him.

1 JOHN 5:13-21 *What We Know as Christians*

ALMOST IMMEDIATELY after his conversion experience at Aldersgate Street, John Wesley struggled for months over the uncertainty of his own salvation. Focusing on his sinful failures, he became increasingly despondent and dejected. Unfortunately, Wesley's problem is the same problem that afflicts many sincere Christians today—a lack of knowledge. The truth is found in this passage.

✐ WARMING UP TO GOD

How well can you relate to Wesley's experience? Explain.

✐ DISCOVERING THE WORD

1. *Read 1 John 5:13-21.* What assurance does John give us in these verses?

2. Verse 13 is a summary statement of purpose for the entire epistle. What then are those "things" that assure us we have eternal life?

3. How can we get to the point where we want what God wants (vv. 14-15)?

4. In light of the whole context of this epistle, what might be the distinction between the sin that does not lead to death and the one that does (vv. 16-17)?

5. How does the coming of God's Son enable us to know the true God in contrast to the false conceptions of God that continually surround us (vv. 20-21)?

✐ APPLYING THE WORD

• What certainties in this passage are the most encouraging to you?

• In what way do you need greater assurance from God?

✐ RESPONDING IN PRAYER

Pray that God will make your desires his own will.

INTRODUCING 2 JOHN

⚘

Like 1 John, 2 John was written by the apostle John between A.D. 85 and 95. It was written to provide guidance about hospitality. During the first century, traveling evangelists relied on the hospitality of church members. Because inns were few and unsafe, believers would take such people into their homes and then give them provisions for their journey. Because Gnostic teachers also relied on hospitality, John warned his readers against taking such people into their homes lest they participate in spreading heresy.

Ron Blankley

2 JOHN 1-13 *Truth and Love*

THERE ARE TWO equally extreme misconceptions many people have concerning the Christian life. One view says, "It doesn't matter what you believe as long as you are sincere and loving." The other says, "It doesn't matter how you live as long as you believe the truth." But the Word of God binds both truth and love inseparably together. They are friends, not enemies.

Nowhere will you see this perspective more clearly than in John's second epistle. His major purpose is to demonstrate how love and truth are designed to support and complement one another as only good friends can.

✎ WARMING UP TO GOD

Have you ever been in a situation where you felt you were torn between doing the right thing and the loving thing? Explain.

✎ DISCOVERING THE WORD

1. *Read 2 John 1-13.* In the brief introductory address and greeting (vv. 1-3), notice how many times truth and love are mentioned together. What does it mean to love someone "in the truth" (v. 1)?

2. We tend to love only those who agree with us or who we feel are compatible with us. What does it mean to love "because of the truth" (v. 2)?

3. In verses 4-6 the unity of truth and love is applied to church relationships. What distinction is made between "his command" and "his commands"?

4. In verses 7-11 the unity of truth and love is applied to relationships outside the church. By denying that Christ had come in the flesh (v. 7), what fundamental truths were the false teachers rejecting?

5. Obtaining a future reward for faithful service was a strong motivation for John (v. 8). In what sense does the prospect of receiving a reward from Jesus Christ motivate you to walk in truth and love?

✎ APPLYING THE WORD

- Would you identify yourself as someone whose truth needs to be balanced by love or whose love needs to be balanced by truth? Explain.

- What can you do to gain a better balance?

✎ RESPONDING IN PRAYER

Pray that your life would reveal an understanding of both truth and love.

INTRODUCING 3 JOHN

Like 2 John, 3 John was written to provide us with guidance about hospitality, but in a much more positive way. Whereas 2 John tells us what we are not to do, 3 John emphasizes what we are to do. For those genuine teachers who are totally dependent on the body of Christ for all of their needs, we are to open not only our hearts but also our homes. This instruction is primarily found in John's commendation of Gaius, who has done this very thing, and in his denunciation of Diotrephes, who has refused. These two men become living examples of good and evil, truth and error. This study will encourage and assure you that you "walk in the truth."

Ron Blankley

3 JOHN 1-14   *Opening Our Hearts and Homes*

IMAGINE LIVING IN a world where there were no bed-and-breakfasts, no hotels and headwaiters. Such was the world of John and his readers. Their hospitality was one of the clearest testimonies of their love for the believers and obedience to God. The same is true today. In the words of Helga Henry, as quoted by V. A. Hall in *Be My Guest,* "Christian hospitality is not a matter of choice; it is not a matter of money; it is not a matter of age, social standing, sex, or personality. Christian hospitality is a matter of obedience to God."

❧ WARMING UP TO GOD

When is showing hospitality difficult?

❧ DISCOVERING THE WORD

1. *Read 3 John 1-14.* Why is Gaius an especially good example for us to follow?

2. How are both love and faithfulness demonstrated in Christian hospitality (vv. 5-6)?

3. Why do you think Christian workers are to look to Christians for support and not to non-Christians (vv. 7-8)?

4. In addition to hospitality, how else can we "work together" with such people?

5. How are the actions of Diotrephes consistent with his true heart's desire (vv. 9-11)?

❧ APPLYING THE WORD

• In contrast to Diotrephes, Demetrius was "well spoken of by everyone" (v. 12). If those who know you best were asked about your love and hospitality, what might they say?

• In light of this passage, what practical steps could you take to develop more of a ministry of hospitality?

❧ RESPONDING IN PRAYER

Pray for an open heart that will lead you to an open home.

Introducing Jude

Jude wrote in the same era as Peter. In fact, much of the information in Jude is also found in 2 Peter 2.

Jude was the brother of James and the half-brother of Jesus. Both Matthew 13:55 and Mark 6:3 speak of James and Jude (along with Joseph and Simon) as brothers of Jesus. Though, according to John 7:5, Christ's brothers were not believers in him during his lifetime, at least these two became converts after his death.

James became a leader in the early church. We see him in action in Acts 12:17, 15:13, and 21:18; 1 Corinthians 15:7; and Galatians 1:19 and 2:9, 12. We hear from Jude only in this book, except perhaps in 1 Corinthians 9:5. It is interesting to note that while Jude claims James as brother, both he and James refer to themselves as servants of Jesus.

The book of Jude was written to oppose false teachers who were sexually immoral and were teaching arrogantly. This letter, Craig Keener notes in his *IVP Bible Background Commentary: New Testament*, would have been used as a sermon in the writer's absence. It serves as a guide and caution for us today so that we do not allow ourselves to be led astray by unbiblical leaders.

Carolyn Nystrom

JUDE 1-24   *The Twisted Fate of Twisted Faith*

IN NOVEMBER OF 1978, more than nine hundred people committed suicide by drinking cyanide-treated punch. Those too young to act on their own were given the punch by their parents. The Jonestown massacre sends a shudder through Christians, because Jim Jones, who prescribed this "White Night" of death, at one time claimed to be among us. It's enough to cause Christians to take a hard, critical look at the life and faith of their leaders—and themselves. The book of Jude shows us how.

✑ WARMING UP TO GOD

How do you think people get tricked into perverted versions of the Christian faith?

✑ DISCOVERING THE WORD

1. *Read Jude 1-24.* What can you know of the circumstances of the people receiving this letter and of Jude's purpose in writing to them (vv. 3-4)?
2. Find as many words and phrases as you can in this letter that describe those "certain men" who have "secretly slipped in among you."
3. What harm could people like these do within a body of believers?
4. Jude used a series of six metaphors in verses 12-13. How does each illustrate the danger of teachers who have perverted the gospel?
5. In the face of this problem, Jude gives his readers two sets of instructions: "Remember" (v. 17) and "build yourselves up" (v. 20). How would remembering, in the way Jude describes, help believers keep the essential ingredients of the Christian faith?
6. How would building ourselves up in the ways Jude outlines (vv. 17-23) help us keep on living in a way that is true to our faith?

✑ APPLYING THE WORD

• What errors in faith and life do you see as dangers for today's Christians?
• How can you protect yourself, and other believers whose lives you touch, from falling into these errors?

✑ RESPONDING IN PRAYER

Pray that you and your church would be protected from false religion.

Introducing Revelation

❦

New Testament Christians eagerly awaited the future. They believed the complete reign of Christ on earth was a more certain reality than the seeming victory of evil. Jesus gave John the strangely beautiful vision recorded in the book of Revelation to give us hope. But how are we to understand this book? Though it is highly symbolic, it is not a lock whose key has been lost. Revelation was meant to be read in one sitting (1:3); we do well to put aside the charts and films we have seen and just read it. A child might hear Revelation and rightly conclude its profound truth: "I'm glad the Lamb won over the beast."

Of the 404 verses in Revelation, 278 allude to Old Testament ideas, symbols, names and themes pulled together through the Spirit's inspiration to form a kaleidoscope effect. We misunderstand Revelation when we treat it as a book of predictions; rather, it is an exposé of spiritual realities that affect us now and will bring history to a worthy end. John shows us how the world looks to someone in the Spirit.

John wrote Revelation between A.D. 90 and 95 from his place of exile on Patmos Island. Tradition tells us that prior to his exile John left Israel to live in Ephesus, capital of the Roman province of Asia. The seven churches to whom this book is addressed were visited by a courier traveling on the circular road through modern Turkey. John's letter describes his vision of Christ as Lord of the churches (1:12—3:22), as the Lamb on the throne (5:1-14), as the liberating Word of God (19:11-16) and as the Leader in the new creation (21—22). This book is truly the Revelation of Jesus Christ (1:1).

John says, "Blessed is the one who reads the words of this prophecy, and blessed are those who hear it" (1:3). Look forward to this blessing as you study Revelation.

R. Paul Stevens

REVELATION 1:1-8 *The Illustrated Letter*

PERSECUTION, imprisonment, martyrdom. These seem far removed from the lives of many Christians today. Yet we do suffer. Who can witness the breakup of families, the deaths of unborn children, the threat of war and the plight of the poor without crying out, "Come, Lord Jesus"? In this passage he does come in a vision to give us hope in a suffering world.

✑ WARMING UP TO GOD

Following Jesus brings many benefits. It also causes new pressures and problems. In what ways have you found being a Christian difficult?

✑ DISCOVERING THE WORD

1. *Read Revelation 1:1-8.* The word *reveal* means "to bring to light what was formerly hidden, veiled and secret." Who and what will be unveiled by the revelation given to John (vv. 1-3)?

2. How would John's description of God be a comfort to his readers (vv. 4-5)?

3. Why would it help discouraged believers to know they are "a kingdom and priests to serve his God and Father" (v. 6)?

4. John presents a vision of Jesus as both coming (v. 7) and already and always here (v. 8). What would it be like to have only one of these two perspectives?

✑ APPLYING THE WORD

• In what ways has a knowledge of Christ's coming encouraged you in the midst of suffering?

• John states that we will be blessed if we hear his message and take it to heart (v. 3). In what ways do you think he expects us to take this message to heart?

✑ RESPONDING IN PRAYER

Ask God to fill your heart with hope.

REVELATION 1:9-20 *Surprised by Magnificence*

THE EXPERIENCE OF meeting a famous person is sometimes disconcerting. That celebrity may be less impressive than we had imagined. But when John sees Jesus face to face, he is overwhelmed with his magnificence. John's experience challenges us to ask whether we have ever met the same Person. Or do we follow a pale, distorted copy of the real Lord?

❧ WARMING UP TO GOD

From all that you have read or experienced before opening Revelation, what images or pictures do you have of Jesus?

❧ DISCOVERING THE WORD

1. *Read Revelation 1:9-20.* John pictures the seven churches as seven golden lampstands (to hold oil lamps). What does John's picture tell us about the function of the churches?

2. How would Jesus' relationship to these churches (v. 13) encourage them to fulfill their function during hard times?

3. John's vision of Jesus is rich with biblical symbolism. Instead of trying to picture all these characteristics at once, allow them to impress you one at a time, like a slide presentation. Which images impress you most with the magnificence of Jesus, and why (vv. 13-16)?

4. Why do you think a godly person like John would be so powerfully overcome by the presence of the One he loved (v. 17)?

5. How would Jesus' words encourage John not to be fearful in his presence (vv. 17-18)?

❧ APPLYING THE WORD

- Revelation was written to churches persecuted under a totalitarian regime. Our society seems friendlier. Yet how is it hostile to us both morally and spiritually?

- How has this passage enlarged your vision of who Jesus is?

- How can this vision of Jesus encourage us to resist the seductions of our society?

❧ RESPONDING IN PRAYER

Praise Jesus for who he is and for what you have learned about him here.

REVELATION 2   *Pardon My Speaking the Truth*

WHAT CAN WE do to help a fellow Christian who is ready to cave in under pressure? Usually we wouldn't say that things are going to get worse before they get better. But that's what Christ does in the seven letters to churches in Asia (Rev 2—3). He confronts believers who have compromised morally and spiritually. But he also encourages them. This kind of tough love is essential for spiritual health.

✎ WARMING UP TO GOD

In what area do you feel pressure (spiritual or otherwise)?

✎ DISCOVERING THE WORD

1. *Read Revelation 2.* Why would "forsak[ing] your first love" (v. 4) be so tragic for the church at Ephesus?

2. Why would Christ's judgment be so severe if they did not repent (v. 5)?

3. Smyrna was noted for emperor worship. Refusal to worship the emperor brought martyrdom to some Christians. What does Jesus know about the believers in Smyrna (vv. 8-11)?

4. The letter to Smyrna mentions no problem and gives no warning. What role does affirmation play in helping Christians under spiritual pressure?

5. Pergamum was also a center of emperor worship. In addition, temple prostitution was prevalent. How had the church responded to the lure of these temptations (vv. 12-17)?

6. Jezebel (v. 20) is an Old Testament character who symbolizes spiritual adultery (1 Kings 16:31). How was the so-called prophetess in Thyatira like her namesake (vv. 18-29)?

✎ APPLYING THE WORD

• Jesus charges the godly and loving church at Thyatira with being too tolerant of evil in their midst. In what areas are Christians today too tolerant?

• Each of the letters (except the one to Smyrna) contains an affirmation, a problem, a warning and a promise. How might Jesus' example guide us as we care for a brother or sister ready to cave in under pressure?

✎ RESPONDING IN PRAYER

Pray for someone you know who is under pressure to compromise.

REVELATION 3 *My Dear Compromised People*

EXPERTS TELL US we are exposed to fourteen hundred advertisements a day. It takes an enormous act of will not to be conformed to our environment. The remaining three letters, sequenced in the order they would be visited by a postal courier, help us resist the powerful temptation to be conformed to the world.

❧ WARMING UP TO GOD

In what ways do Christian groups and churches you know resemble the surrounding culture?

❧ DISCOVERING THE WORD

1. *Read Revelation 3.* In the first century, Sardis exhibited a stark contrast between its past splendor as a Persian capital and its current decay. What indications does the Lord give that the church's reputation does not match its reality (vv. 1-6)? Why is this such a serious problem?

2. The church in Philadelphia received nothing but praise and promises. Why would a weak church be encouraged by an open door of opportunity (v. 8)?

3. As the Philadelphian church faced opposition, how would Jesus' other promises encourage them (vv. 9-13)?

4. Laodicea's northern neighbor, Hierapolis, had famous hot springs. Its southern neighbor, Colosse, had refreshing cool water. A six-mile aqueduct brought water to Laodicea, but by the time it arrived it was lukewarm. How does this help us understand Christ's statements in verses 14-16?

5. Laodicea was so self-sufficient that when they suffered an earthquake in A.D. 60 they rejected help from Rome. How did this attitude affect them spiritually?

❧ APPLYING THE WORD

• Many churches today feel weak, insignificant and discouraged. What can we learn from Christ's words to the Philadelphians?

• As you review all seven letters (Rev 2—3), what has the Spirit taught you about being an overcomer?

❧ RESPONDING IN PRAYER

Pray that the church would be a powerful force in the world.

REVELATION 4—5   *Worship the Omnipotent Lamb*

In a play by George Bernard Shaw, Don Juan says, "Heaven is all right, of course, but for meeting old friends and acquaintances you can't beat hell." There is a powerful truth in this facetious remark. People concerned only about themselves would find the ceaseless praise of God and the Lamb intolerable. Worship on earth, a foretaste of heaven, is just as unpalatable. But worship is the deepest need of the seven churches just described. And it is our deepest need too, as this study will show.

◈ WARMING UP TO GOD

What was the most significant worship experience you have ever had, and what made it so special?

◈ DISCOVERING THE WORD

1. *Read Revelation 4—5.* Instead of trying to decode every part of the throne room of God, try to imagine what can be seen and heard. What are your initial impressions of God's glory as envisioned here in Revelation 4?

2. How do the creatures and the elders respond to God's glory (4:8, 10-11)? How does their reaction help us define and practice worship?

3. While John leaves us in suspense about the contents of the scroll and its seals, there is no doubt about the central figure in the unfolding drama. Why do you think he superimposes the image of the Lamb on the image of the Lion (5:5-6)?

4. The heavenly choir gets larger as the scene unfolds (5:8, 11, 13). What do we see in this heavenly worship that is timelessly relevant?

◈ APPLYING THE WORD

- Worship is not an action but a reaction, a response evoked by a vision of God's glory. If we have difficulty worshiping God, what might we need to do?

- If earthly worship is to be modeled after heavenly worship, what is most lacking in your experience of worship?

◈ RESPONDING IN PRAYER

Take time now to worship the Lamb and the One who sits on the throne.

REVELATION 6   *The Beautiful Wrath of God*

JUDGMENT IS NOT something we normally long for. But if we are suffering unjustly in an evil social system, God's judgment—far from being a dreaded prospect—is our only hope.

In Revelation 6—19 there is a complicated and rather confusing pattern of disaster and suffering. If we seek to unravel these pictures as a timetable for the future, we will be disappointed and perplexed. But if we want to learn how to live in the present and find hope for the future, there is much here to encourage us. These chapters inspire trust in a God who is faithful and just.

↶ WARMING UP TO GOD

As you approach the subject of God's wrath, what thoughts and feelings do you have? Explain.

↶ DISCOVERING THE WORD

1. *Read Revelation 6.* The scene shifts back to earth as the Lamb opens the book of destiny. Summarize the events during the first four seals (vv. 1-8).

2. Are the events during the seals normal bad times (compare vv. 1-8 with vv. 12-14)? Explain.

3. How does the experience of the saints (vv. 9-11) contrast with that of the unbelievers (vv. 15-17) as they anticipate the impending wrath of God?

4. What evidence, if any, do you see of this contrast among people today?

↶ APPLYING THE WORD

- If we realize that the wrath of God will one day be fully expressed, what difference should it make in our attitude toward sin?

- In our attitude toward unjust suffering?

- In our attitude toward non-Christians?

↶ RESPONDING IN PRAYER

Pray for non-Christians you know, that they would come to know the love of the Lord.

REVELATION 7 *Living Faithfully Through the Holocaust*

SOME PREACHERS SPEAK of the Christian life as one great success story. They say that if we attend church, live right, tithe and exercise faith, we will prosper financially and be free of illness and distress. But the relative peace some of us enjoy at this moment is exceptional in the world and in history. From the ascension of Christ to his return, the normal lot of believers is tribulation. Most of the Christians John pictures for us are martyrs. They are dead to the threats of this life but gloriously alive to God. Their experience reminds us that the call to discipleship is a call to radical obedience.

ᢴ WARMING UP TO GOD

Think about a story you've heard about people suffering for their faith. How would you handle a similar situation?

ᢴ DISCOVERING THE WORD

1. *Read Revelation 7.* In verses 1-8 an angel seals 144,000 people. What do you think "the seal of the living God" means (7:2-3; 9:4)?

2. In verse 9 the scene shifts from earth to heaven. How did the great multitude in verse 9 come to stand before the Lamb?

3. Why does the multitude cry out with praise and thanksgiving (vv. 10-12)?

4. How do the blessings these martyred Christians enjoy compare with the tribulations they suffered (vv. 13-17)?

5. How does their experience help us understand the benefit of being faithful?

ᢴ APPLYING THE WORD

• In the first century, persecution of Christians came from three basic sources: emperor worshipers, heretics and those whose commercial interests were threatened by the radical lifestyle of Christians. Why might faithful Christians suffer today?

• This vision comes at the point of maximum dramatic intensity: between the sixth and seventh seals. How can the vision encourage us to be faithful no matter what happens in the world?

ᢴ RESPONDING IN PRAYER

Pray for those who suffer for their faith.

REVELATION 8—9 *The Message of the Angels*

ANGELS ARE QUITE popular these days. We see them depicted on T-shirts, mugs and cards. You can get little pins picturing charming angels. And there's a growing category of books available to show you how to get in touch with your "inner angels" and other such things. None of this has much to do with the angels we meet in Scripture. In the next few passages you will meet some of God's angels—and you will be confronted with their terrible power.

ᥱᷢ WARMING UP TO GOD

What positive feelings or experiences have you had about angels?

ᥱᷢ DISCOVERING THE WORD

1. *Read Revelation 8—9.* List the events that happen when each of the angels blows his trumpet.

2. What similarities do you note between all of these events?

3. The seventh seal (8:1-5) contains the seven trumpet judgments (8:6—11:15). What apparently is God's purpose in allowing these judgments to fall on the whole creation (9:20-21)?

4. Does such a response by God seem justified? Explain.

5. It is sometimes maintained that Christians are removed from the world before God's wrath falls. What alternate view is possibly suggested by 9:4 (see also 7:3)?

ᥱᷢ APPLYING THE WORD

• Those mentioned in 9:20-21 did not repent. How do our sins today compare to theirs?

• Where do you see yourself in this list of sins?

• In what way do you feel that you need to be ready for the judgment that takes place here?

ᥱᷢ RESPONDING IN PRAYER

Repent of your sins before God.

REVELATION 10—11 *God's Messenger*

IN THE OLD TESTAMENT, God often used specific persons to deliver a message to another person, or sometimes to entire groups. Sometimes these messages were positive and easy to hear. However, they were often condemnations of the way things were, and those who delivered the messages, the prophets, were often ridiculed or threatened. In chapter 10, John is given a message that is not easy to deliver. In chapter 11, two of God's prophets have a life experience that roughly parallels Jesus' time on earth. Their example can give us hope that the God who calls us to be a light in the darkness is also the one who will vindicate us.

☙ Warming Up to God

When has God used someone else to give you a message? How did you react to the message and the messenger?

☙ Discovering the Word

1. *Read Revelation 10—11.* What are the actions of the "mighty angel" introduced in 10:1?

2. What is the significance of the mystery of God that will be revealed without further delay (10:6-7)?

3. What happens to the two witnesses empowered by God (11:3-14)?

4. Why do you think the witnesses caused such turmoil?

5. What happens when the seventh trumpet is blown (11:15-19)?

☙ Applying the Word

• The "little scroll" that John eats (10:8-11) probably refers to the gospel. When has the gospel tasted like honey or turned your stomach sour?

• The two witnesses had "tormented those who live on the earth" (11:10). When have you felt that God was calling you to deliver a message of bad news?

• What feelings about God and his actions do you have after reading the description of worship in 11:15-19?

☙ Responding in Prayer

Pray that you will be willing to be God's messenger to those around you.

REVELATION 12 *Conflict with the Accuser*

DRAGONS SYMBOLIZE all that is terrifying, evil and loathsome. In Revelation 12 Satan appears as an enormous red dragon, full of rage. Knowing that his time is short, he unleashes his fury as never before. During such dark moments of history, it seems as though God is absent and Satan is victorious. Yet in this passage John describes a heavenly vision that puts all earthly tribulation in proper perspective.

✍ WARMING UP TO GOD

In what ways have you experienced the reality of spiritual warfare?

✍ DISCOVERING THE WORD

1. *Read Revelation 12.* Three of the characters in this chapter are the woman (perhaps the Lord's people or the Holy Spirit), the red dragon (Satan) and the male child (the Lord Jesus). What conflict does John observe among them (vv. 1-6)?

2. In verses 7-9 John describes a war in heaven. What does the war reveal about the dragon?

3. What does the dragon's defeat mean in heaven (vv. 10, 12) and on earth (vv. 12-17)?

4. What does it mean to overcome Satan's accusations "by the blood of the Lamb and by the word of [our] testimony" (v. 11)?

✍ APPLYING THE WORD

• How can we help a fellow Christian who is no longer under God's condemnation but who still feels condemned and defeated?

• In what other ways do we experience Satan's attacks?

• How can the victory of Christ help us face these battles and struggles of the Christian life?

✍ RESPONDING IN PRAYER

Pray for those who are struggling against Satan.

REVELATION 13 *The Beast*

IN *BRAVE NEW WORLD* Aldous Huxley described a future too close for comfort: "As political and economic freedom diminishes, sexual freedom tends compensatingly to increase. And the dictator will do well to encourage that freedom." Faithful Christianity inevitably involves conflict, tension and suffering for followers of Jesus. We cannot be fully at home in our own culture. Even where we do not face open hostility, we are pressured—indeed seduced—by a seemingly friendly society. Revelation 13 demonstrates that the church must always deal with radical evil. In these visions John unmasks the powers of darkness at work in everyday life and at the end of history.

❧ WARMING UP TO GOD

Why do you think it is so difficult for believers to make substantial changes in society? (For example, in the areas of justice, protection of the unborn or making peace.)

❧ DISCOVERING THE WORD

1. *Read Revelation 13.* How is the beast a satanic imitation of Christ?
2. What is the mission of the beast (vv. 5-8)?
3. Why do you think John tells us about this formidable enemy of the soul?
4. What new powers are given to the second beast (vv. 11-18)?
5. How does this beast ensure that people worship the first beast?

❧ APPLYING THE WORD

- John seems to be describing a conflict with Satan and his puppets that is going on now but will one day be fully realized (see 1 Jn 2:18). How might we expect to see this satanic influence at work today?
- How can we prepare ourselves to face this conflict?

❧ RESPONDING IN PRAYER

Pray that you will be equipped to face Satan.

REVELATION 14—15 *Tale of Two Choices*

AS YOU STRUGGLE to live according to God's laws, do you ever wonder if there will really be any reward? Will there be any difference between those who love God and those who live their life in rebellion against God's love? In these chapters, John makes it clear that the choices we make now will have an impact on God's judgment on us in the future. These chapters are a tale of two choices.

✿ WARMING UP TO GOD

Recall a time you tried to do what is right, only to see those who didn't play by the rules seem to come out better than you. How did the experience impact your relationship with God?

✿ DISCOVERING THE WORD

1. *Read Revelation 14—15.* What differences do you notice between the 144,000 who are with the Lamb (14:1-5) and Babylon (14:8), the beast and those who worship it (14:6-11)?

2. What harvest is reaped in 14:14-20?

3. What connections do you find between the angels who give warnings in 14:6-11 and the beings who reap the harvest?

4. Who sings the hymn to God in 15:1-4?

5. What are the righteous acts that have been revealed (15:4)?

✿ APPLYING THE WORD

- In 14:12 John states that these events call "for patient endurance on the part of the saints." How does this passage encourage you to endure in your faith?

- The hymn beginning in 15:3 is called the song of Moses, which was sung by Moses after crossing the Red Sea. When have you been delivered by God from danger, spiritual or physical?

✿ RESPONDING IN PRAYER

Thank God for the assurance you have of your salvation.

REVELATION 16 *Who's to Blame?*

WHEN SOMETHING GOES wrong, who do we blame? Often God's name is among the first to come up. When we are inclined to blame God, we must ask ourselves what it is we expect out of life. Do we feel that we have an innate right to health, wealth and happiness? In understanding God's working in the world it's important that we learn to see beyond our private world to God's vast creation.

✍ WARMING UP TO GOD

When are you inclined to place blame on God for events in your life?

✍ DISCOVERING THE WORD

1. *Read Revelation 16.* Note the similarity between these "bowls of God's wrath" and the plagues brought on Egypt (blood, frogs, gnats, flies, livestock, boils, hail, locusts, darkness, firstborn). What might be meant by this comparison?

2. How could the same events lead to worship on the part of some (vv. 5-7) and cursing on the part of others (vv. 9, 21)?

3. How can we see this happening in our culture?

4. What is the result of the plagues (vv. 19-21)?

✍ APPLYING THE WORD

• When has God's judgment been a source of praise for you?

• When has God's judgment caused you to curse or blame God?

✍ RESPONDING IN PRAYER

Talk honestly with God about any feelings of blame and responsibility that have been revealed to you during this study.

REVELATION 17—18 *Beneath the Surface*

IN EVERY AGE there is at least one symbol for everything that goes against God. For several of the Old Testament writers it was Babylon, the beautiful city that held captive God's chosen people. Babylon represented everything that was evil and unsightly about humanity. John uses this powerful symbol to interpret his own age and the powers that opposed God in his generation. In these two chapters we see not only John's vision of how those powers opposed God, but also the ultimate outcome of that opposition.

✎ WARMING UP TO GOD

Recall a time you noticed someone or something that looked appealing but on closer scrutiny was unappealing or revolting. How did your reaction change?

✎ DISCOVERING THE WORD

1. *Read Revelation 17—18.* Who or what do you think John had in mind when he described the prostitute (17:3-6)?

2. What is the relationship between the prostitute and the beast, and how does it change (chapter 17)?

3. What are the crimes of the prostitute, identified as Babylon (17:3-6; 18:1-3)?

4. How does the prostitute see herself (18:7-8)?

5. What is the reaction of the kings (18:9-10), merchants (18:11-17) and sea captains (18:17-20) to the fall of Babylon?

✎ APPLYING THE WORD

• Who or what is a contemporary parallel to the prostitute?

• In what way(s) is the modern "prostitute" a temptation to you?

• How can you avoid this temptation?

✎ RESPONDING IN PRAYER

Ask God for protection from the temptations of those who are prideful and oppose God.

REVELATION 19   *Are You Going to the Wedding?*

IN AN ERA THAT takes seriously "interchangeable marriage roles," "five-year renewable relationships" and "serial monogamy," it is difficult to grasp the splendor of marriage as God intends it. John chooses a wedding to describe the consummation of the deepest longing of the human soul: Christ's coming to receive us. Our present engagement (betrothal) to Christ will be followed by the wedding service and a joyous feast. Then and only then can we experience complete unity with Christ. This vision seems a welcome relief after the long passage on tribulation and judgment (chapters 6—18). In fact the marriage is the logical result of all that has gone before, as we shall see.

✧ WARMING UP TO GOD

In your opinion, what are some of the best things about marriage?

✧ DISCOVERING THE WORD

1. *Read Revelation 19.* Why is the great multitude shouting praise in heaven?

2. John does not describe the details of the marriage; he simply proclaims it. Why is marriage such a good image for the believer's hope (vv. 7-9)?

3. Like a champion ready for battle, Jesus appears on horseback. What do we learn about him (vv. 11-16)?

4. Why must this battle take place before the marriage can begin and the kingdom of God fully come (vv. 17-21)?

✧ APPLYING THE WORD

• In what ways would you like to see Christ triumph in your life or in the world around you?

• How can we confidently know we are invited to the "wedding supper of the Lamb" (v. 9)?

✧ RESPONDING IN PRAYER

Allow praise for this future celebration to flow forth out of your prayer.

REVELATION 20 *The Last Battle*

FINALITY IS SOMETHING we crave and God graciously provides. A relationship needs to be broken, an assignment needs to be completed, an extended friendship needs to become a committed marriage—all require closure. The previous study explored our inexpressible hope to be reunited with our Lord. This chapter enlarges our appreciation of God's master plan: his settled decision to be with us forever and to establish his glorious rule over everything.

◌ WARMING UP TO GOD

What do you look forward to most about Christ's return?

◌ DISCOVERING THE WORD

1. *Read Revelation 20.* This chapter, out of the whole book, has sparked the greatest controversy. Why is Satan, previously thrown to earth (12:9), now bound (20:1-3)?

2. The thousand-year reign of Christ (vv. 4-6) has been interpreted as referring to (a) a period of righteousness and peace on earth before Christ's return; (b) Christ's reign in heaven between his first and second coming; (c) Christ's reign on earth after his return. Which view (if any) do you think best fits this passage and the book of Revelation?

3. What is the nature and outcome of Satan's last fling (vv. 7-10)?

4. Who will be judged at the great-white-throne judgment (vv. 11-15)?

5. What does it say about God's character that he should keep a record of each person's deeds?

◌ APPLYING THE WORD

- How can verses 4-6 help us to see life and death in proper perspective?
- How should the ultimate judgment of evil and the reward of faithfulness affect the way we live now?

◌ RESPONDING IN PRAYER

Pray that you will be made faithful in every way.

REVELATION 21—22 *God Dwelling with His People*

W. H. AUDEN SAID, "Nobody is ever sent to hell; he or she insists on going there." Could the same be said of heaven? Far from being "pie in the sky by and by" or a hedonistic longing for pleasure, John's vision of God dwelling with his people is the consummation of faith. Creation is renewed. Evil is finally excluded. The face of God is seen. But John's vision is, at the same time, unsettling to the normal view held by Christians about "last things." It goes beyond not only our imagination but even our faith.

∽ WARMING UP TO GOD

List the things you think about when you hear the word *heaven*.

∽ DISCOVERING THE WORD

1. *Read Revelation 21—22.* What aspects of the "old order" must be eliminated before God can fully dwell with his people (21:1-5)?

2. What in the passage suggests that the new Jerusalem is the church in its final, consummated life (21:10)?

3. Why do you think John gives such a detailed description of the splendor of the city (21:11-21)?

4. Why do you think a city (rather than a glorious garden like Eden) is used to describe our final home?

5. Taken together, chapters 21 and 22 describe a place of exquisite beauty. Yet what statements in chapter 22 indicate that the real significance of the city lies in something else?

6. What are the requirements for entering the city (21:6-7, 27; 22:12, 14)?

∽ APPLYING THE WORD

• Why must the requirements for entering the city be met during the times of testing we experience in this life?

• As you review what you have learned in Revelation, what new insight do you have into the early Christian prayer "Come, Lord Jesus!"?

∽ RESPONDING IN PRAYER

Pray for Jesus' coming.

Introducing Psalms

P eople look at mirrors to see how they look; they look at psalms to find out who they are. We use psalms to present ourselves before God as honestly and thoroughly as we are able. The psalms are poetry and the psalms are prayer. These two features need to be kept in mind always. If either is forgotten, the psalms will not only be misunderstood but also misused.

Poetry gets at the heart of existence. Poets use words to drag us into the depths of reality itself, not by reporting on how life is but by pushing and pulling us into the middle of it. The psalms are almost entirely this kind of language. We will not find in the psalms primarily ideas about God or direction in moral conduct. We will expect, rather, to find exposed and sharpened what it means to be human beings before God.

Our usual approach to God's Word is to ask, "What is God saying to me?" That is almost always the correct question when reading Scripture. But in the psalms the question is "How do I answer the God who speaks to me?" This is hard to get used to. Our habit is to talk *about* God, not *to* him. The psalms resist such discussions. We don't learn the psalms until we are praying them.

One editorial feature of Psalms helps to keep these distinctive qualities of the psalms before us. At the end of Psalms 41, 72, 89, 106 and 150, formula sentences indicate a conclusion. Because of these mini-conclusions Psalms is usually printed (in English translations) as Book I (Psalms 1—41), Book II (42—72), Book III (73—89), Book IV (90—106) and Book V (107—150).

Everything that anyone can feel or experience in relation to God is in these prayers. They are the best place in Scripture to explore the parts of your life and then say who you are and what is in you—guilt, anger, salvation, praise—to the God who loves, judges and saves you in Jesus Christ.

Eugene Peterson

PSALM 1

Praying Our Inattention

PSALM 1 IS THE biblical preparation for a life of prayer. Step by step it detaches us from activities and words that distract us from God, so that we can be attentive before him. Most of us can't step immediately from the noisy, high-stimulus world into the quiet concentration of prayer. We need a way of transition. Psalm 1 provides a kind of entryway into the place of prayer.

↪ WARMING UP TO GOD

Do you feel a gap (or chasm!) between "real life" (work, school, family) and your prayer life? Explain. Ask God to help you begin to make prayer a part of your life.

↪ DISCOVERING THE WORD

1. *Read Psalm 1.* What contrasts do you notice in the psalm?
2. What significance do you see in the progression from walk to stand to sit (v. 1)?
3. "The law of the LORD" (v. 2) is contrasted with the words *counsel, way* and *seat.* What does this contrast bring out?
4. *Tree* is the central metaphor of the psalm (v. 3). Put your imagination to use. How are law-delighting people like trees?
5. In what ways are the wicked like chaff (vv. 4-6)?

↪ APPLYING THE WORD

- How do these two radically different portraits (the tree-righteous and the chaff-wicked) motivate you to delight in God's Word?
- How does meditation—listening to God speak to us through Scripture—prepare us for prayer?
- A life of prayer requires preparation, a procedure for moving from inattention to attention. The same procedure will not suit everyone. If you do not yet have a procedure that fits your circumstances and development, how might you develop one?

↪ RESPONDING IN PRAYER

As you turn to prayer, spend careful time in preparation.

PSALM 2   *Praying Our Intimidation*

WE WAKE UP each day in a world noisy with boasting, violent with guns, arrogant with money. How can we avoid being intimidated? What use can prayer have in the face of governments and armies and millionaires? None, if God is not at work; all, if God is. God is as much at work in the public sphere as he is in the personal, and our prayers are as needful there as in our personal lives.

✎ WARMING UP TO GOD

How do you feel when you consider the needs of our world and try to pray for them? Know that God is in control. Spend time reflecting on that fact before you begin.

✎ DISCOVERING THE WORD

1. *Read Psalm 2.* Compare the opening nouns and verbs in 1:1-3 with those in 2:1-3. What differences in orientation do they suggest between these two psalms?

2. How does the Lord view the vaunted power of nations (vv. 4-6)?

3. "Anointed One" in verse 2 is a translation of the Hebrew word *Messiah*. What in this psalm reminds you of Jesus?

4. The psalm begins and ends with references to kings and rulers (vv. 2-3, 10-12). How do they relate to the King enthroned by the Lord (v. 6)?

✎ APPLYING THE WORD

• It is always easier to pray for personal needs than for political situations. But Psalm 2 is entirely political. Therefore, as citizens of Christ's kingdom, what responsibility do we have as citizens of an earthly nation?

• How does Christ's relationship with kings and rulers impact your prayers for the world?

✎ RESPONDING IN PRAYER

Think of three rulers (presidents, kings, prime ministers or dictators). Pray for them.

PSALM 3 *Praying Our Trouble*

PRAYER BEGINS IN a realization that we cannot help ourselves, so we must reach out to God. "Help!" is the basic prayer. We are in trouble, deep trouble. If God cannot get us out, we are lost; if God can get us out, we are saved. If we don't know that we need help, prayer will always be peripheral to our lives, a matter of mood and good manners. But the moment we know we are in trouble, prayer is a life-or-death matter.

✆ WARMING UP TO GOD

What is the worst trouble you were in this past week? Where did you go for help? Did you get help? God is your help. Talk to him about what you need today.

✆ DISCOVERING THE WORD

1. *Read Psalm 3. Deliver/deliverance* is a key word in this psalm. What do we learn about the nature of deliverance through its various uses here?
2. David's prayer naturally divides into verses 1-2, 3-4, 5-6 and 7-8. What progression do you see from each section to the next?
3. What actions is God described as taking in this psalm?
4. Are you used to thinking of God in these ways? Explain.
5. What actions is David described as taking in the psalm?

✆ APPLYING THE WORD

• David describes his foes in verses 1-2. Do you ever feel overwhelmed by threatening people or circumstances? Give an example.
• What kind of trouble are you in right now?
• What in this psalm do you think will help you to pray your trouble?

✆ RESPONDING IN PRAYER

Take an image or phrase from Psalm 3 and use it to pray your trouble.

PSALM 4 *Dealing with Anger*

ANGER IS AN EMOTION common to all people. Anger in itself is not sin. It is simply an emotion, a God-given part of life as a human being. Anger is a natural reaction to threats or injuries; yet it is all too often expressed in ways that spread the harm around. The Old Testament is full of references to God's righteous anger or indignation against sin, and this emotional aspect of God's character also appears in the New Testament through Christ. How can we learn to be angry without sinning?

✦ WARMING UP TO GOD

How do you generally respond when you are angry? (For example, do you talk about it or do you keep it to yourself?)

✦ DISCOVERING THE WORD

1. *Read Psalm 4.* What is David angry about (v. 2)?
2. How does David deal with his anger (vv. 1, 3)?
3. In verse 4 David suggests that we can be angry and not sin. How do you think that could be possible?
4. What do you think David means by the phrase "search your hearts and be silent" (v. 4)?

✦ APPLYING THE WORD

• How can reflecting on angry feelings be a healthy way of dealing with anger?

• How can knowing the joy of the Lord (vv. 6-7) help you deal with anger?

✦ RESPONDING IN PRAYER

Talk to God about any anger you are dealing with right now. Ask him to help you express it directly and not hold it in.

PSALM 5 *Relying on God*

FEELING BETRAYED, persecuted or fearful are common human experiences. Christians are not immune to such emotions. Indeed, because of the opposition of the fallen world to Christ, we will inevitably face them. How do we pray in these circumstances? Instead of allowing our fear or anger to dominate our thinking, we need to focus on God. Psalm 5 is one example of a prayer written in the face of opposition.

✎ WARMING UP TO GOD

What happens to your relationship with God (especially your prayer life) when you find yourself facing opposition or persecution?

✎ DISCOVERING THE WORD

1. *Read Psalm 5.* List the characteristics of the wicked and the righteous from David's descriptions in the passage.

2. When we are opposed or persecuted by others, it is easy to become aggressive. What is David's strategy for dealing with opposition?

3. David appears confident of God hearing his prayer and shielding him. What grounds are there in the passage for such confidence?

4. What does the passage show us about David's relationship with God?

5. David is clearly accustomed to beginning his day with prayer (v. 3). What are the benefits of this model?

✎ APPLYING THE WORD

- The psalm gives us a clear picture of how God opposes the wicked and deals with them. How does this help you cope with opposition or persecution on a day-to-day basis?

- Both Christians and non-Christians often blame God for the pain, suffering or persecution that they encounter. How does Psalm 5 help us to understand the pain, suffering and persecution from God's perspective?

- What aspects of David's prayer in this passage are helpful models for you?

✎ RESPONDING IN PRAYER

Think of situations that represent a threat or pressure for you. Spend some time praying about those situations, trying to focus on God's power and supremacy over the situation (while being realistic about the difficulties!).

PSALM 6

Praying Our Tears

TEARS ARE A biological gift of God. They are a physical means for express-ing emotional and spiritual experience. But it is hard to know what to do with them. If we indulge our tears, we cultivate self-pity. If we suppress our tears, we lose touch with our feelings. But if we pray our tears, we enter into sadnesses that integrate our sorrows with our Lord's sorrows, and we dis-cover both the source of and the relief from our sadness.

☞ WARMING UP TO GOD

Recall your most recent memory of crying. Was it a negative, positive or mixed experience? Why?

☞ DISCOVERING THE WORD

1. *Read Psalm 6.* Compare the first verse with the last. Are the tears because of the Lord or the enemies? Explain.

2. What is the cumulative effect of the three verbs *turn, deliver* and *save* in verse 4?

3. The emotional center of this prayer is verses 6-7. How many different ways is weeping expressed?

4. Why the tears? (Go through the psalm and note every possible source.)

5. In verses 8-9 there are three phrases in parallel: weeping, cry for mercy and prayer. Are these aspects of one thing or three different things? Ex-plain.

☞ APPLYING THE WORD

• "How long?" (v. 3) is a frequent question in prayer. Considering the fre-quency with which it is uttered in Scripture, God must welcome it. What in your life, past or present, evokes this question?

• Tears are often considered a sign that something is wrong with us—depression, unhappiness, frustration—and are therefore to be either avoided or cured. But what if they are a sign of something right with us? What rightness could they be evidence of?

☞ RESPONDING IN PRAYER

Who do you know who is in grief? Pray for them now, using phrases from Psalm 6 to express their sorrow.

PSALM 8 *Praying Our Creation*

DISORIENTATION IS A terrible experience. If we cannot locate our place, we are in confusion and anxiety. We are also in danger, for we are apt to act inappropriately. If we are among enemies and don't know it, we may lose our life. If we are among friends and don't know it, we may miss good relationships. If we are alongside a cliff and don't know it, we may lose our footing. In Psalm 8, we find out where we are and some important aspects of who we are.

✎ WARMING UP TO GOD

Recall a time you felt disoriented, like you didn't know where you were. How did you react?

✎ DISCOVERING THE WORD

1. *Read Psalm 8.* Browse through the psalm and note every word that refers to what God has created. How do these things reveal God's glory?
2. Why do you think the psalmist contrasts what children and infants say with what foes and avengers say (v. 2)?
3. What evidence do we have that God is mindful of us, that he cares for us?
4. "Ruler" and "under his feet" (v. 6) can be twisted into excuses to exploit and pillage. What is there in this psalm to prevent such twisting?

✎ APPLYING THE WORD

- How does Psalm 8 compare with the way you view yourself?
- What adjustments do you need to make to view yourself as God views you?
- Some people think of themselves as a little higher than the heavenly beings; others, a little lower than the beasts of the field. In what area has Psalm 8 corrected your self-image?

✎ RESPONDING IN PRAYER

Praise God and use this psalm as the basis for your praise.

PSALM 10 *A Prayer of Helplessness*

HELPLESSNESS IS AN experience shared by everyone. There is no way out. There are no alternatives. It is an experience full of fear, rage and despair. Because our culture places such a high value on individualism and self-reliance, the experience of helplessness is full of shame for us. We expect that others will blame us for letting it happen. And we end up blaming ourselves. In times of helplessness, however, shame and blame are not helpful. What might be helpful is to know that God understands helplessness and that he hears our prayers.

✑ WARMING UP TO GOD

Picture God in a situation with you when you felt helpless. How might God serve as your protector and defender?

✑ DISCOVERING THE WORD

1. *Read Psalm 10.* The prayer begins with the question "Why, LORD, . . . do you hide yourself?" Why is this such an urgent question when you are feeling helpless?

2. How does the author describe the person attacking him (vv. 3-11)?

3. What is the attitude of the wicked person toward God (vv. 3-4, 11)?

4. How does the writer describe the victim (vv. 2, 10, 14)?

5. How does the writer describe God and his actions on behalf of people who have been abused (vv. 12, 14-18)?

✑ APPLYING THE WORD

• Notice the author's various perspectives of God. The prayer begins with an absent God: "Why do you hide yourself?" In the middle the author risks asking God to respond on his behalf: "Arise, LORD!" The prayer ends with praise to the God who hears and defends the oppressed. Which of these perspectives of God have you experienced?

• When you feel helpless, how would it help you if you experienced God as acting on your behalf?

✑ RESPONDING IN PRAYER

How would you like God to respond to your feelings of helplessness?

PSALM 13 *A Prayer of Self-Doubt*

"WHY DID GOD let this happen?" "Was he unable to respond to my prayers?" "Was it my fault?" "Was my faith too weak?" These painful questions and the doubts they represent are difficult to discuss with other people. They can also be very difficult to share with God. Fortunately the Bible itself gives voice to these painful questions. God is not shocked by our struggles with doubt. May knowing that God is able to respond to doubt in helpful ways give you the courage to pray when your heart is full of unanswerable questions.

☞ WARMING UP TO GOD

At what times in your life have you struggled with doubt? Talk openly with God about it; he wants to know your true feelings.

☞ DISCOVERING THE WORD

1. *Read Psalm 13.* The psalmist begins with two questions that express his doubts about God. What are his concerns?

2. In verse 2 what reasons does he give for his sorrow?

3. Why is it helpful to express our doubts to God?

4. The author not only has questions about God, he also has questions about himself. He asks, "How long must I wrestle with my thoughts and every day have sorrow in my heart?" What is it about the experience of doubt that causes people to question themselves?

5. The writer ends the prayer of doubt with a statement of trust (vv. 5-6). How is it possible to doubt and trust at the same time?

☞ APPLYING THE WORD

• When is it difficult for you to follow the writer's example in expressing your doubts about God?

• How might it give you courage in your spiritual struggle to know that the Bible gives voice to doubts?

☞ RESPONDING IN PRAYER

What doubts would you like to express to God?

PSALM 15   *A Person of Honesty*

A LIE CONTAMINATES everyone close to it. Worst of all, it rots the character of the person who tells the lie.

ᴥ WARMING UP TO GOD

Reflect on the past week. How have you failed to be honest? Take your feelings to Christ. What does he have to say to you?

ᴥ DISCOVERING THE WORD

1. *Read Psalm 15.* What must a person do to be worthy to approach the Lord ("dwell in your sanctuary"; vv. 2-5)?
2. What, according to this psalm, keeps a person from being shaken?
3. What would it be like to live "on the holy hill" of the Lord?
4. When is it hard to keep a promise (v. 4)?

ᴥ APPLYING THE WORD

- How might this psalm help you to make specific choices for honesty in your dealings with other people?
- What forms of self-discipline would you recommend to someone who wanted to become more truthful?
- What help in being honest do you need?

ᴥ RESPONDING IN PRAYER

Ask God to help you to have a walk that is blameless.

PSALM 16   *Finding Balance in Life*

JOE IS A CHRISTIAN businessman. He has significant responsibility and is productive at his work. He is active in his church, helps at home with the cooking and cleaning, and enjoys spending time with his family. Joe is the Christian many of us strive to be. But does he really exist? This study is about how we can discover God's values for our lives.

✎ WARMING UP TO GOD

In what areas of your life do you struggle for balance?

✎ DISCOVERING THE WORD

1. *Read Psalm 16.* According to this passage, what has the Lord done for David?

2. What body imagery does David use to describe his relationship with God (vv. 5, 7-11)?

3. Describe the spirit of David's comments about the land in verses 5-6.

4. What is the significance of the Lord being at David's right hand (vv. 8-11)?

5. Look back through the entire passage. What is important to people who follow God?

6. How do those values contrast with worldly values?

✎ APPLYING THE WORD

• In what specific ways do you need to bring your values in line with God's values?

• What would help you to do that?

✎ RESPONDING IN PRAYER

Make thanking God for the "inheritance" he has given you a focus for prayer. Try to be aware of the different roles (counselor, protector, sustainer, refuge) God plays in your daily life.

PSALM 18:1-24   *A Prayer for Justice*

IT MAY COME as a surprise that God is angry at those who take advantage of others. God shares our anger at injustice. In the text for this study, the author suggests that God's response to the wicked is anger so intense that the earth itself trembles.

⚜ WARMING UP TO GOD

Recall a time you felt angry at injustice toward you or toward others.

⚜ DISCOVERING THE WORD

1. *Read Psalm 18:1-24.* How does David describe the distress he has experienced (vv. 4-6)?

2. What does the text say God actually does to our enemies (vv. 7-15)?

3. What does the Lord do to help David (vv. 16-19)?

4. For what reasons does God deliver David (vv. 20-24)?

⚜ APPLYING THE WORD

• How do David's feelings compare with your own?

• What thoughts and feelings do you have as you read this powerful description of God's response to a cry for help?

⚜ RESPONDING IN PRAYER

What would you like to say to the God who shares your anger about injustice and delights in you?

PSALM 18:25-50   *A Prayer for Equipping*

WRESTLERS, BOXERS and fencers know that for every move there is a move meant to block it, counterpunch or parry the thrust. So also God provides the right protection and provision for his people. Here God enables David to evade and thwart his enemies, eventually overcoming and crushing them.

✎ WARMING UP TO GOD

Think about what battles God may be leading you into and what you need to emerge victorious. Thank God that he will make every provision to help you overcome enemies and obstacles along the way.

✎ DISCOVERING THE WORD

1. *Read Psalm 18:25-50.* Previously the psalmist noted that the earth "trembled and quaked" as an expression of God's anger (v. 7). Now it's the enemies of God's people who tremble, or quake in their boots (v. 45). What has God done on David's behalf to bring this about?

2. What was David's part in securing this victory with God (vv. 25-29)?

3. In what ways did God specifically equip or provide for David (vv. 30-36)?

4. What reversal of fortune do David and the surrounding nations experience as a result of the Lord coming to his rescue (vv. 37-45)?

5. How does the conclusion of this psalm (vv. 46-50) compare with its beginning (vv. 1-6)?

6. What does that tell you about God the Warrior?

✎ APPLYING THE WORD

• At what points (feelings, circumstances, outcomes) can you identify with David?

• Think about the fights God may be preparing you for. What equipping do you need? (Where can God strengthen a particular weakness of yours? What can you praise him for already?)

✎ RESPONDING IN PRAYER

Trust God to avenge any wrongs done to you. If you have experienced God's justice in the face of evil, praise him. Recount the ways he has led and equipped you.

PSALM 19 *Comfort from Scripture*

SHARING SCRIPTURE may not always be helpful in the moment, but often it is. Psalm 19 describes what Scripture is like and how it can offer comfort.

❧ WARMING UP TO GOD

Reflect on some of your favorite words from Scripture. You may want to turn to that verse or passage and reread it. Drink in the comfort those familiar words bring.

❧ DISCOVERING THE WORD

1. *Read Psalm 19.* What does creation reveal about God (vv. 1-6)?

2. The terms *law, statutes, precepts, commands* and *ordinances* in this passage are synonyms for Scripture. In verses 7-11, how are the Scriptures described?

3. What do they do?

4. What is the overall effect of the psalmist's encounter with God through nature and the Scriptures (vv. 12-14)?

❧ APPLYING THE WORD

- From which of the effects of Scripture listed in verses 7-11 have you benefited?

- How has this psalm been helpful to you by offering insight or comfort?

- Sharing Scripture can be done in three ways. The first and most obvious way is sharing a passage or verse directly. The second is sharing how we have been affected or changed by Scripture. The third is simply living out the principles of Scripture. How might you appropriately and effectively share Scripture with someone in need this week?

❧ RESPONDING IN PRAYER

Ask God to make Scripture alive and active in you this week. Pray that he will help you share his Word, either directly or through actions, with someone in need.

PSALM 22 *A Prayer of Anguish*

THE PRAYER OF anguish in Psalm 22 parallels the experience of Jesus, who spoke it from the cross. No other psalm is quoted as often in the New Testament. Persecuted saints and lonely Christians ever since have used this prayer to draw near to God at times when they felt most abandoned.

✍ WARMING UP TO GOD

Think back on an experience you never want to have again. How does remembering it make you feel?

✍ DISCOVERING THE WORD

1. *Read Psalm 22.* David did not shrink back from asking tough "why" questions. Neither did Jesus in quoting verse 1 (Mt 27:46; Mk 15:34). What were David and Jesus experiencing at the time they prayed this prayer (vv. 1-2, 6-8)?

2. Being abandoned by friends and surrounded by enemies can feel all the more stark in contrast to one's history of being close to God and his people. What kind of relationship have this psalmist and his people enjoyed with their God (vv. 3-5, 9-10)?

3. What are his attackers like (vv. 12-18)?

4. What does David pray for (vv. 11, 19-21)?

5. In anticipating God's deliverance, what does the psalmist vow (vv. 22, 25)?

6. Who joins him in this chorus of praise, and why (vv. 23, 26-31)?

✍ APPLYING THE WORD

• This psalm uses images of sword fights, bullfights, dog fights and a lion's den. What contemporary scenes of violence does it conjure up for you?

• The Gospel writers applied this psalm to Jesus (see Mt 27:35, 39, 43, 46). In what ways does Psalm 22 fit the circumstances of Jesus' crucifixion?

• At what points can you identify with the psalmist or with Jesus?

✍ RESPONDING IN PRAYER

Pour out your anguish before God, as he will listen to your cry for help. Trust God to deliver you from physical circumstances and emotional moods that cause you to feel forsaken. Remember what God has done for you in the past, and join others in praising God for what he will do in the future.

PSALM 23   *Praying Our Fear*

THE WORLD IS a fearsome place. If we manage, with the help of parents, teachers and friends, to survive the dangers of infancy and childhood, we find ourselves launched into an adult world that is ringed with terror: accident, assault, disease, violence, conflicts. Prayer brings fear into focus and faces it. But prayer does more than bravely face fear; it affirms God's presence in it.

✺ WARMING UP TO GOD

Spend some time trying to bring your fears into focus. Know that God is with you in the midst of your fear.

✺ DISCOVERING THE WORD

1. *Read Psalm 23.* There are two large metaphors in this psalm: the shepherd (vv. 1-4) and the host (vv. 5-6). Compare and contrast these two images.

2. Look carefully at the shepherd. How exactly does he care for his sheep (vv. 1-4)?

3. "I will fear no evil" (v. 4) is a bold statement. What does it mean for you to say that?

4. Look carefully at the host. How exactly does he provide for his guest (vv. 5-6)?

✺ APPLYING THE WORD

• Enemies are prominent in the psalm prayers and appear here. Who are your enemies?

• What is the most comforting thing you have experienced in the life of faith?

• Psalm 23 is a weapon against fear. What fear in your life will you go to war against with this prayer as your cannon?

✺ RESPONDING IN PRAYER

Name your fears and ask Christ the Shepherd and Christ the Host to relieve them.

PSALM 24 *A Prayer of Ascension*

DAVID MAY HAVE composed Psalm 24 on the occasion of bringing the ark of the covenant back to Jerusalem or in commemoration of that historic event. This prayer by worshipers ascending to Mount Zion has long been used by the church to celebrate Christ's ascension to the heavenly Jerusalem, paving the way for others to follow and stand in God's holy presence. Psalm 24 affirms that Jerusalem is the royal site for inaugurating the kingdom of God.

✧ WARMING UP TO GOD

What is the longest journey or pilgrimage you have made? What was arriving like for you?

✧ DISCOVERING THE WORD

1. *Read Psalm 24.* Verses 1-2 echo themes from creation in reference to the founding of a city and the temple. What feelings and images does that backdrop evoke for this worshiper?

2. What kind of person may enter the Lord's sanctuary (vv. 3-6)?

3. Do these restrictions render the temple accessible to the public, only to priests or to the one and only King?

4. Who is this "King of glory," and how is he described (v. 7)?

5. What glorious things has he done as Lord of creation (vv. 1-2) and God of Jacob (v. 6)?

✧ APPLYING THE WORD

• What steps in preparation for worship does this psalm conjure up for you?

• Paul quotes verse 1, which had become a Jewish blessing at mealtimes, to underscore the believer's freedom to eat meat without a troubled conscience (1 Cor 10:25-26). What new freedoms does knowing the sovereignty of God, affirmed in Psalm 24, give you?

✧ RESPONDING IN PRAYER

Prepare yourself to meet God's standards of acceptance: pure motives, integrity, trusting totally in God to vindicate you. Then lift up the gates and doors of your life, with thanksgiving and praise, to let the King into your worship.

PSALM 25   *Integrity in Times of Doubt*

PHILIP YANCEY, in his book *Disappointment with God,* tells the story of a new and enthusiastic convert to the Christian faith. When Richard's parents separated, he prayed constantly that God would bring them back together. Then he lost an important job. Then his fiancée jilted him. And his health began to deteriorate.

One night Richard stayed up all night to pray. For four hours he pleaded with God to reveal himself. Finally Richard lit a fire and burned up his Bible and his theology textbooks—and his faith.

Why? As Yancey said, "The theology he had learned in school . . . no longer *worked for him.*" Is faith in God good only as long as it "works"?

◄ WARMING UP TO GOD

When you are in a difficult situation, what kind of things are you likely to say to God?

◄ DISCOVERING THE WORD

1. *Read Psalm 25.* Psalm 25 divides into four stanzas (vv. 1-3, 4-7, 8-15, 16-22). Give a topic-title to each.

2. What does it mean to "lift up" your soul to God (v. 1)?

3. Study stanza 2. What all does David ask God to do?

4. David began his prayer by saying he trusted God. In what ways does stanza 3 show that God has integrity—and therefore ought to be trusted?

5. Study stanza 4. What words and phrases here help you to understand David's current situation?

6. Compare David's position in stanza 4 with what he hopes from God (vv. 12-13). What does David's prayer say about his own integrity?

◄ APPLYING THE WORD

• Three times David uses the term *remember.* What would you want God to remember (and not remember) about you?

• What do you count on God to do and to be?

◄ RESPONDING IN PRAYER

Before you pray, meditate on God's character as David did. Ask God to make you a person of integrity.

PSALM 27 *Waiting for the Lord*

ONE OF SAMUEL BECKETT'S most famous plays is titled *Waiting for Godot*. Throughout the play the characters wait and wait for Godot to appear, but he never does. The play is Beckett's way of saying that hope is futile—especially hope in God. In contrast to Beckett's despair, the Bible offers hope to the sufferer. When we feel overwhelmed and ready to give up, Psalm 27 encourages us to "wait for the LORD." When we see no possibility of relief, David assures us, "I am still confident of this: I will see the goodness of the LORD in the land of the living" (v. 13).

ᗧ Warming Up to God

In what kinds of situations do you find it hardest to wait?

ᗧ Discovering the Word

1. *Read Psalm 27.* Why is David able to be fearless in the face of evil people, armies and even war (vv. 1-3)?

2. What images of safety does David apply to the Lord in verses 1-2 and 5-6?

3. David seeks not only the Lord's protection but also the Lord himself (v. 4). How is David's intense desire for God revealed in this psalm (vv. 4, 8, 11)?

4. David's confident statements about the Lord (vv. 1-6) lead up to his prayer in verses 7-12. What is the substance of his prayer?

5. What real dangers does he seem to be facing?

6. Why must your hope not only be confident but also patient (v. 14)?

ᗧ Applying the Word

• How does it give you hope to know that the Lord is your stronghold (or "mighty fortress") during battle and your shelter from life's storms?

• The psalm ends as it begins—with David's confidence in the Lord's help (vv. 13-14). How can David's view of God help you to "be strong and take heart" in the midst of suffering?

ᗧ Responding in Prayer

Ask God to strengthen your confidence in his promises and to make you patient as you wait for his answers.

PSALM 29   *The Voice of the Lord*

WHAT ARE THE ways God chooses to speak to us? He uses the counsel of friends or the subtlety of our own conscience, and often he uses his own Word. But sometimes he speaks so that he can be heard loud and clear, and so that no one can be mistaken about what he is saying. This passage explores the ways we hear the voice of the Lord.

✒ WARMING UP TO GOD

Recall a time you felt God was speaking to you specifically. Thank him for coming to you. Ask him now to speak to your listening heart.

✒ DISCOVERING THE WORD

1. *Read Psalm 29.* The psalmist addresses a specific audience in verse 1: "mighty ones." Why do you think he speaks to them?

2. David urges his audience to "ascribe to the LORD glory and strength" (v. 1). How does his psalm accomplish this?

3. What does "the voice of the LORD" do (vv. 3-9)?

4. What characteristics of God do these verses bring to mind?

5. What does verse 9 tell us about the proper response to hearing the voice of God?

6. Most of Psalm 29 describes the actions of God as a mighty and powerful rainstorm, inspiring not only awe but even fear. However, the psalm ends describing the actions of God in quite a different fashion (v. 11). How does this complete the picture of God that David has painted?

✒ APPLYING THE WORD

- How does observing the power of God both in nature and in his actions help us understand the nature and role of worship in our lives?

- Sometimes God uses a storm to draw our attention to him, but he also "blesses his people with peace" (v. 11). How can this passage help you to better understand the ways of God and his workings in your life?

✒ RESPONDING IN PRAYER

Take some time to "ascribe to the LORD" some of the marvelous deeds he has done for you.

PSALM 30 *Waiting for Security*

MAJOR CORPORATIONS are laying off large numbers in the latest rage of downsizing. Those who have gotten a pink slip do their best to cover it, but you can see the pain in their eyes. One of our basic human needs is security. In the end, if our security in any area is dependent on our own resources and abilities, then we must live in constant vigilance. How much better if the Creator of the universe were in charge of protecting us! In this psalm David relates the experience of looking to God for his security. He found it both a humbling and a thrilling experience.

✎ WARMING UP TO GOD

Sit for a while in silence. What are your thoughts and impressions?

✎ DISCOVERING THE WORD

1. *Read Psalm 30.* No one knows what the problem was, but from the words *depths, healed, enemies, grave* and *pit,* what dangers may David have been facing?

2. Read the whole psalm again. List the range of emotions that is described.

3. What insight into life does David gain by acknowledging that painful as well as pleasurable experiences come from God (v. 5)?

4. How do verses 6-7 describe David's sense of dependence on God?

5. What reasons does David present to God in favor of his deliverance (vv. 9-10)?

6. Look over the entire psalm. How would you describe David's relationship with God?

✎ APPLYING THE WORD

- Difficult circumstances can cause us to reflect on the character of God. How have your life circumstances affected your relationship with God?

- David expresses some of the ups and downs of his life. Consider the past six months to year of your life and chart your ups and downs.

- Picture the Lord with you through those ups and downs. How does it help you to know that God is with you?

✎ RESPONDING IN PRAYER

Give thanks for the ways God has helped you in the hard places of your life.

PSALM 31 *Rescued from Idolaters*

WE LIVE IN A turbulent time. While the turbulence created by clashing belief systems seems new, the clash has been going on in different forms for thousands of years. In this psalm David affirms his choice to trust in the Lord rather than in the popular idols of his age. In the current culture war we need to do the same.

❧ WARMING UP TO GOD

Make a list of everything you have to do, and give it over to God. If God blesses you with a sense of peace, just sit for a while and enjoy his presence before you move on to study.

❧ DISCOVERING THE WORD

1. *Read Psalm 31.* This is a psalm of urgency. What does David want from God (vv. 1-4)?
2. David feels threatened. What words does he use in these verses to describe his plight?
3. What words and ideas in verses 9-13 convey David's sense of isolation?
4. According to verses 14-18, what are several of the things David wants from God?
5. David's response to God's help is praise. What specific things does David praise God for?

❧ APPLYING THE WORD

- Consider a time in your life when you felt that others (perhaps non-Christians) held you in contempt and avoided you. How did it affect you?
- What was your relationship with God like at that time?
- What encouragement from God do you need to continue in a harsh world?

❧ RESPONDING IN PRAYER

Tell God that you trust him with the "times" of your life. Ask him to make himself known in new ways to you and your family.

PSALM 32   *Confession and Forgiveness*

JUST AS CHOLESTEROL is the silent killer of the physical heart, guilt is the silent killer of our souls. Cholesterol accumulates slowly over the years, residue left by a poor diet, inadequate exercise and perhaps genetics. So it is with guilt. Little by little, with each act of envy, lust, anger, resentment or other sin, guilt accumulates around our spiritual hearts. The good news is that God won't let us succumb to guilt without many warnings. The exposure of guilt is not for the purpose of condemnation (as it is with Satan) but for cleansing our hearts and restoring the flow of his love.

✺ WARMING UP TO GOD

What is causing you to feel frustrated or envious or resentful today? Give your feelings over to God one by one.

✺ DISCOVERING THE WORD

1. *Read Psalm 32.* Verses 1 and 2 begin with the word *blessed.* How would you define *blessed* from the way David uses it in these verses?

2. David had a responsive conscience. How did his unexpressed sin affect him (vv. 3-4)?

3. It feels good to be forgiven. How does David respond in verses 6-11?

4. It is interesting that David experienced a sense of protection after receiving forgiveness (v. 7). How might unconfessed sin have made him feel vulnerable and exposed?

5. In verses 8-9 David records the Lord's promise of guidance. From these verses, what is the condition for receiving God's guidance?

✺ APPLYING THE WORD

• Consider whether there are things in the past for which you are guilty but have never sought forgiveness. Name those things.

• Are there things you feel guilty about though there was really no wrong done? Explain.

✺ RESPONDING IN PRAYER

Ask God's forgiveness for what you have done wrong, and experience his grace.

PSALM 33

Hoping in the Word

THE WORDS THAT God has spoken are never outdated. In Psalm 33 David meditates on the powerful Word of God by which God creates and sustains his world. Because of the nature of God's Word, we need to open our ears to hear as we read to understand.

❧ WARMING UP TO GOD

In order to spend time with God today—stop! Don't try to run your own life, and don't tell God what to do. Present your life to God. Ask God to bring in his order.

❧ DISCOVERING THE WORD

1. *Read Psalm 33.* What is the emotional tone of this psalm?
2. The word of the Lord is one of the themes of this psalm. What can you learn about God's Word from verses 1-11?
3. This psalm gives a big picture of God. Other nations thought of their gods as national deities with limited realms of authority. Over what things does Israel's God have power (vv. 6-11)?
4. According to verses 12-22, what is God's relationship to the world he created?
5. What is his special relationship with "those who fear him" (vv. 18-22)?

❧ APPLYING THE WORD

- Imagine that God watched you conduct your day from beginning to end. What would he see about your actions?
- How do they express your priorities, values and commitments?
- What hopes for success do you have that are misdirected? (Consider whether you are trusting in your skills, your background, your education, your intelligence, your money, your influence, your friends . . . or a thousand other things.)

❧ RESPONDING IN PRAYER

After you have identified your false hopes, turn them over to God. Ask him to take them from you.

PSALM 34 *Deliverance from Trouble*

DAVID WRITES PSALM 34 for the spiritually immature, who need to be instructed in the ways of God. How do we face hard times? When we hurt, we want to know if we have done something wrong. Has God deserted us? What do we need to do to receive God's help? These are good questions. If we pay attention to David, we will get some answers.

✎ WARMING UP TO GOD

List questions you have for God. Don't tell him what to do, just ask. Then sit quietly for a while and listen.

✎ DISCOVERING THE WORD

1. *Read Psalm 34.* What words does David use in verses 1-10 to express his feelings toward God?

2. What benefits are mentioned in verses 1-10 that come to those who seek God's help?

3. What do you think David means by inviting his readers to "taste and see that the LORD is good" (v. 8)?

4. From verses 11-22, describe a righteous person.

5. According to what David writes, righteousness doesn't guarantee a trouble-free life. What assurances of comfort do the righteous have during times of pain?

✎ APPLYING THE WORD

• How can the goodness of God be a means of strength in the problems you face?

• "Fear of the LORD" is an Old Testament term for respect and submission to God. We should be afraid of offending God with conscious acts of disobedience. What temptations are you facing now?

• How can learning the fear of the Lord keep you acting and thinking righteously?

✎ RESPONDING IN PRAYER

Ask God to increase your ability to "taste and see" that he is with you and that he is good.

PSALM 35   *Protection from My Enemies*

YOU MIGHT BE tempted to see Psalm 35 as barbaric and primitive. It contains angry thoughts of revenge. David feels hurt and the anger pours forth in an eloquent torrent. There is no sense of "I'm not supposed to feel this way." Christian maturity is not about reducing the highs and lows of emotions to a level plane, but of feeling deeply in a godly way. The issue is not how or what we feel, but what we do with our emotions. David shows the way.

✑ WARMING UP TO GOD

Those who know God hunger for him. Before you begin your study, allow a desire for God to rise within you.

✑ DISCOVERING THE WORD

1. *Read Psalm 35.* In your own words describe the different kinds of misfortune David would like to see inflicted on those who have hurt him (vv. 4-6, 8, 26).

2. What reasons does David give for being so hurt and angry (vv. 4, 7, 11-16, 19-21)?

3. What do verses 11-16 reveal about David's enemies?

4. What does the cry "How long will you look on?" (v. 17) imply about David's sense of God's help?

5. David continues with the description of his adversaries' behavior. What have his enemies done in verses 19-28 to hurt him?

✑ APPLYING THE WORD

• We may not feel gracious toward those who hurt us, but we choose to act that way, not from feelings but from obedience to Jesus Christ. Who do you feel hostility and anger toward?

• When we come through a trying experience with a sense of victory, it is natural to think about what a good job we have done and how cleverly we have faced our problems. David, however, avoids the temptation of personal boasting and gives praise to God. How does waiting on the Lord for help keep us from taking credit that belongs to God?

✑ RESPONDING IN PRAYER

Ask God to bless those who have hurt you.

PSALM 36   *The Fountain of the Lord's Love*

OUR NEED FOR love means we need people—friends, spouses, family members. However, even if all those people loved us perfectly, we still wouldn't have enough love to meet our need. David celebrates the good news that God's supply of love is more than sufficient. God's love reaches to the heavens and has more substance than the biggest mountains.

☜ WARMING UP TO GOD

Consider how open you are to receiving love from God, your family, friends and fellow Christians. Ask God to soften your heart. Give over to God any hardening factors that you can discern.

☜ DISCOVERING THE WORD

1. *Read Psalm 36.* Describe the character of a wicked person from verses 1-4.
2. Describe the dynamics of a wicked person's relationship to God.
3. What decisions does a wicked person make that lead to a sinful life (vv. 2-4)?
4. David observes that there is no fear of the Lord before the eyes of the wicked (v. 1). From verses 5-9, what is it that they are blind to?
5. David seems to jump abruptly from musing on the wicked to writing on the love of God. However, in verses 10-12 he ties the two themes together. What do these verses tell you about David's experiences?

☜ APPLYING THE WORD

- We all have sinful thoughts from time to time. The wicked, however, do not reject such thoughts. Instead they choose to entertain them and then make a commitment to act on them. What are some thoughts you have chosen to reject recently because you knew they were wrong?
- Consider your own ability to accept the Lord's love and his benefits. What hesitations do you have about the Lord's love for you?
- What would have to happen for you to be more open to his love?

☜ RESPONDING IN PRAYER

Give thanks to God that he has been so active in helping you choose what is right. If you have let some ungodly ideas settle in your heart, ask God to cleanse and redirect your thinking patterns.

PSALM 37:1-17 *The Peace of the Lord*

DAVID SAYS THAT for us to enjoy peace in the land we have to "refrain from anger and turn from wrath" (v. 8). If you pay attention to what he says, then you will find a new way of coping with anger.

❧ WARMING UP TO GOD

The first step in receiving God's peace is to stop shouting so loud. (If we aren't actually shouting out loud, we are usually doing so in our hearts.) Once we stop, he can sort things out. Put down the burdens and fights you face. Give them to God and allow him to speak peace to your heart.

❧ DISCOVERING THE WORD

1. *Read Psalm 37:1-17.* David gives an unusually extensive list of exhortations to his readers in verses 1-7. List them in your own words.

2. What benefits does God give to those who live this way?

3. We are not to worry when those who are evil succeed (v. 6). Why not?

4. What are the contrasts between the righteous and the wicked in verses 8-17?

5. Against the backdrop of the wicked, how is God's promise of peace and land an encouragement?

❧ APPLYING THE WORD

- David encourages you to "delight yourself in the LORD" (v. 4). What do you find delightful about knowing God?

- What hesitations do you have that would keep you from delighting in God?

❧ RESPONDING IN PRAYER

Pray for those who are angry with you. Ask God to bless them.

PSALM 37:18-40   *Our Inheritance*

PSALM 37 IS written from David's perspective of knowing God for more than eighty years. David affirms that God keeps his promises and brings rewards to those who trust him.

❦ Warming Up to God

Consider the staggering fact that the Creator of time and eternity loves you. Write down ten things you can think of about the love of God.

❦ Discovering the Word

1. *Read Psalm 37:18-40.* What are the contrasts between the blameless and the wicked in verses 18-24?

2. What can we know about the future of the wicked (vv. 20, 22, 28, 33-35)?

3. What are the benefits that come to the righteous in the end (vv. 18, 25, 28-29, 33, 37, 39-40)?

4. From verses 25-36, describe the character and actions of the righteous.

5. Describe the relationship between the wicked and the righteous in verses 32-40.

❦ Applying the Word

- David emphasizes the theme of inheritance in these verses. How can the anticipation of a future inheritance affect the way you live today in your relationships and the way you use your money and your possessions?

- If you knew that all you could want would be coming to you in five years, how would it affect your actions and decisions today?

❦ Responding in Prayer

Pray for those you know who are facing hard times. Ask God to bring his comfort, protection and provision.

PSALM 38   *Rebuke and Judgment*

IF I AM WILLING to acknowledge that God blesses me, I must be willing to acknowledge that he disciplines me as well. As the author of Hebrews writes, "the Lord disciplines those he loves" (12:6). God refuses to let me go my own way. This is good news indeed!

At the same time, when I talk about the blessing or the judgment of God, I must be careful. I don't understand all that the Lord does. What appears to be a blessing may not be, while what appears to be judgment may not be either. Let's see if we can gain a little light on this difficult issue from David.

✑ WARMING UP TO GOD

Make a list of thank-yous to God for as many instances of his help as you can think of.

✑ DISCOVERING THE WORD

1. *Read Psalm 38.* David writes during a time of great pain. What images does he use to describe his situation (vv. 2-14)?

2. What reasons can you discover for his all-encompassing pain in these verses?

3. What physical, social and spiritual afflictions is David experiencing in these verses?

4. Describe David's attitude toward God in the midst of his afflictions.

5. What specific things does David want God to do to help him with his pain (vv. 15-16, 21-22)?

✑ APPLYING THE WORD

- What dangers and what benefits come from thinking of our physical, emotional and spiritual states as being the result of the discipline of God?

- Although David is experiencing rejection and persecution, he acknowledges that he shares in the responsibility for his affliction. When have you experienced pain that was at least partly your fault? How did you handle it?

- What can you learn from David's example?

✑ RESPONDING IN PRAYER

Pray for those whom you have offended this past year. Ask for God's blessing on them.

PSALM 39   *Facing Life's End*

JANE WALMSLEY, television correspondent and commentator on American life, says that an essential element of the American psyche is the fervent belief and hope that somehow it is possible to elude death. That hope flies in the face of reality. David would say that only those who have faced their death can really live life properly. In this psalm he asks God to help him take a long-term view of life and, as you shall read, that includes the prospect of impending death.

ᴄ᷍ᴼ WARMING UP TO GOD

While we can never quite get our minds around this, the good news is that an eternal God can offer eternal life. Express praise and thanksgiving to our immortal God.

ᴄ᷍ᴼ DISCOVERING THE WORD

1. *Read Psalm 39.* Remembering that the psalms combine life experience, knowledge of God and emotions, how would you describe David's mood and situation in this psalm?

2. David chooses to be silent in the presence of some hostile people. What effect does his silence have on him in verses 1-6?

3. When David breaks his silence, he offers a prayer to face his mortality. What does he want to know (v. 4), and what does he know (vv. 5-6)?

4. This is a psalm of judgment. In your own words describe God's approach toward sin in verses 7-13.

5. What does David desire from God for himself (vv. 8, 10)?

6. At the end of this passage, how does David come to terms with his death?

ᴄ᷍ᴼ APPLYING THE WORD

• How does considering your own mortality affect the way you think of the present and the future, your possessions and your relationships?

• How does the knowledge of eternal life affect your reflections?

ᴄ᷍ᴼ RESPONDING IN PRAYER

Following David's example, ask God to help you to see as much about your own mortality as you can handle. Sit quietly and wait for the Lord's insight. Write down what benefits you can perceive from facing your own death.

PSALM 40   *Learning to Wait on the Lord*

JUDY HAD A CELL phone beside her. Her son's wife was expecting, and Judy was about to become a grandmother for the first time. During the entire Bible study, Judy contributed to the discussion. However, if that phone had rung with news of her daughter-in-law's labor, Judy would have been out of there in a minute. Just as Judy was prepared to receive a call and ready to respond when it came, so we should be waiting on the Lord.

ᙦ WARMING UP TO GOD

Jesus calls his disciples to deny themselves, take up their cross and follow him. Commit yourself, body and soul, to him. As reservations or objections rise to the surface, ask Jesus to take them from you.

ᙦ DISCOVERING THE WORD

1. *Read Psalm 40.* In response to God's help, David proclaims righteousness, doesn't seal his lips, doesn't hide God's righteousness and does not conceal God's love. From your reading of verses 1-10, what is he eager to make known?

2. Compare verses 1-10 with verses 11-17. How does the tone differ?

3. Put into your own words David's description of life's dilemma. What effect does it have on him?

4. David begins by saying he waited patiently. He concludes by asking that God not delay. What do patience and the need for a speedy answer contribute to your understanding of what it means to wait on God?

ᙦ APPLYING THE WORD

- Waiting in a slimy pit—what a graphic picture of needing God's help! Imagine you are in a pit from which you need deliverance. What things in your life have placed you in that pit, and what makes it "slimy"?

- As you call out for God to deliver you, what is it like to wait on God?

- Imagine that you knew Jesus Christ was coming back in one week. How would you spend your week waiting?

ᙦ RESPONDING IN PRAYER

Pray for your loved ones who don't yet have a relationship with Jesus Christ. Ask the Spirit to give them hungry hearts for his love.

PSALMS 42—43 *Hoping in the Lord*

THE AUTHOR OF Psalms 42—43 was a musician who used to lead worshipers to the temple in Jerusalem. But now the temple of God lies in ruins; the fields and vineyards are burned, and this former spiritual leader sits six hundred miles away—an exile in Babylon. The psalmist grieves over his circumstances. Like the other holy people of his era, he had linked drawing near to God with going up to God's temple. How could he worship God now? And, as his taunters reminded him, where is God anyway?

✑ WARMING UP TO GOD

When is it hard for you to worship God? Talk honestly with God about your struggles.

✑ DISCOVERING THE WORD

1. *Read Psalm 42—43.* A refrain for these psalms is found in 42:5, 11, and 43:5. What in this refrain makes it important enough to repeat?

2. The psalmist speaks honestly and openly to God. What words does he use to tell how he is feeling?

3. Why might the psalmist's honest words with God about his past and his present help to strengthen his faith?

4. Not all of what the psalmist says is about himself and his past. He also focuses on God. What aspects of God's character does he acknowledge (42:5, 8-9; 43:2, 3)?

5. How might a firm belief in a God of this character bring hope—even to an ancient Hebrew in exile?

✑ APPLYING THE WORD

• What kinds of things are likely to throw you into depression?

• What do you talk about with God and others when you are depressed?

• Based on this psalm, when depression comes, what measures can you take to begin to cope with it?

✑ RESPONDING IN PRAYER

Ask God to help you understand your own feelings of depression. Ask him to help you focus on him and to more readily turn to him, both with your own depression and with that of a troubled friend.

PSALM 44 *A Prayer When God Is Silent*

WHAT DO WE DO when God is silent? Do we withdraw in fear? Do we give up all hope? This is certainly our temptation. Psalm 44 shows us another way. It opens the way for us to pursue God even when he is silent.

❧ WARMING UP TO GOD

Think of a time when a friend did not respond to a letter or a phone message for a long time. What was your reaction to your friend's silence?

❧ DISCOVERING THE WORD

1. *Read Psalm 44.* How does the writer contrast God in the past (vv. 1-8) with God in the present (vv. 9-16)?
2. The psalmist argues with God that the situation he and his people find themselves in is not fair. How does he express this (vv. 17-22)?
3. What is the significance of this plea for fairness and justice?
4. The psalmist summarizes his accusations of God in verses 23-24. What does he accuse God of?
5. In the final phrase of the psalm (v. 26), the writer appeals to God's "unfailing love." This is a dramatic contrast to the accusations he has just made. How can these views of God be reconciled?

❧ APPLYING THE WORD

- Think of a time when it seemed God was silent. How did your experience at that time compare with the experiences described in this psalm?
- Think of a time when you experienced God's unfailing love. How would you describe that experience?
- What encouragement does this psalm offer you for times when God seems silent?

❧ RESPONDING IN PRAYER

Ask God to help you to understand his ways and grant you peace when you are waiting for his voice.

PSALM 45   *A Wedding Song*

THE EXCITEMENT OF a wedding day! A bride in beautiful gowns, an abundance of sweet-smelling flowers, a nervous grooms waiting in the wings for the bride to make her entrance—all are overflowing with a sense of expectancy that fills the air. The reason behind all of the extravagance, beyond the legal joining of two individuals together, is to celebrate a wonderful event and to capture it as something to remember for all time. This psalm is a celebration, both for the joy of the day and for the joy that is still to come.

❧ WARMING UP TO GOD

God is a powerful judge and the Creator who flung the stars into space. But he also knows and loves you and became your Savior. Let this knowledge fill you with peace as you look to the words of God.

❧ DISCOVERING THE WORD

1. *Read Psalm 45.* Psalm 45 is a wedding song celebrating the marriage of a king of David's dynasty to a foreign princess. Twice in the psalm the poet refers to himself. What does he say are his purposes for writing (vv. 1, 17)?

2. What are the characteristics of this king?

3. How could these verses (particularly 6-7) refer to more than David's reign?

4. Verses 6 and 7 are quoted in Hebrews 1 to describe the reign of Jesus Christ. How could the description of the king in this passage be applied to Christ?

5. What are the characteristics of the bride, and what is the attitude surrounding her coming (vv. 10-16)?

❧ APPLYING THE WORD

• We are Christ's bride. What promises do you see for yourself in this passage?

• What kind of response does seeing the majesty of Christ cause in your own life?

❧ RESPONDING IN PRAYER

Thank God that your heart has been "stirred by a noble theme"—the promises of the King coming for his bride. Praise him for his majesty and the overwhelming awe that you feel because he has chosen you to be his bride.

PSALM 46 *Still Point in a Turning World*

MARTIN LUTHER'S famous hymn "A Mighty Fortress Is Our God" is based on Psalm 46. This psalm celebrates Jerusalem as the city of God, the sure foundation for the kingdom of God. Today we can find spiritual strength and security in this psalm, especially when everything else is so topsy-turvy.

✎ WARMING UP TO GOD

Recall a time of loss, tragedy or high anxiety. What got you through it?

✎ DISCOVERING THE WORD

1. *Read Psalm 46.* This psalm readily falls into three stanzas (vv. 1-3, 4-6, 8-10) plus two refrains, or chorus lines (vv. 7, 11). What themes emerge in each section?

2. What images of a world falling apart do you see in these verses?

3. What truth about God in contrast to the world is conveyed here?

4. What effect does God's triumph over the nations have on the people who draw their strength from him (vv. 8-10)?

5. Where does one find stillness and security in the midst of violent forces unleashed all around (vv. 10-11)?

✎ APPLYING THE WORD

• What in your life is threatening or pounding away at your sense of security in God?

• How can you remain still (v. 10) and know God's fortresslike strength (vv. 7, 11) in the midst of a world falling apart?

✎ RESPONDING IN PRAYER

As God has triumphed, and will triumph, over all that wars against the city of Jerusalem and the soul of the believer, how can you exalt him among the nations? Spend some time being still and centering on him.

PSALM 47   *Being Devoted to God*

THE SIGN OF a spiritually healthy heart is gratitude and affection. You will discover that after you have spent time with God, there rises from within your heart a deep sense of gratitude. Galatians 4:6 says, "Because you are sons, God sent the Spirit of his Son into our hearts, the Spirit who calls out, 'Abba, Father.'" We can actually sense the Spirit within us as he cries, "Abba, Father."

ᏝᎦ WARMING UP TO GOD

Make a list of things you are thankful for. While you may not be able to express gratitude right now, it will come in time if you continue to walk in this inner spiritual pilgrimage. If you do feel gratitude, sit for a while in heartfelt thanks to God.

ᏝᎦ DISCOVERING THE WORD

1. *Read Psalm 47.* What is the psalmist thankful for (vv. 2-4)?
2. How is God described in each verse?
3. What is revealed about God's relationship with the people?
4. What actions of joy and gratitude do you see in these verses (vv. 1, 5-7)?

ᏝᎦ APPLYING THE WORD

- How would you feel using the same outward expressions of joy as the psalmist?
- The psalmist sings, claps, sacrifices and invites others to share in his joy in God. What ways can you outwardly show your joy in the Lord?
- The Holy Spirit within us is continually offering praise. If you can, allow yourself to join the Spirit in praise. Try to write a psalm to the Lord, including in it reasons you enjoy knowing God. If you haven't come to the place of heartfelt worship, don't try to generate what you don't feel. You might want to sing a song or hymn that you can sing with meaning. Or perhaps play some recorded music that reflects your mood.

ᏝᎦ RESPONDING IN PRAYER

Ask God to give you the courage to walk in honesty until he brings you into the place of inner praise.

PSALM 50 *Offering Thanks*

"HOW ARE YOU?" we ask, and the response generally comes back, "Fine." Often we follow that with the question "Been busy?" and the answer is invariably yes. We live in a culture of busyness, and sometimes that overlaps into our Christian lives. We can become so busy working for God, doing good deeds, that we don't have time to offer him our praise and thanksgiving. This psalm helps us to get our focus back to the fact that we are created to worship God.

ᕦ WARMING UP TO GOD

Recall a time you got caught up in the things you do for God to the extent that you neglected worshiping him.

ᕦ DISCOVERING THE WORD

1. *Read Psalm 50.* How is God described in verses 1-6?
2. God does not say that sacrifices are wrong (v. 8), but what does he want the people to understand about their offerings to him (vv. 9-15)?
3. How does the tone of the psalm change in verses 16-22?
4. What evil deeds have the wicked done (vv. 16-22)?
5. How would "thank offerings" help them to understand salvation (vv. 14-15, 23)?

ᕦ APPLYING THE WORD

- What would a "thank offering" to God look like for you?
- God promised that we can call on him "in the day of trouble" and he will deliver us (v. 15). In what way would you like to call on God today?

ᕦ RESPONDING IN PRAYER

Make your prayers an offering of praise and thanksgiving for God's work in your life.

PSALM 51   *Praying Our Sin*

ALONGSIDE THE BASIC fact that God made us good (Ps 8) is the equally basic fact that we have gone wrong. We pray our sins to get to the truth about ourselves and to find out how God treats sinners. Our experience of sin does not consist in doing some bad things but in being bad. It is a fundamental condition of our existence, not a temporary lapse into error. Praying our sin isn't resolving not to sin anymore; it is discovering what God has resolved to do with us as sinners.

☙ WARMING UP TO GOD

As Christians, we know we are sinful. Why then is it so painful to be confronted with a specific sin? What sin have you been avoiding talking to God about? Take it to God and experience his forgiveness.

☙ DISCOVERING THE WORD

1. *Read Psalm 51.* List the different synonyms for sin in David's prayer.
2. What is God asked to do about sin? (Count and name the verbs.)
3. Verse 10 is the center sentence. How does it center the prayer?
4. Forgiveness is an internal action with external consequences. What are some of them (vv. 13-17)?
5. What do you understand a "broken and contrite heart" to be (v. 17)?
6. According to verses 18-19, what is the relationship between personal forgiveness and social righteousness?

☙ APPLYING THE WORD

• When have you had a "broken and contrite heart"?
• Psalm 51 makes us aware of how sinful we are, and it makes us less actively sinful. How do you see it working that way in you?

☙ RESPONDING IN PRAYER

Be quiet before God. In silence confess your sins to him. Accept his forgiveness and grace.

PSALM 55   *Expressing Feelings to God*

LEARNING TO EXPRESS our feelings to God is not easy. The passionate, emotionally unrestrained prayers of the Bible may not be the kind we grew up with. We may find, in fact, that the prayers of the Bible make us anxious. We wonder how God would respond if we told him what we really felt.

Learning to express our feelings to God is a vital part of growing in intimacy with him. When we can tell him of our sorrow and anger and confusion and joy, we will experience his faithful love in new ways. In his Word we find many models of godly people who openly expressed their deepest feelings to God.

✦ WARMING UP TO GOD

When you are sad or angry and you are talking to God, how do you expect him to respond? Talk to God about your concerns and fears.

✦ DISCOVERING THE WORD

1. *Read Psalm 55.* What feelings are described in each section of Psalm 55?
2. Describe the image of God that you find in this passage.
3. What seems to be causing the psalmist to suffer (vv. 12-15, 20-21)?
4. What does the psalmist expect God to do for him (vv. 16-19, 22-23)?

✦ APPLYING THE WORD

• We often have a negative response to our "negative" feelings. What thoughts do you typically have in response to your feelings of anger, depression or fear?
• How does it affect you to know that God is near to you when you are in pain?

✦ RESPONDING IN PRAYER

How would you like God to help you to grow in your ability to express your feelings to him?

PSALM 57 *A Prayer of Distress*

SOME PEOPLE FEEL that they cannot bring their troubles to God. But God invites us to turn to him when we are in distress. Repeatedly in the Scriptures God says to us something like this: "Call on me in the day of trouble and I will answer you." This is exactly what Psalm 57 helps us to do.

ᐿ WARMING UP TO GOD

What mental pictures does the word *distress* create for you?

ᐿ DISCOVERING THE WORD

1. *Read Psalm 57.* The title and the introduction to Psalm 57 suggest that this psalm was written by David when he fled into a cave, hiding from King Saul, who wanted to kill him. What image does David use in verse 1 to describe his experience of God as a safe shelter?

2. What metaphors does David use in verse 4 to describe the danger he found himself in?

3. In his time of distress David cried out to God (v. 2). What does it mean to "cry out" to God?

4. How did God intervene for David in his time of distress (vv. 3, 6)?

5. David responds to God's care in verse 7 by saying that his heart is steadfast. What is the significance of this response?

ᐿ APPLYING THE WORD

• Think of a time when you were in distress. What was your experience of God like during that time?

• How might this psalm encourage you in times of distress?

ᐿ RESPONDING IN PRAYER

David responds to God's care with praise in verses 9-11. Offer your praises to God for his work in your life.

PSALM 62
A Prayer of Trust

HUMANS COME INTO the world as vulnerable creatures, completely dependent on their parents for their survival. For people to develop a healthy capacity to trust, they need to experience an emotional attachment with a nurturing parent. If children are not greeted with nurturing, empathic responses to their physical, emotional and social needs, or if the relationship with the parent is disrupted, the attachment will be threatened and the capacity to trust will be damaged. Later in life it will be difficult for them to trust God. Trust is based on a person's character, ability and truthfulness. It is an act of committing oneself to another's good intentions and care. Psalm 62 invites us to risk trusting. It calls us to commit ourselves to God's care.

᧗ WARMING UP TO GOD

How do you determine if a person is trustworthy? Recall a time you took a risk to trust someone.

᧗ DISCOVERING THE WORD

1. *Read Psalm 62.* How does the writer contrast God and humanity?

2. The psalmist talks about resting in God. What pictures come to your mind with these words?

3. In verse 8, the psalmist draws a parallel between trusting in God and pouring out one's heart to God. How are these related?

4. Verse 10 warns against trusting in material wealth. Why is this such a strong temptation?

5. The last two verses depict God as strong and loving. What images of a strong and loving God are presented in the psalm?

᧗ APPLYING THE WORD

- Where else might you be tempted to place your trust, other than in God?
- How does seeing God as strong help you to trust him?
- How does seeing God as loving help you to trust him?

᧗ RESPONDING IN PRAYER

Express your hesitations and your desires to trust God.

PSALM 63   *A Prayer of Longing for God*

SOMETIMES WE FEEL separated from God. Many things can create this sense of separation. It might come as a result of a loss or crisis that leaves us feeling forgotten or uncared for by God. It might come during a time of personal sin or failure when we struggle with fear that God might condemn or reject us. It might come, as it did for this psalmist, as a result of being removed from a community of faith. Whatever the reason, a sense of separation from God can generate life's deepest pain, that of an intense longing for God. This psalm helps us express our longing for God in times when we feel separated from him.

✎ WARMING UP TO GOD

Recall a time you felt especially close to God. What was the experience like for you?

✎ DISCOVERING THE WORD

1. *Read Psalm 63.* Longing for God is described in verse 1 as being thirsty in a desert. What does this strong physical image convey?

2. In verses 2-3 the psalmist describes how in the past he experienced God's presence. What did he experience of God?

3. Because of his longing, the psalmist says he will seek God (v. 1), remember God (v. 6) and cling to God (v. 8). What does it mean to seek God?

4. Where, when and how does the psalmist say he "remembers" God?

5. In verse 8 the psalmist describes how he clings to God and how God holds him. What is your response to the image of clinging to God?

✎ APPLYING THE WORD

• Verse 1 describes a thirsty soul. What words or images would you use to describe times you have felt separated from God?

• Verse 5 describes a soul that is satisfied with "the richest of foods." What words or images would you use to describe times when you felt close to God?

• As you think about seeking, remembering and clinging to God, which describes what would be most helpful to you at this time? Explain.

✎ RESPONDING IN PRAYER

Talk to God about your longing for him and your sense of deep satisfaction and joy in his presence.

PSALM 65 *A Prayer of Gratitude*

WHEN WE ARE unable to receive the good things that others offer us, we cheat ourselves and we cheat them. When we are able to say thank you for gifts given, we are able to take the gift in, enjoy it and engage in a personal, intimate way with the giver of the gift. In the same way, when we express gratitude to God, we enter into a cycle of joyful relating with him. We take in his love, feel a deeper connection with him and experience joy. This psalm invites us to express gratitude to God for his good gifts.

✍ WARMING UP TO GOD

What is it like for you to receive a gift or a compliment? What is it like for you to be on the receiving end of someone else's gratitude?

✍ DISCOVERING THE WORD

1. *Read Psalm 65.* God's great power is acknowledged in this psalm. How is God's power a gift to us?

2. In verse 5 God is called "our Savior, the hope of all the ends of the earth and of the farthest seas." In what ways is God the hope of all the earth and seas?

3. The psalmist mentions several of God's awesome deeds in verses 6-7. What other awesome deeds might you add to the list?

4. Verse 8 offers a picture of the fears and joys common to all people of the earth. How do God's wonders cause us to experience fear?

5. How do God's wonders call forth songs of joy?

✍ APPLYING THE WORD

- Verses 9-13 describe the specific ways in which God tenderly loves and cares for the earth. What thoughts and feelings does this description evoke for you?

- What implications does God's care for the earth have for the ways in which we treat the earth?

- What personal value does expressing gratitude to God have for you?

✍ RESPONDING IN PRAYER

What are you grateful for today? Express your thanks to God.

PSALM 66 *A Prayer of Joy*

LIFE WAS NOT intended by God to be a joyless ordeal. As much as it might surprise some of us, it is actually God's desire for us to experience joy. Joy is an act of relating to God with vulnerable, unselfconscious gratitude for the good gifts he gives. Joy comes when we experience and acknowledge God's love and care for us, when we allow ourselves to express our gratitude for his love with great energy. This psalm invites us to experience joy.

৬ WARMING UP TO GOD

Think of a time when you experienced joy. What evoked this feeling in you?

৬ DISCOVERING THE WORD

1. *Read Psalm 66.* The writer calls us to action (vv. 1, 2, 3, 5, 8, 16). What all does he call us to do?

2. How are each of these behaviors related to the experience or the expression of joy?

3. What does the section in the middle of this psalm (vv. 8-12) tell us about the cause for this particular expression of joy?

4. How might this kind of experience lead to joy?

5. Verses 16-20 are a more personal account of what the Lord has done. What does the writer say the Lord has done for him?

6. How might this kind of experience lead to joy?

৬ APPLYING THE WORD

• What other ways of expressing joy to God would you add to the psalmist's list?

• Why is it important to allow ourselves to experience and express joy?

• How might this psalm help you to experience and express joy?

৬ RESPONDING IN PRAYER

What joy would you like to express to God?

PSALM 67   *God's Love for All Creatures*

JESUS LOVES EVERY culture, and he longs for them all to fully experience the healing of his compassion. That's what redemption is all about. Because some of our sincere attempts to bring others into this love have been clumsy and insulting, Christianity is bombarded with accusations of destroying other cultures. Some of those accusations are worth listening to. Yet these mistakes are not the true picture of our ministry. The gospel is good news to all societies, and God has always called and is still calling his people to bear his redemptive love to every place and people group on the earth.

☙ WARMING UP TO GOD

How have you recently seen God's power being revealed in your nation?

☙ DISCOVERING THE WORD

1. *Read Psalm 67.* What words do you notice being repeated throughout this passage?

2. Identify the blessings the Lord wants to bring to the nations.

3. What does this reveal about how God regards the nations?

☙ APPLYING THE WORD

• What would these blessings look like if they came to your own culture?

• How would these blessings affect some other nation in the world (say, Bosnia or South Africa)?

☙ RESPONDING IN PRAYER

Thank God for his compassion for the nations.

PSALM 73 *Praying Our Doubt*

DOUBT IS NOT A SIN. It is an essential element in belief. Doubt is honesty. We see contradictions between what we believe and what we experience. What is going on here? Did God give us a bum steer? Why aren't things turning out the way we were taught to expect? No mature faith avoids or denies doubt. Doubt forces faith to bedrock.

⌘ WARMING UP TO GOD

What doubts have you had or do you have about the Christian life? Express them to God without fear.

⌘ DISCOVERING THE WORD

1. *Read Psalm 73*. How would you paraphrase the doubt expressed in verses 2-12?

2. Who do you know who is, as they say, "getting away with murder"?

3. The key word and the pivotal center of the psalm is *till* in verse 17. What takes place here in the sanctuary?

4. The *yet* in verse 23 links two contrasting statements. What are they?

5. The prosperity of the wicked occupied the first part of the psalm (vv. 1-16). The presence of the Lord occupies the second (vv. 17-28). What is more vivid to you, the wicked or the Lord? Explain.

⌘ APPLYING THE WORD

• Self-pity is like a deadly virus. How would you express, in terms of your own life, what the psalmist says in verses 13-14?

• The appearance of the wicked whom we envy is in utter and complete contrast to their reality (vv. 18-20). How do you discern between what you see (and are tempted to envy) and what is (and so is affirmed in obedience)?

• Worship is the pivotal act in this prayer. The Christian consensus is that it is the pivotal act every week. How can worship become a more pivotal part of your experience?

⌘ RESPONDING IN PRAYER

In your time of prayer, spend five minutes in silence, savoring God's presence, letting him restore your perspective. Then speak your praises.

PSALM 77   *Praying Our Discontent*

"THE ROOM IS TOO COLD. Why were we seated way back in the corner?
You'd think a restaurant like this would have more selection on the menu.
When is our food going to get here? I don't even think this waitress deserves
a tip . . ." Perhaps you've had a meal with a person who complains like this.
Some people are never satisfied with what they are given. Such people are
tiring to be with. In contrast, the person who is aware of God's never-ending
good gifts (and a person who seems to have comparatively less) is a joy to
be around. Where do you fall on this spectrum?

✎ WARMING UP TO GOD

List three things you're grateful for. Reflect on your response. How long did
it take you to think of things you're grateful for? Did they come to mind
quickly or slowly? What did you learn about yourself?

✎ DISCOVERING THE WORD

1. *Read Psalm 77.* What words and phrases does the psalmist use to describe
   his emotion?

2. Why does he "groan" at the memory of God (vv. 3-9)?

3. How does the tone of the passage change in verses 10-15?

4. What is the source of the change?

5. How do verses 16-20 emphasize God's power?

✎ APPLYING THE WORD

- The psalmist's discontent makes him "too troubled to speak" (v. 4). When
  have you experienced this?

- Sometimes our culture leads us to believe that material things and
  achievements, such as a promotion at work, social status, the right relationship, a new car or the perfect house, will bring contentment. What
  false sources of contentment do you put faith in?

- What in this passage could help you reform your thinking?

✎ RESPONDING IN PRAYER

The psalmist finds his source of contentment in who God is. Make God's
character—rather than your needs—a focus of prayer.

PSALM 84   *A Prayer of Yearning*

CONTINUOUS ACCESS and warm intimacy with God are sometimes difficult to maintain. Times of spiritual dryness, busyness and adversity may
capture our attention more and rob us of regular meeting times with God.
Psalm 84 reflects a time of spiritual dryness common to many believers experientially and to Israel historically. This psalmist laments his forced and
prolonged separation from God (likely during the Babylonian exile), which
has robbed him of the appointed duties, freedom of access and the warm intimacy he once enjoyed.

❧ WARMING UP TO GOD

Think back to where you were living when you were twelve years old. What
was the center of warmth in your home then?

❧ DISCOVERING THE WORD

1. *Read Psalm 84.* What is the psalmist yearning for (vv. 2-3, 10)?

2. What names and metaphors for God can you find in this psalm?

3. The Valley of Baca (v. 6) was an arid stretch of desert that brought tears
   of adversity to pilgrims who had to traverse it en route to Jerusalem.
   What does that valley symbolize—historically and spiritually?

4. What are the benefits or blessings of trusting God as this psalmist does
   (vv. 4-5, 11-12)?

❧ APPLYING THE WORD

• If you could have one wish come true regarding your Christian life, what
  one thing would you yearn for?

• How do you usually address God in prayer? Why?

• Try to visualize where and when God has been closest to you. Put yourself in that picture as a "doorkeeper." How do you feel at those intimate
  times?

❧ RESPONDING IN PRAYER

Spend time with the Lord of the universe in prayer, fellowship and worship.

PSALM 86   *A Prayer of Dependence*

OUR RELATIONSHIP WITH God is that of children to a parent, sheep to a shepherd, creatures to the Creator. We are dependent on him for life, for breath, for sustenance, for help in trouble, for love, for forgiveness, for mercy. We may like to think of ourselves as independent and self-sufficient, but we are not. We need God. It is vital that we acknowledge our need for him because it is the beginning place of our relationship with him. This psalm helps us give voice to our dependence on God.

⁌ WARMING UP TO GOD

Think of a time when you needed to rely on someone for emotional or physical support. What feelings did you have about depending on that person for help?

⁌ DISCOVERING THE WORD

1. *Read Psalm 86.* What is the overall sense you get about the nature of the psalmist's relationship with God?

2. List the many requests the psalmist makes of God.

3. The psalmist sees God as loving, powerful and actively involved in caring for him. What are some of the specific statements he makes about God?

4. What impact would this view of God have on a person's ability to depend on God?

5. How does the psalmist show his dependence on God throughout this psalm?

⁌ APPLYING THE WORD

• What reactions do you have to this kind of dependency on God?

• How might the psalmist's dependency on God encourage you to depend more fully on God?

• In what areas of your life do you need to acknowledge your dependence on God?

⁌ RESPONDING IN PRAYER

Freely express your sense of need for God and your struggles to depend on him.

PSALM 88 *A Prayer of Despair*

"I GIVE UP," Nancy said as she buried her face in her hands. Nancy was not a passive person. She worked hard as a single mother to provide for her children. She had developed a good support system for herself. She was actively, compassionately engaged in life. But a series of losses had left her deeply shaken. Everything she had worked so hard for seemed to be gone. Nancy felt defeated. And without hope. Despair is giving up. As the psalmist expresses it, despair is a time when "darkness is [our] closest friend" (v. 18).

✍ WARMING UP TO GOD

What pictures come to mind when you think of a person who is experiencing despair?

✍ DISCOVERING THE WORD

1. *Read Psalm 88.* What evidence is there of despair in this psalm?

2. What emotional impact did you experience as you read this psalm?

3. Contrast the first and last verses of this psalm. Most psalms that express strong doubts end with hope or praise. This psalm ends with doubt and despair. What is it like to be left with unresolved questions?

4. The writer blames God for his desperate situation. What does he say in blaming God (vv. 6-9, 15-18)?

5. In spite of his sense that God has rejected him and hurt him, the psalmist continues to talk with God. What does this say about his relationship with God?

✍ APPLYING THE WORD

- What reactions do you have to the psalmist blaming God?

- Think of a time when it was difficult for you to talk to God. What was that experience like for you?

✍ RESPONDING IN PRAYER

Spend some time talking to God about the areas in life that feel "dark" or hopeless to you.

PSALM 90   *Praying Our Death*

DEATH IS NOT a popular subject. We live in a society characterized by the denial of death. This is unusual. Most people who have lived on this earth have given a great deal of attention to death. Preparing for a good death has been an accepted goal in life. Psalm 90 has been part of that preparation for millions of Christians.

⊰ WARMING UP TO GOD

When you think about your own death, what do you think about? What do you feel?

⊰ DISCOVERING THE WORD

1. *Read Psalm 90.* Death sets a limit to our lives and stimulates reflection on the context of life, which is not death but God. In verses 1-2, how does the psalmist set death within his view of God?

2. How does the psalmist describe God's anger and its effects on our lives (vv. 7-11)?

3. How do you integrate this view of God with the well-known biblical statement "God is love"?

4. Luther commented on verse 12: "Lord, teach us all to be such arithmeticians!" What does it mean to number our days aright?

5. Study the verbs in verses 14-17. What emerges as most important for you—what you do for the rest of your life or what God will do in your life? Explain.

⊰ APPLYING THE WORD

• How long do you expect to live?

• How do you plan to live the years left to you?

• Plato believed that philosophy was nothing more than a study of death. In the Middle Ages pastoral care concentrated on preparing you for a good death. How does your meditation on death affect the way you live your life?

⊰ RESPONDING IN PRAYER

Express your awareness that you will die. In your prayers be conscious of Christ's death.

PSALM 91 *Angels Among Us*

PEOPLE SEE ANGELS as messengers of glad tidings, spirits of people who have died, invisible guardians of our safety, angels in disguise as do-gooders or cherubs of romantic love. Many of the popular depictions of angels have nothing to do with the biblical perspective. The angels invoked in Psalm 91 are heralds and harbingers of God's power. The psalm glows with testimony to the security of godly worshipers.

✧ WARMING UP TO GOD

In your mind's eye, what do angels look like? What do they spend their time doing?

✧ DISCOVERING THE WORD

1. *Read Psalm 91.* The psalm divides into two stanzas: vv. 1-8 and vv. 9-16. What theme is common to the opening couplet of each stanza (vv. 1-2, 9-10)?

2. What threatens the security of the believer, even the one who takes refuge in God (vv. 3-6, 13)?

3. Are godly believers protected from calamity and sorrow, or are they promised God's presence amidst terrible circumstances? Explain your answer from the passage.

4. What is the basis for the psalmist's assurance that he will be safe and secure (vv. 9-12, 14-15)?

5. In this psalm, what does "my [God's] salvation" (v. 16) look like?

✧ APPLYING THE WORD

- What are you particularly anxious about these days, for which God is waiting on you to call his name and acknowledge your need?

- How can you make God your dwelling place, your refuge, your shield in times of trouble?

✧ RESPONDING IN PRAYER

God is waiting to hear from his people who love him and acknowledge their need of him. Tell him whatever is on your mind, whatever fears you have and whatever terrible circumstances you are facing. Trust him to answer.

PSALM 94 *A Prayer of Anger*

MIKE AND JOHN had both been ripped off by their business partners, and they were both angry. As they shared their experiences with each other, however, they discovered an important difference. Mike was baffled by what to do with his strong feelings. His anger frightened him and did not seem very spiritual, so most of the time he kept quiet about his sense of outrage. John, on the other hand, had grown up in a church that prayed the psalms together. Together they had spoken the words of anger and outrage to God. As a result, John knew he could take his anger to God. Psalm 94 can help us speak freely to God about our anger.

✎ WARMING UP TO GOD

Is it difficult or relatively easy for you to tell God about your anger? Explain.

✎ DISCOVERING THE WORD

1. *Read Psalm 94.* The psalmist addresses God as the Judge and as the one who avenges (vv. 1-2). What is the meaning of this for the psalmist?

2. What does the psalmist say the wicked have done (vv. 4-7)?

3. In verses 8-10 the psalmist asks several rhetorical questions of God. What statement is he making in these questions?

4. What hope does the psalmist express in verses 12-15?

5. Verse 16 captures the question the psalmist is wrestling with. What words would you use to express this question?

6. In verses 17-19 the psalmist expresses himself in vulnerable terms. How does he describe the experience of fear that generated his anger?

✎ APPLYING THE WORD

• God will take care of justice. Why is this important to remember when we are feeling powerless?

• This psalm models honesty with ourselves and God, trusting God's care and letting God take care of justice. How might this example help you in times of anger?

✎ RESPONDING IN PRAYER

Talk to God about any feelings of anger—fresh or lingering—that you have.

PSALM 95 *A Psalm of Rest*

SO OFTEN GOD gives us the consequences of our choices; other times he withholds or spares us the punishment our rebellion or hardheartedness deserves. That is an act of his mercy, for which this psalmist and all believers can give thanks. This psalm acknowledges God as Lord of the earth and Shepherd King of his people. The writer reflects on times of rebellion when the Israelites put God to the test and ended up missing out on God's rest.

✐ WARMING UP TO GOD

Picture the place you go to rest from your labors and listen to God. If you don't have a place like that, make one up.

✐ DISCOVERING THE WORD

1. *Read Psalm 95.* Where does this psalmist envision God ruling as Lord and King (vv. 3-5)?
2. Meribah and Massah are places where the Israelites rebelled in the desert and tested the Lord about whether he was with them or not (vv. 8-9). What happened as a result of that testing (vv. 10-11)?
3. What is the "rest" from which the rebellious Israelites were banned by an oath of God, but which a later generation would enjoy (v. 11)?
4. Imagine life without God's promised rest. What must that have been like?
5. What warning does the psalmist derive as he contemplates "Meribah" and "Massah" recurring for the present generation of God's people?

✐ APPLYING THE WORD

• If your life and well-being were constantly threatened with adversaries where you live and work, what would you be praying for?
• During those times in your past when your heart strayed from God's ways (v. 10), how did God bring you back to himself?
• As you listen to God's voice "today" (v. 7), what is he saying to you?

✐ RESPONDING IN PRAYER

Whatever the past or present circumstances of your relationship with God may be, this psalm invites you to come into his presence today. Try kneeling in his presence, acknowledging him as Lord of your life. Soften your heart and give him the praise and thanksgiving he deserves.

PSALM 96   *Worldwide Worship*

OUR GOD IS a missionary God. He wants all nations, every living thing, to bow down in worship of him. And God wants us to take that message—in word and deed, in song and praise—to the ends of the earth. The psalmist bids us to be most inclusive in our worship of the one true God.

✌ WARMING UP TO GOD

What songs come to mind when you feel like praising God for the great things he has done?

✌ DISCOVERING THE WORD

1. *Read Psalm 96.* This psalm is divided into four parts, identifiable by repeated words or refrains: verses 1-3, 4-6, 7-9 and 10-13. What repetition do you see in each section?

2. What "marvelous deeds" (v. 3) come to mind that would prompt a believer to sing God's praises?

3. Why is the Lord "most worthy of" (entitled to) praise (vv. 4-6, 10, 13)?

4. Like an orchestra conductor, the psalmist bids different sections to join in the chorus of praise to God. How extensive or inclusive is this call to "ascribe glory to" (worship) God (vv. 7-13)?

✌ APPLYING THE WORD

- In light of this universal call to worship, think of those around you and on the other side of the globe. What does this psalmist prompt you to do about those who don't know God?

- This psalm invites us to sing a "new song" (v. 1) declaring his glory to others (in witness) and ascribing glory directly to God (in worship). How would someone who is not musically inclined be creative in this kind of witness and worship?

✌ RESPONDING IN PRAYER

Let the joy of knowing God bubble up within you and burst forth in a new song of worship. Be spontaneous and let this psalm be the wellspring for singing out or jotting down words of praise. (Later see if you, or someone you know, could set those words to music.)

PSALM 99 *Hail to the King of Kings*

THE ATTRIBUTES and actions of our holy God inspire praise, awe and obedience in those who call on his name. This psalm calls to mind the special relationship that he had with Moses, Aaron and Samuel—a relationship that is representative and possible for all of God's people.

⌘ WARMING UP TO GOD

How does thinking about God's holiness make you feel about approaching him?

⌘ DISCOVERING THE WORD

1. *Read Psalm 99.* This psalm speaks of the Lord in a total of seven different ways. (Seven is a symbol of completeness.) What aspects or characteristics of this complete Lord does the psalmist affirm?

2. How do or should others respond in relation to the exalted Lord?

3. Consider the cause and effects, also the actions and explanations, in this psalm. Why should God's people worship this Lord (vv. 4-8)?

4. Out of reverence for God's unapproachable holiness, the people went through intermediaries to God. Priests such as Moses, Aaron and Samuel were the go-betweens (v. 6). How did God speak with them (vv. 6-8)?

⌘ APPLYING THE WORD

• God is terribly awesome and holy, forgiving and punishing. What does that say about the casual God-is-my-buddy approach or the presumptuous God-is-my-bellhop approach we often take in worship and prayer?

• What does God expect you to do in response to his holy character and righteous decrees?

• This psalm invites us to tremble, praise, exalt and worship this Lord. How do you do that each day?

⌘ RESPONDING IN PRAYER

Let the awe of knowing this holy God sink in. Pray for a desire to be and do and love the things that characterize this holy God.

PSALM 100   *Seeing Myself as Human*

"IT MAKES ME NERVOUS when people say, 'I'm only human,'" said Bob. "I'm afraid that if I give myself excuses like that I will let myself off the hook instead of doing my best. I don't know why, but I need to keep pushing myself beyond my limits or I become terribly anxious."

To be human is to be a long list of things we would rather avoid. We do not like the vulnerability, the limits or the needs. And so, all too often, we defend ourselves against our fears by trying to be God. But we are not God. The more we are able to embrace this most fundamental of realities—that we are creatures and God is our Creator—the freer our lives can become. The text for this study will help us to see ourselves as belonging to God.

✆ WARMING UP TO GOD

List some obstacles that keep you from seeing yourself as a child of God.

✆ DISCOVERING THE WORD

1. *Read Psalm 100.* According to this psalm, who is God and what is he like?
2. This psalm also tells us about ourselves. According to this psalm, who are we?
3. The text instructs us to "know that the LORD is God" (v. 3). What does it mean to "know that the LORD is God"?
4. What freedom might knowing this provide?
5. What things are we invited to do in response to God?

✆ APPLYING THE WORD

• In what area of your life do you need to quit trying to be superhuman?
• How might it help you personally to "know that the LORD is God," that you are a creature and "the sheep of his pasture" (v. 3)?

✆ RESPONDING IN PRAYER

We are invited by this psalm to worship the Lord with gladness. Offer a brief song or poem or prayer of worship or praise to God.

PSALM 102   *A Prayer of Grief*

GRIEF IS AN experience of deep sorrow over a significant loss. Whether the loss we have suffered is the loss of a loved one, a job, our health or our home, the physical, emotional and spiritual suffering is intense. This psalm speaks our anguish to God in times of grief.

☙ WARMING UP TO GOD

Write down your best attempt to describe the experience of grief.

☙ DISCOVERING THE WORD

1. *Read Psalm 102.* In verses 1-2 the psalmist pleads for God to hear him. Why is this need so urgent in times of grief and distress?

2. How does the psalmist describe his current physical and emotional state (vv. 2-11)?

3. The psalmist seems to be blaming God and pleading with God (vv. 1-2, 24) at the same time. What does he blame God for (vv. 8, 10, 23)?

4. The writer seems to have mixed feelings about God. What positive perspectives does he express about God (vv. 12-22, 25-28)?

5. Mixed feelings about God are common in times of suffering and grief. What is it about times of grief that might create these mixed feelings?

☙ APPLYING THE WORD

- How do the psalmist's descriptions compare with your experiences of grief?

- What experience have you had with mixed feelings toward God in times of grief?

- What grief are you aware of (over a loss you have suffered—recent or long past) that you need to express to God?

☙ RESPONDING IN PRAYER

Express your feelings of grief to God, and pray for others you know who are grieving.

PSALM 103   *Praying Our Salvation*

WHAT GOD HAS done for us far exceeds anything we have done for or against him. The summary word for this excessive, undeserved, unexpected act by God is *salvation*. Prayer explores the country of salvation, tramping the contours, smelling the flowers, touching the outcroppings. There is more to do than recognize the sheer fact of salvation and witness to it; there are unnumbered details of grace, of mercy, of blessing to be appreciated and savored. Prayer is the means by which we do this.

✺ WARMING UP TO GOD

Reflect on the meaning of your salvation. Allow praise for God to arise from your joy.

✺ DISCOVERING THE WORD

1. *Read Psalm 103.* Note the first and last sentences. How does this bracketing affect your understanding of the psalm's contents?
2. Salvation is more richly complex than we sometimes think. What five actions of God add up to salvation (vv. 3-5)?
3. How did God make his ways known to Moses and Israel (v. 7)?
4. What astounding statements about God does the psalmist make in verses 8-14?
5. Carefully observe the contrast between us (vv. 15-16) and God (vv. 17-19). Does this make you feel better or worse about yourself? Explain.

✺ APPLYING THE WORD

- How have you benefited from your salvation?
- How do verses 8-14 show you ways in which you would like to expand your thinking about God?

✺ RESPONDING IN PRAYER

Add your personal praise to the praise in this psalm.

PSALM 104   *Protecting God's Creation*

THE STARS ARE great at camp. They emerge slowly at first. Then more and more come out. The first ones glare trumpetlike against the inky black, while others dance a gentle harmony. A shooting star streaks across the sky, as if to connect the dots in some new constellation. What can we say to a God who made all this and somehow created in us the ability to enjoy it? Perhaps silence is the most sensible part of our prayer.

✑ WARMING UP TO GOD

Recall a time that God's creation helped you to experience him. What did you find particularly helpful?

✑ DISCOVERING THE WORD

1. *Read Psalm 104.* Study verses 1-4. How does the sky serve God?

2. Study verses 5-9. What elements of earth's creation show God at work?

3. Study verses 10-18. What relationships does this description of God's creation reveal?

4. Study verses 19-26. How do these verses express an orderliness to what God has made?

5. Study verses 27-30. How do these verses show that God not only created but also personally takes care of what he has made?

6. Study verses 31-35. What responses to God are triggered by the psalmist's meditation on creation?

✑ APPLYING THE WORD

- When have you enjoyed some aspect of the natural rhythms described here?

- As you meditate on what God has made, how would you like to respond to God?

✑ RESPONDING IN PRAYER

Praise God for the glory of his creation.

PSALM 107 *The Goodness of God*

PSALM 107 IS the classic exposition of God's goodness. In his book *Knowing God*, J. I. Packer writes, "The whole psalm is a majestic panorama of the operations of divine goodness, transforming human lives." God's actions reveal goodness in its highest and purest form. His goodness provides the standard for developing this fruit in our own lives.

✢ WARMING UP TO GOD

Try to imagine what it would be like if God were to withdraw all his goodness from you. How would your life be changed? Respond to God with praise for his presence with you.

✢ DISCOVERING THE WORD

1. *Read Psalm 107.* How do verses 1-3 introduce the major themes of the psalm?
2. The psalmist gives four illustrations of God's goodness in verses 4-9, 10-16, 17-22 and 23-32. What do these illustrations have in common?
3. What needs do the people have in each of these sections?
4. According to the psalmist, what are some ways we should give thanks to God for his goodness and love (vv. 22, 32)?
5. What do verses 33-42 reveal about the ups and downs of life?

✢ APPLYING THE WORD

- Are you likely to call out to God in the midst of your trouble as those in this passage did? Why or why not?
- In what ways can we imitate the goodness of God displayed in this psalm?

✢ RESPONDING IN PRAYER

Thank God for his goodness and unfailing love. Ask him to help you develop the fruit of goodness in your life.

PSALM 109 *Feeling Anger*

FOR MOST OF US, anger is not a comfortable emotion. We know the pain it can cause. We fear our own capacity for evil when we are angry. However, avoiding anger will not make it go away but can instead allow it to grow into bitterness. Feeling anger and expressing it honestly to God and to others makes it possible for us to continue growing toward forgiveness.

✎ WARMING UP TO GOD

What do you usually do when you are angry with someone who is important to you?

✎ DISCOVERING THE WORD

1. *Read Psalm 109.* To what painful experiences is the psalmist reacting (vv. 2-5)?

2. The speaker is particularly outraged at the injustice of his accusers: "They repay me evil for good, and hatred for my friendship" (v. 5). How does this add to his sense of rage?

3. What does the author ask God to do to his enemies (vv. 6-20, 28-29)?

4. What does the author want God to do for him (vv. 20-26)?

✎ APPLYING THE WORD

• God is described in verse 31 as being on the side of the "needy" and "condemned." How could seeing God in this way be a practical help to you when you are angry?

• How would expressing your anger to God be helpful to you?

• How can other people be helpful to you in your struggle with anger?

✎ RESPONDING IN PRAYER

What anger do you want to express to God today?

PSALM 110   *A Psalm of Submission*

THINK OF THE enemies you have. Bring to mind people you know who are opposed to Christianity. Picture them (and yourself) one day coming to Christ. Psalm 110 acknowledges God as the eternal King-Priest who will settle all disputes and judge all nations. This coronation hymn, though used for other kings of Israel, was viewed by Jews and Christians alike as messianic and forward-looking. Writers of the New Testament quote verses 1 and 4 on numerous occasions, making this psalm one of the most prophetic.

⊛ WARMING UP TO GOD

How does the idea that God will judge your actions and behaviors make you feel?

⊛ DISCOVERING THE WORD

1. *Read Psalm 110.* Who is the psalmist referring to as "my Lord" (v. 1; see Mt 22:41-45)?
2. How will that Lord rule, and over whom (vv. 1-3, 5, 6)?
3. What is significant about the Lord swearing with a covenant oath (v. 4; Heb 6:16-18; 7:20-22)?
4. Melchizedek was the original king-priest of God Most High in Jerusalem, who received a tithe from Abraham. His priesthood was a prototype of Christ's eternal priesthood (v. 4). What is significant about a priesthood for God's people that is permanent and irrevocable?
5. What is significant about this Lord sitting at the right hand of God (vv. 1, 5)?

⊛ APPLYING THE WORD

- The troops are freewill offerings (v. 3) in the service of their Lord. What is your sacrificial offering to the Lord?
- The Lord rules over all the powers that be, even enemies of his kingdom, with an iron hand and the undiminished vigor of youth (vv. 2-3). How is that good news to you in the battles you face?

⊛ RESPONDING IN PRAYER

What battles or problem areas can you turn over to God now for his intercession and judgment?

PSALM 115   *A Psalm of Praise*

PSALM 115 PRAISES GOD as the one true Lord and ridicules the cheap imitations and pretenders to the throne in the surrounding culture. The liturgical exchange between people and priests in this psalm makes it a very appropriate lead-in for public worship. In this liturgy, the cares and snares of the world are left behind and the people are called to trust God, who will abundantly bless them and receive the praise of his people.

✎ WARMING UP TO GOD

When has God seemed distant or unresponsive to you (in the past or present)? Open yourself up to the possibilities of God blessing you and your family afresh.

✎ DISCOVERING THE WORD

1. *Read Psalm 115.* This psalm divides into five parts: three stanzas spoken by the respondents—a taunt song (vv. 1-8), confession of trust (vv. 12-13) and the closing doxology (vv. 16-18)—interspersed with an invocation (vv. 9-11) and benediction (vv. 14-15) spoken by the priests. What does this rhythm call forth from the worship participants and leaders?

2. How do the idols that others worship compare to the God Israel worships (vv. 1-8)?

3. Why should everyone, but especially Israel, trust in the Lord (vv. 9-11)?

4. Who will the Lord bless? Why and how (vv. 12-15)?

5. What is the reason for living granted to those who have survived the exile and more (vv. 16-18)?

✎ APPLYING THE WORD

• The Lord is not the only person or object that people trust to get them through the day. What else do people trust in these days for their salvation or their guidance?

• For what have you recently trusted God alone to provide?

• How did God prove to be your help and shield?

✎ RESPONDING IN PRAYER

Consider how vastly superior God is to all idols. Ask God to help you forsake the idols of your culture.

PSALM 116 *Talking to God*

HONESTY IS A necessary ingredient to all intimate relationships. If we are to grow in our intimacy with God, we will need to learn to be honest with him. God invites us to talk to him and has promised to pay attention. He does not require us to do any physical, mental or spiritual gymnastics to get his attention. He does not insist that we have our lives "together" before we can talk to him. We can talk to him even when we are in trouble.

✎ WARMING UP TO GOD

Imagine yourself as a little child standing next to Jesus. How would you talk to him? What thoughts and feelings did you have during this meditation?

✎ DISCOVERING THE WORD

1. *Read Psalm 116.* What images of God are presented here?
2. What did the author of the psalm experience when he called on God?
3. How does the psalmist respond to God (vv. 12-19)?
4. God invites us to talk to him about our troubles. He does not ask us to ignore them or minimize them or take care of them ourselves. How does this compare or contrast with your expectations of God?

✎ APPLYING THE WORD

• Think of a time when you had difficulty calling on God. What made it difficult for you?
• Recall a time when you did call on God and he answered you. What was this experience like for you?

✎ RESPONDING IN PRAYER

What do you need to talk with God about today?

PSALM 118   *Enduring Love*

REMEMBER WHEN your parents used to force you to write thank-you notes for gifts you received from out-of-town relatives? Although it may have been painful at the time, this discipline helped you develop a grateful heart. In like manner, the psalmist expresses thanks to God for delivering Israel from its many enemies. The historic setting of Psalm 118 may have been Israel's defeat of a confederacy of nations or her deliverance from the Babylonian exile. In either event, the Israelites had much to thank God for, especially his love that endures forever. We who know the love of God in Christ have even more reason to give thanks through this psalm.

᧌ WARMING UP TO GOD

Think about your closest, longest relationships. List the differences between them and relationships that have proven temporary.

᧌ DISCOVERING THE WORD

1. *Read Psalm 118.* This psalm divides into five parts: calls to praise at the beginning (vv. 1-4) and end (v. 29) sandwich the leader's song of thanksgiving (vv. 5-21), the people's response (vv. 22-27) and the leader's final prompting (v. 28). What indicators suggest a change of voice or speaker in each section?

2. What is the significance of the repetitions found in this psalm?

3. What has the Lord done for the king or representatively for the people (vv. 5-21)?

4. As an Israelite prompted to give thanks on the occasion of this psalm, what redemptive occasions in the life of your people come to mind?

5. What is the significance of the stone-turned-capstone (v. 22), which is being celebrated on this festive day (vv. 23-24)?

᧌ APPLYING THE WORD

• The early church applied verse 22 to Jesus. How is Jesus like this stone-turned-capstone?

• For what events in your life are you particularly grateful to God?

• How did God prove to be your helper, your strength or your salvation?

᧌ RESPONDING IN PRAYER

Praise God for the day(s) he has given you to rejoice (v. 24).

PSALM 119:1-24   *Searching for God's Wisdom*

FEW SITUATIONS BRING life to a grinding halt like losing a contact lens. Everything necessarily stops while we feel our way to the contact; only then can we regain our vision. If we are going to see life from God's perspective, we will regularly have to stop everything, hunker down and find out just what that perspective is. Like finding a contact lens, God's wisdom is simply worth whatever inconveniences may come in its pursuit.

❧ WARMING UP TO GOD

In what area of your life today do you need God's wisdom?

❧ DISCOVERING THE WORD

1. *Read Psalm 119:1-24.* What different words does the psalmist use to describe God's Word?
2. What benefits of knowing and following God's Word does the psalmist mention in verses 1-8?
3. How does God's Word help us to deal with sin (vv. 9-16)?
4. How does God's Word enlighten us about God's ways (vv. 17-24)?
5. What are the consequences of not knowing or following God's Word (vv. 5-6, 9-11, 21-22)?

❧ APPLYING THE WORD

- What is a way you have experienced frustration in studying Scripture?
- What in the psalmist's example can bring encouragement to us to mediate on and delight in God's Word?

❧ RESPONDING IN PRAYER

Ask God to guide you as you turn to his Word for wisdom.

PSALM 119:25-40 *Seeking God*

PRAYER AND MEDITATION are not easy disciplines. Many of us have used prayer as a magical device for controlling God or for acquiring God's favor. Similarly, many use meditation as a magical tool for control. But there is nothing magical about the spiritual disciplines of prayer and meditation. Both are ways to focus our attention on God. We can talk (pray) openly, honestly and vulnerably to God, and we can listen (meditate) with humility. It is this dynamic of speaking and listening, prayer and meditation that makes it possible for us to increase our contact with God. We can experience loving and being loved by our Creator.

✎ WARMING UP TO GOD

What difficulties do you experience with prayer and meditation?

✎ DISCOVERING THE WORD

1. *Read Psalm 119:25-40.* Restate in your own words the requests the psalmist makes of God.

2. What major needs and desires is the psalmist expressing in these requests?

3. How do these needs and desires compare with your own at this time?

4. How does the psalmist describe what he has done and what he desires to do in his pursuit of God?

5. What benefits does the psalmist suggest might come from prayer and meditation (vv. 32-40)?

✎ APPLYING THE WORD

• The psalmist describes himself as "laid low in the dust" (v. 25) and as "weary with sorrow" (v. 28). Describe a time when you experienced these feelings.

• In your experience, how can prayer and meditation improve our contact with God?

✎ RESPONDING IN PRAYER

Ask God to help you practice the disciplines of prayer and meditation.

PSALM 121 *A Prayer of Assurance*

THE JEWS WERE on an uphill journey to Jerusalem and the temple at Mount Zion. This psalm is among the many "songs of ascent" sung (or inwardly affirmed) by individuals in the caravan along the way. Any pilgrim facing an uphill climb of faith, and all of us on life's pilgrimage from this earthly existence to the heavenly glory, will find assurance in repeating the confession of this psalm.

ᴄ᷾ WARMING UP TO GOD

Imagine a battle of faith that you may be facing. How do you imagine God making a difference in that situation?

ᴄ᷾ DISCOVERING THE WORD

1. *Read Psalm 121.* Judging from the words and phrases most often repeated in this psalm, what is its major theme?

2. How does the second verse in each of the four verse pairs (vv. 2, 4, 6, 8) expand on the mini-theme of the introductory line in each pair (vv. 1, 3, 5, 7)?

3. What kind of help does the Lord provide his people along the journey (in contrast to those idols who may slumber or slouch on the job)?

4. In light of the assurances offered in this psalm, how do you account for the fact that some people do slip and fall into harm's way?

ᴄ᷾ APPLYING THE WORD

• Imagine you are an Israelite making this pilgrimage to Mount Zion and dialoging your way through this psalm of confession and assurance. What parts do you find most reassuring for yourself?

• What parts do you find most reassuring for a fellow pilgrim whom you know is struggling along the way?

• Consider one time, day or night, when you slipped badly and fell into harm's way. How was God watching over you in that situation?

ᴄ᷾ RESPONDING IN PRAYER

Consider using Psalm 121 as an appropriate prayer for all your comings and goings. Offer it at mealtimes, office breaks and bedtimes. Let it influence the prayers and counsel you offer family, friends and work associates, especially anyone facing an uphill battle.

PSALM 122 *A Prayer for Peace*

PRAYER FOR THE "peace of Jerusalem" (vv. 6-9) distinguishes this Zion hymn. (For other Zion songs, see Pss 46, 48, 76, 84, 126, 129, 137.) This prayer is not just for fellow worshipers but for the policies and programs that bring "peace and prosperity" to the city. This call to pray for the decision-makers in government confers a benediction on their work, the result of which would be shalom for the "City of Peace."

ᑋ WARMING UP TO GOD

When you think about doing good and seeking the welfare of others, who comes to mind? Meditate on today's newspaper along with the Bible to see the needs that God cares most about in your city.

ᑋ DISCOVERING THE WORD

1. *Read Psalm 122.* What was it like for these worshipers to go to the house of the Lord in Jerusalem (Mount Zion)?

2. Describe the city of Jerusalem (vv. 3-5).

3. What things does the psalmist pray will be given to the city (vv. 6-9)?

4. What would this psalmist say to someone who wants to meet his own needs or those of his family before seeking the peace and prosperity of the city?

ᑋ APPLYING THE WORD

• Worship at Mount Zion was both a regular obligation (although a joyous event) and a bonding experience for temple-bound worshipers. What is "going to church" like for you?

• Psalm 122 evokes memories of how Jesus wept over Jerusalem (Lk 9:51; 13:31-35; 19:41-44). By comparison, what tears have you shed over your city?

• "Peace within *your* walls" and "security within *your* citadels" (v. 7, emphasis added) will benefit believers, but the city itself is the end in view here. How do you work for the good of the city where you live and worship?

ᑋ RESPONDING IN PRAYER

Scan the city news section of your newspaper for events and people that need God's shalom (peace and prosperity). Bring to God in prayer everyone you know in city hall as well as the key urban areas that need shalom.

PSALM 126 *A Song of Joy*

A GREAT IMAGE OF happiness is the suppertime dance Snoopy does in the *Peanuts* comic strip. His head is flung back, his ears flop about, and his feet pound furiously. Have you ever felt like dancing for joy? In this passage the Israelites do.

✍ WARMING UP TO GOD

What do you do when you are filled with joy?

✍ DISCOVERING THE WORD

1. *Read Psalm 126.* This is a song of celebration by the exiles who returned to Zion. What emotions do you see expressed throughout this psalm?

2. What imagery is used in verses 1-2 to describe the joy the writers feel?

3. How do verses 4-6 reflect a balance between cause and effect?

4. How are sadness and joy intertwined (vv. 5-6)?

✍ APPLYING THE WORD

• The Israelites give God the credit for the "great things" (v. 2) that have happened. How do you do with giving God the credit?

• When do you feel inhibited about freely expressing your joy?

✍ RESPONDING IN PRAYER

What do you need to praise God for? Share your joy with him.

PSALM 127 *Worthwhile Work*

WILL WE ALLOW technology and our society's definition of personhood to drive a wedge into our community? It can and does happen almost naturally—without our help. As we respond to Jesus, there will be purpose in our lives and meaning within our relationships. It is the context of relationships with God and other persons that should give meaning to our work. Unfortunately our culture elevates the possession of things and applauds compulsive work habits. We need to intervene where God's image in people is being destroyed by our society and structures. These passages encourage us to take the lead in bringing God's kingdom back into our relationships.

☙ WARMING UP TO GOD

What challenges to faith are you currently facing in your workplace?

☙ DISCOVERING THE WORD

1. *Read Psalm 127.* What basis is offered in this passage for the worth of our work (v. 1)?

2. Why is it foolish to work long hours (v. 2)?

3. Children (v. 3) are a gift from God and are a sign of his favor on those who do worthwhile work. In what ways has God rewarded you for good work?

☙ APPLYING THE WORD

- How does your attitude toward work shape how you view your personal relationships?

- In what way do you need the rest that the Lord grants "to those he loves" (v. 2)?

☙ RESPONDING IN PRAYER

Ask God to build in you the attitude toward work that he wants you to have.

PSALM 130 *A Prayer of Hope*

HOPE IS NECESSARY. It gives us the strength to keep going through the tough times. It gives life joy and meaning in the good times. However, when hope has been repeatedly disappointed, it slips away. This psalm offers a picture of this struggle. The writer is without much hope. Yet he puts himself in a place of allowing for the possibility of hope. As we pray with him, we too can begin to wait with growing expectation. We too can nurture our hope.

ꙮ Warming Up to God

How would you describe the experience of hope? How would you describe the experience of hopelessness?

ꙮ Discovering the Word

1. *Read Psalm 130.* The psalm begins with a cry to the Lord from "out of the depths" (v. 1). What pictures come to mind as you read this phrase?

2. The psalmist's distress seems to be related to a struggle with guilt. How can guilt lead to hopelessness?

3. Verses 3-4 tell us that God forgives. How does the promise of forgiveness contribute to hope?

4. Verse 5 says, "I wait, . . . my soul waits." What is the relationship between waiting and hope?

5. The psalmist then uses the metaphor of watchmen (v. 6) to describe the experience of hope. What does he convey with this image?

6. What reasons does the psalmist give for hoping in the Lord (vv. 7-8)?

ꙮ Applying the Word

• What area of life is it difficult for you to be hopeful about?

• What reasons do you have for hoping in the Lord?

ꙮ Responding in Prayer

Thank God for being the source of hope. Pray for courage when you face hopelessness.

PSALM 133 *Blessed Unity*

THINK ABOUT THE brother-to-brother and sister-to-sister loyalties celebrated in our society: fraternities and sororities, sports teams, family corporations, even the Mafia (that is, "the Brotherhood"). Can you envision a fraternal unity so blessed that it oozes and drips with sweetness? David can.

☞ WARMING UP TO GOD

How does the "mystic sweet communion" enjoyed by God's people compare to the unity you have witnessed or experienced? Surround yourself with images of warm Christian fellowship.

☞ DISCOVERING THE WORD

1. *Read Psalm 133.* What is so good or pleasant about people living together in unity (v. 1)?

2. To what is this blessedness compared (vv. 2-3)?

3. If the oil of anointing that saturated Aaron's beard and priestly robes was so precious and sanctifying (v. 2; Ex 29:7; Lev 21:10), what does that say about harmony running its course through the fellowship of God's people?

4. Mount Hermon rises nine thousand feet, its many glaciers stretching across twenty miles in northern Israel, watering the Jordan River valleys and cities below. However, during the summer, its snow and glaciers produce a heavy dew that envelops Mount Hermon, leaving much of the surroundings arid. For the "dew of Hermon" to fall on Mount Zion (v. 3) would be most unusual. What does that say about the blessing of brotherly unity?

☞ APPLYING THE WORD

- Where are you experiencing strong brother-to-brother or sister-to-sister bonds and blessings that sanctify and sustain God's people"?

- In what way could you experience more of the "priestly oil" and "Mount Hermon's dew"?

☞ RESPONDING IN PRAYER

Think about the spiritual refreshment and moral accountability that strong fellowship provides you. Thank God for the brothers and sisters he has given you to sanctify and sustain you. Consider ways you can live in harmony with your family of faith, and pray toward that end.

PSALM 137   *Praying Our Hate*

WE PUT ON our "Sunday best" in our prayers. But when we pray the prayers of God's people, the psalms, we find that will not do. We must pray who we actually are, not who we think we should be. Here is a prayer that brings out not the best but the worst in us: vile, venomous, vicious hate.

✑ WARMING UP TO GOD

Everyone has hated at one time or another. It is one of the basic human experiences. Be honest before God. Whom have you hated? Why?

✑ DISCOVERING THE WORD

1. *Read Psalm 137.* This psalm combines the loveliest lyric we can sing with the ugliest emotion we can feel. What makes verses 1-6 lovely?

2. What makes verses 7-9 ugly?

3. Homesickness is understandable. Sometimes it is evidence of loyalty. Sometimes it is simply irresponsibility. Remembering your own experiences of this, how would you evaluate verses 4-6?

4. The two dominant emotions in this prayer are self-pity (vv. 1-6) and avenging hate (vv. 7-9), neither of them particularly commendable. Praying our sins doesn't, as such, launder them. What does it do?

✑ APPLYING THE WORD

• Jesus said, "Love your enemies and pray for those who persecute you" (Mt 5:44). How can we possibly love and pray for such people?

• Most of us suppress our negative emotions (unless, neurotically, we advertise them). The way of prayer is not to cover them up so we will appear respectable, but to expose them so we can be healed. What negative emotion would you like healed?

✑ RESPONDING IN PRAYER

Take any hate or dislike that you have uncovered and give it voice as you pray.

PSALM 139   *Wonderfully Made*

A CRAFTSMAN IN medieval times would work for months on a special piece that displayed his finest artistic skill. Finally, when the work was finished, he would present it to the craftsmen's guild in hopes of achieving the rank of master. The work was called his masterpiece. In Psalm 139 we see God the master craftsman, lovingly at work on his masterpiece. This psalm can have a profound impact on the way we view ourselves.

❧ WARMING UP TO GOD

Do you think of yourself as God's artwork, his masterpiece? Why or why not? Ask God to help you see yourself through his eyes as you begin this study.

❧ DISCOVERING THE WORD

1. *Read Psalm 139.* According to the psalmist, what specific things does the Lord know about us (vv. 1-6)?

2. The psalmist declares that God's knowledge of him is "wonderful" (v. 6). Yet why do you think he also feels an urge to flee from God's presence (vv. 7-12)?

3. What words are used to describe God's activity and artistry in making us (vv. 13-16)?

❧ APPLYING THE WORD

- How do you hide your true self from God?

- How do you hide your true self from others?

- How does this psalm help you to feel more loved and valued by God?

❧ RESPONDING IN PRAYER

Take time to thank God for the fact that you are "fearfully and wonderfully made." Put verses 23-24 in your own words and express them to God in prayer.

PSALM 142   *A Prayer of Desperation*

DESPERATION IS AN experience of extreme need and helplessness. We feel desperate when life's circumstances overpower us. We feel desperate when our well-being is threatened and we feel unable to affect the outcome. This psalm gives voice to our experiences of desperation.

✑ WARMING UP TO GOD

Think of a time when you felt desperate. What phrases or images would you use to describe the situation you faced?

✑ DISCOVERING THE WORD

1. *Read Psalm 142.* David wrote this psalm when he was in a cave, perhaps when he was hiding from Saul. How would you describe David's emotional state?

2. What phrases and images does David use to describe the situation he faces (vv. 3, 6, 7)?

3. What contrast do you see between David's experiences with people and his experience with God?

4. How would you compare his view of his personal power with his view of God's power?

✑ APPLYING THE WORD

• What is the significance of the contrast between our power and God's power when we feel desperate?

• Are you able to pray with this kind of directness and urgency in times of personal need? Why or why not?

✑ RESPONDING IN PRAYER

Write a psalm of your own, allowing yourself to cry out to God on your own behalf or on behalf of someone else who faces a desperate situation.

PSALM 143   *Asking for Guidance*

"THE WAY I was taught to pray," explained Sue, "was to list for God the things I wanted done. I really felt I knew what everyone needed and that my job was to bring these needs to God's attention. I would decide what needed to be done and God would do it.

"I was surprised to discover a humbler way to pray. I learned to say, 'Show me your will today and give me the power to carry it out.' I stopped telling God what to do and started to ask for guidance and help. Now I pray with an awareness that I am talking to my Creator, who knows me better than I know me, who loves me more than I love me, and who is personally involved in my life."

❧ WARMING UP TO GOD

What fears might keep you from seeking to know and to do God's will?

❧ DISCOVERING THE WORD

1. *Read Psalm 143.* What specifically does the psalmist say he longs for in this text (vv. 1, 7)?

2. What does the psalmist fear might happen (vv. 2, 7)?

3. Why does the psalmist need God's help (vv. 3-6)?

4. The psalmist asks for knowledge of God's will and the power to carry it out. What specifically does he ask for (vv. 8-12)?

5. The psalmist reminds God, "I have put my trust in you. . . . To you I lift up my soul. . . . I hide myself in you" (vv. 8-9). What do you think the psalmist is trying to communicate to God?

❧ APPLYING THE WORD

- In what area of life do you feel a need for knowledge of God's will?

- What knowledge of God's will have you received, but are hesitant and needing power to carry out?

❧ RESPONDING IN PRAYER

What guidance would you like to ask God for today?

PSALM 145 *Relying on God*

PEOPLE WHO HAVE experienced repeated disappointments with parents or other significant people can develop an image of an unreliable God. He is seen as a God who cannot be counted on. He makes promises he may not keep. He may be loving one day and unaccountably angry the next. People who have experienced unreliable parents may ask, "How do I know God will keep his promises? How do I know he listens to me? How do I know he will answer me or help me?" The image of an unreliable God stands in stark contrast to biblical images of God. The God of the Bible is the Faithful One, the Rock, the Fortress. He is the same yesterday, today and forever.

⇨ WARMING UP TO GOD

Think of a person whom you see as reliable. Describe the person and your response to his or her reliability.

⇨ DISCOVERING THE WORD

1. *Read Psalm 145.* What descriptive words and phrases are used about God in this prayer?
2. What phrases suggest that God is reliable?
3. How does God help those who are in need (vv. 14-20)?
4. What image of God comes through to you most clearly?

⇨ APPLYING THE WORD

• How does the picture of God here compare or contrast with your image of his reliability?
• Why is it important for you to know that God is reliable?

⇨ RESPONDING IN PRAYER

Offer God your thanks for his faithfulness.

PSALM 146   *The Source of Hope*

"MY OWN MOM and dad failed me," Linda said in her support group meeting. "Then my marriage fell apart. And then my health fell apart. Life has always been hard. I don't see why I should expect it to ever get any better. If anything, it will probably get worse. How is it possible for me to have hope?" The Bible teaches that there is more to the story of our lives than our experiences of loss and disappointment. The planet may be fallen, but it is not forsaken by God. God is actively present in our lives, bringing gifts of life and joy into the midst of our darkness. We can dare to hope because of who God is.

ᕍ WARMING UP TO GOD
In what area of life is it hard for you to find hope?

ᕍ DISCOVERING THE WORD
1. *Read Psalm 146.* How does this psalm contrast the experience of hoping in God with the experience of hoping in people?
2. The psalmist mentions eight kinds of circumstances that might seem hopeless (vv. 7-9). List these situations/conditions and the reasons they might seem hopeless.
3. Describe how God responds to people in each of these situations.
4. What do these responses from God to people in hopeless situations suggest to you about God's character?

ᕍ APPLYING THE WORD
- Which of the eight images of hopelessness do you most strongly relate to at this time? Explain.
- Take a few minutes and allow yourself to picture God responding to you in the way this text describes God's response. What thoughts and feelings do you have in response to this image of God's care for you?

ᕍ RESPONDING IN PRAYER
What would you like to say to God, who is the source of your hope?

PSALM 148   *A Symphony of Praise*

THE CALL TO PRAISE in Psalm 148, if heeded by all of creation, would make for quite a symphony. Perhaps it would sound more like a cacophony than a symphony. Judging from the noises that all of God's creatures make individually, it boggles the mind (never mind the eardrums!) to imagine the concert called for in Psalm 148. Its location at the end of the book suggests that this psalm is meant to wrap everything up on a high praise note.

✑ WARMING UP TO GOD

Think about an exciting time of corporate praise that you have been a part of. How does seeing others engaged in worship inspire your worship?

✑ DISCOVERING THE WORD

1. *Read Psalm 148.* This psalm divides into two six-verse stanzas (vv. 1-6 and 7-12), with a recap that underscores the motivation to praise (vv. 13-14). What two major chorus groups are appealed to here?

2. Within those two major choral divisions, who joins in praising God?

3. Do you see this as mere figurative (symbolic or exaggerated) language used by the psalmist to call all things in heaven and on earth, or is there some way that all the various elements actually praise God?

4. Why praise God at all (vv. 5-6, 13-14)?

✑ APPLYING THE WORD

• What is the closest you have come, this side of heaven, to experiencing a worldwide worship service such as this psalm announces?

• Do you look forward to heaven, when this psalm finds its fulfillment, or does praising God all day long sound boring to you? Explain.

• How does this psalm provide a new or fresh picture of praise for you?

✑ RESPONDING IN PRAYER

Imagine what it would be like to have every man, woman and child—young and old alike—participating in your church's choir. Pray (and practice) toward that end.

PSALM 150   *Praying Our Praise*

ALL PRAYER FINALLY, in one way or another, becomes praise. Psalm 150 is deliberately placed as the concluding prayer of the church's book of prayers. No matter how much we suffer, no matter our doubts, everything finds its way into praise, the final consummating prayer.

✵ WARMING UP TO GOD

What circumstances or feelings in the past year have, however momentarily, made a praising person out of you? Reflect on that again in joy, celebrating with Christ.

✵ DISCOVERING THE WORD

1. *Read Psalm 150.* How many times is the word *praise* used in the psalm?

2. Verse 1 tells us where the Lord is to be praised. What is the meaning of "in his sanctuary" and "in his mighty heavens"?

3. Verse 2 tells us why he is to be praised. What reasons does the psalmist give?

4. Verses 3-5 tell us how to praise the Lord. As you read these verses, what kind of scene do you imagine?

✵ APPLYING THE WORD

• Building on verse 2, what reasons can you give for praising God?

• There are no shortcuts to praise. We can see this in many psalms that express pain. What difficult circumstances in your life have found their way into praise?

• Augustine claimed that a "Christian should be a hallelujah from head to foot." What needs to be done to get to that point?

✵ RESPONDING IN PRAYER

Gather the reflections and insights that have come from your study and turn them into a time of concluding and celebrative praise.

ACKNOWLEDGMENTS
AND PERMISSIONS

The New Testament quiet times were adapted from the following LifeGuide®
Bible Studies:

- *Matthew* ©1987 by Stephen and Jacalyn Eyre.
- *Mark* ©1987 by InterVarsity Christian Fellowship of the United States of America. Written by James Hoover.
- *Luke* ©1992 by Ada Lum.
- *John* ©1990 by Douglas Connelly.
- *Acts* ©1992 by Phyllis J. Le Peau.
- *Romans* ©1986 by InterVarsity Christian Fellowship of the United States of America. Written by Jack Kuhatschek.
- *1 Corinthians* ©1988 by Paul Stevens and Dan Williams.
- *2 Corinthians* ©1990 by Paul Stevens.
- *Galatians* ©1986 by InterVarsity Christian Fellowship of the United States of America. Written by Jack Kuhatschek.
- *Ephesians* ©1985 by InterVarsity Christian Fellowship of the United States of America. Written by Andrew T. and Phyllis J. Le Peau.
- *Philippians* ©1985 by InterVarsity Christian Fellowship of the United States of America. Written by Donald Baker.
- *Colossians and Philemon* ©1989 by Martha Reapsome.
- *1 & 2 Thessalonians* ©1991 by Donald E. Baker.
- *1 & 2 Timothy and Titus* ©1991 by Pete Sommer.
- *Hebrews* ©1991 by James Reapsome.
- *James*, rev. ed. ©1987 by Andrew T. and Phyllis J. Le Peau.

- *1 & 2 Peter and Jude* ©1992 by Carolyn Nystrom.
- *John's Letters* ©1990 by Ron Blankley.
- *Revelation* ©1987 by R. Paul Stevens.

Quiet times for Revelation 10—11; 14—15; 17—18 are by Scott Hotaling.

Quiet times for specified psalms are adapted from the following sources:

- *Caring for Emotional Needs* ©1991 by Phyllis J. Le Peau and NCF (Pss 42—43).
- *Created Male* ©1993 by Brian M. Wallace and Cindy Bunch (Ps 16).
- *Deciding Wisely* ©1992 by Bill Syrios (Ps 119:1-24).
- *Entering God's Presence* ©1992 by Stephen D. Eyre (Ps 47).
- *The Fruit of the Spirit,* rev. ed. ©1987 by Hazel Offner (Ps 107).
- *Healing for Broken People* ©1990 by Dan Harrison (Ps 4).
- *Loving the World* ©1992 by Carolyn Nystrom (Ps 104).
- *Multi-ethnicity* ©1990 by Isaac Canales (Ps 67).
- *People and Technology* ©1990 by Mary Fisher (Ps 127).
- *Prayer* ©1994 by David Healey (Ps 5).
- *Psalms* ©1987 by Eugene H. Peterson (Pss 1—3; 6; 8; 23; 51; 73; 90; 103; 137; 150).
- *Psalms II* ©1994 by Juanita Ryan (Pss 44; 57; 62—63; 65—66; 86; 88; 94; 102; 130; 142).
- *Pursuing Holiness* ©1992 by Carolyn Nystrom (Ps 15).
- *Recovery: A Lifelong Journey* ©1993 by Juanita and Dale Ryan (Pss 119:25-40; 143).
- *Recovery from Abuse* ©1990 by Dale and Juanita Ryan (Pss 10; 13; 18:1-24).
- *Recovery from Bitterness* ©1990 by Dale and Juanita Ryan (Ps 109).
- *Recovery from Depression* ©1993 by Juanita and Dale Ryan (Ps 146).
- *Recovery from Distorted Images of God* ©1990 by Juanita and Dale Ryan (Ps 145).
- *Recovery from Distorted Images of Self* ©1993 by Juanita and Dale Ryan (Ps 100).

- *Recovery from Family Dysfunctions* ©1990 by Dale and Juanita Ryan (Pss 55; 116).
- *Resources for Caring People* ©1991 by Phyllis J. Le Peau and NCF (Ps 19).
- *Self-Esteem* ©1990 by Jack Kuhatschek (Ps 139).
- *Suffering* ©1992 by Jack Kuhatschek (Ps 27).
- *Waiting on the Lord* ©1994 by Stephen D. and Jacalyn Eyre (Pss 30—40).
- *Women Facing Temptation* ©1993 by Cindy Bunch (Ps 77).

Quiet times for Psalms 18:25-50; 22; 24; 46; 84; 91; 95—96; 99; 110; 115; 118; 121—22; 133; 148 are by Dietrich Gruen.

Quiet times for Psalms 37:18-40; 66 are by Linda Gehrs.

Quiet times for Psalms 50; 126 are by Cindy Bunch.

Index of Quiet Time Subjects